MW00387178

CONSTRUCTION DAMAGES AND REMEDIES

Authors:
Leslie O'Neal-Coble
Allen Holt Gwyn
Douglas S. Oles
C. Allen Gibson, Jr.
Charles M. Sink

Editor:
W. Alexander Moseley

Defending Liberty
Pursuing Justice

Cover design by Beth Boulton, Boulton Advertising + Promotions

The materials contained herein represent the opinions of the authors and editors and should not be construed to be the action of either the American Bar Association or the Forum on the Construction Industry unless adopted pursuant to the bylaws of the Association.

Nothing contained in this book is to be considered as the rendering of legal advice for specific cases, and readers are responsible for obtaining such advice from their own legal counsel. This book and any forms and agreements herein are intended for educational and informational purposes only.

© 2004 American Bar Association. All rights reserved.
Printed in the United States of America.

08 07 06 05 04   5 4 3 2 1

Library of Congress Cataloging-in-Publication Data

Construction damages and remedies / by W. Alexander Moseley, editor.
    p. cm.
Includes bibliographical references and index.
   ISBN 1-59031-271-6
   1. Construction contracts—United States. I. Moseley, W. Alexander, 1949–

   KF902.C6125 2003
   343.73'078624—dc22

                                                2003019904

Discounts are available for books ordered in bulk. Special consideration is given to state bars, CLE programs, and other bar-related organizations. Inquire at Book Publishing, ABA Publishing, American Bar Association, 750 North Lake Shore Drive, Chicago, Illinois 60611.

www.abanet.org/abapubs

1) CALL IMMIGRATION

Contents

About the Authors

LESLIE O'NEAL-COBLE

Leslie O'Neal-Coble is the leader of Holland & Knight LLP's national construction practice group. For 25 years, she has focused her practice on construction law issues, representing public and private owners, developers, construction managers, and general contractors in matters of contract drafting, negotiation, claims preparation, and prosecuting and defending claims in mediation, arbitration, and litigation. She has extensive experience in design and construction defect claims, mold litigation, performance and payment bond claims, insurance issues, and delay and disruption claims. She is a former chair of the ABA Forum on Construction and is a Fellow in the American College of Construction Lawyers. Ms. O'Neal-Coble received her B.A. and J.D. from the University of Florida.

ALLEN HOLT GWYN

Allen Holt Gwyn is a principal in the law firm of Conner Gwyn Schenck pllc, in Greensboro and Raleigh, North Carolina. His practice is concentrated in construction, environmental, surety and insurance disputes, and white-collar criminal defense for private industry clients. His practice regularly includes contract drafting and negotiation, prosecution and defense of construction defects, mold and environmental

issues, and design, delay, and interference claims. Mr. Gwyn
is a former chair of the ABA Forum on the Construction
Industry, and a Fellow in the American College of Construction Lawyers. He is a member of the Large Complex Case
Program (LCCP) Panel of Arbitrators, and the Carolinas
Contruction Mediation Panel for the American Arbitration
Association. He is a frequent author and speaker at bar and
industry groups on construction and environmental law, and
on alternative dispute resolution issues. Mr. Gwyn received
his B.A. from the University of North Carolina and his J.D.
from Wake Forest University.

DOUGLAS S. OLES

Douglas S. Oles is a partner in the Seattle firm of Oles Morrison Rinker & Baker LLP. For more than 20 years, Mr.
Oles has assisted construction industry clients with negotiating contracts and litigating issues on complex projects. He
has served as editor of *The Construction Lawyer* and as a member of the ABA Construction Forum Governing Committee.
He currently chairs the Forum Publication Committee. Mr.
Oles has written many articles and spoken on construction
law issues at conferences across the United States and Europe.
Mr. Oles received his A.B. from Stanford University (phi
beta kappa) and his J.D. from the University of Washington,
where he served as executive editor of the law review.

C. ALLEN GIBSON, JR.

C. Allen Gibson, Jr., is a principal in the Charleston, South
Carolina, law firm of Buist, Moore, Smythe & McGee, P.A.
His practice represents parties in the construction industry
in the areas of contract negotiation, arbitration, and litiga-
tion of construction and surety law. He is past chair of the
ABA Forum on the Construction Industry and is a member
of the ABA's Fidelity and Surety Committee of the Torts and
Insurance Practice Section. He is a Fellow in the American
College of Construction Lawyers and is listed in *The Best*

Lawyers in America in the field of Construction Law. Mr. Gibson received his B.A. with high distinction and his J.D. from the University of Virginia, where he was Order of Coif.

CHARLES M. SINK

Charles M. Sink specializes in construction and commercial litigation and claims. For the past 26 years, he has advised clients in all aspects of contract negotiations and has been involved in arbitration and in state and federal litigation. He has worked for many years resolving insurance coverage claims, exclusively for policyholders, arising from construction projects. Mr. Sink is familiar with construction delay claims, defective workmanship and design issues, project management disputes, warranty rights, lien problems, and related construction claims. He also specializes in alternative dispute resolution. He has taught, lectured, and written on arbitration methods and strategies. He is a member of the ABA Forum on Construction and co-authored its 1998 publication *A201 Deskbook*. Mr. Sink received his B.A. from Harvard University and his J.D. from the University of California, Hastings.

About the Editor

W. ALEXANDER MOSELEY

W. Alexander Moseley is a member of the firm of Hand Arendall, L.L.C., practicing in its Mobile, Alabama, office. He heads Hand Arendall's construction and public contract practice group. Mr. Moseley's practice is devoted primarily to advocacy for construction contractors, subcontractors, owners, and designers, in both negotiation of construction and design contracts and dispute resolution, as well as general commercial and business litigation. He is a former division chair and former member of the Governing Committee, and immediate past chair of the Publications Committee, of the ABA Forum on the Construction Industry. He is a member of the Associated General Contractors of America and its Contract Documents Committee. Mr. Moseley received his B.A. from the University of the South and his J.D. from the University of Alabama. He also served as a judge advocate in the United States Air Force. Mr. Moseley is listed in *The Best Lawyers in America* in the field of Construction Law.

Acknowledgments

A book of this kind inevitably requires dedicated efforts by many people. At the highest level, it has received consistent encouragement and support from three consecutive chairs of the ABA Forum on the Construction Industry (Allen Gibson, Deborah Ballati, and John Heisse). It was produced by ABA Publishing under the careful guidance of Rick Paszkiet and Jill Nuppenau. Preliminary research was performed, case citations and West Key Numbers were carefully collected and checked, and other detailed suggestions and initial drafting were contributed by Paul Davis, Arlene Graves, Will Honea, Patrick McKinney, Marion Quinones, Margie Hawkins, and Michael Starks. The authors also wish to thank Boulton Advertising & Promotions for the cover art and Doug Oles for preparing the index.

Introduction

Romeo: *Courage, man; the hurt cannot be much.*
Mercutio: *No, 'tis not so deep as a well, nor so wide as a church-door*
          but 'tis enough, 'twill serve:
          ask for me tomorrow, and you shall find me
          a grave man.
          (Romeo and Juliet, Act III, Scene 1)

As set forth above, Romeo's friend Mercutio assessed his own damages with a grim sense of humor. He also makes fine use of understatement, a tool found infrequently among construction law advocates. Meanwhile, the duels of Montagues and Capulets provide a reminder of the bloody methods by which disputes were often resolved in times before a more orderly system of legal administration took hold.

As Shakespeare recalls an earlier age, this book also begins with a look back on the development of the main theories supporting claims for monetary damages under the American common law of contracting. And just as Mercutio's injuries became famous through his choice of words to describe them, this book will offer specific recommendations on how to articulate claims for damages, or other remedies, after the appropriate theories have been selected. At the core of this book, the authors will outline major principles of identifying, calculating, allocating, and recovering damages in connection with public and private contracts for design, construction, and supply.

This book is of course not the first entry in its field. As its sponsor, however, the ABA Forum on the Construction Industry hopes that it will be a useful reference for lawyers and others who participate actively in construction-related disputes.

One reason for this hope is the fact that the authors collectively combine well in excess of a century of construction claims practice across the United States. Three of the five authors are recent past chairs of the Construction Forum.

A second reason is that the major legal principles are accompanied by experience-based suggestions on how to apply them in the prosecution or defense of claims. Thus, the book combines elements of a treatise with a practical guide.

Third, the authors have adopted an experimental approach of supplementing their legal citations with references to sections in the West Key Number system. Such references should enable readers to keep up to date with legal decisions issued after the publication date of this book. The Forum wishes to thank West Publishing for consenting to this use of its system.

As Mercutio grows weaker in Act III, he offers a list of insults to Tybalt, the adversary whose sword dealt the fatal blow:

> 'Zounds, a dog, a rat, a mouse, a cat,
> to scratch a man to death!
> a braggart, a rogue, a villain,
> that fights by the book of arithmetic!

Apparently, he saved his worst insult for the last. But today, courts increasingly expect claimants and their advocates to articulate their damages by arithmetical calculations rather than by vague estimates. To aid those who undertake this task and also those who defend against them, the authors are pleased to offer this modest contribution to the literature on construction damages and remedies.

Theories of Recovery

1

DOUGLAS S. OLES

HISTORICAL INTRODUCTION

To understand the available theories of damage recovery under modern construction law, one must understand how our current law evolved. Construction law seems to have existed long before money itself was invented, so many centuries passed in which there was no need for rules on how to quantify damages for breach of contract. If an early builder failed to do his work properly, the aggrieved parties were apparently content to choose between requiring corrective work or taking some form of personal revenge.

Around 1780 B.C., King Hammurabi[1] promulgated what is often said to be the oldest surviving codification of construction law. It included some of the following remedial clauses:

> If a builder build a house for some one, and does not construct it properly, and the house

---

1. Hammurabi was the sixth king of the Amorite Dynasty in Old Babylon.

1

that he built fall in and kill its owner, then that builder shall be put to death.

If it kill the son of the owner, the son of that builder shall be put to death.

If it kill a slave of the owner, then he shall pay slave for slave to the owner of the house.

If it ruin goods, he shall make compensation for all that has been ruined, and inasmuch as he did not construct properly this house which he built and it fell, he shall re-erect the house from his own means.

If a builder build a house for some one, even though he has not yet completed it; if then the walls seem toppling, the builder must make the walls solid from his own means.[2]

Over the centuries, however, builders were apparently successful in dissuading owners from using the death penalty as a method of resolving construction disputes. By the sixth century B.C., the dynasty of King Croesus[3] had popularized the use of coinage as a medium of exchange, and it became increasingly accepted that construction errors and omissions should be redressed through monetary compensation.[4]

The word "damage" derives from the Latin word *damnum*, referring to a loss suffered. An older edition of *Black's Law Dictionary* defined "damages" as "A pecuniary compensation or indemnity, which may be recovered in the courts by any person who has suffered loss, detriment, or injury, whether

---

2. *See* Hammurabi Code §§ 229–233 at http://www.yale.edu/lawweb/avalon/medieval/hamframe .htm, cited in 20:3 CONSTR. LAW. 3 (July 2000).

3. Croesus was king of Lydia until he misinterpreted a Delphic oracle and destroyed his own kingdom by attacking his more powerful Persian neighbors. Famous for great wealth, he gave rise to the saying "as rich as Croesus." *See* http://www.icu-cdnx.com/a_croesus_name_m.htm.

4. Arthur Corbin aptly summarized the role of contract law in replacing the more primitive system of personal revenge:

> There is more than one purpose underlying the rules of law that provide for the giving of damages for breach of contract. One of the ends to be obtained is, without doubt, the keeping of the peace. The party injured by the breach has a sense of grievance. In the absence of a public remedy, he would do his best to redress his own wrong. This means private war, with all of the resulting harm that it entails to the interests of other people.

ARTHUR LINTON CORBIN, CORBIN ON CONTRACTS § 1002, at 29 (interim ed. 2002).

to his person, property, or rights, through the unlawful act or omission or negligence of another."[5]

A more recent edition explains damages more simply as "money claimed by, or ordered to be paid to, a person as compensation for loss or injury."[6] In other words, damages are a monetary amount by which the court system quantifies a payment owed by one party to another.

COMPENSATORY DAMAGES

Inherent in the foregoing definitions is a notion that there are some injuries for which the law of contracts awards no damages. The Romans referred to this as *damnum sine injuria*,[7] i.e., damages without actionable wrongful act. To the extent that this principle survives, civil litigants in construction cases are sometimes surprised and disappointed to learn that they may not recover compensation for the emotional damages that they in fact may suffer from another party's breach of contract.

It is sometimes noted as an ironic feature of the common law that a momentary unintentional act of negligence can expose a tortfeasor to broader liability than arises from an intentional breach by a person who is contractually bound to another. In general, however, awards of pecuniary damages (as distinguished from specific performance) in construction contract cases are limited to recovery based upon economic losses that can be established by a preponderance of evidence.

Arthur Corbin explains that the need for flexible legal rules is sometimes at odds with the need for uniformity in assessing contract damages:

> The purpose of awarding damages is always said to be compensation for harm done. The effort is made to put the injured

---

5. BLACK'S LAW DICTIONARY 499 (3d ed. 1933).
6. BLACK'S LAW DICTIONARY 393 (7th ed. 1999).
7. Also referred to as *damnum absque injuria*.

party in as good a position as he would have been put by full performance of the contract, at the least cost to the defendant and without charging him with harms that he had no sufficient reason to foresee when he made the contract. The various difficulties involved in this effort frequently make it impracticable to attain its purpose with any near approach to exactness.

The rules of law governing the recovery of damages for breach of contract are very flexible. Their application in the infinite number of situations that arise is beyond question variable and uncertain. Even more than in the case of other rules of law, they must be regarded merely as guides to the court, leaving much to the individual feeling of the court created by the special circumstances of the particular case. In spite of the difficulties involved, the courts have actually achieved a considerable degree of uniformity. ...[8]

Traditionally, courts have viewed the law of contract damages as protecting three interests of an injured party. The "expectation interest," "reliance interest," and "restitution interest" will each be discussed in this chapter.[9]

FORESEEABILITY

Another fundamental principle is that damages are recoverable only if they are within the scope of what the breaching party "knew or should have been aware of when the contract was made."[10] The nineteenth-century English decision in *Hadley v. Baxendale*[11] is often cited as establishing this "foreseeability" limitation. The Restatement (Second) of Contracts explains that "[d]amages are not recoverable for loss that the party in breach did not have reason to foresee as a probable result of the breach when the contract was made."[12]

---

8. CORBIN, *supra* note 4, § 1002, at 27–28.

9. *See* RESTATEMENT (SECOND) OF CONTRACTS § 344 (1981); Ralph C. Nash & John Cibinic, *Breach-of-Contract Damages: Expectation, Reliance, or Restitution*, 10 NASH & CIBINIC REPORT 51 (October 2001).

10. BLACK'S LAW DICTIONARY 394 (7th ed. 1999); *see also* JUSTIN SWEET, LEGAL ASPECTS OF ARCHITECTURE, ENGINEERING AND THE CONSTRUCTION PROCESS § 6.06(C), at 47 (6th ed. 2000).

11. 9 Ex. 341, 156 Eng. Rep. 145 (1854).

12. RESTATEMENT (SECOND) OF CONTRACTS § 351(1) (1981).

In other words, the breaching party may be liable both for the types of damages that are likely to result from a breach "in the ordinary course of events"[13] and for the particular types of damage of which "the party in breach had reason to know."[14] Especially in breach of contract claims alleging common law damages against the federal government, remote damages will be disallowed.[15]

In a construction context, for example, a defaulting subcontractor or supplier will presumably foresee that its nonperformance can expose the prime contractor to liquidated damages that are contractually payable to the owner. Conversely, an owner who has received pre-bid submissions outlining the contractor's planned methods and sequences of work may have specific knowledge about ways in which the contractor would be adversely affected if the project is unreasonably changed or delayed. Of course, a party's liability for some of these foreseeable damages may in some cases be limited effectively by contract, as will be discussed further in Chapter 9 of this book.

The permissible theories of damage recovery in U.S. construction litigation typically have their roots in large part in the English courts of law and equity. The most common theories of damage recovery are reviewed below.

RELIANCE DAMAGES

When a construction or supply contract is formed and then breached, the nonbreaching party is generally entitled to recover its costs incurred in reasonable reliance on the agreement. This is the principle of "reliance damages."

Black's Law Dictionary defines reliance damages as "damages awarded for losses incurred by the plaintiff in reliance

---

13. *Id.* § 351(2)(a); *see also* CORBIN, *supra* note 4, § 1007 *et seq.*

14. RESTATEMENT (SECOND) OF CONTRACTS § 351(2)(b) (1981); Landmark Land Co. v. FDIC, 256 F.3d 1365, 1378 (Fed. Cir. 2001).

15. *See, e.g.*, San Carlos Irrigation & Drainage Dist. v. United States, 111 F.3d 1557 (Fed. Cir. 1997); Wells Fargo Bank N.A. v. United States, 88 F.3d 1012 (Fed. Cir. 1996).

on the contract."[16] The Restatement (Second) of Contracts summarizes this principle by stating that "the injured party has a right to damages based on his reliance interest, including expenditures made in preparation for performance or in performance, less any loss that the party in breach can prove with reasonable certainty the injured party would have suffered had the contract been performed."[17]

A party's "reliance interest" is defined as its "interest in being reimbursed for loss caused by reliance on the contract by being put in as good a position as he would have been in had the contract not been made."[18] In explanatory Comment (a), the Restatement adds:

> If the injured party was to supply services such as erecting a building, for example, the difference between loss in value of the other party's performance and the cost or other loss avoided by the injured party will be equal to the cost of the injured party's expenditures in reliance, up to the time of breach, plus the profit that would have been made had the contract been fully performed.[19]

These principles are often applied in construction disputes, especially when a project is terminated before it achieves completion. In some cases, termination occurs before any actual work is performed at the designated construction site. For example, an owner may award a construction contract but fail to issue a notice to proceed at the site. In that case, the construction contractor would have a claim for costs reasonably incurred in preparing for the job. A contractor might incur such costs for ordering materials, making nonrefundable deposits for shipment of materials, preparing permit applications or paying permit fees, creating a file system for project records, or specially fitting equipment for the contemplated project.

---

16. BLACK'S LAW DICTIONARY 396 (7th ed. 1999).
17. RESTATEMENT (SECOND) OF CONTRACTS § 349, at 124 (1981).
18. *Id.* § 344(b), at 102.
19. *Id.* § 349, at 124.

A construction supplier may start to incur reliance costs as soon as it begins to set aside shop time for manufacture of required equipment or starts to create special dies, molds, or forms that are uniquely designed for the job in question. The manufacturing of required equipment often begins in reliance on a purchase order, even though on-site construction has not yet started. Thus, even if a purchase order is canceled prior to the first delivery, the supplier may already have incurred or committed to substantial costs.

Once construction has started, claims for reliance damages will generally extend to all costs incurred in performance of the work. As suggested by the Restatement, however, there is a series of limitations on a claimant's right to recover the costs that it incurred in "reliance" on a contract. A nonexhaustive list of those limitations might include:

- Offset for the claimant's savings if the breaching party can prove that the plaintiff would have lost money in completing the contract.

- Offset for costs that can be avoided through reasonable mitigation by the nonbreaching party (for example, reusing materials that can readily be used on other work or sold at market).

- Possible offset for costs that the breaching party can show to have been unreasonable—partly on the theory that unreasonable expenditures are beyond the scope of reasonable foreseeability, as discussed earlier in this chapter.[20]

It should be noted that in some circumstances, a provider of labor, materials, or equipment may have a claim for reliance damages even before it has a written contract. If a prime construction contract has been awarded under circumstances where the prime contractor is obliged to utilize certain subcontractors or suppliers whose prices were incorporated into

---

20. *See Landmark, supra* note 14, 256 F.3d at 1378 ("In order to be entitled to reliance damages, a plaintiff must prove that both the magnitude and type of damages were foreseeable.")

the final bid, those subcontractors and suppliers may reasonably argue that they thereafter have a right to incur costs in reliance on the expectation of receiving a contract under which they will ultimately be reimbursed. A plaintiff's entitlement to reliance damages in these circumstances may depend on a variety of circumstances, including the existence of legal requirements to use listed subcontractors and/or the presence of a stipulation that acceptance of a lower tier contractor's bid is conditional upon negotiation of a contract acceptable to the prime contractor.

It should also be kept in mind that oral contracts may be enforceable in a number of circumstances. Contracts for the supply of goods, however, will generally be subject to the statute of frauds of the Uniform Commercial Code.[21] And contracts for services are usually subject to corresponding restrictions under applicable state laws.[22]

EXPECTATION DAMAGES

When a construction or supply contract is formed and then breached, the nonbreaching party is generally entitled to recover the compensation that it reasonably could have expected if the contract had been performed. This principle of expectation damages is also said to give nonbreaching parties the benefit of their bargain.[23]

Black's Law Dictionary defines "expectation damages" as "compensation awarded for the loss of what a person reasonably anticipated that was not completed."[24] According to the Restatement, "Contract damages are ordinarily based on the injured party's expectation interest and are intended to give him the benefit of his bargain by awarding him a sum of money that will, to the extent possible, put him in as good

---

21. *See* U.C.C. § 2-201 (1992).
22. *See generally* authorities cited at West's ⊕═ 95 CONTRACTS, k30–46.
23. Bluebonnet Savings Bank, F.S.B. v. United States, 266 F.3d 1348, 1355 (Fed. Cir. 2001).
24. BLACK'S LAW DICTIONARY 394 (7th ed. 1999).

a position as he would have been in had the contract been performed."[25]

The Restatement adds that an injured party's "expectation interest"[26] may be measured by:

1. The loss in the value to him of the other party's performance caused by its failure or deficiency, plus

2. Any other loss, including incidental or consequential loss, caused by the breach, less

3. Any cost or other loss that he has avoided by not having to perform.[27]

From the standpoint of a service provider in the construction industry (e.g., contractor, designer, or supplier), the measure of lost value is generally based on the unpaid balance of a mutually agreed contract price. From the standpoint of a project owner, the measure of lost value is generally based on the reasonable cost of securing an alternative service provider to complete the work that was started by a breaching contractor.

In addition, it should be noted that "incidental or consequential" damages are generally a recoverable element of damages unless they are excluded by contract. In contracts for supply of goods, the Uniform Commercial Code specifically allows incidental damages to an injured seller,[28] and it allows both incidental and consequential damages to an injured buyer.[29]

Incidental damages are loosely defined as "losses reasonably associated with or related to actual damages."[30] When a construction owner breaches a contract to purchase goods

---

25. RESTATEMENT (SECOND) OF CONTRACTS § 347, comment a, at 112 (1981).

26. *Id.* § 344(a), at 102 (defining "expectation interest" as a party's "interest in having the benefit of his bargain by being put in as good a position as he would have been in had the contract been performed"); *see also* Glendale Fed. Bank v. United States, 239 F.3d 1374, 1380 (Fed. Cir. 2001).

27. RESTATEMENT (SECOND) OF CONTRACTS § 347 (1981).

28. U.C.C. § 2-710 (1992).

29. *Id.* § 2-715.

30. BLACK'S LAW DICTIONARY 395 (7th ed. 1999).

for a project, it will generally be liable for the supplier's "commercially reasonably charges, expenses or commissions incurred in stopping delivery, in the transportation, care, and custody of goods after the buyer's breach, in connection with return or resale of the goods or otherwise resulting from the breach."[31] When a supplier of construction goods breaches its contract, the buyer goods will generally be entitled to recover all "expenses reasonably incurred in inspection, receipt, transportation and care and custody of goods rightfully rejected, any commercially reasonable charges, expenses or commissions in connection with effecting cover and any other reasonable expense incident to the delay or other breach."[32] In a construction service agreement, unless incidental damages are effectively disclaimed, a breach by one party should allow the nonbreaching party to recover analogous damages. For example, when a builder defaults, the owner's incidental damages might include reasonable costs of inspecting partially completed work, removing defective work, storing materials as required, and retaining a contractor to complete the work as specified.

There does not appear to be a consensus on the definition of consequential damages.[33] In general, they are "losses that do not flow directly and immediately from an injurious act, but that result indirectly from the act."[34] Their status is affected by the requirement that recoverable damages must be reasonably foreseeable.[35] In a construction context, an owner's consequential damages arising from delay or other

---

31. U.C.C. § 2-710 (1992).

32. *Id.* § 2-715(1).

33. Arthur Corbin apparently felt that the expression "consequential damages" was so vague that its use "should be abandoned." CORBIN, *supra* note 4, § 1011, at 75.

34. BLACK'S LAW DICTIONARY 394 (7th ed. 1999).

35. For a thoughtful discussion of these two principles, *see* Howard Goldberg, *Hadley v. Baxendale, Consequential Damages & Modern Contract Law*, AIA CONTRACT DOCUMENTS: GENERATION NEXT at 297 (ABA 1997) (program materials, available at http://www.abanet.org/forums/construction/html/publications.html).

breach by a defaulting contractor are generally thought to include:

- Extended contract inspection and administration
- Lost revenue arising from delayed availability of completed facility
- Loss of use of new facility (e.g., costs of continuing to rent or own a pre-existing facility that must be retained because the new replacement is not ready on time)[36]
- Diminished value of completed facility due to late completion

These elements are often considered by owners in calculating and specifying liquidated delay damages in their contracts.

Examples of contractors' consequential damages arising from owner breaches can include:

- Unabsorbed home office overhead expense (due to extended duration of work)
- Lost profits on other jobs that might otherwise have been performed
- Loss of project financing
- Loss of project bonding

Examples of supplier consequential damages can include:

- Lost profits that could have been earned on purchase orders for other customers, using the shop time allocated to the job where the default occurred
- Costs of expanding staff or production facility to accommodate the contract that was breached

As exemplified in the 1997 edition of the American Institute of Architects A201 General Conditions,[37] there has been a

---

36. *But see* CHARLES M. SINK & MARK D. PETERSEN, THE A201 DESKBOOK 76 (1998) (suggesting that an owner's loss of use of a project building should be treated as a direct damage rather than a consequential damage).

37. AIA Document A201, General Conditions of the Contract for Construction ¶ 4.3.10 (1997 edition) calls for the owner and contractor to waive claims against each other for all consequential damages, provided that the owner may still collect any specified "liquidated direct damages."

recent trend toward mutual contract waivers of consequential damages. This waiver appears to reflect a widespread perception that potential exposure for consequential damages can be very broad and is often out of proportion to the fees being paid for design, construction, and supply services. Suppliers and service contractors who cannot afford to bear such risks (and who cannot obtain or afford insurance against them) may be compelled to insist on being insulated from them as a matter of contract. The enforcement of such waivers will be addressed in Chapter 9.

After determining the lost value resulting from breach and any incidental or consequential damages arising from the same, a calculation of expectation damages must offer credit for costs that the nonbreaching party has avoided on account of the breach. In a construction or supply context, this obviously involves calculating the costs that the nonbreaching party would reasonably have incurred to complete its work but for the breach of contract. If the breaching party can prove that the nonbreaching party would have lost money in completing the job as bid, the damage award should be reduced by a credit for that amount.

The Restatement of Contracts also notes several exceptions to the right to recover expectation damages, suggesting that the nonbreaching party should not recover damages that (a) it reasonably could have avoided without undue risk through mitigation;[38] (b) the breaching party did not have reason to foresee;[39] or (c) could not be established with reasonable certainty.[40]

The requirement for damages to be reasonably foreseeable has previously been discussed in this chapter. The nonbreaching party's duty to mitigate will be addressed in Chapter 9, and the issue of proof will be addressed in Chapter 10.

---

38. RESTATEMENT (SECOND) OF CONTRACTS § 350(1), at 126 (1981).

39. Id. § 351, at 135.

40. Id. § 352, at 144.

The Restatement offers a number of illustrations in the context of construction contracts. For example, an owner's claim for delay in completion of a new hotel must be offset by the avoided cost of operating the hotel during the delay period.[41] When an owner repudiates a contract for construction of a new house, the contractor's claim for the balance of its price is offset by the reasonable cost of completing the house.[42] When an owner's default leaves a contractor with leftover materials that can be readily used on other projects, the contractor's claim for damages must give credit for the saved cost of those materials.[43] The fact that a contractor performs similar work for another owner after being improperly defaulted by the first owner does not bar the contractor from recovering lost profits on the first job, unless the defaulting owner can prove that the contractor's business was incapable of performing both jobs.[44]

EQUITABLE THEORIES

Equitable relief is generally a matter for a court, not for a jury.[45] When a court concludes that an award of money damages is an insufficient remedy for a breach of contract, several alternative remedies may be available under principles of equity.[46]

---

41. Restatement (Second) of Contracts § 347, illustration 5, at 115 (1981).

42. *Id.* illustration 6, at 115.

43. *Id.* illustration 7, at 115.

44. *Id.* illustration 16, at 117.

45. See authorities cited at West's ⚷ 150 EQUITY, k369–92.

46. See authorities cited at West's ⚷ 50 EQUITY, k43–45. The United States Supreme Court has repeatedly held that remedies in equity will not be imposed if there is an adequate remedy at law. *See, e.g.*, Boise Artesian Water Co. v. Boise City, 213 U.S. 276, 281 (1909):

> It is a guiding rule in equity that in such a case it will not interpose where there is a plain, adequate and complete remedy at law. This rule at an early date was crystallized into statute form by the sixteenth section of the Judiciary Act (Revised Statutes, § 723), which, if it has no other effect, emphasizes the rule and presses it upon the attention of courts. *New York & Co. v. Memphis Water Co.*, 107 U.S. 205, 214. It is so well settled and has so often been acted upon that no authority need be cited in its support, though it must not be forgotten that the legal remedy must be as complete, practicable and efficient as that which equity could afford. *Walla Walla v. Walla Walla Water Co.*, 172 U.S. 1, 11.

Rescission

One of the traditional equitable remedies is rescission. It is generally intended to describe a remedy by which parties are returned as closely as possible to their pre-contract positions.[47] When a contractor is put back into its pre-contract position, it is not entitled to recover lost profit, so the rescission remedy is most attractive to contractors working on a project that is unlikely to generate a substantial profit.[48]

Although the traditional definition of rescission seems to have been limited to situations where parties mutually agree to discharge and terminate their duties under an existing contract,[49] the term is also sometimes applied to the unilateral right of a nonbreaching party to be discharged from further performance by the other party's material breach of contract.[50] Courts also hold that a party may unilaterally "rescind" an agreement based on failure of consideration or impossibility of performance.[51]

Arthur Corbin argues cogently that the term "rescission" should not be used to describe the unilateral right of a nonbreaching party.[52] To clarify the issue, Corbin distinguishes contract "rescission" from "termination" or "cancellation,"

---

47. *See* authorities cited at West's ⊕ 95 CONTRACTS, k249–74.

48. *See* discussion of when rescission is favorable to contractors in JOHN D. CARTER, ROBERT F. CUSHMAN, DOUGLAS F. COPPI & PAUL J. GORMAN, PROVING AND PRICING CONSTRUCTION CLAIMS § 7.29, at 235 (2001).

49. *See* CORBIN, *supra* note 4, § 1236, at 26.

50. *See, e.g.,* BLACK'S LAW DICTIONARY 1308 (7th ed. 1999) ("A party's unilateral unmaking of a contract for a legally sufficient reason, such as the other party's material breach"); see also authorities cited at West's ⊕ 95 CONTRACTS, k261. Federal government contractors may also obtain rescission for their own bidding errors, otherwise inexcusable, when regulations require government agencies to inspect bids for mistakes. Giesler v. United States, 232 F.3d 864, 869 (Fed. Cir. 2000).

51. For lack of consideration, see authorities cited at West's ⊕ 95 CONTRACTS, k260. For impossibility of performance, *see* authorities cited at West's ⊕ 95 CONTRACTS, k261(5).

52. *See* CORBIN, *supra* note 4, § 1237, at 36 (citations omitted):
Without doubt a considerable amount of injustice has been done by reason of variation and confusion in the use of the term "rescission." When one party repudiates the contract or otherwise commits a very material breach, this fact may in itself discharge the other party from further duty under the contract. This is not a "rescission" or even an offer of a rescission; yet is it often said that such a breach privileges the other party to "rescind" the contract. This usage has caused serious difficulty; it should not be hopeless to try to eliminate it.
See also id. § 1105, at 18–19.

with "the latter two terms being applicable only to the rendition of further performance as provided in the contract, leaving intact all claims for performance rendered or breaches committed in the past." But he acknowledges that usage of this definitional distinction "is not so uniform as to be decisive in interpretation."[53]

Under the Uniform Commercial Code, this right to undo the original contract is described in terms of a buyer's rights to reject[54] or revoke acceptance[55] of nonconforming goods. In the laws governing contracts for design or construction services, however, even one party's material breach generally does give another party the right to insist on returning to the *status quo ante*. In service contracts, there is no "perfect tender rule," and providers of construction services are generally held merely to the standard of "substantial performance"[56] rather than to the more unattainable standard of "free from defects."

When one contract party repudiates its contract or has committed a vital breach in some other way, it is generally held that the injured party acquires "a legal privilege of performing no further on his own part and a legal right to be compensated in some form for the wrong done him."[57] Whether or not this right is defined as a right of "rescission," it is an important right in an industry where service providers are typically required to invest large sums of money in reliance on contract assurances of receiving periodic (typically monthly) progress payments.

In the construction industry, project owners frequently seek to narrow the foregoing principle by including broadly worded clauses to the effect that contractors are required to continue performing work at their own expense even if there is a pending claim in dispute. However, well-established principles of

---

53. Corbin, *supra* note 4, § 1236, at 30–31.
54. U.C.C. § 2-602 (1992).
55. *Id.* § 2-608.
56. *See* authorities cited at West's 95 CONTRACTS, k293–95.
57. Corbin, *supra* note 4, § 1105, at 20.

equity would appear to place limits on the enforcement of such clauses. For example, a court may find it unreasonable to require that a designer, contractor, or supplier should continue performing unpaid work in the following cases:

- The owner's delay or withholding of earned payments is sufficiently large as to impair the financial ability of the general contractor or its subcontractors to continue work.

- Ongoing work would require contractors to perform changes in scope or schedule entailing a substantially larger cash flow investment than reasonably contemplated when they bid the job.

- The owner is attempting to impose a change outside the scope of the original contract (sometimes termed a "cardinal change").

- The contractor can adduce evidence that the owner's ability to pay for further work is substantially in doubt.

Some contract clauses compromise on this point by linking the contractor's duty to continue work (despite disputes) to the owner's duty to continue making timely payments.[58]

Once a contract is validly formed, and especially when it has been partly fulfilled, most courts will seek to effectuate what they construe as the parties' original mutual intent, and they will seldom grant the unilateral request of one party to restore all parties to their pre-contract positions.

Reformation

One remedy that equitably modifies a contract while leaving it in effect is reformation. This remedy can be defined as

---

58. *See, e.g.,* AIA Document A201, General Conditions of the Contract for Construction ¶ 4.3.3 (1997 edition) ("Pending final resolution of a Claim except as otherwise agreed in writing or as provided in Subparagraph 9.7.1 and Article 14, the Contractor shall proceed diligently with performance of the Contract and the Owner shall continue to make payments in accordance with the Contract Documents.") Paragraph 9.7.1 provides a right to stop work in the face of delayed payment, and paragraph 14.1.1.3 ultimately gives the unpaid contractor a right to terminate the agreement on this basis.

revising a written agreement "to reflect the actual intent of the parties, usu[ally] to correct fraud or mutual mistake."[59] The most common application of reformation is the latter, which can be summarized as follows:

> Where a writing that evidences or embodies an agreement in whole or in part fails to express the agreement because of a mistake of both parties as to the contents or effect of the writing, the court may at the request of a party reform the writing to express the agreement, except to the extent that rights of third parties such as good faith purchasers for value will be unfairly affected.[60]

An intended third-party beneficiary or a party's successor in interest may also have standing to request reformation of a contract based on mutual mistake.[61]

Examples of circumstances that might justify a contract reformation include:

- Correcting a technical error in execution of a document[62]

- Correcting an error in the legal description of the mutually contemplated project site[63]

- Revising a plan sheet or specification to incorporate the mutually agreed substance of a negotiated change order

- Clarifying any portion of the contract documents when the parties mutually intended something different than what is stated

It must be noted, however, that errors in business judgment and negligent failure to read specifications do not qualify as mutual mistakes justifying reformation.[64] Erroneous bids

---

59. BLACK'S LAW DICTIONARY 1285 (7th Ed. 1999).

60. RESTATEMENT (SECOND) OF CONTRACTS § 155, at 406 (1981).

61. RESTATEMENT (SECOND) OF CONTRACTS § 155, comment e, at 410 (1981); *see also* authorities cited at West's ⊕⟹ 328 REFORMATION OF INSTRUMENTS, k17, k19.

62. *See* authorities cited at West's ⊕⟹ 328 REFORMATION OF INSTRUMENTS, k12.

63. *See* authorities cited at West's ⊕⟹ 328 REFORMATION OF INSTRUMENTS, k13.

64. Giesler v. United States, 232 F.3d 864, 870–71 (Fed. Cir. 2000).

based on mistakes in judgment generally do not entitle contractors to contract reformation.[65]

Correction of a mutual mistake may in some cases justify an equitable adjustment to the contract in question. If, for example, an owner and contractor both assume erroneously that a specified design detail will meet building codes, the correction of that assumption may have to be addressed by a change to the contract. If the governing code authority in fact requires a different method of installation, and if that change necessitates an increase in the cost or time of contract performance, the contractor should receive an equitable change order. Thus, the right to contract reformation may be separate from the issue of whether the corrective change is compensable.

Many current construction contract forms provide that if one clause is legally invalidated, the others shall remain in effect unless enforcing those remaining terms on their own would be substantially inequitable. The term "reformation" may also be applied to the equitable remedy by which a contract is modified to remove a specific provision that is for some reason unenforceable.

Restitution

In cases where the more traditional remedies of reliance or expectation damages are insufficient, courts sometimes allow the remedy of restitution. The Restatement offers the following as part of its introduction to this topic:

> Restitution is a common form of relief in contract cases. It has as its objective not the enforcement of contracts through the protection of a party's expectation or reliance interests but the

---

65. United States v. Hamilton, 711 F.2d 1038, 1048 (Fed. Cir. 1983). In very limited contexts, unilateral error may constitute grounds for reformation where necessary to prevent injustice. *Giesler, supra* note 64, 232 F.3d at 869, *quoting* Liebherr Crane Corp. v. United States, 810 F.2d 1153, 1157 (Fed. Cir. 1987) ("a contractor may obtain reformation or rescission of the contract only if the contractor establishes that its bid error resulted from a 'clear cut clerical or arithmetical error, or a misreading of the specifications.' If the contractor's error does not constitute one of these kinds of mistakes, then the contractor is not eligible for reformation of the contract.")

prevention of unjust enrichment through the protection of his restitution interest. See § 344. A party who has received a benefit at the expense of the other party to the agreement is required to account for it, either by returning it in kind or by paying a sum of money.[66]

Because restitution is based on compensation for a benefit conferred, it is available only to a claimant who either has started performing a contract or has incurred costs in reliance thereon.[67] On the other hand, restitution will generally not be available if the contract is fully performed, because at that point the plaintiff usually has an adequate remedy at law (e.g., a claim for payment of the stipulated contract price).[68] Like rescission, restitution is a backward-looking remedy that can allow an injured contractor to avoid a losing contract situation.[69]

Restitution damages are typically measured in either of two ways:[70]

1. The reasonable value to the defendant of what it received,[71] in terms of what it would have cost to

---

66. RESTATEMENT (SECOND) OF CONTRACTS § 370, introductory note, at 199 (1981). Section 344 defines "restitution interest" as a party's "interest in having restored to him any benefit that he has conferred on the other party."

67. *Id.* at § 370; *see also* Mobil Oil Exploration, Prod. Southeast, Inc. v. United States, 530 U.S. 604, 608 (2000).

68. *See* CORBIN, *supra* note 4, §§ 1110–11, at 34 *et seq.*

69. JUSTIN SWEET, SWEET ON CONSTRUCTION LAW § 11.7, at 409 (1997) ("Most courts allow the contractor in a losing contract to use restitution and ignore any possible losses, as long as, paradoxically, he has *not completed* performance. He can establish the amount of money that his work has enhanced the owner."); *see also* Landmark Land Co. v. FDIC, 256 F.3d 1365, 1372 (Fed. Cir. 2001) ("The idea behind restitution is to restore—that is, to restore the non-breaching party to the position he would have been in had there never been a contract to breach.").

70. RESTATEMENT (SECOND) OF CONTRACTS § 371, at 202 (1981); *see also* Landmark, *supra* note 69, 256 F.3d at 1372.

71. CORBIN, *supra* note 4, § 1109, at 31–33:

One who has rendered service or supplied work, labor, and materials under a contract with another, but who has been wrongfully discharged or otherwise prevented from so far fully performing as to earn the agreed compensation, may regard the contract has terminated and get judgment for the reasonable value of all that the defendant has received in performance of the contract. This rule is applicable to contracts of personal service and to all kinds of construction contracts. The defendant's breach may have been a repudiation, a discharge, a prevention of performance by the plaintiff, or a failure to perform the agreed exchange due from the defendant.

obtain the same benefit from another person in the plaintiff's position; or

2. The extent to which the value of the defendant's property has been increased or other interests of the defendant have been advanced.

Courts may be more generous in granting restitution where a benefit has been conferred by way of part performance, as distinguished from reliance in some other way, and uncertainties as to the value of the benefit conferred are likely to be resolved against the claimant if it has also breached the agreement.[72]

In the context of damages for breach of a construction contract, an agreed contract price (or, arguably, a mutually agreed schedule of values within the contract price) may operate as a limit on recoverable damages, because justice does not permit an injured plaintiff to recover more than it specifically agreed to accept in full compensation for the work that it was not permitted to finish.[73] Restitution should, however, be available where unresolved changes in the scope, sequence, or duration of work are of sufficient magnitude to render the original contract price an inadequate basis for calculating full equitable compensation.

For a plaintiff to receive restitution based on a breach of contract, the breach must be "vital"—i.e., affecting a fundamental term of the agreement.[74] In the construction context, a material failure to make progress payments when due would generally be an example of such a breach. There are, however, many cases in which "a plaintiff is entitled to restitution even though no contract whatever has been made, or even though the defendant has been discharged from duty under an existing contract and has been guilty of no breach whatever."[75] Thus, restitution can be available both

---

72. RESTATEMENT (SECOND) OF CONTRACTS § 371, comment a, at 202–03 (1981).

73. *Id.* § 373, comment b, at 210.

74. CORBIN, *supra* note 4, § 1104.

75. *Id.* at 11.

as a remedy for breach and as a quasi-contractual remedy.[76] For example, a party who confers a benefit on another party under a contract that is later voided (e.g., due to illegality, impracticability, lack of capacity, mistake, or duress) may be able to claim restitution if there is no sufficient alternative remedy at law.[77]

Implied Contracts and *Quantum Meruit*

In proper circumstances, equity provides monetary relief where the injured party has no adequate remedy at law and where (a) an existing contract has been fundamentally breached, (b) a contract is voided as a matter of law, or (c) the existence of a contract must be implied to prevent unjust enrichment. The previously described remedy of restitution is sometimes available in each of these three circumstances.

So-called constructive contracts do not depend upon mutual assent, but are generally implied by law when it would be unjust for a recipient to retain a benefit without paying for it.[78] The restitutionary mirror image of unjust enrichment is *quantum meruit* ("the amount he deserves"), a theory grounded on the notion that one who has provided goods or services should be compensated for doing so.[79]

In an unjust enrichment case, damages are set by the value to the defendant of the benefit received; in a *quantum meruit* case, however, damages are measured by the reasonable value

---

76. *See, e.g.*, Bill v. Gattavara, 209 P.2d 457 (Wash. 1949) ("restitution" and "unjust enrichment" are modern designations for the older doctrine of "quasi contracts"); *see generally* authorities cited at West's ◈═ 205H IMPLIED AND CONSTRUCTIVE CONTRACTS, k4.

77. *See, e.g.*, RESTATEMENT (SECOND) OF CONTRACTS §§ 375, at 219 (1981) (contract voided due to statute of frauds); 376, at 222 (contract voidable for other reasons); 377 (contract discharged by impracticability, frustration, or nonoccurrence of essential condition).

78. *See* authorities cited in West's ◈═ 205H IMPLIED AND CONSTRUCTIVE CONTRACTS, k1–3. Hercules Inc. v. United States, 516 U.S. 417, 424 (1996), *quoting* Baltimore & Ohio R. v. United States, 261 U.S. 592, 597 (1923) ("an agreement implied in law is a 'fiction of law' where 'a promise is imputed to perform a legal duty' ").

79. *See* Barrett Refining Corp. v. United States, 242 F.3d 1055, 1061 (Fed. Cir. 2001) (*quantum meruit* "provides an equitable remedy allowing recovery of the value of goods or services provided, and accordingly, only the provider of the goods or services has such a claim").

of work and materials provided by the plaintiff.[80] The theory of *quantum meruit* exists separately from unjust enrichment in order to address those situations where it would be fundamentally unfair to deny recovery to a plaintiff for his efforts simply because they conferred no value on the defendant.[81]

In cases where equitable payments are collected from a project owner who repudiates or otherwise fundamentally breaches a contract to pay for construction services or materials, courts are likely to apply the label of restitution. Where equitable relief is granted because a contractor's costs, sequences, method, or schedule are pervasively changed, however, courts often prefer to characterize the basis for compensation as *quantum meruit*.[82] Courts may likewise apply *quantum meruit* as a theory of recovery in proper circumstances where the contract has been voided (illegality, fraud, duress).[83]

Although we noted above that restitution is traditionally not available to a contractor that has completed its performance of a contract with an agreed price, *quantum meruit* recovery is afforded to such a contractor. Such relief is allowed, however, only where the project was sufficiently changed, delayed, or otherwise disrupted by causes attributable to the owner so that recovery based on the originally agreed contract price is inequitable.

Some courts may hold that *quantum meruit* recovery is available only to compensate for changes, delays, or other

80. *See* 66 AM.JUR.2D *Restitution and Implied Contracts* § 37 (2001).

81. *See, e.g.,* United States v. Amdahl Corp., 786 F.2d 387, 393 (Fed. Cir. 1986) (citing example of contract voided for illegality, with substantial start-up costs incurred by contractor, but no actual benefit accruing to government, as a situation where unjust enrichment recovery would not adequately compensate contractor but *quantum meruit* would).

82. For authorities addressing quantum meruit recovery by parties furnishing labor, materials, or other expenses, see authorities cited at West's ☞ IMPLIED CONTRACTS k30–32. The term *quantum valebant* is occasionally used interchangeably with the term *quantum meruit*. The former applies to goods, the latter to services, and there seems to be "functionally no difference" in applying these two principles. Urban Data Sys., Inc. v. United States, 699 F.2d 1147, 1154 n.8 (Fed. Cir. 1983).

83. *Amdahl, supra* note 81, 786 F.2d at 393 ("it would violate good conscience to impose upon the contractor *all* economic loss from having entered an illegal contract") (emphasis in original).

disruptions that are beyond the scope or reasonable contem plation of the contracting parties.[84] This type of analysis is not particularly helpful, however, because there is usually no clear basis on which a trier of fact can determine how many owner changes, differing site conditions, delays, and other impacts should have been contemplated (especially in a competitive award situation where bidders typically cannot afford to inflate their prices with allowances for speculative contingencies).

Most construction contracts and some supply contracts contain clauses that specifically provide for equitable adjustments in price and schedule when a project is impacted by owner changes, differing site conditions, and other specified events. To the extent that cost impacts of such events can reasonably be segregated and quantified, a claimant contractor will often have an adequate remedy of damages at law—e.g., applying agreed unit prices, agreed rates for extended overhead costs, or traditional principles of reliance damages.[85] Where changes or disruptions to the scope, sequence, or duration of a project are sufficiently pervasive, however, a contractor's only adequate remedy may lie in replacing the original contract pricing with payment on an equitable theory of *quantum meruit*.

EXEMPLARY DAMAGES

Exemplary damages, also known as punitive damages, are damages awarded in addition to actual damages when the party liable for damages acted in some especially reprehensible way.

---

84. *See* authorities cited at West's ⊕═ 205H IMPLIED AND CONSTRUCTIVE CONTRACTS, k64.

85. In discussing labor productivity, the Defense Contract Audit Agency's CONTRACT AUDIT MANUAL (January 2001) states at § 9-504.6:

> Causes and effects can be separately measured, provided the change is sufficiently pronounced and not obscured by other factors. A change in tools or the introduction of a highly improved production process might be related to a specific reduction in the required labor hours; or a change in design might be related to an increase in labor hours. Factors which affect productivity operate interdependently, and it is difficult to evaluate separately the effect of any one factor.

emplary damages may arise either under the
r by statute. The general understanding of
es is that they are intended both to punish
wrongdoing and to make an example of wrongdoers so as to
deter others from similar conduct.

Under common law, the traditional and prevailing rule is
that "[p]unitive damages are not recoverable for a breach of
contract unless the conduct constituting the breach is also a
tort for which punitive damages are recoverable."[86] For
example, injuries to persons and damage to property may be
tortious even if they also breach contractual promises to perform work with due care.

Efforts to explain why punitive damages are allowed in
tort cases while being excluded in most contract cases sometimes appear strained, but there are practical reasons to support the distinction.[87] Due to the latitude typically given to
triers of fact in calculating damages, the broad range of potential liability for punitive damages (if widely available in
contract cases) would make it highly difficult to calculate and
allocate risk in commercial transactions. Compensatory awards
of actual damages are much easier to predict and can more
effectively be covered by bonds, insurance, and other risk transfer tools that are essential to the orderly flow of commerce.

Although government agencies generally rely on their
"sovereign immunity" to bar any liability for punitive damages as a result of their own misconduct, they have enacted
a number of laws imposing punitive damages on private
parties. Such liabilities can arise either in dealings with the
government or in transactions between private parties.

One of the best-known such statutes at the federal level
is the False Claims Act,[88] which imposes a minimum civil

---

86. Restatement (Second) of Contracts § 355 (1981); *see also* Richard J. Bednar, Herman M. Braude & John Cibinic, Construction Contracting 783 (1991).

87. *See, e.g.*, Corbin, *supra* note 4, § 1077, at 380 (1964) ("Breaches of contract. . .do not in general cause as much resentment or other mental and physical discomfort as do the wrongs called torts and crimes.")

88. 31 U.S.C. § 3729 *et seq.* (2000).

penalty and treble damages on a contractor who knowingly "makes, uses, or causes to be made or used, a false record or statement to conceal, avoid, or decrease an obligation to pay or transmit money or property to the Government."[89] Punitive damages are imposed both on persons who have actual knowledge of the false information and on those who act in deliberate ignorance of or reckless disregard for its truth or falsity. At the state level, breaches of contract may also constitute violations of laws enacted to protect consumers against unfair trade practices, to punish improper handling of hazardous materials, or even to protect certain favored industries or resources.[90] As the courts appear to impose tort liability in an expanding range of circumstances, the potential exposure to punitive damages in connection with contract breaches increases correspondingly.[91]

---

89. *Id.* § 3729(a)(7).

90. It is beyond the scope of this book to survey the various states and their respective punitive damage statutes. Most readers are probably already familiar with such damages being available under certain consumer protection statutes and basic environmental statutes in their respective jurisdictions. As an illustration of the last category of laws, states with valuable forestry industries may impose punitive damages on contractors who injure trees on land belonging to others. *See, e.g.,* OR. REV. STAT. § 105.810 (2001); WASH. REV. CODE § 64.12.030 (2002).

91. *See, e.g.,* JUSTIN SWEET, LEGAL ASPECTS OF ARCHITECTURE, ENGINEERING AND THE CONSTRUCTION PROCESS § 27.10, at 540 (6th ed. 2000); RESTATEMENT (SECOND) OF CONTRACTS § 355, comment b, at 155 (1981).

Elements of Damages

2

DOUGLAS S. OLES

In most construction and supply contracts, the owner reserves a right to direct additive or deductive changes in the scope of work. Such contracts also typically specify certain events (e.g., differing site conditions, compensable delays, suspensions of work) that will entitle the supplier of services or goods to an adjusted contract price. Some agreements attempt to set forth in advance a detailed formula for calculating such adjustments. More often, however, the contract provides for an "equitable adjustment" or some similar assurance that the change in compensation will be priced fairly.

There is, of course, considerable room for contract parties and their attorneys to argue about what constitutes reasonable payment for a single compensable event or combination of such events. Regardless of how damages are calculated, price negotiations typically include an examination of the principal components in a contractor's price. This chapter will concentrate on how to identify and evaluate the elements of construction cost that are most frequently at issue in pricing disputes.

DIRECT VERSUS INDIRECT COSTS

In discussing construction-related costs, it is customary to distinguish between so-called "direct costs" and "indirect costs." There is no universal consensus on the meanings of these terms.[1] Many people in the industry simply refer loosely to all productive craft labor as "direct" while referring to all management and supervisory labor as "indirect." Part 31 of the Federal Acquisition Regulation (FAR) provides a more complex distinction.

To appreciate the FAR definitions, one must understand that the federal cost principles and procedures are designed to help allocate items of cost to specific "cost objectives." Such cost objectives may be particular contracts, or they may be certain work units within a contract for which pricing is desired.[2]

In this context, FAR 31.202(a) defines a "direct cost" as

> any cost that can be identified specifically with a particular final cost objective. No final cost objective shall have allocated to it as a direct cost any cost, if other costs incurred for the same purpose in like circumstances have been included in any indirect cost pool to be allocated to that or any other final cost objective. Costs identified specifically with the contract are direct costs of the contract and are to be charged directly to the contract. All costs specifically identified with other final cost objectives of the contractor are direct costs of those cost objectives and are not to be charged to the contract directly or indirectly.

---

1. The Federal Circuit Court of Appeals has defined direct costs as those that "arise solely because of and are attributable directly to performance of a specific contract" and indirect costs as those that "are not attributable to one contract in particular but arise because of its general operations." West v. All State Boiler, Inc., 146 F.3d 1368, 1372 (Fed. Cir. 1998).

2. *See* definition of "cost objective" in FAR 31.001. The FAR is generally located at Title 48 of the CODE OF FEDERAL REGULATIONS. Citations in this chapter are to the September 2001 edition.

By contrast, FAR 31.203(a) defines an "indirect cost" as

> any cost not directly identified with a single, final cost objective, but identified with two or more final cost objectives or an intermediate cost objective. It is not subject to treatment as a direct cost. After direct costs have been determined and charged directly to the contract or other work, indirect costs are those remaining to be allocated to the several cost objectives. An indirect cost shall not be allocated to a final cost objective if other costs incurred for the same purpose in like circumstances have been included as a direct cost of that or any other final cost objective.

Although the foregoing distinctions may not be readily apparent, they incorporate several basic principles. The first is that a "direct cost" must be allocable only to the single contract or work activity (i.e., cost objective) that is being priced. Thus, the cost of a worker who pours concrete into forms will be a direct cost of concrete construction. Payments to the working foreman who directs the forming crew will also constitute a direct cost of concrete labor. Payments to the superintendent who divides his time between observing the concrete crews and preparing daily reports in the site office may be part of the overall project's direct labor cost (because all of his time is allocable to that job), but his compensation will be an indirect cost with respect to pricing the concrete labor. The salary of the contractor's project manager who spends part time at the construction site and part time in the home office is almost certain to be treated as an indirect cost.

In pricing adjustments to compensation under a construction or supply contract, it is important to identify each element of direct cost that is affected and then to add whatever portion of indirect cost is reasonably allocable to the change in direct cost.

ALLOWABLE COSTS

The cost principles and procedures established by Part 31 of the FAR are both the most detailed and the most thorough rules of contract pricing in the construction industry. By their terms they apply only to federal contracts or to state and local projects being funded (in whole or in part) with federal money. Even where federal cost principles are not technically controlling, however, they may be regarded by courts or arbitrators as persuasive precedent, especially in identifying and allocating indirect costs.

The FAR indicates that contract pricing changes should be granted only with respect to "allowable" costs. To meet this standard, a particular cost must pass four tests:[3]

1. The cost must be reasonable.[4]

2. The cost must be allocable to the work being priced.

3. The cost must be consistent with generally accepted accounting principles (GAAP) and any other statutorily mandated requirements.[5]

4. The cost must not be disallowed by terms of the applicable contract.

To the extent practicable, and recognizing that the level of required cost analysis should not be disproportionate to the sums at issue, contract pricing should apply the foregoing tests to each element of affected cost.

---

3. *See* FAR 31.201-2(a).

4. FAR 31.201-3 provides in part that "[a] cost is reasonable if, in its nature and amount, it does not exceed that which would be incurred by a prudent person in the conduct of competitive business." Although the same regulation goes on to say that "[n]o presumption of reasonableness shall be attached to the incurrence of costs by a contractor," that statement is probably contrary to the weight of authority in cost disputes governed by state law. If a contractor or supplier has voluntarily incurred a cost under a fixed price contract, common sense would normally suggest that the contractor believed such cost to be reasonable for what was being received in return. It therefore seems fair that an owner who challenges such costs should generally bear the burden of proving that they were unreasonable.

5. For example, FAR 31.205-14 disallows business "entertainment costs" and requires that they be removed from home office overhead pools before allocating parts of those pools to a federal contract cost objective. This and other similar rules tend to make cost accounting on federal contracts complex and time consuming, with a result that the detailed federal regulations on cost allowability have generally not been followed outside the realm of federal contracting.

DIRECT LABOR

The most ancient and in some ways least controversial element of compensable damages is the cost of labor. Before any tools or equipment were invented, humans built buildings by hand. Even in the technology-rich world of the early twenty-first century, construction remains dependent on hand labor, and it remains a central element of estimating and pricing a construction project.

Labor costs on a construction project typically comprise a number of components. They are likely to include (a) direct wages paid to employees, (b) additional sums withheld or designated for payment of federal and state tax obligations, (c) sums that may be payable to unions pursuant to applicable collective bargaining agreements, (d) sums that may be designated for premiums on insurance provided to the employee and/or the employee's family, and (e) contributions made to pension or retirement plans on behalf of the employee. Craft labor is usually paid on an hourly basis, and the total package of payments owed for an hour of work is generally referred to as the employee's "fully burdened" labor rate.

The reasonableness of labor rates paid can be challenged on a number of bases. Some of the most common challenges include:

- The hourly wages paid were above prevailing market rates.[6]

- Premiums paid for overtime would have been unnecessary if the work had been better managed.

- Premiums paid for overtime should have been anticipated in the original bid and were not necessitated by changes during the project.

---

6. Labor rates are seldom challenged on public projects, where craft wages are normally set by the Davis-Bacon Act or its state law counterparts. Typically, there will also be no challenge to the reasonableness of hourly rates dictated by union collective bargaining agreements with which an employer is legally bound to comply. Labor rates are, however, more often challenged on small private contracts, where labor rates are commonly not mandated by law or specified by written agreement.

Aside from challenging the rate of labor paid, a defendant may argue that the labor hours for which payment is requested were inherently unnecessary and unreasonable. Subject to the factual evidence, labor may be criticized as unnecessarily inefficient due to such factors as the following:

- Lack of sufficient advance planning and scheduling
- Failure to provide workers with proper tools and equipment
- Failure to provide workers with proper light, heat, water, or temporary power
- Lack of sufficiently experienced supervision
- Lack of sufficient on-site supervisors
- Insufficient coordination of trades by the general contractor
- Workers' lack of proper experience for the required work

Defendants in labor pricing disputes also frequently argue that the labor in question should have been expected under the initially specified scope of work.

It is beyond the scope of this book to describe the wide variety of cases that have been decided on these issues. In general, a party claiming damages based on labor cost must show (a) that it actually paid the costs claimed, (b) that it was reasonable to incur costs for the labor at issue, (c) that the labor in question was properly allocable to the work being priced, and (d) that the labor costs being claimed are not in violation of any applicable law or contract provision.

If a dispute arises as to the reasonableness of the labor rates that were actually paid, the burden of proof should at some point shift to the defendant who challenges them. The degree of *prima facie* proof required from the claimant on this issue may vary, depending on whether the contract at issue is based on a fixed price (i.e., where costs are generally at the contractor's risk) or on a cost reimbursable arrangement. At least in fixed price contracts, it seems reasonable that proof of wage rates voluntarily and actually paid by a contractor or supplier should normally constitute *prima facie* evidence of their reasonableness. A claimant may, however, be held to a higher initial standard of proof if labor costs are paid to one of claimant's relatives, close friends, or other affiliated persons in circumstances that raise significant doubt as to whether the employment of labor was at arm's length.

It is not uncommon for labor rates to be increased pursuant to collective bargaining agreements or other normal adjustments for rising costs of living. Subject to the normal test that costs must be reasonable, this type of escalation is usually included in calculating the costs of labor affected by changes, delays, or other compensable events.[7]

DIRECT MATERIALS

Costs of materials on construction projects generally fall into two categories. The first comprises materials that are furnished to become incorporated into the final facility (e.g., gravel for roads or concrete or steel for a building). The second consists of consumables that are used up in the construction process (e.g., acetylene for welders or wood for concrete forms). Both are generally priced at the direct cost of the contractor making a claim. Of course, a general contractor's "cost" of providing materials is likely to include overhead and profit charged by the subcontractor or supplier who provides the materials, but those elements are nonetheless part of the general contractor's direct material cost.

To avoid disputes, it is advisable to agree at the beginning of a project on when material costs are to be reimbursed. Although such payment is generally due no later than the time at which they are incorporated into the work, many contracts provide for payment to be made as soon as

---

7. *See* RICHARD J. BEDNAR, HERMAN M. BRAUDE & JOHN CIBINIC, CONSTRUCTION CONTRACTING 721 (1991) (hereinafter "CONSTRUCTION CONTRACTING"), *citing* U.S. Steel Corp. v. Missouri Pac. R.R., 668 F.2d 435 (8th Cir. 1982) and other cases.

the materials have been safely delivered and deposited at or near the construction site in an owner-approved storage facility.[8]

Claims for material costs are typically supported by copies of invoices, but certain materials may be provided from a pre-existing supply in the contractor's inventory for which no invoices have been preserved. If a contractor makes use of such materials from its own inventory, a question may arise whether they should be priced based on the contractor's historical cost or based on the (typically higher) current market value of such materials. Of course, an owner generally cannot require a contractor to provide materials from its own inventory at below-market prices, so an owner who wishes to obtain this benefit may have to negotiate for it.

A party claiming reimbursement of direct material costs will generally bear the burden of showing (a) that it actually paid the costs claimed, (b) that it was reasonable to incur the costs of procuring the materials at issue, (c) that the materials in question were properly allocable to the work being priced, and (d) that the charge for material costs does not violate any applicable law or contract provision.

At least in fixed price contracts (where contractors have an incentive to minimize expenses), proof of costs voluntarily and actually paid to third parties for materials should normally constitute *prima facie* evidence as to their reasonableness. As with labor costs, however, a claimant may be held to a higher initial standard of proof if materials are purchased in circumstances that raise significant doubt as to

---

8. For example, AIA Document A201, General Conditions of the Contract for Construction ¶ 9.3.2 (1997 edition), states as follows:

> Unless otherwise provided in the Contract Documents, payments shall be made on account of materials and equipment delivered and suitably stored at the site for subsequent incorporation in the Work. If approved in advance by the Owner, payment may similarly be made for materials and equipment suitably stored off the site at a location agreed upon in writing. Payment for materials and equipment stored on or off the site shall be conditioned upon compliance by the Contractor with procedures satisfactory to the Owner to establish the Owner's title to such materials and equipment or otherwise protect the Owner's interest, and shall include the costs of applicable insurance, storage and transportation to the site for such materials and equipment stored off the site.

whether their procurement was at arm's length.[9] Another test for reasonableness of material costs is whether they are incurred in the same or similar manner that the claimant typically obtains materials on other projects.[10]

DIRECT EQUIPMENT

When construction equipment is rented at arm's length from a third party, its pricing is generally a straightforward matter based on invoices. Similar to the rules governing material costs, costs of rented equipment are generally reasonable if they are incurred at prevailing market prices.[11] With respect to contractor-owned equipment, however, the preferred method of pricing is to calculate the contractor's actual cost of owning and operating the equipment in question.[12] It is often difficult, if not impracticable, to determine such costs precisely.[13] There has accordingly been considerable controversy in pricing of contractor-owned equipment.

For purposes of pricing, costs of contractor-owned construction equipment are generally analyzed in terms of two main components. The first is the cost of operating the equipment, which obviously varies according to the degree and duration of use. The second component is a fixed cost of owning the equipment and preparing to replace it when it wears out. The variable operating cost of construction equipment typically includes fuel, oil, grease, spare parts, and items of maintenance that are tied to hours of operation. These operating costs can be highly variable from one climate zone

---

9. The test of "arm's length bargaining" is one of the federal tests under FAR 31.201-3(b)(2).

10. This test is applied to federal contracts under FAR 31.201-3(b)(4).

11. One cross-check for the reasonableness of third-party rental costs is the AED GREEN BOOK, a compilation of nationally averaged rental rates, published annually by K-III Directory Corporation.

12. *See* the detailed discussion of equipment pricing in JOHN D. CARTER, ROBERT F. CUSHMAN, DOUGLAS F. COPPI & PAUL J. GORMAN, PROVING AND PRICING CONSTRUCTION CLAIMS, Chapter 10 (3d edition 2001) (hereinafter "PROVING AND PRICING CONSTRUCTION CLAIMS").

13. *See* Philip L. Bruner & Craig M. Jacobsen, *Pricing Equipment Claims*, CONSTRUCTION BRIEFINGS 92-5, at 4 (April 1992).

to another,[14] just as they can vary from one geological setting to another. [15]

Meanwhile, the costs of equipment ownership are likely to be fixed, including such elements as depreciation, insurance, taxes, and cost of facilities capital.[16] It should also be noted that depreciation allowance by itself does not cover a contractor's cost of replacing a particular item of equipment when it reaches the end of its useful life. While depreciation is generally based on historical acquisition cost,[17] purchase of a replacement machine may cost substantially more. An equitable price for owning and operating equipment must be sufficient not only to cover depreciation based on historical cost; it should also include a reasonable allowance for the cost of purchasing a replacement machine.

Defendants often prefer to base compensation on the internal equipment rates that contractors develop for use in pricing their bid estimates because such rates are often well below what it would cost to rent the same pieces of equipment from third parties on the open market. A contractor's reliance on such rates for bid purposes does not, however, necessarily render an equitable basis of compensation for the use of such equipment, especially when pricing changed or

---

14. Extremes of temperature can strain many types of equipment and can effectively shorten their operating lives. In arctic climates, for example, some equipment must be kept running continuously to avoid damage from freeze-up; in tropical zones, extremely high temperatures may promote overheating. See, e.g., Philbin v. Matanuska-Susitna Borough, 991 P.2d 1263, 1264 (Alaska 1999) (cold weather causes breakdowns to contractor's equipment).

15. For example, drilling foundations in hard rock tends to accelerate wear and tear on drilling equipment, as compared with excavating in soil. Working in fine sands or dusty environments can clog engine intakes. Off-road work may wear down equipment in a variety of ways, as compared with work on a smooth paved surface. See, e.g., Al Johnson Constr. Co. v. Missouri Pac. R., 426 F. Supp. 639, 644 (D.Ark.1976) (unexpected drilling of hard rock wears out contractor's equipment and increases costs).

16. FAR 31.205-10(a)(1)(i) defines facilities capital cost of money (cost of capital committed to facilities) as "an imputed cost determined by applying a cost-of-money rate to facilities capital employed in contract performance."

17. FAR 31.205-11(a) defines depreciation as "a charge to current operations which distributes the cost of a tangible capital asset, less estimated residual value, over the estimated useful life of the asset in a systematic and logical manner." Depreciation is based on the historical cost of acquiring a piece of equipment rather than on the market value of that equipment.

impeded work.[18] The goal in pricing contractor-owned equipment should be to fairly reimburse the costs of owning and operating that equipment.

Contractor internal equipment rates may be lower than third-party rental rates for a number of reasons, including the following:

- The contractor in business for many years may own highly depreciated equipment that can be provided without loss at well below what a commercial rental business must charge.

- The contractor that maintains its own equipment may experience lower repair costs than a commercial rental company renting to strangers who lack a proprietary interest in the longevity of the equipment.

- For competitive reasons or through lack of proper accounting, contractors may simply utilize rates that fail to include reasonable allowances for the ultimate costs of replacing the equipment in question.

In any case, it is fairly common for project owners to argue that a contractor should be permitted to recover no more than the rates used internally by the contractor in preparing its initial project bid. If such internal rates are ultimately used in pricing a claim, they should be used because they are realistic and not merely because the contractor was willing to use them in a bid.

Under many contracts (and especially on public jobs), potential disputes over equipment pricing are resolved by referring to published rates that are intended to reflect industry-wide experience as to the costs of owning and operating certain items of equipment.[19] Of course, such rates may not cover certain specialized types of construction equipment,

---

18. *See* Philip L. Bruner & Patrick J. O'Connor, Jr., Bruner and O'Connor on Construction Law § 19:81, at 270-71 (2002).

19. The authors would like to thank John J. Reed, C.P.A., for providing input to this discussion of published equipment rates.

and they must be properly adjusted for special factors that may cause the equipment in question to have sustained a higher than normal rate of wear and tear.

Perhaps the most widely known published equipment rates appear in the *Rental Rate Blue Book*.[20] A 1992 study reported that 41 states and the District of Columbia were using it as the sole basis for pricing equipment usage.[21] Notwithstanding its title, this three-volume publication does not in fact collect rates at which equipment is customarily "rented." More accurately, as indicated in its introduction, the *Blue Book* is a comprehensive guide for cost recovery by a company that operates its own equipment. The *Blue Book* segregates between ownership cost[22] and operating cost,[23] quoting rates per month, week, day and hour, and includes tables by which rates can be adjusted for regional differences in annual use hours, costs of labor, freight, taxes, etc. It also includes tables for adjusting depreciation rates on older equipment. The *Blue Book* does not include (a) general overhead or profit allowances, (b) costs of wages or benefits payable to operators, (c) costs of special attachments, or (d) adjustments that may be appropriate for use of equipment in severe job conditions. The *Blue Book* includes volumes dedicated to older equipment that is no longer being manufactured.[24]

The leading publication in use under federal contracts is the *Construction Equipment Ownership and Operating Expense Schedule,* published by the U.S. Army Corps of Engineers. This schedule of rates is generally approved for use on fed-

---

20. The *Blue Book* is currently published by Primedia Information Inc., but was previously published by Dataquest.

21. Bruner & Jacobsen, *supra* note 13, at 9.

22. Equipment ownership costs are segregated between costs of depreciation, indirect costs (insurance, taxes, mechanics' supervision, storage, licenses, and record keeping), cost of facilities capital, and major overhaul.

23. Equipment operating costs generally consist of labor and parts for routine daily servicing and operating consumables (e.g., fuel, lubrications, and drill teeth). They do not include costs of an equipment operator.

24. Volume II of the *Blue Book* covers models discontinued between five and 10 years ago. Volume III covers models discontinued between 11 and 20 years ago.

eral construction and architect-engineer contracts[25] as an indication of "average ownership and operating rates for construction equipment,"[26] with the proviso that "actual cost data shall be used when such data can be determined for both ownership and operations costs for each piece of equipment, or groups of similar serial or series equipment, from the contractor's accounting records."[27] Like the *Blue Book*, the Corps of Engineers rates generally do not include costs of labor, mobilization, demobilization, overhead, or profit, which must therefore be considered separately.[28] It has been noted that the Corps rates are slightly less inclusive than the *Blue Book* rates because they do not cover equipment insurance or taxes.[29] Rather than providing regional adjustments like the *Blue Book*, the Corps rates are published separately for each of 12 regions, ranging from New England to Kwajalein Island.[30] The Corps schedule is accompanied by appendices with adjustments for varying operating conditions.[31]

A few states, notably California, have chosen to publish their own rates for pricing equipment. The California Department of Transportation rates are generally used on state-funded projects in California but have not been followed elsewhere. Some respected industry organizations, such as the Associated General Contractors of America (AGC),[32] the National Electrical Contractors Association, and the Mechanical Contractors Association of America, have at various times published tool and equipment rates schedules for items commonly used by their members.

---

25. FAR 31.105(a) generally does not, however, apply to federal contracts with educational institutions, state and local governments, and nonprofit organizations.

26. FAR 31.105(d)(2)(i)(B).

27. FAR 31.105(d)(2)(i)(A).

28. *See* FAR 31.105(d)(2)(i)(B).

29. Bruner & Jacobsen, *supra* note 13, at 7.

30. Kwajalein Atoll, in the Marshall Islands, lies at the western extreme of the regions for which the Corps of Engineers publishes equipment rates.

31. The Corps allows for average, difficult, or severe conditions, both with respect to tire wear and with respect to the equipment as a whole.

32. The AGC manual was the most widely used manual in federal contract pricing before the Corps of Engineers schedule became widely used. *See, e.g.,* CONSTRUCTION CONTRACTING 74.

It is sometimes argued that contractors who own older equipment should be permitted to depreciate their equipment only until its book value reaches zero (i.e., full depreciation from an accounting standpoint). The theory behind this argument is that a contractor should not be paid more than the historical cost of the equipment that has already been reimbursed through depreciation. This argument is fundamentally unfair and should be rejected. Of course, a contractor may not depreciate its equipment more than once for income tax purposes, but mobilization of useful equipment has value in the marketplace. That value exists because the project owner would have to pay rent if it obtained similar equipment from someone else. The fact that the equipment may be fully depreciated for tax purposes should not deprive the equipment owner of reasonable market-based compensation for the value of providing it to a job.

One important issue in connection with construction equipment is how to price items that are idled or on "standby." After noting that no industry standard exists regarding the computation of standby rates, the *Blue Book* suggests that equipment be priced by adding together three components of equipment ownership cost: depreciation, cost of facilities capital, and indirect costs. The Corps of Engineers rate is computed from the average operating condition, allowing full allowance for facilities capital cost of money plus one-half of the hourly depreciation rate (not to exceed 40 hours in a week). As a rough rule, a number of courts have calculated standby rates as one-half of the normal rate charged for owning the equipment when it is operating.[33]

The rates discussed above generally apply to substantial items of equipment that are typically capitalized and depreciated by the contractors who own them. However, smaller hand-held tools (costing less than $1000) are often expensed

33. *See, e.g.*, PROVING AND PRICING CONSTRUCTION CLAIMS, *supra* note 12, § 10.06, at 331 (*citing* Appeal of J.D. Shotwell Co., 65-2 BCA ¶ 5,243 at p. 24,689 (ASBCA 1965)).

on the theory that they tend to be consumed in a year or two during performance of the contracts to which they are assigned. Small tools may be charged either to company overhead or to jobs where they are used.[34] In construction cost estimating, it is common to price small tools and equipment as a fixed percentage markup on direct labor. When labor is added by change order, it may be appropriate to add a markup allowance for small tools, unless evidence indicates that the change did not in fact increase the contractor's use of small tools on the job.

Again, the guiding principle in equipment pricing should be to compensate fully and fairly (but not excessively) for the contractor's costs of ownership and operation. If those costs cannot readily be ascertained from the contractor's own records, the use of published rates is often a practical solution.

SITE OVERHEAD

Unless a construction project happens to be performed immediately next door to the contractor's office, it is usually necessary for the contractor to maintain a separate site office through the duration of the project. Certain costs are inherent in maintaining such a facility. Examples often include costs of supervisory and office personnel, trailer rental, office equipment and furniture, telephone and telecopy costs, temporary utilities, toilets, and pickup trucks or other vehicles for personnel. These costs tend to be a function of project duration, and some contracts impose a limitation on the number of dollars per day that will be allowed for site overhead costs in the event of a project delay. To the extent owner-caused changes or disruptions to work sequence reasonably necessitate an increase in the contractor's site overhead expenses, however, the contractor may be able to claim

---

34. *See* PROVING AND PRICING CONSTRUCTION CLAIMS, *supra* note 12, § 10.04, at 330 (quoting from the AICPA AUDITING AND ACCOUNTING GUIDE ON CONSTRUCTION CONTRACTORS).

that the specified per diem allowance for site overhead cost should be subject to equitable adjustment.[35]

From an owner's standpoint, it is often helpful to compare the claimant contractor's site overhead costs with the allowances in the contractor's initial budget. If the contractor began the job with a larger or more expensive site office operation than budgeted, its ability to allocate cost overruns to later compensable events may be limited. From a contractor's standpoint, it is helpful to keep track of any supervisory or office personnel who are added due to unexpected problems with design errors, owner changes, or other compensable events.

If properly documented, added site overhead expenses may be charged as direct costs of a proposed change. Alternatively, field overhead can be added as an indirect cost, either a percentage markup on direct costs or a per diem charge on changes that extend the duration of a contract. [36]

It should be noted that when site overhead is treated as an indirect cost (at least on federal contracts), the claimant must utilize a consistent method of allocating that cost to changes. For example, in *Appeal of M.A. Mortenson Co.*,[37] the Armed Services Board of Contract Appeals held that a contractor that regularly treated job site overhead as a per diem charge on changes that extended the contract could not also allocate indirect job site overhead as a percentage markup on direct costs of changes that had no schedule impact. The Board relied in part on language in FAR 31.203(d), which required a "contractor's method of allocating indirect costs" to be "consistently applied." The Armed Services Board followed the *Mortenson* decision in *Appeal of Caddell Construction Co.*,[38] notwithstanding recognized case authority that allows

---

35. *See, e.g.*, Kinetic Builders Inc. v. Peters, 226 F.3d 1307, 1315-6 (Fed. Cir. 2000) (disallowing extended site overhead adjustment caused by owner delay where contractor had not substantially completed contract).

36. *See, e.g.*, CONSTRUCTION CONTRACTING 748-51.

37. 98-1 BCA ¶ 29,658 (ASBCA 1998).

38. 00-1 BCA ¶ 30,859 (ASBCA 2000), *affirming* 00-1 BCA ¶ 30,702 (ASBCA 1999).

home office overhead (G&A) expenses to be recovered both as percentage markups on direct cost and as per diem allowances under the *Eichleay* formula discussed below.[39] One possible rationale for this distinction between site and home office overhead is that home office resources typically flow in greatest concentration to the jobs where changes or delays require negotiation, while job site overhead more often involves a fairly fixed level of staffing that is fully committed to the job regardless of how many changes may require implementation.

HOME OFFICE GENERAL AND ADMINISTRATIVE EXPENSES

In the FAR, home office general and administrative expense (often known as "G&A") is defined as:

> any management, financial, and other expense which is incurred by or allocated to a business unit and which is for the general management and administration of the business unit as a whole. G&A expense does not include those management expenses whose beneficial or causal relationship to cost objectives can be more directly measured by a base other than a cost input base representing the total activity of a business unit during a cost accounting period.[40]

In other words, G&A expense is typically the type of management expense that benefits (and should therefore be allocated to) the full activities of a specific company or business unit, as distinguished from expenses relating only to a narrower portion of the business in question.

G&A expenses typically include such items as:

- Salaries and benefits paid to officers and home office employees[41]

---

39. See discussion at 00-1 BCA at 152, 336–37.

40. See definition of "General and administrative (G&A) expense" in FAR 31.001. The same FAR provision defines "home office" as "an office responsible for directing or managing two or more, but not necessarily all, segments of an organization."

41. *See, e.g.,* FAR 31.205-6.

- Bid and estimating expenses[42]
- Depreciation of company-owned assets[43]
- Employee morale and entertainment expenses[44]
- Equipment maintenance not charged to specific jobs[45]
- Insurance and bonding costs[46]
- Labor relations costs[47]
- Patent costs[48]
- Services of professionals and consultants (when not working on a specific project)[49]
- Public relations and advertising expenses[50]
- Relocation costs[51]
- Service and warranty costs (in some companies)[52]
- Taxes[53]
- Training and education costs[54]

Because these indirect costs are seldom allocable to specific price objectives (e.g., to specific claims for changes, delays, or differing site conditions), they are generally allocated on some kind of formula basis.

When pricing an equitable adjustment based on change in the scope and cost of work, the traditional approach has been to add a percentage markup to the direct costs of the affected work. Percentage markups under design contracts

42. *See, e.g.,* FAR 31.205-18.
43. *See, e.g.,* FAR 31.205-11.
44. *See, e.g.,* FAR 31.205-13 & FAR 31.205-14.
45. *See, e.g.,* FAR 31.205-24.
46. *See, e.g.,* FAR 31.205-4 & FAR 31.205-19.
47. *See, e.g.,* FAR 31.205-21.
48. *See, e.g.,* FAR 31.205-30.
49. *See, e.g.,* FAR 31.205-33.
50. *See, e.g.,* FAR 31.205-1.
51. *See, e.g.,* FAR 31.205-35.
52. *See, e.g.,* FAR 31.205-39.
53. *See, e.g.,* FAR 31.205-41.
54. *See, e.g.,* FAR 31.205-44.

tend to be substantially higher than under construction contracts, in part because designer markup is usually applied
only to labor whereas a contractor can also apply markup to
materials and equipment that have been supplied by third
parties. On federal projects and on other complex projects,
G&A markups are subject to audit by the owner, and the
allowable percentage is usually based on the relationship
between the claimant's G&A expense and its aggregate project revenues. A G&A markup is usually reasonable if it fairly
reflects the claimant's actual ratio between home office cost
and project revenue, notwithstanding that the ratio may be
somewhat higher than those of other companies in the same
industry.[55]

In addition to claiming overhead as a percentage markup
on additive changes, a delayed contractor may also recover
"unabsorbed home office overhead" for periods of compensable delay,[56] even if the overall scope of work is unchanged.
Claims for unabsorbed overhead are based on the theory that
delays prevent a contractor from obtaining and performing
other contracts through which its fixed home office expenses
can be recovered (i.e., absorbed). In such circumstances, the
delayed project must arguably absorb a larger share of the
contractor's fixed home office overhead expenses than was
originally covered by the contractor's contract price.

The best known method of pricing such extended home
office overhead is the so-called *Eichleay* formula, derived
from a 1960 decision of the Armed Services Board of Contract Appeals.[57] The formula essentially allocates home office

---

55. In the construction industry, it is usually very difficult if not impossible to make "apples to
apples" comparisons between competing designers or competing contractors. Each company's G&A
expense is a product of its unique financing structure, the risks inherent in its customary work, the
age of its owned equipment, and other factors that cannot fairly be evaluated by a simple comparison
between G&A percentages. Therefore, allowable G&A percentages are typically determined by look-
ing only at the cost experience of the claimant company.

56. *See* James F. Nagle, Federal Construction Contracting § 24.7, at 358 (1992) ("the concept of unabsorbed overhead in a delay claim is well recognized. ... The impossibility of tracing
home office overhead precisely dollar-for-dollar in a particular contract forces contractors to use a
formula to calculate the recoverable amount.")

57. *See* Eichleay Corp., 60-2 BCA ¶ 2688 (ASBCA 1960).

overhead expense to each day of delay based on prorating such expense to the percentage of company revenue being earned on the contract at issue. The formula for this allocation is as follows:

$$\frac{\text{contract billings for contract period}}{\text{total firm billings for contract period}} \times \frac{\text{total overhead for contract period}}{} = \frac{\text{overhead allocable to the contract}}{}$$

$$\frac{\text{overhead allocable to the contract}}{\text{days of performance}} = \text{daily contract overhead}$$

$$\text{daily contract overhead} \times \text{days of delay} = \text{dollar amount recoverable}$$

The *Eichleay* formula has been much criticized over the decades since it was promulgated.[58] Some courts have ruled that it should be applied only where the compensable delay amounts to a full suspension of the contractor's work or that the claimant contractor must prove its inability to secure additional contracts by which its overhead could have been absorbed.[59] In *Melka Marine, Inc. v. United States*,[60] it appeared that the Court of Appeals for the Federal Circuit was retreating from this extreme, holding:

> The Eichleay formula is the only means approved in our case law for calculating recovery for unabsorbed home office overhead. See E.R. Mitchell Constr. Co. v. Danzig, 175 F.3d 1369, 1372 (Fed. Cir. 1999). Home office overhead typically includes accounting and payroll services, salaries for upper-level managers, general insurance, utilities, taxes, and depreciation. See Interstate Gen. Gov't Contractors, Inc. v. West, 12 F.3d 1053, 1058 (Fed. Cir. 1993).
>
> Melka must satisfy two requirements in order to show that it is entitled to Eichleay damages: (1) the government required

---

58. *See, e.g.,* Howard N. Kenyon, Nash & Cibinic Report 13:6, at 94 (June 1999).

59. *See, e.g.,* Satellite Elec. Co. v. Dalton, 105 F.3d 1418, 1421 (Fed. Cir. 1997) and other authorities cited in West's ⌖ 393 UNITED STATES k72–74, 113.

60. 187 F.3d 1370 (Fed. Cir. 1999).

the contractor to stand by during government-caused delay of indefinite duration; and (2) while and because of standing by, the contractor was unable to take on other work. Interstate, 12 F.3d at 1056. If the contractor can make out a prima facie case of (1) above, i.e., that the government-imposed delay was uncertain and that the government required the contractor to remain on standby, ready to resume full work immediately, the burden shifts to the government to show either (1) that it was not impractical for the contractor to obtain "replacement work" during the delay, or (2) that the contractor's inability to obtain such work, or to perform it, was not caused by the government's suspension. See West v. All State Boiler, Inc., 146 F.3d 1368, 1376 (Fed. Cir. 1998).[61]

In *Melka Marine*, the Federal Circuit added that a "heavy burden ... falls on the government once a contractor has established its *prima facie* case of entitlement to *Eichleay* damages."[62]

In *P.D. Dick Inc. v. Principi*,[63] however, the Federal Circuit recently undertook to "clarify" the rules for use of the *Eichleay* formula, stating them in a new and seemingly more restrictive way. It confirmed that the formula may appropriately be used when "much, if not all" of a contractor's work is effectively suspended for an indefinite time while the contractor must remain on the site.[64] The Federal Circuit indicated, however, that the contractor must initially prove (a) the existence of a government-caused suspension or delay that was not concurrently caused by the contractor, (b) a resulting prolongation of the work, and (c) that the contractor was therefore required to remain on standby during the

---

61. *Id.* at 1374–75; *see also* Charles G. Williams Constr. Inc. v. White, 271 F.3d 1055, 1058 (Fed. Cir. 2001) (vacating an ASBCA denial of *Eichleay* damages, in part due to an apparent lack of proof by the government that it was practical for the delayed contractor to take on other work). *But see* Sauer Inc. v. Danzig, 224 F.3d 1340, 1348 (Fed. Cir. 2000) ("Before a contractor can recover *Eichleay* damages, it must show that a government-imposed delay occurred, that the contractor was required to stand by during the delay, and that while standing by it was unable to take on additional work.") (*citing Satellite Electric*).
62. 187 F.3d at 1377–78 (citing authorities).
63. 324 F.3d 1364, 1370–71 (2003).
64. *Id.* at *14.

delay.[65] If these elements are proved, the Federal Circuit held that the burden shifts to the government to show "that it was not impractical for the contractor to take on replacement work and thereby mitigate its damages."[66] If the government carried this burden, the Federal Circuit says that the contractor must thereupon bear "the burden of persuasion that it was impractical for it to obtain sufficient replacement work."[67]

The significance of *P. D. Dick* lies in its requirements for establishing the "standby" element of the test described above. If a Contracting Officer has issued a *written* order suspending *all* contract work, for an *uncertain duration*, and requiring the contractor to remain ready to resume performance "*immediately or on short notice*," the contractor has established standby.[68] On the other hand, in the common situation where the government has issued no such detailed written order, the contractor may be required to prove standby through indirect evidence, showing: (a) that the government-caused delay was not only substantial but of indefinite duration; (b) that during the delay the contractor was required to be ready to resume work at full speed and immediately (a showing negated if a "reasonable time" for remobilization was allowed or if a partial and gradual remobilization was permitted); and (c) that most, if not all, of the contract work was effectively suspended.[69] The elements may be difficult to establish, even in cases of expensive contract interruption, particularly if well-informed Contracting Officers take steps to avoid their existence (for example by expressly permitting partial or gradual remobilization).

In many cases of delay, the contractor must respond by devoting more of its home office efforts than originally planned to the affected job. Such contractors are often

---

65. *Id.* at *9–10.
66. *Id.* at *10.
67. *Id.*
68. *Id.* at *12.
69. *Id.* at *13–17.

restrained from pursuing or committing to new contracts while they remain uncertain as to how long their efforts will be tied up on the project that is being delayed. If delays are attributable to the owner, traditional rules of equity support the principle that some form of added compensation for home office overhead should usually be appropriate. Unfortunately, complicated formulae such as the ones outlined in *P. D. Dick* tend to require elaborate exchanges of proof on facts that involve a significant degree of subjectivity.

Although the *Eichleay* approach has received limited state law support in calculating delay damages,[70] most states have not adopted a specific rule for determining damages based on extended home office overhead. It is reasonable to expect, however, that many of them would tend to look to federal case law as a source of persuasive precedent.

Traditionally, failure to mitigate damages has been an affirmative defense on which the defendant bears the burden of proof. Following that tradition, a party defending against an *Eichleay* claim should logically bear the burden of proving that the claimant should reasonably have mitigated its damages by seeking to recover unabsorbed overhead by performing other jobs during the period in question. It will be difficult for a defendant to carry this burden unless the delayed contractor was given information that would allow it to foresee the duration of delay with sufficient certainty to reassign its work crews and equipment to other jobs while the delayed job was partly or entirely on standby. The reasonableness and availability of such mitigation will of course depend on the facts of each case.

Recovery of unabsorbed overhead for delays (on a per diem basis) does not necessarily preclude recovering an allowance for home office overhead as a percentage markup on additive changes.[71] When a construction project sustains

70. *See, e.g.*, Golf Landscaping, Inc. v. Century Constr. Co., 696 P.2d 590 (Wash. Ct. App. 1984).

71. *See, e.g.*, Altmayer v. Johnson, 79 F.3d 1129 (Fed. Cir. 1996); Community Heating & Plumbing Co. v. Kelso, 987 F.2d 1575 (Fed. Cir. 1993); C.B.C. Enters. v. United States, 978 F.2d 669 (Fed. Cir. 1992), *discussed in* Appeal of Caddell Constr. Co., 00-1 BCA ¶ 30,859 (ASBCA 2000).

both additive change orders and compensable delays, however, an *Eichleay*-based claim for extended overhead costs may in some cases duplicate some of the overhead costs that have been claimed or paid as percentage markups on changes. The extent of such duplication may depend on whether the additive changes were performed without reducing the efficiency of other activities. If added work was inefficient or if impacts on unchanged activities were disproportionate to the cost of the added work, a simple percentage markup on the direct cost of added work may fall short of equitable compensation for increased home office expenses. For example, if the amount of added work was insufficient to keep the contractor's crews and equipment fully occupied during the period of compensable delay, a markup based on the direct cost of increased work scope is likely to be insufficient. On the other hand, if change orders have little or no impact on the efficiency of project labor (e.g., adding an expensive mechanical unit that requires minimum installation labor and has little effect on the completion date), a reimbursement of home office overhead based on a percentage of the increased direct costs may be ample compensation for delay.

In recent years, a number of contracts have included clauses that impose limits (typically a percentage) on the amounts of home office overhead that will be paid for changes and/or delays. Writers of such clauses have a strong argument for enforcing them, to the extent that ultimate changes and delays on the job are reasonably within the contemplation of the parties at bid time. If changes or delays exceed that reasonably expected scope of work, however, the specified limits on overhead recovery may themselves become unenforceable and subject to equitable adjustment.

MARKUPS FOR BOND PREMIUMS, INSURANCE PREMIUMS, AND TAXES

The premiums charged for many project bonds and insurance policies are calculated as a small percentage of the contract price. Contractors are often required by their insurance or surety companies to agree that any increase to the insured party's contract price will necessitate an increase in premium. In many circumstances, increases in contract price also subject the contractor to an increased obligation to pay state taxes. Such increases in premiums and taxes should in some manner be compensated in the process of equitable price adjustments.

With regard to bond and insurance premiums, the contractor may bear an initial burden of showing that increases to its price will in fact affect its premiums. Upon carrying this burden, the contractor is typically entitled to recover percentage markups to cover its liability for increased premiums. When defending against claims for bond and insurance premiums, it will be helpful to check whether the contractor is really bound to pay an increased premium on either its bond or its insurance coverage. An owner may decline to pay such markups without some evidence that they will in fact be passed through to a third party surety or insurer.

Sales and use tax liabilities are also typically handled as percentage markups on change order pricing. If additional taxes are imposed on the contractor's gross business receipts,[72] they should arguably be reimbursed as a direct markup on each additive change order. In most states, however, it is customary for taxes on company-wide income to be carried as an element of the contractor's home office overhead cost pool.

PROFIT

Without earning a profit or "fee," a provider of construction-related services cannot continue in business. Profit is therefore an essential element of every equitable price adjustment.[73] In pricing for contract terminations, federal regulations instruct

---

72. For example, Washington State imposes a business and occupation tax based on the gross receipts rather than the net profits of a business.

73. *See* authorities cited at West's ⊕═ 393 UNITED STATES, k74(15), k113.

the government termination contracting officer to "compensate the contractor fairly for the work done, ... including a reasonable allowance for profit."[74] There is, however, no clear consensus on what percentage markup constitutes a fair or equitable return.[75]

Construction is a relatively high-risk business, and contractors must earn a sufficient rate of return to justify taking such risk. If the rate of profit earned on a successful project is not greater than what can be earned on safer investments (like insured bank savings or certificates of deposit), there will be no contractors. Over a number of years, it became widely accepted that direct costs were marked up for home office overhead and then again for profit. A profit markup in the range of 10 percent was often cited as reasonable. Especially on fixed price public contracts, however, this rate of return is often challenged, typically on the basis that it tends to be higher than the profit markup appearing in the contractor's original bid summary.

Skeptics argue that fixed price contractors deliberately bid a low profit markup to get new contracts and plan to make up for it through change orders. Given the costs and risks associated with change order recovery, however, this theory does not appear to have broad application. More often, a contractor expects to improve on its as-bid rate of profit through a careful "buy out" of the job—obtaining subcontractors, materials, and equipment for lower prices than

---

74. FAR 49.201(a); *see also* discussion of computing termination profit in FAR 49.202.

75. Even among federal agencies, a variety of procedures are used to determine reasonable profit. For example, the Defense Contract Audit Agency's CONTRACT AUDIT MANUAL (January 2001) states in Section 9-904 as follows:

> NASA uses the structured approach which considers contractor effort in each cost category, cost risk, investment, performance, socioeconomic programs, and special situations. DOE uses weighted guidelines which consider sub-levels of the cost elements, contract risk, capital investment, independent research and development, special program participation, and other considerations. DOT uses weighted guideline methods for manufacturing contracts, research and development contracts, and services contracts. Risk percentage ranges are provided by contract type for each of the contract categories. GSA uses a structured approach which considers material acquisition, conversion direct labor, conversion related indirect costs, other costs, and general management. Other factors include contract cost risk, capital investment, cost control and other past accomplishments, Federal socioeconomic programs, and special situations and independent development.

the allowances in the bid. The contractor may also incorporate contingencies in its bid allowances from which it hopes to generate savings if the job goes well. For these reasons, it is often not always fair to calculate a "reasonable" profit on the basis of the percentage markup stated on the face of a contractor's initial bid summary. A trier of fact should at least look at the contractor's post-award budget and consider what rate of profit in fact was likely to result if the work had not been affected by the acts or omissions at issue.

When circumstances make such an assessment difficult or impossible, another useful indication of reasonable profit may be the range of profit that the same contractor has earned on other similar projects in recent years. Two commentators have suggested that a reasonable profit might be determined by considering such factors as (a) complexity of work, (b) risk of undertaking a fixed price before work is performed, (c) extent of capital investment, and (d) extent of technical contributions required to resolve the problem at hand.[76]

In an effort to make the calculation of profit more objective, the U.S. Department of Defense Federal Acquisition Regulation Supplement (DFARS) requires its departments and agencies to utilize "a structured approach for developing a prenegotiation profit or fee objective" on fixed price negotiated contract actions when cost or pricing data is obtained.[77] Under what it calls the "weighted guidelines method," the DoD formula evaluates three "profit factors," including performance risk, contract type risk, and facilities capital employed.[78]

Under the DoD guidelines, "performance risk" assigns numerical values to (a) the technical uncertainties of performance and (b) the degree of management necessary to perform the work in question.[79] The "contract type risk" assigns

---

76. Bruner & O'Connor, *supra* note 18, § 19:87, at 288.
77. DFARS 215.404-4(b)(1) (2002). The DFARS is available online at http://www.acq.osd.mil/dp/dars/dfars.html.
78. *Id.* 215.404-71-1.
79. *Id.* 215.404-71-2.

a numerical risk factor to the "degree of cost risk" involved in performing the work for a fixed price, including an adjustment to allow for the contractor's cost of working capital.[80] A third factor "focuses on encouraging and rewarding aggressive capital investment in facilities that benefit DoD."[81]

Supporters of the DoD weighted guidelines point to the reasonableness of their attempt to match profit markup with the level of risk assumed by the contractor. They also provide a potentially useful checklist of factors to consider in calculating an equitable rate of profit. Critics argue, however, that the DoD guidelines give the illusion of objectivity when they are in essence merely a sum of smaller subjective allowances. They also argue that the weighted guidelines are complex and difficult to apply consistently. At the time of this writing, the DoD weighted guideline approach does not appear to have attracted much following in pricing profit for contracts governed by state law.

It should be noted that recoverable profits may be limited by contract. For example, a contractor may not add profit to a claim for costs under the federal Suspension of Work clause,[82] and many contract forms preclude recovery of lost profits on work that was not yet complete when a termination for convenience is implemented.[83]

In recent years, a number of prime contractors have drafted clauses allowing them to augment their subcontract backcharges with a markup percentage to cover the prime contractor's home office G&A expense and/or profit. It is not yet clear whether such clauses will find favor in the courts. They generally seem to appear in situations where the prime contractor has substantially greater bargaining power than the subcontractor, and they run counter to the

---

80. *Id.* 215.404-71-3.

81. *Id.* 215.404-71-4.

82. *See* FAR 52.242-14(b).

83. *But see* AIA Document A201, General Conditions of the Contract for Construction ¶ 14.4.3 (1997 edition) (allowing "reasonable overhead and profit on the Work not executed").

traditional understanding that a contractee's damages for breach are limited to reasonably foreseeable costs and losses that result proximately from the breach. If a prime contractor is permitted to earn profit from performing remedial work (or if an owner may similarly profit from taking over work from its contractor), the result would appear to create an unhealthy incentive for contractees to declare contractors in default.

ATTORNEY'S FEES AND COSTS

Lengthy treatises have been written on the right of parties to recover attorney's fees and costs in construction-related claims. In general, prevailing parties in federal construction cases are not entitled to awards of their attorney's fees unless such fees are authorized by a specific statute.[84] This is a product of the so-called American Rule that has a long history in our jurisprudence.[85]

One statute that permits attorney's fee awards under federal contracts is the Equal Access to Justice Act,[86] but its remedy is limited to relatively small claimants.[87] To recover attorney's fees against the government under the Act, an eligible claimant must prevail in litigation and must generally prove that the government position in the case was not "substantially justified."[88] As will be discussed in the next section of this chapter, the FAR also allows limited recovery of certain legal fees as "professional and consultant services."

---

84. *See* Fed. R. Civ. P. 54(d).

85. *See* Alyeska Pipeline Serv. v. Wilderness Soc'y, 421 U.S. 240 (1975); Stephen B. Shapiro & Michelle D. Hertz, *Recovery of Attorney's Fees in Federal and State Construction Cases*, 19:3 Constr. Law. 37 (July 1999).

86. P.L. 96-481, codified at 5 U.S.C. § 504 and 28 U.S.C. § 2412 (2000).

87. To qualify under EAJA, a prevailing corporation or partnership may not have net worth in excess of $7 million, and awards of attorney fees will not exceed $125 per hour unless the "court determines that an increase in the cost of living or a special factor, such as the limited availability of qualified attorneys for the proceedings involved, justifies a higher fee." 28 U.S.C. § 2412(d)(1)(D)(2) (1994).

88. *See, e.g.*, Sheila C. Stark, *Collecting Fees and Costs from the U.S. Government*, 20:4 Constr. Law. 15 (Oct. 2000).

If a federal contract is terminated for the government's convenience, the reasonable costs allowed to the contractor include "[a]ccounting, legal, clerical and other expenses reasonably necessary for the preparation of termination settlement proposals and supporting data."[89]

In disputes governed by state law, the general rule again denies attorney's fees to the prevailing party,[90] but several exceptions are typically recognized. Fees may be awarded in any of these instances:

- The governing contract provides for them.

- An applicable statute or court rule provides for them.

- A recognized equitable principle supports their award.

Although most of the nationally published standard contract forms do not include provisions awarding attorney's fees, many standard forms developed for particular companies include such clauses, often on a one-sided basis. It is sometimes said that the party most likely to breach the contract is the one who should most fear inclusion of a clause awarding attorney's fees in case of a dispute. Each party's exposure to liability for the legal expenses of both parties can certainly provide an incentive to be reasonable if a dispute arises.

Contract clauses awarding attorney's fees to a prevailing party are enforceable on a broad basis across the United States. Statutory authorization for attorney's fees is likely, however, to vary considerably from one state to another.[91] There is also a considerable body of case law relating to

---

89. FAR 52.249-2(g)(3)((i).

90. *But see* Alaska Civil Rule 82, which generally awards attorney's fees to the prevailing parties in civil cases as a percentage of the damages recovered.

91. *See* BRUNER & O'CONNOR, *supra* note 18, § 19:98, at 307–08 ("At the state level various construction related statutes governing mechanic's liens, bond claims, prompt payment, consumer protection, indemnity, and small business statutes frequently authorize claimants to recover legal fees and expenses."); *see also* Shapiro & Hertz, *supra* note 78; Frank Hughes & Debera Massahos, *Statutes Permitting Recovery of Attorney's Fees in Construction Cases*, 17:4 CONSTR. LAW. 33 (Oct. 1997).

attorney's fee awards and the means of determining which parties are "prevailing" for that purpose.[92]

If attorney's fees are available by way of contract, statute, or some other recognized equitable theory, their calculation is likely to reflect an evaluation of the prevailing party's legal bills that includes the following:

- To what extent did the prevailing party prevail on issues in the case, comparing issues won with issues lost?

- Were the prevailing party's attorney's fees reasonable in proportion to the size and complexity of the matter at issue?

- Were the prevailing party's legal fees needlessly increased by excess staffing of depositions and other activities in the litigation?

- Were the prevailing party's attorney's fees reasonable when viewed in the context of the levels at which it and the opposing party offered to settle the case?

- Did the prevailing party expend substantial legal fees on conducting depositions or other discovery that was not used at trial?

- Did the prevailing party expend substantial legal fees on unsuccessful motions or other pre-trial activities that were not reasonably justified?

The recovery of "costs" includes a potentially broad category of litigation-related expenses. Typical categories include court reporter fees, photocopy costs, word processing, computer-aided legal research, telephone bills, and certain categories of paralegal services. Except to the extent that such costs are designated as recoverable in a specific contract clause or statute, they are typically not awarded. State laws vary on this issue and should be consulted in each individual case.

---

92. *See* West's ⊕═ 115 DAMAGES, k70–73.

CONSULTANT FEES

As the technology of litigation support continues to undergo advances, the variety of available consulting services expands correspondingly. Consultants are regularly utilized not merely to offer expert opinions on technical subjects but also to assist in organizing and understanding complex data. It becomes increasingly economical to transfer paper documents into electronic databases, in which word-based searches can assist lawyers in distilling relevant facts. While claimants in federal contract disputes seldom recover their attorney's fees, there are some bases for recovering consultant service costs.

In federal contracting, FAR 31.205–33(b) provides that "costs of professional and consultant services" are generally allowable "when reasonable in relation to the services rendered and when not contingent upon recovery of the costs from the Government."[93] Examples of such services are those "acquired by contractors or subcontractors in order to enhance their legal, economic, financial, or technical positions."[94] Of course, such costs must be reasonable and must be properly allocable to the cost objective being priced, but there is at least a regulatory vehicle by which to pursue such recovery.

When a federal contract is terminated for the government's convenience, we have already noted that FAR 52.249–2(g)(3)(i) provides for recovery of "accounting, legal, clerical, and other expenses reasonably necessary for the preparation of termination settlement proposals and supporting data." In private contracts, contract provisions provide increasingly that reasonable costs of consultants shall be awarded to the prevailing party (if any) in case of a dispute. Under state law, however, the rapid growth of consulting services has generally not been matched by increases in the ability of

---

93. *See* James M. Weitzel Jr., *The Professional & Consultant Service Cost Principle,* CP&A REPORT 13 (October 1989).
94. FAR 31.205-33(a).

prevailing parties to recover the expense of using them in trial.

INTEREST

Awards of interest to prevailing parties are normally considered in two categories. The first is prejudgment interest, claimed from the date a claim began accruing until the date it is granted by judgment. The second category is interest that accrues from the date judgment is entered. Legal rights to recover these two types of interest and the rates at which they accrue vary considerably from one state to another.

Under the Contract Disputes Act of 1978 and the federal Disputes clause,[95] interest is allowed at rates that are not affected by entry of a judgment.[96] Simple interest starts to accrue from "(1) the date that the Contracting Officer receives the claim (certified, if required); or (2) the date that payment otherwise would be due, if that date is later, until the date of payment."[97] This interest continues accruing until the claim is paid. The rate of interest is adjusted every six months by the Secretary of the Treasury under criteria established by the Renegotiation Act of 1971.[98]

On federal contracts, compound interest is generally recoverable under the Prompt Payment Act,[99] a statute requiring the federal government to pay interest when it fails to make payments for approved work (a) within 14 days after receipt of a proper payment request or (b) within a such longer time as the contract may specifically allow for such payment.[100] This federal law also requires prime contractors to pay interest to subcontractors when government payments are not

---

95. *See* 41 U.S.C. § 611 (2000); FAR 52.233-1.

96. On the general subject of recovering interest from the federal government, *see* authorities cited at West's ⊕═ 393 UNITED STATES, k110.

97. *See* FAR 52.232-17; FAR 52.233-1(h).

98. For current and previous rates, *see* http://www.publicdebt.treas.gov/opd/opdprmt2.htm.

99. 31 U.S.C. §§ 3901–3906 (2000).

100. *See id.* § 3903(a)(6).

promptly passed through to them.[101] Many states have similar statutes, designed both to ensure prompt payments by public agencies and to ensure that such payments are promptly passed through to lower-tier contractors and suppliers.

For many years, interest on judgments entered in federal diversity actions was based on rates allowed under state law. Since enactment of the Federal Courts Improvement Act of 1982,[102] however, interest on most civil money judgments is computed at a unified rate, subject to periodic market-based adjustments. A successful litigant's entitlement to pre-judgment interest in diversity actions remains governed by the applicable state law.[103]

Under state law, applicable rates of interest will generally be established by statute but may also be subject to contract limitations. In most states, pre-judgment interest will be allowed only on portions of a claim that are "liquidated"[104] or on unliquidated elements of a claim that are ascertainable by computation and without resort to speculation.[105] When a judgment is entered or settlement is reached, however, the amount in dispute is thereby liquidated, so that interest should definitely accrue unless expressly waived by the party to whom payment is due.

Recovery has also been allowed for the cost of borrowing money or the imputed cost of using the claimant's own equity capital to finance cost overruns, subject to reasonable proof that links such costs to compensable events.[106]

---

101. *Id.* § 3905.

102. P.L. 97-164, codified at 28 U.S.C. § 1961 (2000).

103. *See* 17A JAMES WM. MOORE, MOORE'S FEDERAL PRACTICE § 124.07[3][a] (3d ed. 1997).

104. A claim is generally liquidated if its amount is fixed (e.g., suit for an agreed progress payment or contract balance) or determinable by objective calculation. See authorities cited at West's ⊕═ 219 INTEREST, k39(2.5).

105. *See* authorities cited at West's ⊕═ 219 INTEREST, k39(2) and ⊕═ 115 DAMAGES, k67, k68. For factors affecting recovery of pre-judgment interest under state law, *see* CONSTRUCTION CONTRACTING 770–74 (George Washington University 1991). *But see* CAL. CIVIL CODE § 3287(b) (2002) (giving California courts discretion to award prejudgment interest on unliquidated claims from the date of filing); Fairbanks Builders, Inc. v. Morton DeLima, Inc., 483 P.2d 194, 195 (Alaska 1971) (allowing Alaska courts to award prejudgment interest on unliquidated contract claims from the date when the cause of action arose).

106. *See* BRUNER & O'CONNOR, *supra* note 18, § 19:86.

FEDERAL COST ACCOUNTING STANDARDS

In certain negotiated federal contracts and subcontracts in excess of $500,000,[107] Part 30 of the FAR imposes a special set of Cost Accounting Standards (CAS). They do not apply to sealed bid contracts or to any contract with a small business concern.[108] These complex rules of accounting are intended to promote uniformity and certainty but are not easily understood by most contractors.[109] Due to their complexity and lack of broad application, the federal Cost Accounting Standards are beyond the scope of this book.

---

107. The general rules of CAS applicability are set forth in 48 C.F.R. § 9903.201-1 (2001).

108. FAR 30.000.

109. *See* John Cibinic Jr., NASH & CIBINIC REPORT 14:5, at 67 (May 2000):

The reason we need "the expert accounting witness community" is that the ... CAS are so complex and lengthy that the "common man" (COs, contractors, lawyers, judges, and, yes, even some accountants) do not have the time and energy to parse them. In its quixotic quest for certainty in cost accounting, the CAS Board has created an impenetrable forest of detail.

Statutory and Other Sources of Remedies and Damages **3**

LESLIE O'NEAL-COBLE

There are numerous sources for remedies and damages in construction disputes, in addition to the rights and obligations arising under the parties' express contracts and those established by the law of torts, both discussed in subsequent chapters. Some of these remedies have roots in the English common law, while others have sprung from more recent case law and from federal or state statutes or regulations. When handling a construction claim, the lawyer should carefully consider all possible avenues of relief for the client.

EQUITABLE AND IMPLIED REMEDIES[1]

The chaos and complexity of construction projects require equitable remedies in some cases.

---

1. See Chapter 1 for a discussion of the history of equitable theories. *See also* authorities cited at West's ☞ 205H IMPLIED AND CONSTRUCTIVE CONTRACTS, k1, k2, k30, k31–39; ☞ 316A PUBLIC CONTRACTS, k15.

Courts sometimes struggle to balance claimants' requests for relief with defendants' reliance on contract language and adherence to legal principles. Lack of understanding and misuse of terms have resulted in numerous opinions that blur the distinctions between *quantum meruit*, restitution, and unjust enrichment. Some opinions use these terms interchangeably, adding to the confusion.

IMPLIED CONTRACTS AND *QUANTUM MERUIT*

Courts may find a contract created by the parties' conduct even when no formal agreement exists. This constitutes a contract "implied—in fact," distinguished from a contract "implied—in law," which exists without regard to the parties' intentions or conduct.[2] Over time the distinction between these two concepts has been eroded by lack of precision in judicial opinions, by legal commentators, and by modern legal trends.[3] "Because of these confusing influences, it is not unusual to find judicial decisions, which address restitutionary relief on similar facts 'all over the map.' ... As a practical matter, contracts implied in fact and implied in law are guided by the same objective of preventing 'unjust enrichment' by 'benefits conferred.'"[4] *Quantum meruit* is legal restitution, although courts sometimes exacerbate readers' confusion by referring to *quantum meruit* as "equitable."[5]

The number of *quantum meruit* claims in construction disputes might seem surprising given the general rule that such claims are not allowed where there is a written contract and the fact that written contracts are the norm in construction projects.[6] Further, "[t]his bar to recovery in *quantum*

---

2. Philip L. Bruner & Patrick J. O'Connor, Jr., Bruner & O'Connor on Construction Law § 2:5 (West 2002) (hereafter "Bruner & O'Connor").

3. *Id.* § 19:36.

4. *Id.*

5. Doug Rendleman, *Quantum Meruit for the Subcontractor: Has Restitution Jumped off Dawson's Dock?* 79 Tex. L. Rev. 2055, 2060 (June 2001) (hereinafter Rendleman).

6. *See* authorities cited at West's 205H IMPLIED AND CONSTRUCTIVE CONTRACTS, k55–65.

meruit applies whether a contract exists between the parties (as where a general contractor sues the owner) or between strangers (as where a subcontractor sues the owner)."[7] Nonetheless, *quantum meruit* is often pleaded as an alternative theory of recovery in addition to claims for breach of contract and lien foreclosure.[8]

Some common fact situations where *quantum meruit* recovery may be allowed are where (1) a subcontractor provides services outside the scope of its written subcontract at the owner's request and under the owner's supervision;[9] (2) the owner receives the benefit of a subcontractor's work, but the owner does not pay the general contractor for those services;[10] (3) the parties intend to execute a written contract and the contractor provides services as if there were a contract, but the contract is not executed;[11] (4) while performing the original scope of work, there is an accident or act of God (e.g., a fire or flood) requiring additional work to prevent further damage;[12] (5) during performance of the original scope of work, the owner requests the contractor to make changes, but no written change order is executed; or (6) while performing the original scope of work, the contractor encounters unforeseen conditions making performance of the work more difficult.[13]

---

7. *See generally* Thomas C. Galligan, Jr., *Extra Work in Construction Cases: Restitution, Relationship and Revision*, 63 Tul. L. Rev. 799 (March 1989); *Quantum Meruit Recovery in Construction Industry Disputes*, 7–8 Constr. Lit. Rptr. 265 (July–August 2001).

8. The Federal Rules of Civil Procedure and the procedural rules of most states allow plaintiffs to plead alternative theories of recovery. Some states require an election of remedies at trial, while others allow trial on alternative theories. *E.g.*, Wingate Land & Dev. LLC v. Robert C. Walker, Inc., 558 S.E.2d 13 (Ga. Ct. App. 2001). However, some jurisdictions do not permit subcontractors to pursue *quantum meruit* claims if the subcontractor could have perfected a mechanics' lien. *See* Rendleman at 2070 and cases cited therein.

9. John Wade, *Restitution for Benefits Conferred Without Request*, 19 Vand. L. Rev. 1183 (1966).

10. Ind. Code § 32-8-3-9 (1998) allows a subcontractor to give written notice to a property owner that the subcontractor is holding the owner responsible for an amount owed by an employer or lessee to the subcontractor, to the extent that payment is due or may become due from the owner to the employer or lessee. *See* Annotation, *Building and Construction Contracts: Right of Subcontractor Who Has Dealt Only With Primary Contractor to Recover Against Property Owner in Quasi Contract*, 62 A.L.R. 3d 288 (1975).

11. *Wingate Land & Dev. LLC v. Robert C. Walker, Inc., supra* note 8.

12. Berry v. Barbour, 279 P.2d 335 (Okla. 1954).

13. Most standard form contracts address these issues; *quantum meruit* recovery may be available when there is no "changes" clause.

For example, in *Original Grasso Construction Co. v. Shepherd*,[14] the contractor sent the owner a quote of $49,200 for the cost of construction work at a horse boarding and riding facility, including reconstruction of the existing riding ring. The owner did not sign the quote, but returned it with a check in the amount of $10,000 with the notation "ring const." in the memorandum line. The owner paid the contractor $43,200 for work on the riding ring and $32,781.38 for other work, but the owner became dissatisfied with the contractor. The contractor sent a final invoice for $14,620.33, recorded a mechanic's lien, and filed suit to foreclose it. The owner counterclaimed for delay damages, alleging that the ring was not completed on time.

The trial court entered judgment for the contractor, and the owner appealed, arguing that the evidence did not support the findings and the damages award. The appellate court upheld the judgment, holding that the owner's payments to the contractor pursuant to the quote evidenced an intent to enter into the contract. Similarly, where two subcontractors working together under a fixed price contract did not agree about change-order pricing, but continued working under the contract, the court found there was an implied-in-fact contract to use the contract provisions for change orders in the owner's fixed price contract.[15]

In *quantum meruit* claims, the claimant must prove the reasonable value of the services it provided to the recipient.[16] The price specified in an unenforceable contract may be considered as evidence of the reasonable value of the services provided. For example, in *Davis v. McQueen*[17] a landowner hired a contractor to clear some land, push up a fence row, and burn the "stuff" that was in the fence row. The contractor claimed that the owner agreed to pay $55 per hour for

14. 799 A.2d 1083 (Conn. Ct. App. 2002).
15. Fox v. Mountain W. Elec., Inc., 52 P.3d 848 (Idaho 2002).
16. RESTATEMENT OF RESTITUTION § 1, cmt. e (1936); *see also* authorities cited at West's ⊕═ 205H IMPLIED AND CONSTRUCTIVE CONTRACTS, k110.
17. 842 S.W. 2d 376 (Tex. Ct. App. 1992).

use of his big bulldozer and $40 per hour for the small bull-dozer, while the owner claimed that the contractor agreed to do the work for a flat fee of $450 per acre. After the contractor began working, the owner requested him to do additional work, such as demolishing an old house and an old barn and cleaning up rubbish and debris. The contractor testified that he performed twice the amount of work originally requested.[18]

At trial the contractor introduced his daily records showing the hours worked by each bulldozer and testimony from another clearing contractor regarding the value of the work performed. The jury found that there was a contract between the owner and contractor for bulldozer services, and that the contractor was to be paid $55 per hour for the large bull-dozer and $40 per hour for the small bulldozer, but failed to award the contractor any damages. The trial court entered judgment in favor of the contractor on the theory of *quantum meruit* based upon the hourly rate, and the appellate court affirmed, holding that, despite the jury verdict, there was no express agreement as to the *total* compensation to be paid. The dissenting judge noted that the jury's finding that there was an express agreement should have precluded contractor's recovery in *quantum meruit.*

Claimants sometimes assert quasi-contract theories to recover damages that are not recoverable under their existing contracts. These actions are generally not successful because courts are reluctant to reward claimants who were dilatory in protecting their contract rights or to rewrite existing contracts.

For example, in *County Commissioners of Caroline County v. J. Roland Dashiell & Sons,*[19] a contractor that failed to send contractually required notices for time extensions was held not entitled to recover on a *quantum meruit* theory, the court noting that "[the contractor's] attempt to recover under a

---

18. *Id.*
19. 747 A.2d 600 (Md. 2000).

theory of quasi-contract is nothing more than a unilateral attempt to amend the agreement in a manner that the law does not allow."[20] Similarly, in *Hensel-Phelps Construction Co. v. King County*,[21] the court rejected a subcontractor's claim for damages on a *quantum meruit* theory, where the plaintiff "never asked for an extension of time or gave written notice of change of conditions, although such remedies were included in the subcontract." The appellate court affirmed dismissal of the *quantum meruit* claim because each of the plaintiff's specific complaints was contemplated by the contract, which provided a procedure for remedial relief that the contractor failed to follow.

The *Hensel Phelps* decision was applauded by owners who felt it was the end of *quantum meruit* recovery for contractors. However, some commentators consider *Hensel Phelps* a misapplication of the *quantum meruit* doctrine and note that later decisions appear to limit the application of the *Hensel Phelps* case.[22]

The California Supreme Court recently reversed a $2.2 million judgment in favor of a contractor on a *quantum meruit* theory.[23] The contractor claimed that the public owner had abandoned the contract by making excessive changes and that it was entitled to recover for additional costs in *quantum meruit*. In reversing the judgment, the California Supreme Court noted that "[allowing contractors] to recover in *quantum meruit* for the actual as opposed to the bid cost of a project would encourage contractors to bid unrealistically low with the hope of prevailing on an abandonment claim based on the numerous changes inherent in any large public works project."[24] The court did not decide whether

---

20. *See also* L.K. Comstock & Co. v. Becon Constr. Co., 932 F. Supp. 906 (E.D. Ky. 1993).

21. 787 P.2d 58 (Wash. Ct. App. 1990).

22. *E.g.*, Comment, *The Ties of Natural Justice: Restoring Quantum Meruit for Contractors in Washington*, 69 Wash. L. Rev. 431 (1994), *citing* Douglas Northwest, Inc. v. Bill O'Brien & Sons Constr., 828 P.2d 565 (Wash. Ct. App. 1992).

23. Amelco Elec. v. City of Thousand Oaks, 38 P.3d 1120 (Cal. 2002).

24. *Id.*

California law recognizes such abandonment claims against private owners.

Many other jurisdictions recognize the "abandonment" or "cardinal change" doctrines and allow contractors to recover in *quantum meruit* for "added costs caused by excessive changes beyond the general scope of work of the contract."[25] Twenty-two states have adopted some form of the abandonment or cardinal change doctrine;[26] however, Mississippi has expressly rejected these theories.[27] Oregon law allows *quantum meruit* recovery by a party whose performance has been made substantially more onerous by the breaches of the other party, but does not require proof that the parties intended to abandon the contract.[28]

Many courts have held that a public body cannot be held liable to a contractor on a *quantum meruit* theory if an express contract between the owner and contractor is invalid for failure to comply with the competitive bidding law.[29] Some courts have denied contractors *quantum meruit* recovery against public bodies on sovereign immunity grounds.[30]

IMPLIED WARRANTIES

In many states the courts have recognized an implied warranty of habitability in sales of residences and condominiums.[31]

---

25. Aaron Silberman, *Beyond Changes: Abandonment and Cardinal Change*, 22:4 CONSTR. LAW. 5 (Fall 2002).

26. *Id.* at 10 n.3 (list of jurisdictions adopting cardinal change or abandonment doctrines).

27. Litton Sys., Inc. v. Frigitemp Corp., 613 F. Supp. 1377 (S.D. Miss. 1985).

28. City of Portland v. Hoffman Constr. Co., 596 P.2d 1305 (Or. 1979), *citing* McDonald v. Supple, 190 P. 315 (Or. 1920), and Hayden v. City of Astoria, 164 P. 729 (Or. 1917).

29. *See generally* Annotation, *Liability of Municipality on Quasi Contract for Value of Property or Work Furnished Without Compliance With Bidding Requirements*, 33 A.L.R. 3D 1164 (1970).

30. *E.g.*, Southern Roadbuilders, Inc. v. Lee County, 495 So.2d 189 (Fla. Dist. Ct. App. 1986) (contractor's *quantum meruit* claims for extra work not included in written change orders were barred by sovereign immunity). *But see* Champagne-Webber, Inc. v. City of Ft. Lauderdale, 519 So.2d 696 (Fla. Dist. Ct. App. 1988) (sovereign immunity did not bar claims for breach of either express or implied covenants arising from an express written contract).

31. *See* Cochran v. Keeton, 252 So.2d 313 (Ala. 1971); Coney v. Stewart, 562 S.W. 2d 619 (Ark. 1978); Carpenter v. Donohoe, 388 P.2d 399 (Colo. 1964); Gable v. Silver, 264 So.2d 418 (Fla. 1972); Hanavan v. Dye, 281 N.E. 2d 398 (Ill. 1972); Theis v. Heuer, 280 N.E. 2d 300 (Ind. 1972);

(continued)

This change from the old rule of caveat emptor in real estate transactions[32] is a result-oriented concept based on specific public policy considerations including

> the propriety of shifting the costs of defective construction from consumers to builders who are presumed better able to absorb such costs; the nature of the transaction which involves the purchase of a manufactured product, a house; the buyer's inferior bargaining position; the foreseeable risk of harm resulting from defects to consumers; consumer difficulty in ascertaining defective conditions; and justifiable reliance on a builder's expertise and implied representations.[33]

The implied warranty covers defects in construction that impair a home's essential purpose as shelter from the elements, and as a reasonably safe place to live without fear for injury to person, health, safety, or property.[34] However, the warranty does not cover mere aesthetic defects that do not affect the owner's ability to use the residence for its intended purpose.[35]

The implied warranty applies to the sale of new homes and condominiums and related fixtures, such as garages.[36] One court explained that the implied warranty of habitability

---

Weck v. A.M. Sunrise Constr. Co., 184 N.E. 2d 728 (Ill. 1962); Vanville v. Huckins, 407 A.2d 294 (Me. 1979); Loch Hill Constr. Co. v. Fricke, 399 A.2d 883 (Md. 1979); Oliver v. City Builders, Inc., 303 So.2d 466 (Miss. 1974); McDonald v. Mianecki, 398 A.2d 1283 (N.J. 1979); Lyon v. Ward, 221 S.E. 2d 727 (N.C. 1976); Jeanguneat v. Jackie Hames Constr. Co., 576 P.2d 761 (Okla. 1978); Yepsen v. Burgess, 525 P.2d 1019 (Or. 1974); Elderkin v. Gaster, 288 A.2d 771 (Pa. 1972); Bolkum v. Staab, 346 A.2d 210 (Vt. 1975); House v. Thornton, 457 P.2d 199 (Wash. 1969); Tavares v. Horstman, 542 P.2d 1275 (Wyo. 1975); *see also* authorities cited at West's ☞ 400 VENDOR AND PURCHASER, k37(1). Some states have codified the implied warranties; *see, e.g.*, VA. CODE ANN. § 55–70.1 (A)–(C) (2002). Some states also impose an implied warranty of good workmanship, although this warranty is sometimes treated as part of the implied warranty of habitability.

32. *See* Note, *Liability of the Builder-Vendor Under the Implied Warranty of Habitability: Where Does It End?* 13 CREIGHTON L. REV. 593 (1979).

33. Centex Homes v. Buecher, No. 00-04791, 2002 Tex. LEXIS 130 (Tex. Aug. 29, 2002), *citing* Timothy Davis, *The Illusive Warranty of Workmanlike Performance: Constructing a Conceptual Framework*, 72 NEB. L. REV. 981, 1019 (1993). Texas recognizes two separate implied warranties: workmanship and habitability. "The implied warranty of good workmanship focuses on the builder's conduct, while the implied warranty of habitability focuses on the state of the completed structure." *Centex, supra,* at *15–16, citing* Note, *Implied Warranties of Quality in Texas Home Sales: How Many Promises to Keep?* 24 HOUS. L. REV. 605, 617–18 (1987).

34. *See* authorities cited at West's ☞ 95 CONTRACTS, k205.35, k337(2).

35. Goggin v. Fox Valley Constr. Corp., 365 N.E.2d 509 (Ill. App. Ct. 1977); *see also* authorities cited at West's ☞ 95 CONTRACTS, k205.40.

36. Herlihy v. Dunbar Builders Corp., 415 N.E.2d 1224 (Ill. App. Ct. 1980).

means both that "the dwelling, together with all its fixtures, is sufficiently free from major structural defects" and that it is "constructed in a workmanlike manner, so as to meet the standard of workmanlike quality then prevailing at the time and place of construction ... [and] that a builder-vendor impliedly warrants to the initial purchaser that a house and all its fixtures will provide the service or protection for which it was intended under normal use and conditions."[37]

Damages for breach of the implied warranty of habitability are calculated based on the cost to repair the defects, or the diminution in value if the cost of repair constitutes "economic waste." (See Chapter 5 for a discussion of the "economic waste doctrine.") However, in some cases, courts have awarded cost-of-repair damages that exceeded the original cost of construction where there was evidence that the structure was useless for its intended purpose without repair.[38] In *Lapierre v. Samco Development Corp.*,[39] the court affirmed a jury's award to homeowners of $21,477.24 to repair a defective garage, although it cost only $4,500 to build because "[w]ithout the repairs, the garage is virtually useless for its intended purpose."[40]

However, the implied warranty of habitability has been held inapplicable to nonresidential buildings, such as clubhouses, on the grounds that it applies only to defects that interfere with the dweller's use of the unit as a residence.[41] This is the key distinction between the implied warranty of habitability and other building construction warranties.[42] The mere existence of an express warranty providing for specified protection for a limited period of time does not, without an express agreement to the contrary, displace the obligations

---

37. Lapierre v. Samco Dev. Corp., 406 S.E. 2d 646, 648 (N.C. Ct. App. 1991) [internal citations omitted].
38. *See* authorities cited at West's 92H CONSUMER PROTECTION, k40; West's 115 DAMAGES, k123.
39. 406 S.E.2d 646 (N.C. Ct. App. 1991).
40. *Lapierre v. Samco Dev. Corp., supra* note 37, at 650.
41. *See* authorities cited at West's 95 CONTRACTS, k205.40.
42. Bd. of Directors of Bloomfield Club Recreation Ass'n v. Hoffman Group, Inc., 712 N.E.2d 330 (Ill. 1999).

arising by operation of law under an implied warranty of habitability.[43] Though the implied warranty normally applies only to new properties, in some cases the warranty may apply even if the residence has been occupied for a short period of time before being resold to the claimant.[44] Most jurisdictions have not extended the warranty to commercial projects.[45]

Many jurisdictions allow the implied warranty of habitability to be disclaimed;[46] however, most courts require the disclaimer to be in clear and conspicuous language to be effective.[47] The Supreme Court of Missouri not only required clear and unambiguous language for a valid waiver, but also required the builder to prove that the buyer actually understood what he or she was waiving:

> One seeking the benefit of such a disclaimer must not only show a conspicuous provision which fully discloses the consequence of its inclusion, but also that such was in fact the agreement reached. The heavy burden thus placed on the builder is completely justified, for by his assertion of the disclaimer he is seeking to show that the buyer has relinquished protection afforded him by public policy. A knowing waiver of this protection will not be readily implied.[48]

Other courts have held that the implied warranty of habitability cannot be waived except in specific circumstances. In *Centex Homes v. Buecher*,[49] the Texas Supreme Court stated,

> [W]e hold that the implied warranty of habitability may not be disclaimed generally. This latter implied warranty, however, only extends to defects that render the property unsuitable for

---

43. Bridges v. Ferrell, 685 P.2d 409 (Ok. App. 1984).

44. Park v. Sohn, 433 N.E. 2d 651 (Ill. 1982); Gaito v. Auman, 327 S.E.2d 870 (N.C. 1985).

45. *See* Leslie K. O'Neal, *Warranties in Construction*, 6:2 CONSTR. LAW. 3 (January 1986).

46. Sloat v. Matheny, 625 P.2d 1031 (Colo. 1981); Petersen v. Hubschman Constr. Co., 389 N.E. 2d 1154 (Ill. App. Ct. 1979).

47. *Bridges v. Ferrell, supra* note 43, at 410; *see also* authorities cited at West's ⊕══ 95 CONTRACTS, k205.35(4).

48. Crowder v. Vandendeale, 564 S.W. 2d 879, 881 (Mo. 1978) *(en banc)*.

49. *Supra* note 33.

its intended use as a home because it endangers the life, health or safety of the resident. Further, the implied warranty of habitability extends only to latent defects. It does not include defects, even substantial ones that are known by or expressly disclosed to the buyer.[50]

In the absence of a specific statute regarding residential warranties, to enforce breach of an implied warranty claim an owner must establish (1) the existence of the warranty; (2) that a defective condition exists; (3) that the warrantor was notified of the defective condition; and (4) that the warrantor failed to respond to the notice within a reasonable time. These are essentially the same requirements to prove a prima facie case under a written warranty.[51]

STATUTES

During the years since King Hammurabi enacted his famous code (discussed in Chapter 1), governments have enacted numerous laws, statutes, rules, and regulations creating bases for damages claims in construction disputes.

Federal Statutes[52]

False Claims Act

Contractors presenting claims against the federal government may be distressed to receive counterclaims seeking treble damages and penalties for violations of the civil False Claims

---

50. *Id.*

51. *See* Lorence H. Slutzky, *Warranties: Fully Understanding and Utilizing the Call Back Warranty*, 23:4 CONSTR. LAW. 13 (Winter 2003).

52. *See generally* Kathleen Olden Barnes, *The Contract Disputes Act and the Truth in Negotiations Act*; Larry D. Harris, *The Brooks, Buy American, Davis Bacon and Equal Access to Justice Acts—An Overview*; Christine M. McAnney, *False Claims Act*; Christine M. McAnney, *Prompt Payment Act*; and Christine M. McAnney, *Miller Act*, presented at Tab XIII of REVOLUTION AND EVOLUTION IN BOSTON: CHANGES & INNOVATIONS IN THE CONSTRUCTION INDUSTRY (May 2003), ABA Forum on the Construction Industry Annual Meeting program materials, *available at* http://www.abanet.org/forums/construction/html/registration.html.

Act.[53] Contractors have asserted that the government uses the Act's substantial penalties as a weapon to intimidate and dissuade contractors from pursuing legitimate claims, while government officials claim they are protecting the public purse from claims by unscrupulous contractors.[54] The *qui tam*[55] provisions of the False Claims Act (also called the "whistleblower statute") also allow a private citizen to file a civil lawsuit in the name of the United States when in possession of nonpublic information that an entity has submitted false claims for payment to the federal government. The federal government may investigate the claims and intervene in or take over the lawsuit. If the government chooses not to intervene, the whistleblower can pursue the action alone and, if the suit is successful, receive a substantial portion of the proceeds.

The False Claims Act was enacted in 1863 to deal with problems of corruption in wartime contracts. The current version of the Act provides that violators can be liable for up to $10,000 per false claim, plus three times the amount of damages that the government has sustained, and attorney's fees.[56] Consequently, there is a real incentive for whistleblowers (who are frequently former employees of the defendant) and their lawyers to look for possible violations.

The statutory elements of a False Claim Act violation are: "(1) the defendant presented or caused to be presented to an

---

53. 31 U.S.C. §§ 3729–3733 (1994); *see generally* John T. Boese, Civil False Claims and Qui Tam Actions (1993); Daniel D. McMillan, *Federal and State False Claims Acts and Public Construction Projects*, Construction Business Handbook (2003).

54. *See* Krista Pages, *The Civil False Claims Act—Legislation in Turmoil*, 19:1 Constr. Law. 42 (January 1999); Paul Dauer, *False Claims: A New Threat in State and Local Government Contracting*, paper presented at ABA Public Contract Section Fall Meeting, San Francisco (November 1994); Krista Pages, *Defending Against a Mighty Government Weapon: The False Claims Act*, paper presented at the annual meeting of the ABA Forum on the Construction Industry, Washington, D.C. (May 2000).

55. *Qui tam* derives from the Latin phrase *qui tam pro domino rege quam pro se ipso in hac parte sequitur*, meaning "he who brings an action for the King as well as for himself." *See* William Blackstone, Commentaries on the Law of England 160 (1768).

56. 31 U.S.C. § 3729(a) (2000); *see also* Annotation, *Measure and Elements of Damages under False Claims Act*, 35 A.L.R. Fed. 805 (1977).

agent of the United States a claim for payment; (2) the claim was false or fraudulent; and (3) the defendant knew that the claim was false or fraudulent."[57] No proof of specific intent to defraud is required.[58] However, mere negligence or innocent mistake is insufficient.[59] A defendant must act with "deliberate ignorance" or "reckless disregard" of the truth or falsity of the information. It is not necessary that the defendant received payment on the claim.[60] A "claim" is any request for money or property submitted to the government for payment, or submitted to a contractor if any of the money or property requested will be reimbursed to the contractor by the federal government. The defendant need not be aware that the federal government provided funding.[61]

Most state and local governments use federal grants or other financial assistance in public works programs such as highways, mass transit systems, airports, waste treatment plants, and water treatment plants. This federal funding can create liability under the False Claims Act for contractors on these projects.[62]

In 1986, the False Claims Act was amended to include what are described as the "reverse false claim" provisions.[63] These provisions allow awards of damages and penalties against "any person who makes false or fraudulent statements to the United States for the purpose of decreasing, concealing, or avoiding an obligation to transfer money or

---

57. *See* 31 U.S.C. § 3729(a); Wilkins *ex rel.* United States v. State of Ohio, 885 F. Supp 1055 (S.D. Ohio 1995); *see also* authorities cited at West's ☞ 393 UNITED STATES, k122.

58. 31 U.S.C. § 3729(b) (2000). *But see* Annotation, *Specific Intent to Defraud Government as Necessary to Impose Liability Under Provisions of False Claims Act (§§ 31 U.S.C.A. 231 et seq.) Pertaining to "False" or "Fictitious" Claims or Statements*, 26 A.L.R. Fed. 307 (1976).

59. United States *ex rel.* Hagood v. Sonoma County Water Agency, 929 F.2d 1416, 1421 (9th Cir. 1991).

60. United States v. Killough, 848 F.2d 1523, 1533, 1534 (11th Cir. 1988).

61. United States v. Montoya, 716 F.2d 1340 (10th Cir. 1983) (holding the Act applied to a contractor with the State of New Mexico because the project received federal funds).

62. *See* Lewis J. Baker, *Procurement Disputes at the State and Local Level: A Hodgepodge of Remedies*, 25 Pub. Cont. L. J. 265, 289 (Winter 1996).

63. 31 U.S.C. § 3729(a) (2000); *see* Annotation, *Measure and Elements of Damages Under False Claims Act (§§ 31 U.S.C.A. 231 et seq.)*, 35 A.L.R. Fed. 805 (1977).

property to the United States government, thus causing the government to incur a loss."[64]

Other statutes that the government may use in conjunction with the False Claims Act are (1) the Forfeiture Statute, 28 U.S.C. 2514 (2000); (2) the Truth in Negotiations Act, 41 U.S.C. § 255(g) (2000) and 10 U.S.C. § 2306a (2000); a fraud provision in the Contract Disputes Act, 41 U.S.C. §§ 601–613 (2000); the Program Fraud Civil Remedies Act of 1986, 31 U.S.C. §§ 3801–3812 (2000); the Major Fraud Act, 18 U.S.C. § 1031 (2000); and the False Statements Act, 18 U.S.C. § 1001 (2000).

There is considerable conflict in the case law regarding whether a corporation may be held vicariously liable under the False Claims Act for fraud committed by its agent. In considering the issue, courts have considered whether the agent acted with apparent authority and whether the agent acted for his or her own benefit or for the benefit of the principal.[65]

The split of authority among the federal appellate courts as to whether local government entities can be held liable for making false claims to the U.S. government[66] was recently resolved. The Third and Fifth Circuits had held that local government units are not liable for damages under the False Claims Act,[67] basing their views on the U.S. Supreme Court's decision in *Vermont Agency of Natural Resources v. United States ex rel. Stevens*,[68] where the Court held that states were not "persons" as defined and covered in the False Claims Act. In reaching the opposite conclusion, the Seventh Circuit, in *United States ex rel. Chandler v. Cook County*,[69] acknowledged *Stevens*, but concluded that it applied only to states, not to local gov-

---

64. 31 U.S.C. § 3729(a) (2000); *see also* Annotation, *Construction and Application of "Reverse False Claim Provision" of False Claims Act*, 162 A.L.R FED. 147 (2000).

65. *See* Annotation, *Corporation's Vicarious Liability for Fraud of its Agent under False Claims Act*, 107 A.L.R. FED. 665 (1992).

66. *See* authorities cited at West's ⊕══ 393 UNITED STATES, k122; ⊕══ 268 MUNICIPAL CORPORATIONS, k743.

67. United States *ex rel.* Dunleavy v. County of Delaware, 279 F.3d 219 (3rd Cir. 2002); United States *ex rel.* Garibaldi v. Orleans Parish Sch. Bd., 244 F.3d 486 (5th Cir. 2001).

68. 529 U.S. 765 (2000).

69. 277 F.3d 969 (7th Cir. 2002).

ernments. The United States Supreme Court affirmed *Chandler*, holding that local governments are "persons" subject to liability under the False Claims Act;[70] clearly henceforth municipalities, county governments, and entities owned or operated by local governments that receive any type of federal funding[71] could be targets of False Claims Act litigation.

The False Claims Act casts a wide net of possible violations, and each violation may be subject to separate penalties. For example, a general contractor may be held liable for a false claim related to subcontractors' nonperformance or for passing a false or fraudulent subcontractor claim through to the government owner. Thus, contractors should carefully review subcontractors' pay requests and claims before submitting them to a public owner. Additionally, a subcontractor may be liable to a public body for a false claim, despite lack of privity.

Federal Prompt Payment Act

The Federal Prompt Payment Act[72] requires agencies to pay contractors by the "required payment date" failing which the agency is subject to an interest penalty. The interest penalty accrues the day after the required payment date and continues until payment.[73] The Act requires the Director of Management and Budget to issue regulations to carry out the Act, including a regulation providing for payment of interest on a progress payment on a construction project that remains unpaid for more than fourteen days or a specified longer period for inspection of the work[74] and for payment of interest on retainage if not paid by the date specified in the contract, or, if no date is specified, within thirty days after final inspection.[75]

---

70. 123 S. Ct. 1239 (March 10, 2003).

71. For example, county hospitals, ambulance services, water treatment facilities, municipally owned facilities, schools, community colleges, library systems, transit authorities, and sanitary districts.

72. 31 U.S.C. § 3901 *et seq.* (2000).

73. *Id.* 3902(b).

74. *Id.* §§ 3903(a)(6)(A)(i), (ii).

75. *Id.* § 3903(6)(B).

Another section of the Act requires general contractors to include payment clauses in their subcontracts obligating themselves to pay subcontractors for satisfactory performance within seven days after receipt of payments from the owner. This section further requires the general contract to include a clause obligating the general contractor to pay an interest penalty to the subcontractor if payment is not made according to the subcontract payment clause.[76] However, one court has held that this section does not give subcontractors an additional cause of action for a general contractor's alleged contract breach or create a fiduciary duty to the subcontractor.[77]

Miller Act

Enacted by Congress in 1935, the Miller Act[78] requires prime contractors to provide bonds on federal public works projects. The Miller Act applies to any contract in excess of $100,000 for the construction, alteration, or repair of any United States public building or public work. The Act requires a prime contractor to provide a performance bond for the protection of the United States in an amount deemed adequate by the contracting officer, as well as a payment bond for the protection of persons supplying labor or materials in the prosecution of the work under the contract, and specifies procedures for suits to collect on payment bonds. The payment bond must be in an amount equal to the contract price, unless the contracting officer makes a written determination, supported by specific findings, that it is impractical to obtain a payment bond in that amount. In such a case, the contracting officer shall set the amount of the payment bond, which amount cannot, however, be less than the amount of the performance bond. The Fifth Circuit has held that a Miller Act suit may be combined with a claim for attorney's fees, where allowed under applicable state law.[79]

---

76. *Id.* § 3905.
77. *In re* Thomas, 255 B.R. 648 (Bankr. N.J. 2000).
78. 40 U.S.C. §§ 270a–270f (2000).
79. Cal's A/C & Elec. v. Famous Constr. Group, 220 F.3d 326 (5th Cir 2000).

Federal Antitrust Law

Contrary to popular belief, antitrust laws do not apply only to huge corporations. In reality, antitrust laws may affect companies of all sizes, including those involved in construction. While the federal government is usually the plaintiff in antitrust prosecutions, antitrust laws may provide avenues for private recovery in construction disputes in certain circumstances.

Federal antitrust law is based primarily on three statutes: the Sherman Act,[80] the Clayton Act,[81] and the Federal Trade Commission (FTC) Act.[82] Under the FTC Act, the Federal Trade Commission has broad power to regulate "unfair methods of competition." The Sherman and Clayton Acts prohibit specific types of activity, such as: (1) agreements in restraint of trade (e.g., "bid-rigging"); (2) unjustifiable pricing practices (e.g., "tying" arrangements); (3) monopolistic activities; and (4) anticompetitive mergers.[83] In some instances trade associations may be targets of antitrust actions, usually alleging that the trade association engaged in price fixing or discrimination in granting benefits to members and nonmembers.

Under the Sherman Act, agreements between two or more persons that unreasonably restrain trade are prohibited. Some practices, such as price fixing, are always considered unreasonable restraints of trade. Bid-rigging is a form of price fixing most commonly found in the construction industry. For example, contractors may agree that each will submit a predetermined price for a job, with one contractor's price being sufficiently lower than the others to guarantee that he will receive the contract. Alternatively, one or more contractors may agree not to bid on a project, so that another contractor can get the award. Any type of agreement on who

---

80. 15 U.S.C. §§ 1 *et seq.* (2000).

81. *Id.* §§ 22 *et seq.*

82. *Id.* § 41.

83. *See* Warwick Furr, III & Thomas Brownell, *Antitrust Considerations in Construction*, 81-4 CONSTR. BRIEFINGS 293 (July 1991).

will bid on public or private projects or what prices will be offered is considered bid-rigging. Market division, where contractors divide a territory geographically, is another type of price fixing device prohibited under the Sherman Act. An agreement among contractors to bid only on projects in specific counties or only for specific agencies could constitute market division.

Although antitrust violations are generally prosecuted by the government, there are circumstances in which private actions are available. For example, a contractor that learns its suppliers have been indicted or convicted for price fixing or other violations may have an action for damages resulting from having paid an excessive price for goods. Since remedies under antitrust statutes may include treble damages and attorneys' fees, construction attorneys should review these statutes to see if a client's circumstances could support a claim under one of them.

State Statutes

State False Claims Acts

Some states have enacted their own "false claims" acts, similar to the federal False Claims Act but limited to state or local projects.[84] Some of these statutes provide for treble damages plus civil penalties and attorney's fees. In a recent California trial, the jury awarded the Los Angeles Metropolitan Transportation Authority $29.5 million for false claims and unfair business practices.[85] The judge awarded an additional $2.5 million in interest and $22 million in attorney's

---

84. *See, e.g.*, Cal. Gov't. Code Ann. § 12650 (2002); Del. Code Ann. tit. 6, § 1201 (2001); D.C. Code Ann. §§ 2-308.14–.16, .19 (2001); Fla. Stat Ann. § 68.082 (2001); Hawaii. Rev. Stat. §§ 46-171 and 661-21 (2002); Idaho Code Ann. § 18-2706 (2002); 740 Ill. Comp. Stat Ann. 175/3 (2002); Mass. Ann. Laws ch. 12, § 5B (2002); Mont. Code Ann. § 17-8-231 (2002); Nev. Rev. Stat. § 357.040 (2002); Tenn. Code Ann. § 4-18-103 (2002).

85. Metro. Transp. Auth. v. Tutor-Saliba Corp., Los Angeles Superior Court, No. BC123559, August 1, 2001, reported on at http://www.construction.com/NewsCenterHeadlines/ENR/20010716a.asp. The case is on appeal and has been assigned docket number B158407.

fees. The case is on appeal. Unlike the federal whistleblower statutes, however, some state false claims statutes do not provide for a private right of action,[86] perhaps to prevent competitors from bringing such suits.

Prompt Payment Statutes

Most states and the District of Columbia have enacted public and private "prompt payment" laws, requiring that contractors and subcontractors be paid undisputed amounts owed within certain time periods. Failure to pay as required may subject owners and general contractors to interest and other penalties.[87]

Appendix A contains tables summarizing the major provisions of the state prompt payment statutes applicable to public and private projects. Table 1 identifies major provisions for payment from public entities to prime contractors by state. Table 2 identifies laws governing payments from prime contractors to subcontractors on public projects. Table 3 identifies laws governing payments from owners to prime contractors on private projects.

Prompt payment acts can yield substantial awards. For example, in *Morton Engineering & Construction, Inc. v. Patscheck*,[88] the court held that a subcontractor suing under the California Prompt Pay Act[89] was entitled to prejudgment interest, attorney's fees, and a two-percent-per-month penalty in addition to the amount due.

Unfair and Deceptive Trade Practices Statutes

Many states have enacted "unfair and deceptive trade practices" acts, sometimes known as "Little FTC" acts.[90] While

---

86. *See* Pelletier v. Zweifel, 921 F.2d 1465 (11th Cir. 1991) (no private right of action under Georgia false claims law).

87. Allen Holt Gwyn, *Contractor/Subcontractor Prompt Pay Acts—Public and Private Projects*, 16:1 Constr. Law. 61 (Jan. 1996).

88. 104 Cal Rptr. 2d 815 (Cal. Ct. App. 2001).

89. Cal. Bus. & Prof. Code § 7108.5 (2002).

90. *See, e.g.*, Fla. Stat. Ann. § 501.204 (2002); Mass. Gen. Laws ch. 93A, §§ 1 *et seq.* (2003); Mich. Comp. Laws §§ 445.901–922 (2002); Tex. Bus. & Com. Code Ann. §§ 17.41–.63 (2001). A list

(continued)

these acts were originally intended to cover "consumer" transactions, in many jurisdictions their coverage is broad enough to include aspects of construction projects.[91] Because these laws often provide for awards of attorney's fees and enhanced damages, claims under them are now common in construction cases. However, in most cases, it is necessary for a claimant to show more than a mere breach of contract to make a claim for unfair and deceptive trade practices.[92]

Each act defines the elements necessary to establish a private claim for damages.[93] For example, to establish a deceptive practices claim under the Illinois Consumer Fraud Act,[94] the plaintiff must prove: (1) misrepresentation or concealment; (2) an intent that the misrepresentation be relied upon; and (3) that the deception occurred in the course of conduct involving trade or commerce.[95] An intent to defraud is not required, as an innocent or negligent misrepresentation may be actionable.[96] However, the claimant must prove both that an unfair or deceptive trade practice was committed and that such act or practice caused its damages.[97] To be

---

of state unfair and deceptive trade practices statutes is attached as Appendix B. "Deceptive" business practices are those verbal or written statements that have "the tendency to deceive." *See* Cornell Legal Information Institute site devoted to "Unfair Competition Law," www.law.cornell.edu/topics/unfair_competition.html. *See also* authorities cited at West's ⊕ 92H CONSUMER PROTECTION, k4, 6. *See also* Richard D. O'Connor, Cynthia A. Hatfield, Carmen J. Stuart, *Unfair and Deceptive Trade Practices in Construction Litigation and Arbitration*, 40 S.C.L. Rev. 977 (1989).

91. General contractors may be sued for violating the Florida Unfair and Deceptive Trade Practices Act. Anden v. Litinsky, 472 So.2d 825, 826 (Fla. Dist. Ct. App. 1985).

92. "Mere proof that a contractor is a second-rate builder who does not live up to industry standards does not tend to establish unfair or deceptive solicitation of the consuming public." Eastlake Constr. Co. v. Hess, 686 P.2d 465, 479 (Wash. 1984) (Dimmick, J., concurring in part, dissenting in part); *see also* authorities cited at West's ⊕ 92H CONSUMER PROTECTION, k34.

93. *See* Annotation, *Practices Forbidden by State Deceptive Trade Practice and Consumer Protection Acts*, 89 A.L.R. 3D 449 (1979); *see also* authorities cited at West's ⊕ 92H CONSUMER PROTECTION, k4.

94. 815 ILL. COMP. STAT. 505/2 (2003).

95. *See generally* Neil A. Helfman, *Proof of Statutory Unfair Business Practices*, 36 AM. JUR. PROOF OF FACTS 3D 221 (1996).

96. The defendant need not have had any intent to defraud. Bockenstette v. FTC, 134 F.2d 369 (10th Cir. 1943); D.D.D. Corp. v. FTC, 125 F.2d 679 (7th Cir. 1942); *see* Annotation, *What Constitutes False, Misleading or Deceptive Advertising or Practices Subject to Action by Federal Trade Commission*, 65 A.L.R. 2D 225 (1959).

97. *See* Marshall A. Leaffer & Michael H. Lipson, *Consumer Actions Against Unfair or Deceptive Acts or Practices: The Private Uses of Federal Trade Commission Jurisprudence*, 48 GEO. WASH. L. REV. 521

actionable in Massachusetts, a business act or practice "must either be within the penumbra of some common-law, statutory or other established concept of unfairness, or must be immoral, unethical or unscrupulous, and cause substantial injury to competitors or other businessmen."[98] Merely insisting on enforcement of unfavorable contract terms does not constitute an unfair and deceptive trade practice.[99]

Breaches of contract or failure to live up to industry standards alone will not be considered "unfair and deceptive trade practices."[100] For example, a court in North Carolina overturned a homeowner's judgment against a contractor under the unfair and deceptive trade practices act, holding that, absent additional egregious circumstances, even a willful breach of contract is insufficient to support a finding of unfair and deceptive trade practices.[101] A contractor's failure to remedy construction defects in the home was held not to be the type of conduct that would mislead or deceive an average consumer.

In *Eastlake Construction Co. v. Hess*,[102] the Washington Supreme Court reversed dismissal of a homeowner's claim against a general contractor under the Washington Consumer Protection Act. The homeowners presented proof that Eastlake committed numerous unfair and deceptive acts (including misrepresentations and substitutions with unauthorized materials) during the subject project, and offered to prove similar violation on projects with other individuals. The court held that under the Washington Consumer Protection Act, a claimant must show that the conduct complained of

(1980); Annotation, *Scope and Exemptions of State Deceptive Trade Practice and Consumer Protection Acts*, 89 A.L.R. 3D 399 (1979).

98. Northborough Eng'g, Inc v. Vazza, No. 00-0964B, 2002 Mass Super. LEXIS 309 (Mass. Super. Ct. July 18, 2002).

99. *Id.*

100. *See* authorities cited at West's 92H CONSUMER PROTECTION, k34.

101. Mitchell v. Linville, 557 S.E. 2d 620, 623 (N.C. Ct. App. 2001). *But see* Lapierre v. Samco Dev. Corp., 406 S.E.2d 646 (N.C. Ct. App. 1991) (holding builder liable for unfair and deceptive trade practices for failing to build a deck as shown on brochures and blueprints, where defendant knew it was impossible to build deck in that location).

102. 686 P.2d 465 (Wash. 1984).

(1) is unfair or deceptive; (2) is within the sphere of trade or commerce; and (3) has an impact on the public interest.[103]

Under Washington law, conduct has an impact on the public interest if: (1) the defendant, by unfair or deceptive acts or practices in the conduct of trade or commerce, has induced the plaintiff to act or refrain from acting; (2) the plaintiff suffers damage brought about by such action or failure to act; and (3) the defendant's deceptive acts have the potential for repetition.[104] The purpose of the public interest requirement is to limit claims under the Consumer Protection Act to those related to a company's generalized course of conduct and to exclude actions related to a single transaction.

The *Eastlake* court found that the contractor's bid constituted an inducement to the homeowners to hire the contractor in the same way that an advertisement would induce a customer to make a purchase. The court noted, "A contractor does not provide 'estimates' ... merely to be helpful to the purchaser, but to influence the purchaser to buy the contractor's product or to rely upon the contractor's services to remedy defects in the product. The purchaser will likely rely upon such 'estimates.'"[105] The court remanded the case to the trial court for further proceedings.

Not all jurisdictions follow the trend toward broadening coverage of the consumer protection statutes, however. For example, some courts have declined to apply the unfair and deceptive trade practices statutes in situations where there is state regulation of contractors.[106] Similarly, a window supplier's claim against the manufacturer of a wood preservative product under the Minnesota unlawful trade practice statute was dismissed because the court held that the statute was

---

103. *Id.* at 475, *citing* Anhold v. Daniels, 614 P.2d 184 (Wash. 1980).

104. *Id.* at 476.

105. *Id.*

106. *See, e.g.,* Forton v. Laszar, 622 N.W. 2d 61 (Mich. 2001). *See also* RCDI Construction Inc. v. Space/Architecture Planning, Inc., 148 F. Supp. 2d 607 (W.D.N.C.), *aff'd* 29 Fed. Appx (4th Cir. 2002) (unpublished opinion) ("learned professional" exception precludes architect liability), *but see*

designed to protect consumers, not merchants.[107] In the Minnesota case, Marvin Lumber & Cedar Company, a manufacturer of custom windows and other products, sued PPG Industries, a supplier of wood preservatives, on a variety of theories, including breach of warranty, negligence, strict liability, fraud, and violations of the unfair trade practices, consumer protection, and false advertising statutes. The trial court's summary judgment for PPG was affirmed. Likewise, a New York court upheld dismissal of a commercial owner's consumer protection claim against a concrete panel manufacturer, holding that New York's unfair trade practices statute applied to consumer-oriented conduct and modestly sized transactions, not to large commercial projects involving sophisticated business entities.[108]

Some "deceptive and unfair trade practices" statutes include an antitrust component because they prohibit unfair methods of competition in the conduct of any trade or commerce. The relationship between such statutes and state antitrust laws is discussed later in this chapter. These statutes may also provide "a flexible and potent weapon for asserting claims against manufacturers or suppliers"[109] by owners and contractors.

Unfair Claims Settlement Practices Statutes

In addition to the unfair and deceptive trade practices laws, insurance companies and sureties are subject to "unfair claim settlement practices statutes" in many jurisdictions.[110] The Massachusetts statute defines an unfair claim settlement practice as: "Failing to effectuate prompt, fair and equitable

---

Moore v. Bird Engineering Co., 41 P.3d 755 (Kansas 2002) (engineers liable under consumer protection act).

107. Marvin Lumber & Cedar Co. v. PPG Indus., Inc., 232 F.3d 977 (8th Cir. 2000).

108. *See* St. Patrick's Home for the Aged & Infirm v. Laticrete Int'l, Inc., 696 N.Y.S. 2d 117 (A.D. 1999).

109. Daniel S. Brennan, *Construction Defect Claims Against Manufacturers and Suppliers*, 23:2 CONSTR. LAW. 15, 24 (Spring 2003).

110. *See* MASS. GEN. LAWS ch. 176D, § 3(9) (2003); *see also* FLA. STAT. ANN. §§ 626.9541(1)(i) (2002) (unfair claim settlement practices) and 624.155(2002) (insurer civil remedy); Mo. REV. STAT.

(continued)

settlements of claims in which liability has become reasonably clear" or "Compelling insureds to instigate litigation to recover amounts due under an insurance policy by offering substantially less than the amounts ultimately recovered in actions brought by such insureds."[111]

In *R. W. Granger & Sons v. J & S Insulation, Inc.*[112] there was a dispute between a subcontractor (J&S) and the general contractor (Granger) and its payment bond surety (USF&G) related to construction work at Boston's Logan Airport. J&S claimed that Granger breached the subcontract and violated the Massachusetts Deceptive Trade Practices Act by failing to pay J&S on its subcontract. J&S claimed USF&G was similarly liable on its payment bond. Immediately after obtaining a $203,867 jury verdict against Granger, J&S demanded payment from USF&G. After four months during which USF&G had not responded, J&S amended its complaint against USF&G and sought treble damages for willful and knowing violation of the Deceptive Trade Practices Act. Following a hearing at which USF&G introduced no evidence, it offered $230,000 in settlement, which was rejected. Several months thereafter, judgment was entered against Granger on the subcontract and against USF&G on the payment bond claim. USF&G paid those judgments, then tried again, unsuccessfully, to settle the remaining claims against it.

The unfair and deceptive practices claim against USF&G was tried in November 1998. USF&G offered no evidence at trial. The trial judge entered judgment against USF&G for $845,653 (double the amount of the original judgment) for USF&G's violations of the unfair and deceptive trade practices law as well as for violation of the Massachusetts unfair claim practices law. The trial court found there was no evidence to explain the more than four-month delay from J&S's demand for payment after the jury verdict until USF&G's settlement offer, and that in light of the jury verdict and the anticipated interest and attorney's fees awards,

---

§§ 375.930–.948 (2003); Va. Code Ann. § 38.2-517 (2002); authorities cited at West's ⊕ 217 INSURANCE, k3140.

    111. Mass Gen. Laws ch. 176D §§ 3(9)(f) and (g).

USF&G's $230,000 settlement offer was "wholly inadequate." The court also found that USF&G failed to conduct a reasonable investigation of Granger's dispute with J&S, both before and after the jury verdict, and that USF&G failed to "affirm or deny coverage of claims within a reasonable time after proof of loss statements have been completed." Further, USF&G failed to effectuate "prompt, fair, and equitable settlements of claims in which liability has become reasonably clear." USF&G's actions constituted "willful or knowing unfair and deceptive acts and practices ... in violation of G.L. c. 93A."[113]

The *J&S* court noted that:

> The statutory mandate that a surety who engages in bad faith settlement practices must pay multiples of the amount of the underlying judgment against it fulfils the important public policy of encouraging the fair and efficient resolution of business disputes. ... As evidenced by this case, protracted litigation is almost certain to follow where a surety fails to pay, or to make reasonable efforts to settle, an indisputably valid claim under a surety bond. The specter of a punitive sanction many times the loss directly caused by the surety's bad faith settlement practices provides an important disincentive to sureties who would force a claimant into litigation to recover monies to which it is clearly entitled.[114]

Successful claimants under unfair claims settlement statutes may recover attorney's fees and punitive damages in addition to traditional breach of contract damages.[115]

Courts in other states have rejected efforts to make sureties liable for the "tort of bad faith" that often exists in the first-party insurance context. In *Norwood Co. v. RLI Insurance Co.*,[116] a general contractor sued on a subcontractor's performance bond, alleging that the subcontractor had defaulted

112. 754 N.E. 2d 668 (Mass. Ct. App. 2001).
113. *Id.* at 675.
114. *Id.* at 684 (internal citations omitted).
115. *See* authorities cited at West's 217 INSURANCE, k3374, k3375, and k3376.
116. No. CIVA 01-6153, 2002 WL 485694 (E.D. Pa. April 1, 2002); *see also* Masterclean, Inc. v. Star Ins. Co., 556 S.E. 2d 371 (S.C. 2001) (principal could not recover against surety for bad faith failure to pay performance bond claim).

on the subcontract and that the surety had failed to remedy the default, thereby breaching the bond obligations. The general contractor asserted that the surety's failure to take any action constituted "bad faith" under the Pennsylvania insurance code.[117] The district court, noting that neither the Pennsylvania Supreme Court, the intermediate appellate courts, nor the Third Circuit had addressed the issue, held that because the statute applied to "actions on insurance policies," it did not apply to the contractor's bond claim.

Lien Statutes and Equitable Liens

Each state has enacted a mechanics' lien or a construction lien statute, allowing those who provide services to improve real property (such as design professionals, general contractors, subcontractors, suppliers, laborers and, others) to obtain a lien on the real property for unpaid amounts due. "Mechanics' liens protect persons whose labor and materials add value to a property owner's land. The goal of the statutes is to provide a way for those who improve real property to be repaid out of that property."[118] Lien laws vary widely in their scope and in their requirements to perfect a lien. While a complete discussion of the various lien laws is beyond the scope of this chapter, a list of the lien laws in each state is attached as Appendix C.

Although mechanics' or construction liens are creatures of statute, a claimant must have a valid contract to support the lien claim:[119]

> Most statutes define a mechanics' lien as a right in favor of a contractor for the purpose of securing the payment of the price or value of the work performed or materials furnished in the creating or repairing of a building or other structure or in

---

117. 42 Pa. Cons. Stat. Ann. § 8371 (2002).

118. Rendleman at 2069; *see also* authorities cited at West's 257 MECHANICS', LIENS, k1.

119. *See* authorities cited at West's 257 MECHANICS', LIENS, k61. In some states a written contract is necessary to support a lien claim, while in others an implied contract is adequate. *See* authorities cited at West's 257 MECHANICS', LIENS, k73(3).

the making of improvements on the land, or improvements which may attach to the land and/or the building thereon.[120]

Public property is generally exempt from liens, but California, Colorado, New York, and Kentucky have statutes allowing claimants to impose a lien on the funds owed to a general contractor on a public project, providing an alternative source of recovery.[121] Some states recognize a contractor's or a sub-contractor's right to an equitable lien on the contract funds held by the owner or lender.[122] The states differ widely in their recognition of the equitable lien remedy. Some states do not recognize it at all, while others place severe restrictions on its application. [123]

Contractor Trust Fund Statutes

Many lien statutes provide that monies paid to a general contractor are held in trust on behalf of subcontractors, laborers, or materialmen.[124] Some states have specific construction trust fund statutes.[125] Violation of such statutes may subject contractors to civil and criminal remedies, including treble damages and attorney's fees. In *Tri-Tech Corp. of America v. Americorp Services, Inc.*,[126] a general contractor was held liable

---

120. 2 STEVEN G. M. STEIN, CONSTRUCTION LAW ¶ 9.02 (2003).

121. CAL. CIV. CODE §§ 3179–3214 (2003); COLO. REV. STAT. § 38-26-107 (2002); KY. REV. STAT. ANN. § 376.210 (2002); N.Y. LIEN LAW § 42 (2002); *see also* authorities cited at West's ⌘ 316A PUBLIC CONTRACTS, k25.

122. Annotation, *Building and Construction Contracts: Contractor's Equitable Lien Upon Percentage of Funds Withheld by Contractee or Lender*, 54 A.L.R. 3D 848 (1973); *see also* authorities cited at West's ⌘ 239 LIENS, k7.

123. *See* Ten Hoeve Bros. v. City of Hartford, No. CV93-0704020S, 1996 Conn. Super. LEXIS 1211 (Conn. Super. Ct. May 8, 1996) (unpublished opinion).

124. *E.g.*, FLA. STAT. ANN. § 713.345 (2001); *see* THE NATIONAL PROMPT PAY DIGEST (2002) (a summary of public and private prompt pay laws including trust fund information); Judah Lifschitz, Randal Wax, Daniel Lasar, *Construction Trust Fund Statutes and the Misappropriation of Contract Funds/Edition II*, 99-12 CONSTR. BRIEFINGS 1 (Nov. 1999); Annotation, *Validity and Construction of Statute Providing Criminal Penalties for Failure of Contractor Who Has Received Payment from Owner to Pay Laborers or Materialmen*, 78 A.L.R. 3D 563 (1977); *see also* authorities cited at West's ⌘ 257 MECHANICS', LIENS, k115.

125. *See, e.g.*, ARK. CODE ANN. § 5-37-525 (2002); DEL. CODE ANN. tit 6, § 3502 (2001); MICH. COMP. LAWS. § 570.151 (2001); OKL. STAT. ANN. tit. 42, § 152 (2002).

126. 633 N.W.2d 683 (Wis. Ct. App. 2001).

for violation of the Wisconsin contractor theft statute for failure to pay a subcontractor and was assessed treble damages plus attorney's fees and litigation costs. Because of the potential for attorney's fees or even criminal prosecution in some cases, alleging violation of a contractor trust fund statute may provide a claimant with additional ammunition in pursuing a payment claim.

Courts have reached conflicting results in determining whether a contractor's misapplication of construction funds in violation of a contractor trust fund statute constitutes "defalcation while acting in a fiduciary capacity," making the debt nondischargeable in bankruptcy.[127]

Uniform Commercial Code

The Uniform Commercial Code (UCC) can provide a basis for claims by remote purchasers and a source for consequential and incidental damages that might otherwise not be available.[128] Because Article Two of the Uniform Commercial Code applies only to transactions in goods and not in services,[129] the first question is whether the UCC applies to the construction contract at issue. Courts employ two tests in making the factual determination[130] whether a contract is predominantly for goods or services: (1) The "predominant factor test" looks to the transaction as a whole to determine whether the predominant factor in the transaction is the rendition of services, with goods incidentally involved (e.g., a contract with an artist for painting) or is a sales transaction with labor incidentally involved (e.g., installation of a water heater in a bathroom);[131] (2) the "gravamen test" looks to

---

127. *See* authorities cited at West's 🔑 51 BANKRUPTCY, k3357.

128. Robert Wachsmuth, *Applying Article 2 of the Uniform Commercial Code to Construction Contracts*, 18:3 Constr. Law. 13 (July 1998).

129. U.C.C. § 2-102 (1992).

130. Birwelco-Montenay, Inc. v. Infilco Degremont, Inc. 827 So. 2d 255 (Fla. Dist. Ct. App. 2002), *denying rehearing en banc and citing* BMC Indus., Inc. v. Barth Indus., Inc., 160 F.3d 1322, 1331 (11th Cir. 1998), *cert. den.*, 526 U.S. 1132 (1999).

131. Bonebake v. Cox, 499 F.2d 951 (8th Cir. 1974).

that portion of the transaction on which the complaint is based to determine if it involved goods or services.[132] The majority of jurisdictions use the predominant factor test to analyze mixed contracts for goods and services.

In applying these tests, courts look to the parties' intent when the contract was negotiated and signed.[133] Courts have considered the following factors in determining whether a contract is primarily one for sales or for services: (1) whether contract wording focuses on the goods or the services; (2) whether the goods and labor are billed separately or as part of an overall price; (3) the ratio of the cost of the goods to the overall contract price; and (4) the buyer's expectations of acquiring a property interest in the goods.[134]

In *Tacoma Athletic Club, Inc. v. Indoor Comfort Systems, Inc.*,[135] a Washington appellate court held that a contract for the sale and installation of a dehumidification system at a health club was primarily a contract for the sale of goods rather than services, upholding the buyer's claim for breach of an implied warranty of merchantability under the UCC. In so holding, the court noted, "The negotiations leading up to the contract focused on the goods, not the services, aspect of the sale. ... The written contract primarily lists the goods being sold, although it also refers to services."[136]

In *Kaitz v. Landscape Creations, Inc.*,[137] the plaintiff sued a landscape company for damages to trees that were damaged or destroyed in a storm several years after the landscape company installed them. The plaintiff claimed the contract

---

132. Pass v. Shelby Aviation, Inc., No. W1999-00018-COA-R9-DV, 2000 Tenn. App. LEXIS 247 (Tenn. Ct. App. Apr. 13, 2000); *see generally* Jennifer R. Levy & Mark D. Gruskin, *The Uniform Commercial Code and the Construction Industry: "Do the Warranties Really Apply?"*, Construction Advocacy and All That Jazz (April 1997), ABA Forum on the Contruction Industry Annual Meeting program materials, *available at* http://www.abanet.org/forums/construction/cipubs.html#5 at tab G, p.1; Annotation, *Applicability of UCC Article 2 to Mixed Contracts for Sale of Goods and Services*, 5 A.L.R. 4th 501 (1981); *see also* authorities cited at West's 343 SALES, k1.5, k3.1.

133. *See also* authorities cited at West's 343 SALES, k1.5, 3.1.

134. *Levy & Gruskin, supra* note 132, at 2.

135. 902 P.2d 175 (Wash Ct. App. 1995).

136. *Id.* at 179.

137. 2000 Mass. App. 140 (Mass. Dist. Ct. 2000).

was for services. The defendant claimed that the contract was for goods and that suit was barred by the UCC's four-year statute of limitations; the trial court agreed. The appellate court reversed, holding the contract to be for landscape services rather than for goods. The court considered the following factors: (1) the scope of the project was extensive, spanning several months; (2) the project entailed the development of a landscape design and preparation of the soil and beds in addition to the purchase and planting of trees and shrubs, thus making the project more labor-intensive; (3) plaintiff's primary complaint related to the landscaping services provided rather than to the trees themselves.[138]

Where the UCC applies to a transaction, it allows a buyer to recover direct damages[139] as well as incidental and consequential damages[140] resulting from a breach of an express warranty. Consequential damages include "[a]ny loss resulting from general or particular requirements and needs of which the seller at the time of contracting had reason to know and which could not reasonably be prevented by cover or otherwise."[141] Since consequential damages may not be available under other theories, a ruling that the UCC applies can be very helpful to a plaintiff in such cases.

State Antitrust Law

Most states have adopted antitrust laws related to intrastate activity. These laws generally parallel the federal antitrust laws. Because the federal antitrust laws have been broadly applied, most antitrust enforcement occurs under federal law. However, in some instances, a state's "unfair and deceptive trade practices act" may encompass unfair methods of

---

138. *Id.* at 141.
139. UCC § 2-714 (1992).
140. *Id.* § 2-715.
141. *Id.*

competition as well as deceptive trade practices. This may give competitors an additional weapon, including allowing indirect purchasers to file class action litigation against anti-competitive conduct.[142]

Other Statutes

Virginia has a law providing civil remedies for conspiring to injure another in his or her trade or business.[143] One portion of the law makes such a conspiracy a criminal offense (Class I misdemeanor). Another section provides a civil remedy, available regardless of whether criminal charges are brought, that includes treble damages, lost profits, and attorney's fees to victims of such conspiracies.

Under California law,[144] the state may require the owner of a building that substantially endangers the health and safety of residents to pay the agency's inspection costs, investigation costs, enforcement costs, attorney's fees, and prosecution costs, and also pursue a civil remedy. If the owner is required to make repairs, it may also be responsible for tenants' moving costs and additional rental costs. If the owner refuses to make repairs, the state may seek appointment of a receiver for the building.

California recently enacted a detailed law creating specific procedures for resolving construction defect disputes and limiting the damages that a homeowner can recover in a claim for construction defects.[145] The law provides:

> If a claim for damages is made under this title, the home-owner is only entitled to damages for the reasonable cost of repairing any violation of the standards set forth in this title,

---

142. *See* David Federbush, *FDUPTA for Civil Antitrust*, LXXVI Fla. Bar. J. 52 (December 2002).

143. Va. Code. Ann. §§ 18.2-499, 18.2-500 (2003).

144. Cal. Health & Safety Code §§ 17980–17922 (2002).

145. Cal Civ. Code §§ 896 *et seq.* (2003). See the discussion of this reform legislation in Roger B. Coven, *California Attempts to Resolve Construction Defect Cases*, 23:2 Constr. Law. 35 (Spring 2003). *See also* Fla. Stat. Ann. §§ 558.001–558.007 (2003).

the reasonable cost of repairing any damages caused by the repair efforts, the reasonable cost of repairing and rectifying any damages resulting from the failure of the home to meet the standards, the reasonable cost of removing and replacing any improper repair by the builder, reasonable relocation and storage expenses, lost business income if the home was used as a principal place of a business licensed to be operated from the home, reasonable investigative costs for each established violation and all other costs or fees recoverable by contract or statute.[146]

Other states have laws providing civil remedies for violations of state building codes in certain circumstances.[147]

The Texas Residential Construction Liability Law applies to actions "to recover damages resulting from a construction defect, except a claim for personal injury, survival, or wrongful death or for damage to goods."[148] The law excludes damages resulting from normal wear, tear, deterioration, or shrinkage. The claimant must give the contractor written notice specifying the construction defects before filing suit. The contractor may make a written settlement offer, including an agreement to repair or a monetary settlement offer.[149] Under this law, the claimant may recover: (1) the reasonable cost of repairs necessary to cure any construction defect; (2) the reasonable expenses of temporary housing reasonably necessary during the repair period; (3) the reduction in market value, if any, to the extent caused by structural failure; and (4) reasonable and necessary attorney's fees. However, the total damages awarded in a suit under this chapter may not exceed the claimants' purchase price for the residence.[150]

---

146. CAL CIV. CODE § 944 (2003).
147. See, e.g., FLA. STAT. ANN. § 553.84 (2001).
148. TEX. PROP. CODE ANN. § 27.002(a) (2002).
149. Id. §§ 27.004(a), (b).
150. Id. § 27.004(h).

SETOFF AND RECOUPMENT

Under Fed. R. Civ. P. 13(a) and the corresponding civil rule in state courts, a defendant is generally required to allege any counterclaim that "arises out of the transaction or occurrence that is the subject matter of the opposing party's claim and does not require for its adjudication the presence of third parties of whom the court cannot acquire jurisdiction." For example, when a subcontractor claims additional compensation from a prime contractor, the latter may be required to counterclaim for any backcharges arising from the same work. Such offsetting claims involving the same transaction are referred to as "recoupment."

Under Fed. R. Civ. P. 13(b) and its state law equivalents, a defendant is generally permitted but not required to assert offsetting claims that it may have on other projects or transactions. Such permissive counterclaims are referred to as "setoff."

Although authority is not uniform on this point, the better rule seems to hold that recoupment defenses may be raised without privity between the parties. Thus, in a Miller Act lawsuit, a general contractor may be able to assert backcharges for defective work against an unpaid supplier to an insolvent subcontractor.[151]

Once bankruptcy is filed, a creditor must obtain relief from the automatic stay to exercise its right of setoff on unrelated transactions.[152] The case law is split, however, on whether a credit must obtain such relief before effecting a recoupment.[153]

---

151. *See* United Structures of America, Inc. v. G.R.G. Eng'g, S.E., 9 F.3d 996 (1st Cir. 1993) (Judge Breyer, distinguishing between setoff and recoupment), *but see* U.S. *ex rel.* Martin Steel Constructors v. Avanti Steel Constructors, 750 F.2d 759 (9th Cir. 1984), *cert. denied*, 474 U.S. 817 (1985) (recoupment defense not available in Miller Act claim absent privity).

152. *See* 4 Collier Bankruptcy Practice Guide, ¶ 66.10, at p. 66-28 (1988).

153. *Compare In re* Norsol Industries, 147 B.R. 85, 89 (Bankr. E.D.N.Y. 1992) (automatic stay does not apply to recoupment) *with In re* Hiler, 99 B.R. 238, 242 (Bankr. D.N.J. 1989) (recoupment should be subject to automatic stay).

CONCLUSION

While no modern government has yet enacted remedies as stringent as those in Hammurabi's code, construction lawyers should research available statutory remedies and consider implied and other unwritten obligations that may provide for enhanced damages and other relief in construction disputes.

Appendix A

Table 1

State Laws Governing Payment on Public Contracts from Public Owner to Prime Contractors[1]

State	Citation	# of Days in Payment Period	Interest Penalty
Alabama	ALA. CODE § 8-29-3 (2003)	30 days after presentation of invoice	1% per month
Alaska	ALASKA STAT. §§ 36.90.200–36.290 (2003)	30 days from date payment request received	As set forth in § 45.45010(a) (as of this printing, 10.5% per year) 1% per month
Arizona	ARIZ. REV. STAT. ANN. § 34-221 (2002)	14 days after estimate is certified & approved	
Arkansas	ARK. CODE ANN. § 19-4-1411 (2002)	20 days after invoice received	8% per year
California	CAL. PUB. CONT. CODE § ANN. § 20104.50 (2003) (local governments)	30 days after receipt of payment request	As set by §685.010, as of this printing, 10% per year
	CAL. GOVT. CODE § 927.4 & § 927.6 (2003)	45 days from receipt of invoice	1% above rate accrued on June 30 of prior year by Pooled Money Investment Account, not to exceed 15%

[1] Note: Most statutes require payment only of "undisputed" invoices or amounts owed and provide time limits for owners to give contractors notice of objection to the invoice.

State	Citation	# of Days in Payment Period	Interest Penalty
Colorado	§ 24-91-103	None	None
Connecticut	CONN. GEN. STAT. § 42-158j	15 days after date of payment request	1% per month
Delaware	DEL. CODE ANN. tit. 29, § 6516 (2002)	30 days after invoice	Not more than 12% per year
District of Columbia	D.C. CODE ANN. § 2–221.02 (2003) (formerly § 1–1171–76)	30 days after date invoice received or per contract	As determined by mayor, not less than 1%
Florida	FLA. STAT. § 218.735 (2003) (local governments) tit. XIV, ch. 218	25 business days after invoice received	Greater of 1% per month or per contract
	FLA. STAT. ANN. § 337.141 (West 2003) tit. XXVI, ch. 337 (public transportation construction)	Final payment within 75 days of final field acceptance and receipt of documents required for payment	As set forth in § 55.03 (interest payments)
Georgia	GA. CODE ANN. § 13–11–1-11	15 days	1% per month
Hawaii	HAW. REV. STAT. ANN. § 103–10 (Michie 2003)	30 days after receipt of statement or delivery of goods	Prime rate as posted in *Wall St. Journal* on first business day of month for preceding calendar quarter plus 2% but not to exceed 12%
Idaho	IDAHO CODE § 67–2302 (2002)	60 days after receipt of billing	As provided in § 63–3045

State	Citation	# of Days in Payment Period	Interest Penalty
Illinois	30 ILL. COMP. STAT. ANN. 540/3–2 (2003)	60 days after receipt of bill	1% of amount approved
Indiana	IND. CODE ANN. § 5–17–5-1 (West 2002)	35 days after receipt of goods & services or claim	1% per month
Iowa	IOWA CODE ANN. § 421.40 (2003)	60 days after receipt of claim or furnishing of services or materials	1% per month
	§ 573.12(2) (a)(i)	14 days after receipt of payment request or per contract (not to exceed 30 days)	As set forth in §12C6
Kansas	KAN. STAT. ANN. § 75–6403 (2002)	30 days after later of receipt of goods & services or invoice	1.5% per month
Kentucky	KY. REV. STAT. ANN. § 45.453, .454 (Banks-Baldwin)	30 working days after receipt of goods & services or invoice	1% per month
Louisiana	LA. REV. STAT. ANN. §§ 39:1695–:1697 (West 2002)	90 days after due date in contract	As established in LA. CIV. CODE § 2924(B)(3), as of this printing 12%
Maine	ME. REV. STAT. ANN. tit. 5, § 1554 (West 2003)	25 days after receipt of invoice or 15 days after contract date for payment	Reasonable late fee not to exceed normal late charge imposed by vendor

State	Citation	# of Days in Payment Period	Interest Penalty
Maryland	MD. CODE ANN., STATE FIN. & PROC. § 15–103 (2003)	Later of 30 days after contract payment date or receipt of invoice	9% per year
Massachusetts	MASS. ANN. LAWS ch. 30, § 39K (Law. Co-op, 2003)	15 days after receipt of invoice; 30 days for Commonwealth or local housing authority	3% above rediscount rate charged by Federal Reserve Bank of Boston
Michigan	MICH. COMP. LAWS § 125.1562 (2003)	Later of 30 days after architect/ engineer certifies payment or 15 days after public agency receives state or federal funds	"Reasonable" interest
Minnesota	MINN. STAT. ANN. § 16A.124 (West 2002)	Later of 30 days after receipt of invoice or receipt of goods & services	1.5% per month
Mississippi	MISS. CODE ANN. § 31–5-25 (2003)	60 days after contract payment date	1% per month
Missouri	MO. REV. STAT. § 34.057 (2003)	Later of 30 days after date of delivery of materials or service or receipt of invoice or notice of approval	1.5% per month
Montana	MONT. CODE ANN. § 17–8-242 (2002)	30 days or per contract whichever is later	0.05% per day
Nebraska	NEB. REV. STAT. ANN. § 81–2403–2404 (Michie 2002)	45 days after receipt of invoice or per contract	As specified in § 45–104.02
Nevada	NEV. REV. STAT. ANN. §§ 338.515, .530 (Michie 2003)	30 days after receipt of bill	Highest rate by 3 financial institutions for 90-day certificate of deposit
New Hampshire	None		

State	Citation	# of Days in Payment Period	Interest Penalty
New Jersey	N.J. Stat. Ann. § 52:32–34 (West 2003)	60 days after receipt of invoice	Interest set by state treasurer based on rate of new 5-year loan
New Mexico	N.M. Stat. Ann. § 57–28–5 (Michie 2002)	21 days after receipt of invoice; 45 days if grant money is source of funding if provided by contract	1.5% per month
New York	N.Y. Pub. Auth. Law § 2880 (Consol. 2003)	30 days after receipt of invoice	Overpayment rate set by commissioner of taxation and finance pursuant to § 1096(3) of N.Y. Tax Law
	N.Y. Gen. Mun. Law § 106b (Consol. 2003) (municipalities)	45 days after receipt of invoice	Interest rate in effect at time payment is made
North Carolina	N.C. Gen. Stat. § 143–1341.1(a) (2003)	Per contract	1% per month or per contract
North Dakota	N.D. Cent. Code §§ 13–01.1 to 13–01–1.06 (2002)	45 days after receipt of invoice	1.75% per month
Ohio	Ohio Rev. Code Ann. § 126.30 (Banks-Baldwin 2002)	30 days after approved pay request or per contract	1/12 rate set in § 5703.47
Oklahoma	Okla. Stat. tit. 61, § 113.3 (2002)	30 days after work completed	0.75% per month (final payment only)
Oregon	Or. Rev. Stat. §§ 279.435–.445 (2001)	30 days after request for payment or 15 days after payment is approved by agency	3 times discount rate on 90-day commercial paper in as established by Federal Reserve Bank in Federal Reserve District for Oregon (not to exceed 30%)

State	Citation	# of Days in Payment Period	Interest Penalty
Pennsylvania	PA. STAT. ANN. tit. 62, § 3932 (West 2002)	45 days of receipt of payment application	As determined by Sec. of Revenue for interest on overdue taxes as provided in §§ 806 and 806.1 of the Fiscal Code
Rhode Island	R.I. GEN. LAWS § 42–11.1–3 (2002)	30 working days after receipt of invoice	Based on prime interest rate as reported on the money market page of *The Wall St. Journal* published on the 1st business day of each month
South Carolina	S.C. CODE ANN. §§ 29–6–30, 29–6–50 (Law. Co-op. 2002)	21 days after receipt of invoice	1% per month
South Dakota	S.D. CODIFIED LAWS § 5–26–3 (Michie 2002)	45 days after receipt of invoice or per contract	1.5% per month
Tennessee	TENN. CODE ANN. § 12–4.701–707 (2002)	45 days after receipt of invoice unless otherwise contractually agreed upon	1.5% per month unpaid interest at end of each 60-day period will be added to principal amount due
Texas	TEX. GOVT. CODE ANN. §§ 2251.021, .025 (Vernon 2001)	30 days after later of receipt of invoice or date services were last performed or materials supplied	1% per month

State	Citation	# of Days in Payment Period	Interest Penalty
Utah	UTAH CODE ANN. § 15–6-2 (2002)	60 days after receipt of invoice or as contractually agreed upon	2% above rate IRS pays on refund claims
Vermont	VT. STAT. ANN. tit. 9, § 4002 (2002)	20 days after receipt of invoice or 20 days after end of billing period, whichever is later	Interest rate at rate set by tit.12, § 2903(b) (as of this printing, 12% per year)
Virginia	VA. CODE ANN. § 2.2–4355 (Michie 2003)	7 days after receipt of invoice or per contract	Prime rate of U.S. commercial banks as reported in *The Wall St. Journal*
Washington	WASH. REV. CODE § 39.76.011 (2003)	Later of 30 days after receipt of invoice or within 30 days of receipt of grant or federal money	1% per month (but at least $1 per month)
West Virginia	W.V. CODE ANN. § 14–3-1 (Michie 2002)	90 days after certified completion of contract	Current interest at rate determined by state tax commissioner per 17a Article 10, Chapter 11
Wisconsin	WIS. STAT. ANN. § 16.528 (West 2003)	31 days after receipt of invoice	Interest at rate per § 71.82(1)(d) compounded monthly (as of this printing, 12% per year)
Wyoming	WYO. STAT. ANN. § 16–6-602 (Michie 2002)	45 days after receipt of invoice unless otherwise contractually agreed upon	1.5% interest per month

Table 2
State Laws Governing Payment on Public Contracts Due from Prime Contractor to Subcontractors

State	Citation	# of Days in Payment Period	Interest Penalty
Alabama	ALA. CODE § 8-29-3	Per contract or 7 days from GC's receipt of payment from owner	1% per month
Alaska	ALASKA STAT. § 36.90.210 (2003)	8 working days after GC's receipt of payment from state	Interest rate equal to amount set forth in § 45.45.010(a) (as of this printing, 10.5% per year)
Arizona	ARIZ. REV. STAT. ANN. § 34–221 (2003)	7 days after receipt of process payment or per contract	1% per month
Arkansas	None		
California	CAL. BUS. & PROF. CODE § 7108.5 (West 2003)	10 days after receipt of progress payment or per contract	2% per month
Colorado	COL. REV. STAT. § 24–91–103 (2002)	7 calendar days after receipt of payment from public entity	15% per year or per contract
Connecticut	CONN. GEN STAT. § 49–41a (2001)	30 days after GC's receipt of payment from state	1% per month

State	Citation	# of Days in Payment Period	Interest Penalty
Delaware	DEL. CODE ANN. tit. 6, §§ 2301, 3506 (2002)	30 days after date of payment to GC	Not in excess of 5% over the Federal Reserve discount rate including any surcharge as of the time from which interest is due
District of Columbia	D.C. CODE ANN. § 2–221.02 (2003) (formerly § 1–1171–76)	7 days after receipt of funds from government	Not less than 1%, as determined by the mayor or by regulation
Florida	FLA. STAT. ANN. § 287.0585 (West 2002)	7 working days after GC's receipt of payment	One-half of 1% per or per day not to exceed 15% of amount due
Georgia	GA. CODE ANN. § 13–11 (2003)	10 days after payment GC's receipt of from state	1% per month
Hawaii	HAW. REV. STAT. ANN. § 103–10.5 (2003)	10 days after GC's receipt of funds	1.5% per month
Illinois	ILL. COMP. STAT. ANN. 540/0.01–540/7 (2002)	15 days after receipt of invoice per contract	2% per month
Indiana	IND. CODE ANN. § 5–17–5-4 (2003)		1% per month; interest accrues when contractor is unable to pay subcontractor because of late payments by state agency
Iowa	IOWA CODE § 573.12 2 b (2003)	7 days after GC's receipt of payment by state	As set forth in § 573.14 and 12C.6 (interest rate for public funds)
Kansas	None		
Kentucky	None		
Louisiana	LA. REV. STAT. ANN. § 2784	14 days after receipt of payment from owner	One-half of 1% per day not to exceed 15% of amount due

State	Citation	# of Days in Payment Period	Interest Penalty
Maine	ME. REV. STAT. ANN. (West)	Later of 7 days after GC's receipt of payment from state or 7 days of receipt of sub's invoice	As specified in tit. 14, §1602A(2): as of this printing, the weekly average one-year constant maturity Treasury yield, as published by the Board of Governors of the Federal Reserve System, for the first calendar week of the month prior to the date from which the interest is calculated, plus 7%
Maryland	MD. CODE ANN., STATE FIN. & PROC. § 15–226 (2003)	10 days after GC's receipt of payment	Penalty not to exceed $100 per day
Massachusetts	MASS. ANN. LAWS ch. 30, § 39F (Law. Co-op, 2003)	65 days after substantial completion or occupancy	Not specified
Michigan	None		
Minnesota	MINN. STAT. ANN. § 16A.1245 (West 2002)	10 days after GC's receipt of payment from state	1.5% per month
Mississippi	MISS. CODE ANN. § 87-7-5 (2002)	15 days after GC's receipt of payment from state	1.5% per day, not to exceed 15% of amount due
Missouri	MO. ANN. STAT. § 34.057 (West 2003)	15 days after receipt of payment from owner	1.5% per month
Montana	MONT. CODE ANN. § 28-2-103 (2002)	3 working days after GC's receipt of payment	Not specified
Nebraska	NEB. REV. STAT. §§ 16–626, 17–520, 17–925, 17–975, 17–995, 18–2003, 19–2406, 19–2419, 19–2412, 23–3624, 39–1619, 39–1645 (2002)	45 days after certification of amounts due by engineer in charge and approval by governing body	8% per year

State	Citation	# of Days in Payment Period	Interest Penalty
Nevada	NEV. REV. STAT. §§ 338.160–.170	15 days after GC's receipt of payment from public agency	No
New Hampshire	None		
New Jersey	N.J. STAT. ANN. §§ 52:32–32 et. seq. (West 2003)	60 calendar days after GC's receipt of payment from state or 60 days after contract date	Prime rate plus 1%
New Mexico	None		
New York	N.Y. GEN. MUN. LAW § 106b (Consol. 2003); N.Y. TAX LAW § 1096 (Consol. 2003)	15 days after GC's receipt of payment from state or public agency	Fed short-term rate plus 2%
North Carolina	N.C. GEN. STAT. § 143–134.1 (2003)	7 days after GC's receipt of payment by state	1% per month
North Dakota	N.D. CENT. CODE § 13–01–1.06 (2002)	45 days after GC's receipt of payment from state	1.75% per month
Ohio	None		
Oklahoma	None		
Oregon	OR. REV. STAT. §§ 279.435–.445 (2001)	10 days after GC's receipt of payment from state	3 times Fed. discount rate on 90-day commercial paper, but no more than 30%
Pennsylvania	PA. STAT. ANN. tit. 73, § 507 (West 2002)	Later of 14 days after GC's receipt of payment from owner or 14 days after receipt of sub's invoice	1% per month
Rhode Island	R.I. GEN. LAWS §§ 42–11.1–3–.1–6 (2002)	10 days after GC's receipt of payment by state	Prime interest rate as reported on the money market page of *Wall Street Journal* published on the first regular business day of each month

State	Citation	# of Days in Payment Period	Interest Penalty
South Carolina	S.C. CODE ANN. §§ 29–6–30, 29–6–50 (Law. Co-op. 2002)	7 days after GC's receipt of payment	1% per month
South Dakota	S.D. CODIFIED LAWS § 5–26–1–8 (Michie 2003)	30 days after GC's receipt of payment from state	1.5% per month
Tennessee	TENN. CODE ANN. § 12–4.701–707 (2002)	30 days after GC's receipt of payment from state	1.5% per month
Texas	TEX. GOVT. CODE ANN. §§ 2251.022, .025 (Vernon 2002)	10 days after GC's receipt of payment by state	1% per month
Utah	UTAH CODE ANN. § 15–6–1–6 (2002)	45 days after GC's receipt of payment from state	15.5% per year (interest begins to accrue on 31st day after payment is due)
Vermont	VT. STAT. ANN. tit. 9, §§ 4001–4009 (2003)	7 days after GC's receipt of payment from state or 7 days after GC's receipt of invoice, whichever is later	Established by tit. 12, § 2903(b) (as of this printing, 12% per year)
Virginia	VA. CODE ANN. § 2.2–4354 (Michie 2002) (formerly § 11.62.1–11)	7 days after GC's receipt of payment from state	1% per month
Washington	WASH. REV. CODE § 39.04.250 (2003)	10 days after GC's receipt of payment from state	Interest at highest rate allowed under § 19.52.025
	§ 39.76.011 (2003)	8 working days after GC's receipt of payment from state	1% per month
West Virginia	None		

State	Citation	# of Days in Payment Period	Interest Penalty
Wisconsin	WIS. STAT. § 16.528 (2002)	7 days after GC's receipt of payment from state	The rate specified in § 71.82(1)(a) compounded monthly (as of this printing, 12% per year)
Wyoming	None		

Table 3
State Laws Governing Payment on Private Contracts from Owners to Prime Contractors

State	Citation	# of Days in Payment Period	Interest Penalty
Alabama	ALA. CODE § 8–29–3 (2003)	Per contract or 30 days after receipt of invoice	1% per month
Alaska	None		
Arizona	ARIZ. REV. STAT. § 32–1129.03 (2003) (formerly § 21–1129.01)	7 days after date billing or estimate is certified or approved per contract	1.5% per month
Arkansas	None		
California	CAL. CIV. CODE § 3260.1, 3260(g) (West 2001)	30 days after receipt of demand for payment	2% per month
Colorado	None		
Connecticut	CONN. GEN STAT. § 42–158 (2001)	15 days after payment request	1% per month
Delaware	DEL. CODE ANN. tit. 6, § 3507 (2002)	Per contract	Not specified
District of Columbia	None		
Florida	FLA. STAT. ANN. § 715.12 (West 2002)	14 days after date payment is due	As specified in § 55.03

State	Citation	# of Days in Payment Period	Interest Penalty
Georgia	GA. CODE ANN. §§ 13–11–1–13–11–11 (2002)	15 days after receipt of invoice	1% per month
Hawaii	None		
Idaho	IDAHO CODE § 29–115 (2003)	Provides retention must be released within 35 days of substantial completion	Not specified
Illinois	None		
Indiana	None		
Iowa	None		
Kansas	None		
Kentucky	None		
Louisiana	None		
Maine	ME. REV. STAT. ANN. tit. 10, ch. 201-A § 1113 (2003)	Later of 20 days after end of billing period or 20 days after delivery of invoice	As provided in tit. 14, § 1602A(2)
Maryland	MD. CODE ANN., REAL PROP. § 9–301–9–304 (2003)	Within 7 days of contract time for payment or 30 days after occupancy permit granted or 30 days after owner takes possession, whichever is earlier	Not specified; court may award interest, costs, and attorney's fees
Massachusetts	None		
Michigan	None		
Minnesota	None		
Mississippi	MISS. CODE ANN. § 87-7-3 (2003)	60 days after date payment due	1% per month
Missouri	None		
Montana	MONT. CODE ANN. § 28-2-2104 (2002)	30 days from date required in contract	1.5% per month

State	Citation	# of Days in Payment Period	Interest Penalty
Nebraska	None		
Nevada	NEV. REV. STAT. ANN. §§ 624.609–.610 (Michie 2002)	Per contract or 21 days after contractor submits pay request	Per contract or prime rate of largest bank in state
New Hampshire	None		
New Jersey	None		
New Mexico	N.M. STAT. ANN. § 57–28–5 (Michie 2002)	21 days after receipt of undisputed request for payment	1.5% per month
New York	N.Y. GEN. BUS. LAW ch. 20 §§ 756-a, 756-b (Consol.) (effective Jan. 14, 2003)	30 days or as per contract	Per contract or 1% per month
North Carolina	None		
North Dakota	None		
Ohio	None		
Oklahoma	None		
Oregon	None		
Pennsylvania	PA. STAT. ANN. tit. 73, § 505 (West 2002)	7 days after due date	1% per month
Rhode Island	None		
South Carolina	S.C. CODE ANN. §§ 29–6-30, 29–6-50 (Law. Co-op. 2002)	21 days after receipt of invoice	1% per month
South Dakota	None		
Tennessee	TENN. CODE ANN. §§ 66–34–202, -205, 66–34–601 (2002)	Per contract	Per contract or as established in § 47–14–121
Texas	TEX. PROP. CODE ANN. § 28.001–010 (Vernon 2002)	35 days after receipt of invoice	1.5% per month

State	Citation	# of Days in Payment Period	Interest Penalty
Utah	None		
Vermont	VT. STAT. ANN. tit. 9, § 4002 (2002)	Later of 20 days after invoice or 20 days after end of billing period or per contract	As established by tit. 12, § 2903(b)
Virginia	None		
Washington	None		
West Virginia	None		
Wisconsin	None		
Wyoming	None		

APPENDIX B
Summary of State Unfair and Deceptive Trade Practices Acts

Alabama	ALA. CODE § 8–19–1 (2002)
Alaska	ALASKA STAT. § 45.50.471 (2001)
Arizona	ARIZ. REV. STAT. § 44–1522 (2001)
Arkansas	ARK. CODE ANN. § 4–88–107 (2002)
California	CAL. BUS. & PROF. CODE § 17500 (West 2003)
Colorado	COLO. REV. STAT. § 6-1-105 (2002)
Connecticut	CONN. GEN. STAT. § 42–1100 (2001)
Delaware	DEL. CODE ANN. tit. 6, §§ 2531–2536 (2001)
District of Columbia	D.C. CODE ANN. § 28–3904 (2002)
Florida	FLA. STAT. ANN. §§ 501.202 *et seq.* (West 2002)
Georgia	GA. CODE ANN. § 10-1-370 (2002)
Hawaii	HAW. REV. STAT. § 481A-3 (2003)
Idaho	IDAHO CODE § 41–1301 (2002)
Illinois	815 ILL. COMP. STAT. § 510/2 (2002)
Indiana	IND. CODE ANN. § 24–5-0.5–3 (West 2002)
Kansas	KAN. STAT. ANN. § 50–626 (2001)
Kentucky	KY. REV. STAT. ANN. § 367.170 (Banks-Baldwin 2001)
Louisiana	LA. REV. STAT. ANN. § 51:1409 (West 2003)
Maine	ME. REV. STAT. ANN. tit. 10, § 1212 (2001)
Maryland	MD. CODE ANN., COM. LAW I/II § 13–303 (2002)

Massachusetts	Mass. Ann. Laws ch. 93A, § 4 (Law. Co-op, 2002)
Michigan	Mich. Comp. Laws § 445.911 (2002)
Minnesota	Minn. Stat. § 3250.45 (2001)
Mississippi	Miss. Code Ann. § 83–57–59 (2001)
Missouri	Mo. Rev. Stat. § 407.020 (2003)
Montana	Mont. Code Ann. § 30–14–142 (2001)
Nebraska	Neb. Rev. Stat. § 87–302 (2001)
Nevada	Nev. Rev. Stat. § 598.0925 (2002)
New Hampshire	N.H. Rev. Stat. Ann. § 358-A:2 (2002)
New Jersey	N.J. Stat. Ann. § 56.12–17 (West 2002)
New Mexico	N.M. Stat. Ann. § 57–12–1 (Michie 2002)
New York	N.Y. Gen. Bus. Law § 350-e (Consol. 2002)
North Carolina	N.C. Gen. Stat. § 75–1.1 (2002)
North Dakota	N.D. Cent. Code § 51–10–06 (2002)
Ohio	Ohio Rev. Code Ann. § 4165.02 (2002)
Oklahoma	Okla. Stat. tit. 78, § 53 (2002)
Pennsylvania	Pa. Stat. Ann. tit. 73, § 201–3 (West 2002)
Rhode Island	R.I. Gen. Laws § 6–13.1–1 (2001)
South Carolina	S.C. Code Ann. § 39–5–10 (Law. Co-op. 2001)
South Dakota	S.D. Codified Laws § 58–33–3 (Michie 2002)
Tennessee	Tenn. Code Ann. § 56–8-104 (2001)
Texas	Title 2, Chap. 7, subchap. e §§ 17.41–.63 (2003)
Utah	Utah Code Ann. § 13–11–1 (2002)
Vermont	Vt. Stat. Ann. tit. 9, § 2453 (2002)
Virginia	Va. Code Ann. §§ 59.1–196–.1–207 (Michie 2003)
Washington	Wash. Rev. Code § 48.30.010 (2002)
West Virginia	W.Va. Code § 46A-6-104 (2002)
Wisconsin	Wis. Stat. §§ 421.102 *et seq.* (2001)
Wyoming	Wyo. Stat. Ann. §§ 40–12–107 *et seq.* (Michie 2002)

APPENDIX C
Bond and Lien Law Summary*
State Lien Laws and Public
Payment Bond Laws

Each state has adopted its own mechanics' lien or construction lien law. In addition, most states have adopted "little Miller Act" laws requiring contractors (and, in some cases, subcontractors) to provide payment bonds.[†] These laws are cited below:

Alabama   Mechanics' liens — ALA. CODE §§ 35–11–210 *et seq.* (2002)
Bonds on public projects — ALA. CODE §§ 39–1-1 *et seq.* (2002)

Alaska   Mechanics' lien — ALASKA STAT. §§ 34.35.0005 *et seq.* (2002)
Bonds on public projects — ALASKA STAT. § 36.25.010 (2001)

Arizona   Mechanics' liens — ARIZ. REV. STAT. § 33–993 (2001)
Bonds on public projects — ARIZ. REV. STAT. § 33–1004(B) (Supp. 1998)

Arkansas   Mechanics' liens — ARK. CODE ANN. §§ 18–44–101 *et seq.* (2002)
Bonds on public projects — ARK. CODE ANN. § 18–44–503 (2002)

California   Mechanics' liens — CAL. CIV. CODE §§ 3179 *et seq.*; § 1369 (liens on condominiums) (2002)
Bonds on public projects — CAL. CIV. CODE §§ 3247 *et seq.* (2001); CAL. PUB. CONT. CODE § 4108 (2001); CAL. PUB. CONT. CODE § 10221 (2001); CAL. PUB. CONT. CODE § 204261 (2001)

---

* For a more complete discussion of the bond and lien laws in the fifty states, see FIFTY STATE CONSTRUCTION BOND AND LIEN LAW (Robert F. Cushman, Stephen D. Butler, & Laurance Schor eds., 2000); and Construction Lien Law (ch. 9) and State by State Lien and Bond Claim Summary (app. J) in CONSTRUCTION LAW (Steven G. M. Stein ed., 1986).

[†] For a more complete discussion on payment bonds and payment bond claims, see Kevin L. Lybeck & H. BRUCE SHREVES, THE LAW OF PAYMENT BONDS (1998) and Daniel Toomey & Tamara McNulty, Surety Bonds: A Basic User's Guide for Payment Bond Claimants and Obligees, 22 CONST. LAW. 5 (Winter 2002).

Colorado	Mechanics' liens — Colo. Rev. Stat. §§ 38–22–101 *et seq.* (2001) Bonds on public projects — Colo. Rev. Stat. §§ 38–26–105 *et seq.* (38–26–102) (railroad and irrigation contracts) (2002); lien on funds (public projects) — §§ 10–3-1113, 11004(1)(h)(I) to (XIV)
Connecticut	Mechanics' lien — Conn. Gen. Stat. §§ 49–33 *et seq.* (2001) Bonds for public projects — Conn. Gen. Stat. §§ 49–41 *et seq.* (2001)
Delaware	Mechanics' liens — Del. Code Ann. tit. 25, §§ 2702 *et seq.* (2001) Bonds for public projects — Del. Code Ann. tit. 29, § 6962 (2001)
District of Columbia	Mechanics' liens — D.C. Code Ann. § 40–30307 (2002) Bonds for public projects — D.C. Code Ann. § 2–201.02 (2002)
Florida	Mechanics' liens — Fla. Stat. §§ 713.01 *et seq.* (2002) Bonds for public projects — Fla. Stat. § 255.05 (2002)
Georgia	Mechanics' liens — Ga. Code Ann. § 44–14–320 and § 44–14–360 *et seq.* (2002) Bonds for public projects — Ga. Code Ann. § 13–10–60 (2002)
Hawaii	Mechanics' liens — Haw. Rev. Stat. § 507–47 (2002) Bonds for public projects — Haw. Rev. Stat. § 103–10.5 (2001)
Idaho	Mechanics' liens — Idaho Code §§ 45–505 *et seq.* (2002) Bonds for public projects — Idaho Code §§ 54–1925 *et seq.* (2002)
Illinois	Mechanics' liens — 70 Ill. Comp. Stat. 60/1 *et seq.* (2002) Bonds for public projects — 30 Ill. Comp. Stat. 550/1 (2002)
Indiana	Mechanics' liens — Ind. Code Ann. §§ 32–28–31 *et seq.* (Michie 2001) Bonds for public projects — Ind. Code Ann. § 4–13.6–7-6 (Michie 2002)
Iowa	Mechanics' liens — Iowa Code §§ 572.2 *et seq.* (2002) Bonds for public projects — Iowa code § 573.2 (2002)
Kansas	Mechanics' liens — Kan. Stat. Ann. §§ 60–1102 *et seq.* (2001) Bonds for public projects — Kan. Stat. Ann. 2001 Supp. 60–1111 (amended by 2002 Kan. A.L.S. 73)
Kentucky	Mechanics' liens — Ky. Rev. Stat. Ann. § 376.010 (2001, amended by 2002 Ky. Acts 66) Liens on funds due contractor on public projects — Ky. Rev. Stat. Ann. § 376.210 (Banks-Baldwin 2001) Bond to discharge lien on funds due contractor on public projects — Ky. Rev. Stat. Ann. § 376.212 (Banks-Baldwin 2001) Bonds for public projects — Ky. Rev. Stat. Ann. § 45A.190 (Banks-Baldwin 2001)
Louisiana	Mechanics' liens — La. Rev. Stat. Ann. §§ 9:4802 *et seq.* (West 2002) Bonds for public projects — La. Rev. Stat. Ann. § 38:2241 (West 2002)

Maine	Mechanics' liens — ME. REV. STAT. ANN. tit. 10, §§ 3251–3255 (2002) Bonds for public projects — ME. REV. STAT. ANN. tit. 14, § 871 (2001)
Maryland	Mechanics' liens — MD. CODE ANN., REAL PROP. § 9–102 (2001) Bonds for public projects — MD. CODE ANN., STATE FIN. & PROC. §§ 17–103 *et seq.* (2001)
Massachusetts	Mechanics' liens — MASS. ANN. LAWS ch. 254, § 2 (Law. Co-op, 2002) Bonds for public projects — MASS. ANN. LAWS ch. 149, § 29 (Law. Co-op, 2002)
Michigan	Mechanics' liens — MICH. COMP. LAWS §§ 570.1104 *et seq.* (2002) Bonds for public projects — MICH. COMP. LAWS §§ 129.201 *et seq.* (2002); § 570.101 (2002)
Minnesota	Mechanics' liens — MINN. STAT. §§ 514.01 *et seq.* (2001) Bonds for public projects — MINN. STAT. § 574.26 (2001)
Mississippi	Mechanics' liens — MISS. CODE ANN. §§ 85–7-131 *et seq.* (2002) Bonds for public projects — MISS. CODE ANN. § 31–5-51 (2001)
Missouri	Mechanics' liens — MO. REV. STAT. §§ 429.010 *et seq.* (2001) Bonds for public projects — MO. REV. STAT. § 107.170 (2001)
Montana	Mechanics' liens — MONT. CODE ANN. §§ 71–3-522 *et seq.* (2001)* Bonds for public projects — MONT. CODE ANN. § 18–2-201 (2001)
Nebraska	Mechanics' liens — NEB. REV. STAT. §§ 52–131 *et seq.* (2001) Bonds for public projects — NEB. REV. STAT. §§ 14–365, 39–1407 (2002)
Nevada	Mechanics' liens — NEV. REV. STAT. §§ 108.221–.246 (2001) Bonds for public projects — NEV. REV. STAT. § 309.340 (2001)
New Hampshire	Mechanics' liens — N.H. REV. STAT. ANN. § 447:12–1 (2002) Bonds for public projects — N.H. REV. STAT. ANN. § 447:16 (2002)
New Jersey	Mechanics' liens — N.J. STAT. §§ 2A:44A-22 *et. seq.* (West 2002) Bonds for public projects — N.J. STAT. § 2A:44–143 (West 2002)
New Mexico	Mechanics' liens — N.M. STAT. ANN. §§ 48–2-2 *et seq.* (Michie 2002) Bonds for public projects — N.M. STAT. ANN. § 13–4-18 (Michie 2002)

* Note: The 49th Montana legislature appointed an interim committee to examine Montana's lien laws and to report its findings to the 50th legislature.

New York   Mechanics' liens — N.Y. Lien Law § 3 (Consol. 2002)
                      Lien on public funds — N.Y. Lien Law § 42 (Consol. 2002)
                      Bonds — N.Y. High. Law § 38 (Consol. 2002); N.Y. Unconsol.
                      Law ch. 214-A, § 8 (health care) (Consol. 2002); N.Y. State Fin.
                      Law § 137 (bond for prompt payment) (Consol. 2002)

North Carolina   Mechanics' liens — N.C. Gen. Stat. § 44A-10 (2001)
                      Bonds for public projects — N.C. Gen. Stat. § 44–26 (2002)

North Dakota   Mechanics' liens — N.D. Cent. Code § 35–27–02 (2002)
                      Bonds for public projects — N.D. Cent. Code § 48–02–06.2 (2002)

Ohio   Mechanics' liens — Ohio Rev. Code Ann. §§ 1311.02 *et seq.*
                      (Anderson 2002)
                      Bonds for public projects — Ohio Rev. Code Ann. § 153.54
                      (Anderson 2002)

Oklahoma   Mechanics' liens — Okla. Stat. tit. 42, §§ 142–143 (2001)
                      Bonds for public projects — Okla. Stat. tit. 61, § 1 (2002)

Oregon   Mechanics' liens — Or. Rev. Stat. §§ 1311.02 *et seq.* (2001)
                      Bonds for public projects — Or. Rev. Stat. § 279.029 (2001)

Pennsylvania   Mechanics' liens — Pa. Stat. Ann. tit. 49 §§ 1201 *et seq.* (West
                      2001)
                      Bonds for public projects — Pa. Stat. Ann. tit. 8 § 193 (West 2002)

Rhode Island   Mechanics' liens — R.I. Gen. Laws § 34–28–1 (2001)
                      Bonds for public projects — R.I. Gen. Laws §§ 37–2-41, 37–12–1
                      (2001)

South Carolina   Mechanics' liens — S.C. Code Ann. § 29–5-40 (Law. Co-op. 2001)
                      Bonds for public projects — S.C. Code Ann. § 11–35–3030 (Law.
                      Co-op. 2001)

South Dakota   Mechanics' liens — S.D. Codified Laws § 44–9-1 (Michie 2001)
                      Bonds for public projects — S.D. Codified Laws § 5–21–1 (Michie
                      2001)

Tennessee   Mechanics' liens — Tenn. Code Ann. §§ 66–11–102 *et seq.* (2002)
                      Bonds for public projects — Tenn. Code Ann. § 54–5-119 (2001)

Texas   Mechanics' liens — Tex. Prop. Code Ann. § 53.021 (Vernon 2002)
                      Bonds for public projects — Tex. Gov't Code § 2253.021 (2002)

Utah   Mechanics' liens — Utah Code Ann. § 38–1-3 (2002)
                      Bonds for public projects — Utah Code Ann. §§ 14–1-18 *et seq.*
                      (2002)

Vermont   Mechanics' liens — Vt. Stat. Ann. tit. 9, § 1924 (2001)
                      Bonds for public projects — Vt. Stat. Ann. tit. 19, § 10 (2001)

Virginia   Mechanics' liens — Va. Code Ann. §§ 43–1 *et seq.* (Michie 2002)
                      Bonds for public projects — Va. Code Ann. § 2.2–4337 (Michie
                      2002)

Washington   Mechanics' liens — Wash Rev. Code §§ 60.04.011 *et seq.* (2002)
                   Bonds for public projects — Wash. Rev. Code § 39.08.010 (2002)

West Virginia Mechanics' liens — W. Va. Code § 38–2-1 (2001)
                   Bonds for public projects — W. Va. Code § 38–2.39 (2001)

Wisconsin   Mechanics' liens — Wis. Stat. §§ 779.01 *et seq.* (2001)
                   Bonds for public projects — Wis. Stat. § 779.14 (2001)

Wyoming   Mechanics' liens — Wyo. Stat. Ann. § 29–2-101 (Michie 2002)
                   Bonds for public projects — Wyo. Stat. Ann. § 9–2-1016 (Michie 2002)

Contractors' and Subcontractors' Remedies Related to Bidding

4

LESLIE O'NEAL-COBLE

Bidding is a critical component of the construction process. Some private projects and most public works projects are awarded on the basis of competitive bidding. Absent unlawful discrimination, owners on private projects are generally free to accept or reject any bid for design or construction services. On public projects, however, the bidder submitting the lowest responsible price on a competitively advertised job may have certain rights if this bid is rejected. Generally, these rights are limited to injunctive or declaratory relief or compensation for bid preparation expenses. This chapter will deal exclusively with the rights and remedies available to bidders on public projects, but will not discuss all the procedural aspects of bid protests on state and federal projects.[1] Owners' remedies related to bidding are discussed in Chapter 5.

---

1. For a comprehensive discussion of procedures for bid protests on state and federal projects, *see* 1 STEVEN G. M. STEIN, CONSTRUCTION LAW § 2.03 (2002).

(continued)

Bid protests are governed by statute and by the rules and regulations of the particular public agency involved in the bidding. Because the time for filing a bid protest is usually very short, familiarity with the applicable rules and procedures is essential. Many states have enacted procurement codes containing bid protest procedures for all state agency purchases. However, such codes may not apply to municipal or other types of agencies. Bid protests may also be governed by a state's administrative procedure act and protestors may be required to exhaust their administrative remedies before filing a lawsuit.

STANDING

As with other types of legal actions, plaintiffs in bid protests must have standing to maintain the action.[2] Generally this means that a plaintiff must be a bidder whose substantial interests are affected by the public agency's bid award.[3] Except in extraordinary circumstances, in order to have standing the bid protestor must have submitted a bid or proposal and must have been reasonably likely to receive the contract if its protest is to be successful.[4] Before filing a

---

For a review of bid protest procedures for the U.S. General Accounting Office, *see* Office of General Counsel, U.S. Gen. Accounting Office, *Bid Protests at G.A.O.: A Descriptive Guide* (7th edition 2003), *available at* http://www.gao.gov/decisions/bidpro/bid/d03539sp.pdf. For a discussion of the defense of bid protests *see* Steve R. Patoir, *Bid Protests: An Overview for Agency Counsel*, 2002 ARMY LAW. 29 (July 2002).

2. See generally Note, *Disappointed Bidder Standing to Challenge a Government Contract Award: A Proposal for Change in Kentucky Procurement Law*, 88 KY. L. J. 161 (2000); Annotation, *Standing of Unsuccessful Bidder for Federal Procurement Contract to Seek Judicial Review of Award*, 23 A.L.R. FED. 301 (1975).

3. Brasfield & Gorrie General Contractor, Inc. v. Ajax Constr. Co. of Tallahassee, 627 So.2d 1200 (Fla. Dist. Ct. App. 1993), *rev. den.*, 639 So.2d 974 (Fla. 1994). The federal regulations require a protestor to be "an actual or prospective bidder or offer or whose direct economic interest would be affected by the award or a contract or of the failure to award a contract." 4 C.F.R. § 21.0 (2003); *see also* authorities cited at West's ⬅ 316A PUBLIC CONTRACTS, k5.1; ⬅ 13 ACTION, k13.

4. *But see* Fairbanks, Inc. v. Dep't of Transp., 635 So.2d 58 (Fla. Dist. Ct. App. 1993), *rev. den.*, 639 So.2d 977 (Fla. 1994) (allowing a supplier that did not submit a bid to maintain a bid protest).

lawsuit, a protestor usually must also exhaust any administrative remedies under the state's procurement code.[5]

The law regarding bid protest standing is anything but uniform. Before filing a bid protest, counsel should check the applicable law regarding standing. Courts in several states have held that bidders on public projects lack standing to challenge bid awards because doing so benefits the bidder's interest rather than the public interest.[6] However, some jurisdictions will allow bid protests by bidders who are also "taxpayers" in that jurisdiction, because a "taxpayer" protest would (at least in theory) be on behalf of the general public.[7] And some courts have held that disappointed bidders have standing to challenge government contract awards on public policy grounds.[8] In some jurisdictions bid protest suits are permitted only where there are allegations of fraud, collusion, or dishonesty in the bidding process.[9] For example, Kentucky courts have held that "absent a showing of fraud, collusion or dishonesty, a disappointed bidder has no standing to challenge the award of a contract to another bidder."[10]

---

5. *E.g.,* ALASKA STAT. tit. 36, chap. 30 (2002); LA. REV. STAT. ANN. tit. 39, subtitle III, chap. 17 (2003); MD. CODE ANN. Div. II, tit. 15 (2003); S.C. CODE ANN. tit. 11, chap. 35 (2002).

6. *E.g.,* Communications Sys., Inc. v. City of Danville, 880 F.2d 887 (6th Cir. 1989); Sowell's Meats & Services, Inc. v. McSwain, 788 F.2d 226 (4th Cir. 1986); Apcoa, Inc. v. City of New Haven, No. CV9503702205, 1995 WL 155434 (Conn. App. 1995); Garling Constr., Inc. v. City of Shellsburg, 641 N.W. 2d 522 (Iowa 2002); State *ex rel.* Mid-Missouri Limestone, Inc. v. County of Calloway, 962 S.W.2d 438 (Mo. App. 1998); ISC Distrib., Inc. v. Trevor, 903 P.2d 170 (Mont. 1995); Spencer, White & Prentis, Inc. v. Southwest Sewer Dist., 477 N.Y.S.2d 681 (App. Div. 1984); *see also* authorities cited at West's ☞ 268 MUNICIPAL CORPORATIONS, k336(1).

7. *E.g.,* Gannett Co. v. Delaware, Civil Action No. 12815, 1993 WL 19714 (Del. Ch. Jan. 11, 1993).

8. Metro. Express Servs., Inc. v. City of Kansas City, 23 F.3d 1367 (8th Cir. 1994); AT/ COMM, Inc. v. Illinois State Toll Highway Auth., No. 96C6961, 1997 WL 222875 (N.D. Ill. April 23, 1997); Walt Bennett Ford, Inc. v. Pulaski County Special Sch. Dist., 624 S.W. 2d 426 (Ark. 1981); M.A. Stephen Constr. Co. v. Borough of Rumson, 308 A.2d 380 (N.J. Super. Ct. 1973); Albert Elia Bldg. Co. v. New York State Urban Dev. Corp., 388 N.Y.S.2d 462 (App. Div. 1976); Browning-Ferris Indus. v. City of Oak Ridge, 644 S.W.2d 400 (Tenn. Ct. App. 1982).

9. *See, e.g.,* authorities cited at West's ☞ 316A PUBLIC CONTRACTS, k5.1; ☞ 360 STATES, k98.

10. HealthAmerica Corp. v. Humana Health Plan, Inc. 697 S.W.2d 946 (Ky. 1985); Ohio River Conversions, Inc. v. City of Owensboro, 663 S.W.2d 759 (Ky. Ct. App. 1984); *see also Gannett Co. v. Delaware, supra* note 7.

DAMAGES

After a government bid opening, a disappointed bidder who feels that the bidding process was unfair may seek relief through an administrative bid protest or a lawsuit for damages or injunctive relief. Such a claimant may feel that the appropriate damages are the anticipated profits from the contract it should have received. However, with few exceptions, state and local governments, and the federal government, are not liable to unsuccessful bidders for lost profits on public contracts.[11] The majority rule is that a bid protestor may be awarded its bid preparation expenses and, in some cases, its bid protest costs.[12] However, some courts hold that bid protestors are not entitled to any damages, including bid preparation costs.[13] As stated in *Peerless Food Prods, Inc. v. State*:[14] "Allowing damages to a low bidder when that bidder is denied a public contract and the contract is awarded to a higher cost bid is a remedy inherently conflicting with the primary purpose behind public bidding law: the protection of the public purse."[15] While it could be argued that the public purse would be best served by allowing

---

11. See David E. Rosengren & Thomas G. Librizzi, *Bid Protests: Substance and Procedure on Publicly Funded Construction Projects*, 7:1 CONSTR. LAW. 1 (Jan. 1987); Note, *The Private Rights of a Bidder in the Award of a Government Contract: A Step Beyond Scanwell*, 24 CASE W. L. REV. 559 (1973); Annotation, *Public Contracts: Low Bidder's Monetary Relief Against State or Local Agency for Non-Award of Contract*, 65 A.L.R. 4th 93 (1988); *see also* authorities cited at West's ⊕ 268 MUNICIPAL CORPORATIONS, k330(3); ⊕ 316A PUBLIC CONTRACTS, k5.1; ⊕ 360 STATES, k98; ⊕ 104 COUNTIES, k116; ⊕ 393 UNITED STATES, k64.

12. *See generally* Annotation, *Recovery from United States of Costs Incurred by Unsuccessful Bidder in Preparing and Submitting Contract Bid in Response to Government Solicitation*, 30 A.L.R. FED. 355 (1976); *see also* Owen of Georgia, Inc. v. Shelby County, 648 F.2d 1084 (6th Cir. 1996); City of Scottsdale v. Deem, 556 P.2d 328 (Ariz. Ct. App. 1976); City of Atlanta v. J.A. Jones Constr. Co., 398 S.E.2d 369 (Ga. Ct. App. 1990), *cert. den.*, 500 U.S. 928 (1991); Nielsen & Co. v. Cassia, 647 P.2d 773 (Idaho 1982); Telephone Assocs. v. St. Louis County, 364 N.W. 2d 378 (Minn. 1985); Planning & Design Solutions v. City of Santa Fe, 885 P.2d 628 (N.M. 1994); authorities cited at West's ⊕ 268 MUNICIPAL CORPORATIONS, k336(5); ⊕ 316A PUBLIC CONTRACTS, k5.1. Such expenses do not include costs incurred in proving that a bidder was "responsible." Lion Raisins, Inc. v. United States, 52 Fed. Cl. 629 (2002).

13. *See* authorities cited at West's ⊕ 268 MUNICIPAL CORPORATIONS, k241, k336(1).

14. 44 P.3d 865 (Wash. Ct. App. 2002).

15. *Id.* at 871.

rejected bidders to recover sufficient damages to encourage enforcement of the public bidding laws, this reasoning has not been adopted by most courts.

Although there is a strong public policy interest in having fair competitive bidding for public contracts, most courts have balanced that interest against the "longstanding public policy against requiring the public to pay both the contract price to the entity awarded the contract and also the profits that would have been earned by the entity that should have been awarded the contract,"[16] and have declined to award lost profits as damages to unsuccessful bidders. Despite the fact that bid preparation costs alone are acknowledged to be an inadequate remedy in such cases,[17] these are usually the only damages allowed.[18] As stated in *Paul Sardella Construction Co. v. Braintree Housing Authority:*[19]

> The "honest and open procedure for competition" among the various bidders that is one of the fundamental objectives of the competitive bidding statute must necessarily entail fair consideration of all the submitted bids in accordance with the applicable sections of the statute. We hold that where such consideration has not been given by public contracting authorities in violation of statutory provisions, the proper measure of recovery is the reasonable cost of preparing the bid.[20]

Some courts hold that invitations for bid on public projects contain an implied condition that each bid submitted will be fairly considered pursuant to applicable statutes. A public agency's failure to give each bid fair consideration is deemed a breach of this implied condition.[21] The majority rule is

---

16. State Mech. Contractors, Inc. v. Vill. of Pleasant Hill, 477 N.E. 2d 509, 512 (Ill. App. Ct. 1985).

17. General Elec. Co. v. Seamans, 340 F. Supp. 636 (D.D.C. 1972).

18. *See* authorities cited at West's ⊕⟹ 268 MUNICIPAL CORPORATIONS, k376; ⊕⟹ 316A PUBLIC CONTRACTS, k11; ⊕⟹ 393 UNITED STATES, k64.60(6).

19. 329 N.E. 2d 762 (Mass. App. Ct. 1975), *superseded by* 356 N.E.2d 249 (Mass. 1976).

20. 329 N.E. 2d at 766, 767.

21. *See* authorities cited at West's ⊕⟹ 316A PUBLIC CONTRACTS, k11.

that the appropriate measure of damages for such breach is an award of bid preparations costs[22] because awarding these costs will encourage challenges to improper contract awards, thus deterring public agency misconduct, while not unduly burdening the public treasury. A number of states have enacted laws providing that bid preparation costs are the only monetary relief available to bid protestors.[23] The same limitation prevails in the Court of Federal Claims, which "may award any relief that the court considers proper, including declaratory and injunctive relief except that any monetary relief shall be limited to bid preparation and proposal costs."[24]

In *Swinerton & Walberg Co. v. City of Inglewood-Los Angeles County Civic Center Authority*,[25] the public agency awarded a public works contract to a contractor that was not the lowest responsible bidder. The disappointed bidder was allowed to sue the public body for monetary damages on a theory of promissory estoppel.[26] The court there reasoned that by inviting bids, the authority had promised to award the contract to the lowest responsible bidder and should be estopped from acting otherwise if the bidder necessarily relied on that promise.

In a recent case, *Kajima/Ray Wilson v. Los Angeles County Metropolitan Transportation Authority*,[27] the California Supreme

22. Cincinnati Elec. Corp. v. Kleppe, 509 F.2d 1080 (6th Cir. 1975); William F. Wilke, Inc. v. Dept. of Army, 485 F.2d 180 (4th Cir. 1973); Merriam v. Kunzig, 476 F.2d 1233 (3d Cir. 1973), *cert. den. sub nom.* Gateway Ctr. Corp. v. Merriam, 414 U.S. 911 (1973); M. Steinthal & Co. v. Seamans, 455 F.2d 1289 (D.C. Cir. 1971); Armstrong & Armstrong, Inc. v. United States, 140 F. Supp. 409 (Ct. Cl. 1956).
23. *E.g.*, ALASKA STAT. § 36.30.585 (2002); ARK. CODE ANN. § 19-11-244 (2002); COLO. REV. STAT. § 109-104 (2002); D.C. CODE ANN. § 1-1189.8, subd.(f)(2)(2002); HAWAII REV. STAT. § 103D-701(2002); LA. REV. STAT. ANN. § 39:1671, subd. G (2002); MD. CODE ANN., STATE FIN. & PROC. § 15-221.1, subd. (a) (2002); MINN. STAT. § 471.345(14) (2002); S.C. CODE ANN. tit. 63, chap. 56, § 63-56-47 (2002).
24. 28 U.S.C. § 1491(b)(2) (2000).
25. 500 P.2d 601 (Cal. Ct. App. 1974).
26. *See* RESTATEMENT (SECOND) OF CONTRACTS § 90 (1981), which provides: "A promise which the promisor should reasonably expect to induce action or forbearance of a definite and substantial character on the part of the promisee and which does induce such action or forbearance is binding if injustice can be avoided only by enforcement of the promise."
27. 1 P.3d 63 (Cal. 2000); *see also* Ritchie Paving, Inc. v. City of Deerfield, 61 P.3d 699 (Kan. 2003) and authorities cited at West's 🔑 268 MUNICIPAL CORPORATIONS k336(1) and 🔑 316A PUBLIC CONTRACTS k11.

Court followed *Swinerton,* allowing a bid protestor to recover on a promissory estoppel theory, but limited its recovery to bid preparation costs. The court noted that:

> [w]hile nothing precludes application of a promissory estoppel theory to the disappointed bidder context, it fits these circumstances imperfectly. Promissory estoppel was developed to do rough justice when a party lacking contractual protection relied on another's promise to its detriment. Here, we use promissory estoppel primarily to further certain public policies by creating a damages remedy for a public entity's statutory violation. Moreover, unlike the typical promissory estoppel situation, the MTA retains discretion to reject all of the bids as it did in round 1; the lowest bidder has no absolute right to be awarded the contract. These peculiarities play a role in determining the measure of damages available under a promissory estoppel theory.[28]

Other courts have rejected application of a promissory estoppel theory to support a disappointed bidder's claim for relief, reasoning that "not every promise is sufficiently binding to support a cause of action based on promissory estoppel. Such a promise should be enforced only when necessary to avoid injustice."[29] Courts taking this approach have noted that it is an agency's *acceptance* of a bid for public work, rather than the issuance of an invitation for bids, that creates a contract.[30]

If a plaintiff can prove that a public agency acted in bad faith in awarding a contract, lost profits may be recoverable. In *Bradford & Bigelow, Inc. v. Commonwealth,*[31] Bradford & Bigelow (B&B) was the low bidder for a contract with the Commonwealth of Massachusetts to print ballots for the 1984 election. The second low bidder objected to award of

---

28. *Id.* at 69.

29. City of Cape Coral, Florida v. Water Servs. of Am., Inc. 567 So.2d 510 (Fla. Dist. Ct. App. 1990); *see also* authorities cited at West's 🗝 156 ESTOPPEL, k85.

30. Mottner v. Town of Mercer Island, 452 P.2d 750 (Wash. 1969); *see also* authorities cited at West's 🗝 268 MUNICIPAL CORPORATIONS, k335; 🗝 316A PUBLIC CONTRACTS, k10.

31. 509 N.E. 2d 30 (Mass. App. Ct.), *rev. den.,* 513 N.E. 2d 1288 (Mass. 1987).

the contract to B&B, alleging that B&B did not pay the required "prevailing wage." After conducting an investigation and holding a hearing on the prevailing wage issue, the Commonwealth rejected both bids and re-bid the contract. In the second bidding, B&B was not the low bidder.[32] B&B filed a suit for injunctive and declaratory relief and for damages. The case was tried before a jury on the issues of whether the state officers or agencies had acted in bad faith in depriving B&B of the ballot contract and whether B&B was entitled to recover lost profits. The defendants presented no evidence at trial. B&B presented evidence, apparently without objection, that its estimated profit was ten percent of the $1.5 million contract prices. The jury awarded B&B $160,000 in damages plus interest. On appeal, the court upheld this award, but reduced the damages by $10,000, B&B's bid preparation costs. These were considered costs of performing the work that did not result from denial of the award. The application of this case may be limited to its unique factual circumstances.

INJUNCTIVE OR OTHER RELIEF

Even if monetary damages are not available, bid protestors have been successful in obtaining other types of relief, including injunctions against contract award, writs of *mandamus*, and declaratory judgments. Federal statutes and regulations and many state statutes provide that filing a bid protest stays award of the contract;[33] however, protestors

---

32. When it submitted its new bid, B&B carefully reserved in writing its rights to damages and to reinstatement of the prior contract award.

33. *E.g.*, 31 U.S.C. § 3553 (c)(d)(3)(A)(ii) (2000); FEDERAL ACQUISITION REGULATION (hereinafter FAR) § 33.103(f) (48 C.F.R. § 33.103(f)); FLA. STAT. ANN. § 120.57(3)(c) (2001). *But see* CAL. PUB. CONT. CODE div. 2, part 2, ch. 3.6 §§ 12125–12130 (2003) and CAL. CODE REGS. tit.1, div. 2, ch. 5 § 14000-1440 (2003) regarding the California pilot project eliminating the automatic stay in bid protests. This pilot project will continue until applied to at least twenty-five contracts or until December 31, 2005, whichever is later. This project has been criticized by some commentators. *See* Brett E. Bacon, *The California Alternative Protest Pilot Project: Eviscerating the Protestant's Due Process Rights and Remedies to Improve Administrative Efficiency and Reduce Costs*, 29 PUB. CONT. L.J. 511 (2000).

would be wise to file an action seeking an injunction against award of the contract also to avoid claims of waiver.

The recent Florida decision of *City of Sweetwater v. Solo Construction Corp.*[34] dealt with a municipality that decided after the bids were opened to award its contract to what it considered "the most responsible bidder" instead of to the plaintiff, a responsible bidder with the lowest price. Determining that the city's actions not only violated the competitive bid law, but also were arbitrary and capricious, the appellate court affirmed the trial court's injunction prohibiting contract award to any other entity, issuance of a writ of *mandamus* ordering the contract awarded to the plaintiff, and award of attorney's fees and costs.

Similarly, a Louisiana appellate court[35] required a public agency to award a contract to the third-lowest bidder because the two lowest bidders failed to comply with the Disadvantaged Business Enterprise (DBE) listing requirements. The third-lowest bidder had sued for an injunction and for a writ of *mandamus* to compel award of the contract to it. Reversing the trial court's denial of plaintiff's claims, the appellate court held that the DBE requirements were not informalities that could be waived. Because the time for the agency to reject all bids and to resolicit had expired, the appellate court ordered the agency to award the contract to the plaintiff.[36]

A bid protestor's allegation that it had a right to participate in a fair bidding process and that interference with that right would result in irreparable harm was held sufficient to state a claim for injunctive relief in *Keefe-Shea Joint Venture v. City of Evanston.*[37] The court noted that the public agency owed a duty to a bidder to award the contract to the lowest responsive, responsible bidder and, as a corollary to this

---

34. 823 So.2d 798 (Fla. Dist. Ct. App. 2002).

35. Wallace C. Drennan, Inc. v. Sewerage & Water Bd., 798 So.2d 1167 (La. Ct. App. 2001).

36. *See* authorities cited at West's ⊕═ 250 MANDAMUS, k3(5), k72, k84; ⊕═ 268 MUNICIPAL CORPORATIONS, k336(1).

37. 773 N.E.2d 1155 (Ill. App. Ct.), *appeal denied*, 2002 Ill. LEXIS 1594 (Ill. Oct. 2, 2002).

duty, "a bidder has the right to participate in a fair bidding process."[38] The court further held that the plaintiff was not required to present evidence of its bid preparation costs or of lost profits, noting that lost profits were not available and that recouping bid preparation costs was not an adequate legal remedy.

Federal courts have enjoined contract awards pending resolution of a bid protest in some cases.[39] In considering whether injunctive relief was appropriate, these courts have held that an award of bid preparation costs was an inadequate legal remedy and, therefore, that the protestor would be irreparably harmed if the government's contract award were not enjoined.[40] In *General Electric Co. v. Seamans*,[41] the court granted the bid protestor's request for a preliminary injunction against a contract award. The court considered the adequacy of an award of bid preparation costs as damages and stated: "[T]his remedy does not adequately compensate the frustrated bidder's losses entirely, since it provides damages only to the extent of the bid preparation costs. This is not sufficient in cases such as the case at bar."[42] Accordingly, the court found that the availability of damages did not preclude injunctive relief. The court further held that the protestor was likely to prevail on the merits because there was evidence that the Air Force had failed to comply with its own regulations during negotiations prior to contract award.

Protestors should be sure to seek an injunction in addition to *mandamus* or other relief to prevent the contract's being awarded and performed while the protest is pending, thus making the petition moot.[43]

---

38. *Id.* at 1162.
39. *See* authorities cited at West's ⊕ 212 INJUNCTION, k138.63.
40. Ainslie Corp. v. Middendorf, 381 F. Supp. 305 (D. Mass 1974).
41. General Electric Co. v. Seamans, 340 F. Supp. 636 (D.D.C. 1972).
42. *Id.* at 640.
43. Strand Century, Inc. v. Dallas, 683 P.2d 561 (Or. Ct. App. 1984); *see* authorities cited at West's ⊕ 250 MANDAMUS, k16(1).

California has a line of cases following the "void contract" rule, which allows a disappointed bidder to sue for rescission of the public agency's contract with the successful bidder on the grounds that it is void.[44] For example, in *Valley Crest Landscape, Inc. v. City Council of the City of Davis*,[45] an unsuccessful bidder persuaded the court to rescind the city's contract with the low bidder, North Park Construction, even though North Park had substantially performed the contract. The bid specifications required the contractor to perform at least 50 percent of the work with its own forces. North Park's original bid showed that 83 percent of the work would be performed by subcontractors. After Valley Crest objected, claiming North Park's bid was unresponsive, the city allowed North Park to correct an alleged mistake in its bid by revising the subcontracted percentages to 44.65 percent. The city awarded the contract to North Park, and Valley Crest filed a petition for a writ of mandate, for a writ of administrative *mandamus*, and for declaratory and injunctive relief. Valley Crest sought to have North Park's contract declared void and to have the city award the contract to Valley Crest.

Rejecting the city's claim that it merely waived an "immaterial irregularity" in North Park's bid by allowing it to correct the subcontracted percentages, the court concluded that North Park was given an unfair advantage and held the contract was void. The court noted that North Park could have withdrawn its bid. The *Valley Crest* decision has been criticized[46] but remains good law in California.[47]

---

44. *See* Monterey Mech. Co. v. Sacramento Reg'l County Sanitation Dist., 52 Cal. Rptr. 2d 395 (Cal. Ct. App. 1996); Valley Crest Landscape, Inc. v. City Council of Davis, 49 Cal. Rptr. 2d 184 (Cal. Ct. App. 1996); *see also* authorities cited at West's ☞ 250 MANDAMUS, k3(5), k84; ☞ 316A PUBLIC CONTRACTS, k11.

45. *Supra* note 44.

46. Ghilotti Constr. Co. v. City of Richmond, 53 Cal. Rptr. 2d 389 (Cal. Ct. App. 1996).

47. Allowing disappointed bidders to sue to set aside a contract award on account of bid irregularities is uncommon. A number of jurisdictions allow a public body or a taxpayer to sue to recover payments made under a contract that violated the public bid statutes. *See* note 16 in Chapter 5 of this text.

STATUTORY PROVISIONS

Some states have statutes providing specific remedies for bid protestors. Before filing a bid protest action, attorneys should research the law in the particular jurisdiction to determine if such relief is available. For example, Oregon has a statute[48] allowing an action against a successful bidder if the protestor can show that the successful bidder knowingly violated certain Oregon statutes or failed to pay the Department of Revenue all sums withheld from employees. The Oregon statute provides that

> any person that loses a competitive bid for a contract involving the construction, repair, remodeling, alteration, conversion, modernization, replacement or renovation of a building or structure may bring an action within two years of substantial completion of the project. If successful in establishing that a violation occurred, the plaintiff is entitled to recover attorney's fees and liquidated damages of $5,000 or ten per cent of the total amount bid, whichever is greater.[49]

Alabama statutes permit suits by any interested citizen or by an unsuccessful bidder to enjoin the letting or execution of a public works project in violation of the competitive bid law and, in the case of a disappointed bidder, to recover "reasonable bid preparation costs."[50] Additionally, either the state attorney general or an interested citizen may sue, in the name and for the benefit of the awarding authority, within three years after settlement of a public contract let in violation of the competitive bid law and recover funds paid under the contract if there is clear and convincing proof that the contractor or other defendant knew of the violation before the contract was executed.[51]

---

48. OR. REV. STAT. § 279.03 (2001).

49. Id.

50. ALA. CODE § 39-5-4 (2002).

51. Id. § 39-5-3; see Annotation, *Right of Municipal Corporation to Recover Back from Contractor Payments Made Under Contract Violating Competitive Bidding Statute*, 33 A.L.R. 3D 397 (1970).

A minority of courts have allowed disappointed bidders to maintain actions for unlawful deprivation of a property interest under 42 U.S.C. § 1983.[52] In those cases the courts found that state law gave the low bidder a legally protected property right in the contract award. However, most courts have held that bidders have no legally protected property interest to support a Section 1983 claim.[53]

CONTRACTOR'S REMEDIES FOR SUBCONTRACTOR'S WITHDRAWAL OF BID

General contractors often submit written bids on projects based upon oral bids received from subcontractors. For various reasons subcontractors may refuse to honor these oral bids after the general contractor is awarded the contract. There is considerable conflict in the case law in the various states regarding whether a general contractor may sue the recalcitrant subcontractor for damages resulting from failure to honor its bid.

Drennan v. Star Paving[54] is the leading case allowing a general contractor to sue a subcontractor that refused to honor its oral bid on a promissory estoppel theory. In *Drennan*, the general contractor took a telephone bid from a subcontractor and used it as part of the basis of the general contractor's estimate.[55] After being awarded the contract, the general contractor went to the subcontractor's office. The

---

52. *E.g.*, Pataula Elec. Membership Corp. v. Whitworth, 951 F.2d 1238 (11th Cir. 1992); Three Rivers Cablevision, Inc. v. City of Pittsburgh, 502 F. Supp. 1118 (W.D. Pa. 1980); Haughton Elevator Div. v. State, 367 So.2d 1161 (La. 1979); *see generally* Annotation, *Standing of Disappointed Bidder on Public Contract to Seek Damages Under 42 USCS § 1983 for Public Authorities' Alleged Violation of Bidding Procedures*, 86 A.L.R. FED. 904 (1988).

53. Indep. Enters. v. Pittsburgh Water & Sewer Auth., 103 F.3d 1165 (3rd Cir. 1997); Sowell's Meats & Servs., Inc. v. McSwain, 788 F.2d 226 (4th Cir. 1986); ARA Servs., Inc. v. Sch. Dist., 590 F. Supp. 622 (E.D. Pa. 1984); Kendrick v. City Council, 516 F. Supp. 1134 (S.D. Ga. 1981); J. P. Mascaro & Sons, Inc. v. Bristol, 497 F. Supp. 625 (E.D. Pa. 1980); Hill v. Ford, 449 F. Supp. 27 (E.D. Tenn. 1978).

54. 333 P.2d 757 (Cal. 1958).

55. The general contractor listed the paving subcontractor as part of its proposal. 333 P.2d at 760.

subcontractor immediately advised the general contractor that it had made a mistake in its bid and could not perform the work for the price quoted. The general contractor sued the subcontractor for damages and was awarded the difference in price between the nonperforming subcontractor's bid and the replacement subcontractor's price. On appeal the California Supreme Court held that the general contractor's reliance on the subcontractor's bid made the bid irrevocable, noting, "Reasonable reliance serves to hold the offeror in lieu of the consideration ordinarily required to make the offer binding."[56] This case has been widely discussed in law reviews and law journals[57] and, despite considerable criticism, is the majority rule.[58]

The rationale of *Drennan* was that, between the general contractor who reasonably relied on the subcontractor's bid and the subcontractor who made the mistake, the loss should fall on the party who caused it: the subcontractor. The court noted that the general contractor had no reason to know that the subcontractor had made a mistake in its bid. Such knowledge would make reliance on the bid unreasonable and would defeat recovery under promissory estoppel. The court further noted that "a general contractor is not free to delay acceptance after he has been awarded the general contract in the hope of getting a better price. Nor can he re-open

---

56. *Id.*

57. *E.g.*, Christopher J. Daus & G. Steven Ruprecht, *The Pit and the Pendulum: Balancing the Equities in the Construction Bidding Process*, 10:3 Constr. Law. 3 (Aug. 1990); Francis J. Hughes & William K. Hurley, *Home Electric/Hall versus Drennan/Star Paving: Mutuality Is No Substitute for Equity*, 10:3 Constr. Law. 25 (Aug. 1990); Eric C. Rowe & Allen Holt Gwyn, *Home Electric v. Star Paving Promissory Estoppel Debate: The Rules of Offer and Acceptance Have Not Been Abandoned*, 11:1 Constr. Law. 7 (Jan. 1991); Steven M. Siegfried & Mark Lawrence, *Home Electric v. Hall & Underdown Heating & Air Conditioning: Mutuality Remains the Only Solution to the Construction Bidding Problems*, 9:4 Constr. Law. 3 (Nov. 1989) [hereinafter Siegfried]; Comment, *Construction Bidding Problem: Is There a Solution Fair to Both the General Contractor and the Subcontractor?* 19 St. Louis U. L.J. 522 (1975); Comment, *Maryland's Application of Promissory Estoppel in Construction Industry Bidding Disputes: Eliminating Further Confusion*, 30 U. Balt. L. Rev. 171 (Fall 2000); Comment, *The Subcontractor's Bid: An Option Contract Arising Through Promissory Estoppel*, 34 Emory L.J. 421 (Spring 1985); Note, *Promissory Estoppel: Subcontractors' Liability in Construction Bidding Cases*, 63 N.C. L. Rev. 387 (Jan. 1985).

58. *See* authorities cited at West's ☞ 156 ESTOPPEL, k85; ☞ 95 CONTRACTS, k19, k218.

bargaining with the subcontractor and at the same time claim a continuing right to accept the original offer."[59] Thus, the *Drennan* court attempted to prevent general contractors from engaging in "bid shopping," a practice much criticized by subcontractors' counsel.[60]

Subcontractors' counsel prefer the result in the earlier case of *James Baird v. Gimbel Bros.*,[61] a case factually similar to *Drennan*. *Baird* was a suit by a general contractor against a linoleum subcontractor that withdrew its bid after the general contractor submitted an estimate incorporating that bid, but before the general contractor was awarded the contract. The general contractor sued to recover the additional costs incurred by the subcontractor's withdrawal of its bid. Judge Learned Hand, writing for the majority, rejected the general contractor's claim because the general contractor had never formed a contract by accepting the subcontractor's bid. Therefore, the subcontractor was free to revoke its offer until there was an acceptance. A minority of courts have followed *Baird*.[62]

Courts and legal commentators have struggled to define a rule in these cases that adequately balances the interest of the general contractor in relying on the subcontractor's bid and the subcontractor's interest in withdrawing erroneous bids and in negotiating necessary contract terms.[63] Applying a strict contract approach yields a harsh result for the general contractor, while using promissory estoppel may allow subcontractors to be abused. However, most courts have followed *Drennan*. As stated in *Alaska Bussell Electric Co. v.*

---

59. 333 P.2d at 760.

60. *E.g.*, Siegfried, *supra* note 57, at 3: " 'Bid shopping' occurs when a contractor, after being awarded the overall contract, uses a subcontractor's low bid as a tool in negotiating lower bids from other subcontractors."

61. 64 F.2d 344 (2d. Cir. 1933).

62. *E.g.*, Home Elec. Co. v. Hall & Underdown Heating & Air Conditioning Co., 358 S.E.2d 539 (N.C. Ct. App. 1987), *aff'd.*, 366 S.E.2d 441 (N.C. 1988); *see also* authorities cited at West's ☞ 343 SALES, k22.

63. Of course, general contractors are also interested in withdrawing erroneous bids. *See* Annotation, *Right of Bidder for State or Municipal Contract to Rescind Bid on Ground That Bid Was Based Upon His Own Mistake or That of His Employee*, 2 A.L.R. 4th 1991 (1980).

Vern Hickel Construction Co.: "[W]e believe that *Drennan* is better case law than *Baird*. As applied in *Drennan*, promissory estoppel has the practical effect of encouraging subcontractors to be cautious when formulating their bids. Furthermore, it satisfies the needs of the modern construction industry."[64] To prevail in such an action, the contractor must demonstrate that the subcontractor made a clear and unambiguous promise on which the contractor reasonably relied to its detriment.[65]

SUBCONTRACTOR LISTING STATUTES

As noted above, subcontractors have few rights related to bidding. However, because of the concern that "bid shopping" has a deleterious effect on public contracting, many states have enacted statutes requiring general contractors to list the subcontractors they intend to use on a project as a part of their bid proposal.[66] Under these laws, the general contractor is prohibited from replacing a subcontractor except in specified circumstances. Unfortunately, most of these statutes lack an effective enforcement mechanism, which greatly limits their usefulness in terms of actually preventing "bid

---

64. 688 P.2d 576, 580 (Alaska 1984) (citing Michael L. Closen & Donald G. Weiland, *The Construction Industry Bidding Cases: Application of Traditional Contract, Promissory Estoppel and Other Theories to the Relations Between General Contractors and Subcontractors*, 13 J. Marshall L. Rev. 565 (1980).

65. Bunkoff Gen. Contractors, Inc. v. Dunham Elec., 753 N.Y.S.2d 156 (App. Div. 2002).

66. *E.g.*, Cal. Pub. Cont. Code § 4101 (2002): "The Legislature finds that the practices of bid shopping and bid peddling in connection with the contraction ... of public improvements often result in poor quality of material and workmanship to the detriment of the public, deprive the public of the full benefits of fair competition among prime contractors and subcontractors and lead to insolvencies, loss of wages to employees and other evils." *See also* Conn. Gen Stat. § 4b-95 (2003); Haw Rev. Stat. § 103D-302 (2002); Nev. Rev. Stat. § 338.141 (2002); N.M. Stat. Ann. § 13-4-34 (2002); Utah Code Ann. § 63A-5-208 (2002); *see generally* Allen Holt Gwyn, *A Review of Subcontractor-Listing Statutes*, 17:1 Constr. Law. 35 (Jan. 1997). H.R. 1348, 108th Cong. (2003) is a federal "anti-bid shopping" act now pending in Congress. *See* http://thomas.loc.gov/cgi-bin/query/C?c107:./temp/~c107CTFvyl for text of bill.

shopping."[67] One possible remedy for this is to use the "subcontractor listing" statute in conjunction with a state's unfair and deceptive trade practices statute (discussed in Chapter 3). At least one court has allowed a subcontractor to make a claim under such a statute, where it alleged that, after the general contractor listed the subcontractor, it hired another company because the listed subcontractor refused to lower its bid to match another bidder.[68] The combination of the subcontractor listing statute and the unfair and deceptive trade practices statute (many of which provide for treble damages and attorney's fees) could provide a major weapon against bid shopping.

Because public works projects are such a significant part of the construction industry the bidding and award of these contracts will always be a source of disputes. Even though these cases seldom involve large damages awards, they are critical to maintaining confidence that the process is fair and impartial.

---

67. *E.g.*, McCandlish Elec., Inc. v. Will Constr. Co., 25 P.3d 1057 (Wash. Ct. App. 2001) (no private cause of action under subcontractor listing statute, before enactment of R.C.W. 39.30.060(2)). *But see* S. Cal. Acoustics Co. v. Holder, Inc., 456 P.2d 975 (Cal. 1969) (anti–bid shopping statute confers the right on the listed subcontractor to perform the subcontract unless statutory grounds for a valid substitution exist. Moreover, that right may be vindicated by an action for damages against the prime contractor to recover the benefit of the bargain the listed subcontractor would have received had he not been wrongfully deprived of the subcontract).

68. Johnson Elec. Co. v. Salce Contracting Assocs., Inc., 805 A.2d 735 (Conn. App. Ct. 2002), *app. den.*, 812 A.2d 864 (Conn. 2002).

Remedies and Damages Available to Owners

5

LESLIE O'NEAL-COBLE

INTRODUCTION

The owner's role in the construction process is that of a hopeful visionary. All projects, whether skyscrapers or cottages, begin with an owner's vision. The owner's vision for the project must be communicated to the design professional with the hope that the designer will capture and interpret this vision in the plans and specifications. The owner then hopes that the plans and specifications communicate the same vision to the builder who will construct the project. In the meantime, the owner is usually responsible for financing these activities, with the hope that once the project is completed, it will be both functional and profitable.

The owner's relationship with the design professional and the builder is one of "trust and confidence." These words are used in many standard form agreements between owners and contractors.[1] During the hubbub that characterizes most construction projects, the parties give little or no thought to this aspect of their relationship. Yet it plays a vital part in the construction process. Owners put their trust and confidence—and often their financial futures—in the hands of the design professional and constructor.

Courts have struggled to develop and to apply rules that will fairly compensate owners when the contractor's or designer's performance is inadequate or defective, yet not provide the owner with an economic windfall. As the cases discussed in this chapter show, the struggle has yielded varying results.

OWNER DAMAGES RELATED TO BIDDING

Owners' damages in bid disputes are limited. If there is a bid bond or other bid security, the owner may make a claim on the security if the low bidder fails to execute the contract after bid award. If the contract is void because of bid improprieties, in some jurisdictions the owner may be able to recover payments it has made to the contractor.

Bid Bonds

Most invitations to bid on public projects require bidders to post a bid bond[2] or other security[3] to protect the owner in the event the selected bidder fails or refuses to sign the contract

---

1. *E.g.*, AIA Document A111, Standard Form of Agreement Between Owner and Contractor, where the basis for payment is the cost of the work plus a fee with a negotiated maximum price, Article 3 (1997 edition): "The Contractor accepts the relationship of trust and confidence established by this Agreement."

2. *See generally, Bid Bonds*, in The Law of Suretyship (Edward G. Gallagher ed., 1983).

3. Some public bodies permit cashier's or certified checks, letters of credit, or securities to be deposited as bid security in lieu of a bid bond, *e.g.*, Federal Acquisition Regulation [hereinafter FAR] §§ 28.200 *et seq.* The FAR is generally located at Title 48, Code of Federal Regulations; citations to the FAR in this work are to the September 2001 revision. Claims on letters of credit will be governed by the terms of the letter of credit and by Article 5 of the U.C.C. *See* Leslie K. O'Neal, *They're Back: Letters of Credit Provided in Lieu of Surety Bonds*, 13:1 Constr. Law. 3 (Jan. 1993).

upon award. The bid bond is usually five or ten percent of the total bid amount. Owners should review the bond form carefully and be sure to fulfill all of the required conditions.[4] As with all surety obligations, the surety's liability on a bid bond is limited by the terms and conditions of the bond.

For example, the AIA Document A310 Bid Bond form (1970) is conditioned on the occurrence of each of the following acts: (1) the owner accepts the bid; (2) the bidder fails to enter into the contract or to give the bonds required; and (3) the bidder fails to pay the owner the difference between the amount of its bid and any larger amount for which the owner may in good faith contract with another party to perform the work (not to exceed the penal sum of the bid bond). Although not specifically stated in the bond form, the third term implies that the owner must make a demand on the original bidder to pay this excess amount before the surety is liable on the bid bond. In making a claim on the bond, the owner may request its actual damages (the difference between the original low bid and the next low bid) up to the bond's penal sum or, in some instances, the total amount of the bid bond may be forfeited as liquidated damages.[5]

The bidder's failure to execute the contract may be excused in certain circumstances. For example, in *Central Contra Costa Sanitary District v. National Surety Corp.*,[6] the public agency requested bids for construction of a sewer system. The successful bidder died after the bid was accepted, but before he signed the contract. The District sued the bid bond surety to recover the difference between the low bid and the actual contract price as damages. In denying the owner's claim, the court noted that the owner had made no demand on the contractor's estate to execute the contract or

---

4. *See* authorities cited at West's 316A PUBLIC CONTRACTS, k9; *see also* Annotation, *Surety's Liability on Bid Bond for Public Works*, 70 A.L.R. 2D 1370 (1960).

5. PHILIP L. BRUNER & PATRICK J. O'CONNOR, JR., BRUNER & O'CONNOR ON CONSTRUCTION LAW § 2:69 (2002) [hereinafter BRUNER & O'CONNOR].

6. 246 P.2d 150 (Cal. Ct. App. 1952). It is not clear from the opinion if the contractor's bid was in a corporate or an individual name.

to perform the work. The court also considered that the contract could be considered one for personal services, which would be discharged by a party's death. The court held that the owner could not recover under the bid bond, since the contractor's death excused the execution and performance of the contract, and in turn discharged the surety.[7]

Contractors frequently make mistakes in calculating their bids and notify owners of their intent to withdraw the bid before the contract is awarded. In such circumstances, most jurisdictions allow a contractor that made a mistake in its bid to withdraw the bid without forfeiting the bid bond.[8] As noted in illustration 1 from Section 153 of the Restatement (Second) of Contracts (1981):

> In response to B's invitation for bids on the construction of a building according to stated specifications, A submits an offer to do the work for $150,000. A believes that this is the total of a column of figures, but he has made an error by inadvertently omitting a $50,000 item, and in fact the total is $200,000. B, having no reason to know of A's mistake, accepts A's bid. If A performs for $150,000, he will sustain a loss of $20,000 instead of making an expected profit of $30,000. If the court determines that enforcement of the contract would be unconscionable, it is voidable by A.[9]

Corbin has a similar comment:

> Suppose ... a bidding contractor makes an offer to supply specified goods or to do specified work for a definitely named price, and that he was caused to name this price by an antecedent error of computation. If, before acceptance, the offeree knows, or has reason to know, that a material error has been made, he is seldom mean enough to accept; and if he does

---

7. 246 P.2d at 155 (this case may have been decided on the basis of sympathy rather than on legal principles). *See also* authorities cited at West's ⬥ 309 PRINCIPAL AND SURETY, k91.

8. *See* authorities cited at West's ⬥ 95 CONTRACTS, k19; ⬥ 268 MUNICIPAL CORPORATIONS, k333, k335.1; ⬥ 104 COUNTIES, k120.

9. *See also* Annotation, *Right of Bidder for State or Municipal Contract to Rescind Bid on Ground That Bid Was Based Upon His Own Mistake or That of His Employee,* 2 A.L.R. 4th 1991 (1980); authorities cited at West's ⬥ 316A PUBLIC CONTRACTS, k12.

accept, the courts have no difficulty in throwing him out. He is not permitted 'to snap up' such an offer and profit thereby. If, without knowledge of the mistake and before any revocation, he has accepted the offer, it is natural for him to feel a sense of disappointment at not getting a good bargain, when the offeror insists on withdrawal; but a just and reasonable man will not insist upon profiting by the other's mistake.[10]

Illustrating this principle, in *R. J. Taggart, Inc. v. Douglas County*,[11] shortly after submitting its bid and bid bond to the county, the contractor learned that certain materials needed were not available. After the bids were opened, but before the contract was awarded, the contractor filed a written withdrawal of its bid. The following day, the county awarded the contract to the contractor as the lowest bidder. The contractor sued for a declaratory judgment that there was no contract; the owner counterclaimed for forfeiture of the bid bond. The trial court entered judgment for the county on the bid bond. The appellate court reversed, finding that nothing in the specifications, the bid, or the bid bond prohibited the contractor from withdrawing its bid and that the county had not detrimentally relied on the contractor's bid before it was withdrawn. The court noted: "[U]nless the parties *agree* that a bid is to be irrevocable for a period of time, or unless a relevant statute or municipal ordinance specifically so provides, the general rule is that bids are freely revocable prior to acceptance."[12]

To avoid this situation, owners should specify when and under what circumstances a bid may be withdrawn without penalty. Many states have enacted statutes specifically providing when bids may be withdrawn without forfeiting the

---

10. Arthur Linton Corbin, 7 Corbin on Contracts § 28.49 (interim ed. 2002).

11. 572 P.2d 1050 (Or. App. 1977); *see also* First Baptist Church v. Barber Contracting Co., 377 S.E.2d 717 (Ga. Ct. App. 1989).

12. 572 P.2d at 1052, *citing* Eugene McQuillan, Municipal Corporations § 29.67 (3d ed. 1966); this is in contrast to the holding in *Drennan v. Star Paving* regarding withdrawal of subcontractor bids, discussed in Chapter 4 of this text.

bid security.[13] California has a statute allowing a bidder to bring an action against the awarding authority to recover the amount forfeited, without interest or costs. However, if the bidder fails to recover judgment, it is liable to pay the public body's attorney's fees and other costs of defending the suit.[14]

On the other hand, some courts have held that bids on public projects may not be withdrawn, based upon the wording of the governing competitive bidding statute. In *City of Cheyenne v. Reiman Corp.*,[15] for example, the Wyoming Supreme Court held that the Wyoming competitive bidding statute essentially made the contractor's bid irrevocable and gave the City no authority to relieve the contractor from its mistaken bid.[16]

Recovery of Payments Made Under Contract Violating Competitive Bidding Statute

Where a contractor has secured a contract in violation of a competitive bidding statute, a public body may be able to recover payments made to the contractor, particularly if there is evidence of fraud, collusion, or other misconduct.[17] In *K & R Engineering Co. v. United States*,[18] a government employee secretly received a percentage of the contractor's profits in return for assisting the contractor in obtaining three government contracts. The employee was also the contracting officer responsible for overseeing the projects and, in that role, allowed the contractor to cut corners and to make unsubstantiated claims for additional costs. While work

---

13. *E.g.*, ALA. CODE § 39-2-11 (2002); CAL. PUB. CONT. CODE § 10169 (2003); LA. REV. STAT. ANN. § 2214 (2002); OHIO REV. CODE ANN. § 5525.01 (2003); 73 PA. STAT. ANN. tit. 73, § 1602 (2002); VA. CODE ANN. § 2.2-4330 (2002).

14. CAL. PUB. CONT. CODE § 5101 (2003).

15. 869 P.2d 125 (Wyo. 1994).

16. *Id.* at 128, *citing* WYO. STAT. § 15-1-113; *see also* authorities cited at West's ⊕═ 268 MUNICIPAL CORPORATIONS, k333, k335.1; ⊕═ 316A PUBLIC CONTRACTS, k44.

17. Annotation, *Right of Municipal Corporation to Recover Back from Contractor Payments Made Under Contract Violating Competitive Bidding Statute*, 33 A.L.R.3d 397 (1970); *see also* authorities cited at West's ⊕═ 393 UNITED STATES, k75(1).

18. 616 F.2d 469 (Cl. Ct. 1980).

on the third contract was still in progress, the scheme was discovered and the employee resigned. The government then terminated the contract. The contractor sued for payment of the remaining contract balance, and the government counterclaimed to recover the amounts paid to the contractor under all three contracts. The court rejected the contractor's argument that the government was required to show a pecuniary loss from the transaction.

Granting summary judgment for the government, the court stated:

> Effective implementation of the conflict-of-interest law requires that once a contractor is shown to have been a participant in a corrupt arrangement, he cannot receive or retain any of the amounts payable thereunder. Permitting the contractor to retain amounts already received would create the danger that "[m]en inclined to such practices, which have been condemned generally by the courts, would risk violation of the statute knowing that, if detected, they would lose none of their original investment, while, if not discovered, they would reap a profit for their perfidy."[19]

However, in *Bozied v. City of Brookings*,[20] a South Dakota court held that, while a contractor who performed work for the city under void change orders could not recover additional payments under those change orders, neither could the plaintiff taxpayers (who brought the action on behalf of the city) require a forfeiture of the $548,001 already paid to the contractor. The court stated that,

> if the change orders are found to violate SDCL 5-18-3, we hold that in the absence of fraud, collusion or undue influence, consistent with the precept that parties to a void contract must be left where they are found, the contractor may still retain those funds previously received on the two change orders.[21]

---

19. *Id.* at 476, *citing* Boca Raton v. Raulerson, 146 So. 576, 577 (Fla. 1933).
20. 638 N.W. 264 (S.D. 2001).
21. *Id.* at 267.

OWNER DAMAGES FOR DEFECTIVE OR INCOMPLETE WORK

Standing

The first issue involved in an owner's claim for damages for defective or incomplete work is whether the plaintiff has standing to bring the claim or the action. This issue may arise in a number of circumstances. For example, a remote purchaser of a commercial building may lack standing to bring an action against the original contractor or designer for design and construction defects.[22] Certain types of remedies, such as claims for breach of an implied warranty of habitability, apply only to residential dwellings.[23] Consequently, a board of directors of a homeowners' association may lack standing to bring such claims related to commonly held amenities.[24]

MEASURE OF DAMAGES

The measures of owners' damages for defective work are easily stated but difficult to apply. There are two basic techniques to calculate an owner's damages for defective or incomplete work: the cost to repair and diminution in value.[25] Courts' applications of these rules are highly fact-dependent, resulting

---

22. Krusi v. Amoroso Constr. Co., 97 Cal. Rptr. 2d 294 (Cal. Ct. App. 2000) (fourth purchaser of building lacked standing to bring action against original contractor and designer). However, many courts allow subsequent purchasers of residences to bring claims for breach of implied warranty of habitability. *E.g.*, Lempke v. Dagenais, 547 A.2d 290 (N. H. 1988); Sewell v. Gregory, 371 S.E.2d 82 (W.Va. 1988); Moxley v. Laramie Builders, Inc., 600 P.2d 733 (Wyo. 1979); *see also* authorities cited at West's ⬧ 272 NEGLIGENCE, k481, k1205.

23. *See* authorities cited at West's ⬧ 95 CONTRACTS, k205.35(1).

24. Bd. of Directors of Bloomfield Club Recreation Association v. Hoffman Group, 712 N.E. 2d 330 (Ill. 1999) (board lacked standing to bring action for breach of implied warranty of habitability regarding clubhouse in residential development).

25. Some states have enacted statutes regarding damages in construction cases. *E.g.*, CALIFORNIA CIVIL CODE § 3300 (2001) contains a damage recovery rule requiring that the measure of damages for breach of contract is the amount that will compensate the party aggrieved for all the detriment proximately caused thereby, or which, in the ordinary course of things, would be likely to result therefrom.

in many apparently conflicting decisions. However, as one commentator noted,

> These conflicts are more apparent than real. What seems to be at work is a judicial effort to find the just solution for the particular case by balancing the opposing policy objectives of giving the owner substantially what the contract requires, but doing so without exacting a forfeiture from the contractor. Viewed in this light, the case results are generally reconcilable.[26]

The two different approaches to owner damages are stated in the two versions of the Restatement of Contracts. The Restatement (First) adopted the cost of repair approach as the primary method of computing damages, stating:

> (1) For a breach by one who has contracted to construct a specified product, the other party can get judgment for compensatory damages for all unavoidable harm that the builder had reason to foresee when the contract was made, less such part of the contract price as has not been paid and is still not payable, determined as follows:
>
> (a) For defective or unfinished construction he can get judgment for either
>
> (i) the reasonable cost of construction and completion in accordance with the contract if this is possible and does not involve unreasonable economic waste; or
>
> (ii) the difference in value that the product contracted for would have had and the value of the performance that has been received by the plaintiff, if construction and completion in accordance with the contract would involve unreasonable economic waste.[27]

---

26. Annotation, *Modern Status of Rule as to Whether Cost of Correction or Difference in Value of Structures Is Proper Measure of Damages for Breach of a Construction Contract*, 41 A.L.R. 4th 131, 132 (1985). *But see* Carol L. Chomsky, *Of Spoil Pits and Swimming Pools: Reconsidering the Measure of Damages for Construction Contracts*, 75 Minn. L. Rev. 1445 (May 1991); Mark Kadi, *Applications of the Substantial Performance Doctrine in Private and Federal Government Contracts*, 22 Ohio N.U.L. Rev. 295 (1995); *see also* authorities cited at West's ⊕ 115 DAMAGES, k120(3).

27. Restatement of Contracts § 346(1)(a)(i) (1932).

Professor Corbin also states that the appropriate measure of damages for breach of a construction contract by a contractor is the cost or repair or replacement:

> For a breach by defective construction, whether it is partial or total ... the injured party could get a judgment for damages measured by the reasonable cost of reconstruction and completion in accordance with the contract, if this is possible and does not involve unreasonable economic waste. ... [T]he cost of repairs or the cost of replacement, if replacement is necessary to obtain the promised performance, is the appropriate approach without reference to the value of the building as an entity. ... [A]ll substantial doubt as to the usefulness and value of the defective structure should be resolved against the building contractor. ... The damages ... should be determined by the cost of completion (the cost of curing the defects) except in a case in which actual completion (the actual curing of the defects) would cause unreasonable economic waste. ... [To determine] whether the "economic waste" involved in any specific tearing down and rebuilding is "unreasonable" ... prevailing practices and opinions (the mores) of men, involving their emotion as well as reasons and logic must be taken into account. ... [28]

A number of courts have adopted the First Restatement's "cost of repair" measure of damages.[29]

By contrast, the Restatement (Second) adopted the diminution in value test as the primary approach to damages computation, stating:

> § 348 Alternatives to Loss in Value of Performance
>
> (2) If a breach results in defective or unfinished construction and the loss in value to the injured party is not proved with sufficient certainty, he may recover damages based on
>
> (a) the diminution in the market price of the property caused by the breach, or

---

28. Arthur Linton Corbin, 11 Corbin on Contracts § 28.49 at 421–28 (interim ed. 2002), *citing* 525 Main Street Corp. v. Eagle Roofing Co., 168 A.2d 33 (N.J. 1961).

29. *E.g.*, Grossman Holdings, Ltd. v. Hourihan, 414 So.2d 1037 (Fla. 1982); *see also* authorities cited at West's ⊕ 115 DAMAGES, k123.

(b) the reasonable cost of completing performance or of remedying the defects if that cost is not clearly disproportionate to the probable loss in value to him.[30]

The Second Restatement adopts the premise that the owner is entitled to receive the difference in value between the performance promised and the value delivered. If the difference in value cannot be proved with sufficient certainty, the owner may recover cost of repair damages if these costs are not clearly disproportionate to the probable loss in value to the owner.

The classic case on the choice between the "cost to complete" and "diminution in value"[31] approaches is *Jacob & Youngs, Inc. v. Kent*,[32] in which the contractor used a different type of pipe from that specified in building a house. The homeowner demanded that the contractor replace the pipe to conform to the specifications and refused to pay the contract balance. The contractor sued for the balance and offered proof that the pipe installed was the same quality and value as the specified pipe. However, the trial court refused this evidence and entered judgment for the homeowner. The appellate court reversed, concluding in an opinion by Judge Cardozo that the owner was not entitled to the cost of completion if it was "grossly and unfairly out of proportion to the good to be attained."[33]

Economic Waste

Where the cost of repair is substantial, defendants often assert the "economic waste" doctrine as a basis to reduce the owner's damages claim.[34] What constitutes "economic waste"

---

30. RESTATEMENT (SECOND) OF CONTRACTS § 348(2) (1981).

31. The "cost of repair" measure of damages may be applied to some defects while the "diminution in value" measure is applied to other defects in the same project. Harrison v. McMillan, 828 So.2d 756 (Miss. 2002).

32. 129 N.E. 889 (N.Y. 1921).

33. *Id.* at 891.

34. Hal J. Perloff, *The Economic-Waste Doctrine in Government Contract Litigation*, 43 DEPAUL L. REV. 185 (Fall 1993); *see generally* authorities cited at West's ⊕═ 115 DAMAGES, k123.

in repair of a construction project is a fact question that is often hotly contested. Courts in different jurisdictions have reached varying conclusions on what constitutes "economic waste" based on the peculiar facts in each case.

Two situations in which the "economic waste" doctrine is frequently applied are where (1) the cost of repair greatly exceeds the original cost of construction (the "disproportionate value rule") and (2) repairing the defect will result in destruction of usable property (the "destruction rule").[35]

For example, in *Eastlake Construction v. Hess,*[36] the Washington Supreme Court held that the cost to replace nonconforming kitchen cabinets in a condominium building constituted "economic waste" and limited the owner's recovery to the difference in value between the cabinets installed and those specified. The court noted that the cost to repair the cabinets was disproportionate to the increase in market value produced by installing the correct cabinets.

In another case, where the cost to repair a floor and heating system was estimated at $97,000 and the market value of the building was between $107,900 and $145,300, the jury's finding that repair would constitute "economic waste" was upheld. In that case, the appellate court found that the trial court correctly applied the diminished value rule.[37] The court held that where the contractor's performance is so faulty or incomplete that the resulting structure is unusable and has no value, the appropriate measure of damages is the diminution in value, to be measured by the cost of removing the useless structure and restoring the site to its original condition.[38]

---

35. The comments to Section 346 of the First Restatement suggested that economic waste would result if the finished product had a value much less than the cost of producing it or if the defects could not be remedied without tearing down and rebuilding, at a cost that would be imprudent and unreasonable.

36. 686 P.2d 465 (Wash. 1984).

37. Metz v. Prism Corp., 551 N.W. 2d 870 (Wis. Ct. App. 1996); *see also* Hancock v. H & M Constr., 808 P.2d 251 (Alaska 1991) (reversing award of cost to demolish and rebuild house as economic waste).

38. Mayfield v. Swafford, 435 N.E. 2d 953, 957 (Ill. App. Ct. 1982).

In *Grossman Holdings v. Hourihan*,[39] the homebuilder constructed a "mirror image" of the model home that the owners had requested. The owners had wanted the house situated on the lot in a specific way to benefit from the sea breezes. The builder oriented the house in the opposite direction. The owners sued for the cost to tear the house down and rebuild it as requested. The Florida Supreme Court held this would amount to "economic waste" and held that the owners were entitled only to "diminution in value" damages. Facts in that case suggest, however, that the builder in *Grossman Holdings* should not have been entitled to limit his damages to the owners' "diminution in value," since it appeared that he *intentionally* breached the contract by building the house with the wrong exposure.

Prior to the decision in *Granite Construction Co. v. United States*,[40] the economic waste doctrine had "a sporadic and confusing application in construction contract litigation where the United States government was a party."[41] In that case Granite was hired to construct a lock and dam for the U.S. Army Corps of Engineers. The contract required Granite to install a PVC waterstop between the vertical joints of a series of concrete monoliths in the wall system. After approximately 10 percent of the waterstop was installed, the Corps tested it, determined that it did not meet the specifications, and required Granite to remove and replace virtually all of it. Granite filed a $3.8 million claim with the contracting officer for the cost to remove and replace the waterstop, arguing that the installed material was stronger than necessary for the project and that the cost to remove and replace it was economic waste. The government refused to evaluate Granite's repair options for the waterstop material and performed no tests to determine if the installed material was adequate. The Claims Court reversed the denial of

---

39. 414 So.2d 1037 (Fla. 1982).
40. 962 F.2d 998 (Ct. Cl. 1992).
41. Perloff, *supra* note 34, at 187.

Granite's claim for equitable adjustment, holding that the government's requirement to tear out the waterstop material was economically wasteful.

In some cases the owner's aesthetic objectives for a structure may overcome a contractor's economic waste arguments. For example, in *City School District v. McLane Construction Co.*,[42] the school district contracted for construction of a swimming pool building featuring a roof consisting of natural wood decking supported by laminated wood beams. The appearance of the beams was central to the aesthetics of the architectural scheme. The building was intended to be a showplace, the site of large regional swimming competitions. When delivered to the site, the beams were discolored. The owner accepted them based on representations that they could be cleaned. However, it was later determined that the beams were permanently discolored. The school board sued the contractor to recover the cost to replace the beams, $357,000, and recovered a verdict in this amount. On appeal, the court rejected the defendant's claim that the owner's damages were limited to the cost of repairing the beams ($37,500) or the diminution in value in the structure ($3,000).[43] The court distinguished the holding in *Jacob & Youngs v. Kent*, stating, "[H]ere the defect, in relation to the entire project, was not of inappreciable importance. One of the school district's principal objectives was to have an aesthetically prepossessing structure, and that goal has by all accounts been frustrated."[44]

Most courts hold that the breaching contractor has the burden of proving that the cost to repair constitutes economic waste.[45] "Without question, the contract breaker should pay the cost of construction and completion in accordance with

---

42. 445 N.Y.S.2d 258 (App. Div. 1981); *see also* Lyon v. Belosky Constr., Inc. 669 N.Y.S.2d 400 (App. Div. 1998).

43. The owner argued that the diminution in value concept was inapplicable because this was a specialty structure with no market value.

44. 445 N.Y.S.2d at 260.

45. *See* authorities cited at West's ⊕ 115 DAMAGES, k123.

his contract unless he proves affirmatively and convincingly that such construction and completion would involve an unreasonable economic waste."[46] "Once the injured party has established the cost to remedy the defects, the contractor bears the burden of challenging this evidence in order to reduce the award, including providing the trial court with evidence to support an alternative award."[47]

Exceptions to Application of the Economic Waste Doctrine

Courts have refused to allow a contractor who intentionally or willfully breaches a contract to use the economic waste rule to avoid cost of repair damages.[48] Courts have also refused to apply the economic loss doctrine where there are significant safety concerns with the construction.[49] For example, in *Bhattaria v. Stein*,[50] the court awarded the owner the cost to reconstruct a driveway to reduce the slope, noting that "this expensive correction does not constitute economic waste." The driveway had a 37.5 percent slope, nearly twice the maximum grade permitted by city ordinance. The court agreed with the Construction Contractors Board that

> [t]he safety of the public is in jeopardy as a result of the negligent and improper work performed by the respondent. The extraordinary [*sic*] steep driveway is akin to a loaded gun just waiting to go off. While the claimant *may* learn to live with the problem, no one knows if a deliveryman, visitor or some other person using the driveway may cause injury to the

---

46. Moss v. Speck, 306 N.W. 2d 156 (Neb. 1981), citing 5A Charles Linton Corbin, Corbin on Contracts § 1089 at 488 (1964); *see also* County Asphalt Paving Co. v. 1861 Group, Ltd., 908 S.W.2d 184 (Mo. Ct. App. 1995).

47. Panorama Vill. Homeowners Ass'n v. Golden Rule Roofing, Inc., 10 P.3d 417, 428 (Wash. Ct. App. 2000).

48. City Sch. Dist. v. McLane Constr. Co., *supra* note 42; *see also* Shell v. Schmidt, 330 P.2d 817 (Cal. Ct. App. 1958); authorities cited at West's ⊕══ 95 CONTRACTS, k295(1); ⊕══ 115 DAMAGES, k120(3).

49. *See* authorities cited at West's ⊕══ 115 DAMAGES, k123, k140.

50. 849 P.2d 1153 (Or. Ct. App. 1993); *see also* Moss v. Speck, 306 N.W. 2d 156 (Neb. 1981) (award of cost of roof repair was appropriate where structure as completed was totally without value for the purpose for which it was intended).

claimant's family, themselves, or some other member of the public.[51]

Similarly, where the defects in construction were so major as to make the structure virtually useless for its intended purpose without repairs, a court found that the cost to repair was the appropriate measure of damages and did not constitute economic waste, even though the repair cost was substantially greater than the cost of the original construction.[52]

The contractor has the burden of proving that an alternative measure of damages should be used and what the damages would be using that method.[53] Unless the contractor presents evidence of economic waste and an alternative measure of damages, it cannot complain about the trial court's award of repair cost damages to the owner.

Proof of Cost of Repair

To prove the cost to repair, an owner must present either competent testimony regarding the estimated costs or, if the repairs have been done, evidence of the actual costs, such as cancelled checks.[54] In addition, the owner may recover engineering and architectural fees reasonably necessary to accomplish the repairs and relocation and finance costs.[55] The owner's testimony about the amount paid to complete the project may not be sufficient without additional testimony by an expert or by a subsequent contractor to show that the

---

51. 849 P.2d at 1155.

52. Worthen Bank & Trust Co. v. Silvercool Serv. Co., 687 P.2d 464 (Col. Ct. App. 1984) (roof unusable as constructed); LaPierre v. Samco Dev. Corp., 406 S.E.2d 646 (N.C. Ct. App. 1991) (garage unusable as constructed).

53. Gough Constr. Co. v. Tri-State Supply Co., 493 N.E.2d 1283 (Ind. Ct. App 1986); *see also* authorities cited at West's 115 DAMAGES, k163(4).

54. Centex-Rooney Constr. Co. v. Martin County, 706 So.2d 20 (Fla. Dist. Ct. App. 1997), *rev. den.*, 718 So.2d 1233 (Fla. 1998); *see also* Barile Excavating & Pipeline Co. v. Kendall Props., Inc., 429 So.2d 1129 (Fla. App. 1984) (error to rely on evidence of estimated costs for completion when actual costs available); authorities cited at West's 115 DAMAGES, k122.

55. Temple Beth Shalom v. Thyne Constr. Corp, 399 So.2d 525 (Fla. Dist. Ct. App. 1981); *see also* authorities cited at West's 115 DAMAGES, k123.

amount spent was reasonable.[56] "The determination of the cost of repairs is necessarily a matter of estimate by a person qualified in the class of work in question and is a proper subject of opinion testimony when given by properly qualified witnesses such as architects."[57] The contractor has the burden of showing that the owner's actual expenditures were unreasonable.[58]

Loss of Use

The owner's loss of use of a new project may be proved by evidence of the reasonable rental value of the new project.[59] This can be difficult with public projects, such as courthouses or athletic facilities. In such cases, the owner should provide testimony from a qualified expert, such as a real estate appraiser, as to the difficulty in proving the rental value for the new facility. Thereafter the owner may be able to offer evidence of the cost of renting alternative facilities to prove its damages for loss of use.

Diminution in Value

There are two measures of diminution in value: (1) the loss in value to the owner and (2) the loss of market value. Most courts have applied the "loss of market value" approach, although this has been criticized as providing inadequate

---

56. Oertel v. Ransone, No. 143176, 1997 Va. Cir. LEXIS 588 (Va. Cir. Ct., March 27, 1997).

57. Blecick v. Sch. Dist. No. 18, 406 P.2d 750, 757 (Ariz. Ct. App. 1965), *citing* 20 AM. JUR. *Evidence* § 833.

58. Tuttle/White Constructors, Inc. v. Montgomery Elevator Co., 385 So.2d 98, 100 (Fla. App. 1980), *citing* 5 CHARLES LINTON CORBIN, CORBIN ON CONTRACTS § 999 at 24–25 (1964); *see also* authorities cited at West's ☞ 115 DAMAGES, k163(4).

59. *E.g.*, Int'l Fid. v. County of Rockland, 98 F. Supp. 2d 400 (S.D. N.Y. 2000); Seaway Painting, Inc. v. D.L. Smith Co., 242 B.R. 834 (E.D. Pa. 1999), *on remand*, In re: Cornell & Co., No. 96-316500AS, Adversary No. 98-374, 2000 WL 3888838 (Bankr. E. D. Pa., April 12, 2000); Advance Tank & Constr. Co. v. City of DeSoto, 737 F. Supp. 383 (N.D. Tex. 1990). *But see* Miami Heart Inst., Inc. v. Heery Architects & Eng'rs, 765 F. Supp. 1083 (S.D. Fla. 1991), where the court held that the damages were measured by the difference between the reasonable rental value of the new facility and the reasonable rental value of the old facility).

compensation to the owner.[60] The diminution in value rule applies where the contract has been substantially complied with, the structure as completed will serve substantially as well as it would if completed according to contract, and completion in accord with the contract terms would either endanger the balance of the structure or be possible only at inordinate cost.[61]

Some courts have held that a contractor can invoke "diminution in value" as a limitation on its liability for damages only if he has substantially performed the contract or has not intentionally deviated from the terms of the contract. A contractor who raises this defense may bear the burden of proving substantial performance of the contract or lack of intentional deviation.[62]

In *Shell v. Schmidt*,[63] the plaintiffs purchased similar houses in a tract built by the defendant contractor. Plaintiffs contended that the builder made major deviations from the contract specifications, including improper sheathing and stucco of exterior walls and installation of incorrect capacity furnaces. Plaintiffs sued for damages sufficient to make the houses conform to the plans and specifications. The contractor contended that it had substantially performed the contract in good faith and should be entitled to payment of the contract price, less damages for its failure to perform, asserting that its breaches were not willful or fraudulent and did not "substantially affect the usefulness of the building for the purpose for which it was intended."[64] The court did not limit the notion of "willfulness" to "malice or fraud" on the part of the contractor. It ruled that the contractor could not,

---

60. Chomsky, *supra* note 26, at 1496: "[T]he present standard leaves significant opportunity for undercompensation if courts reject cost to complete in favor of an award of diminution in market value, because the loss is often of greater value to the owner than to the market."

61. *See* authorities cited at West's ⬤ 115 DAMAGES, k120(3); ⬤ 95 CONTRACTS, k295(1).

62. Shell v. Schmidt, 330 P.2d 817, 820, 827 (Cal. Ct. App. 1958); *see also* authorities cited at West's ⬤ 115 DAMAGES, k120(3), k163.

63. *Shell v. Schmidt*, *supra* note 62.

64. *Id.* at 820.

as a matter of law, be held to have performed in "good faith" if "there had been willful and intentional major deviations from the terms of the contract."[65]

Diminution in value is far more difficult to prove than the cost to repair, particularly in cases where the contractor's performance is defective rather than incomplete.[66] In such cases, the Second Restatement observes that it may be more appropriate to award damages based on the owner's cost to repair the defects, even if this results in recovery of more than the loss of value. "[I]t is better that he [the owner] receive a small windfall than that he be undercompensated by being limited to the resulting diminution in the market price of his property."[67]

Proving estimated fair market value of a partially completed construction project may be difficult. "Determining fair market value is a complex and inexact task. ... The difficulties are likely to be compounded when the aim is to ascertain what the fair market value would have been if the property were in a different condition than it is presently."[68] In a recent case, an architect and a contractor were held liable to the owner for the diminution in value of a building resulting from window leaks, as evidenced by the reduction in sales price.[69]

Another problem in determining diminution in value is the fact that there usually is no market value for specialty projects such as sports facilities, courthouses, schools, and infrastructure projects such as bridges. In such situations, the reasonable cost of repair may be the only appropriate measure of damages. While the general rule allows a property

---

65. *Id.* at 822.

66. RESTATEMENT (SECOND) OF CONTRACTS § 348(2)(b), cmt. c (1981).

67. *Id.*

68. Chomsky, *supra* note 26, at footnote 60, *citing* AMERICAN INSTITUTE OF REAL ESTATE APPRAISERS, THE APPRAISAL OF REAL ESTATE (8th ed. 1983), and ALFRED A. RING & JAMES H. BOYKIN, THE VALUATION OF REAL ESTATE 58-64 (3d ed. 1986).

69. Commerce Ctr. of Greenville, Inc. v. W. Powers McElveen & Assocs., Inc., 556 S.E. 2d 718 (S.C. Ct. App. 2001).

70. Kenney v. Medlin Constr. & Realty Co., 315 S.E. 2d 311, 313 (N.C. Ct. App. 1984): "Generally the owner is considered competent to testify to the fair market value of his property, even if his knowledge would not qualify him as a witness were he not the owner. The only recognized exception

(continued)

owner to testify as to the value of his own property,[70] expert testimony by a real estate appraiser may be required to prove "diminution in value" damages.[71] The expert witness should be prepared to testify regarding the fair market value of the subject property with and without the alleged defects. The owner should also present testimony regarding the cost to repair the alleged defects. Failure to present adequate evidence of such damages could result in the owner's winning the battle on liability, but losing the war on damages by receiving only a nominal damages award.[72]

Direct and Consequential Damages

Direct damages are defined as those that arise in the ordinary course of events because of a breach of contract.[73] These include the cost to repair defective or incomplete work, increased finance costs, additional management fees, and extended overhead. Direct damages are routinely compensable.[74] Consequential damages' recoverability is more unpredictable.

"Consequential damages are those that arise from the intervention of 'special circumstances' not ordinarily predictable. Consequential damages are compensable only if it is determined that the special circumstances were within the 'contemplation' of both parties."[75] Whether damages are direct or consequential is a question of law.[76] Whether special

---

to the general rule is where it affirmatively appears that the owner does not know the fair market value." The owner's testimony of value must be more than a mere guess; see Hall v. Lovell Regency Homes L.P., 708 A.2d 344 (Md. Ct. Spec. App. 1998) (homeowner's testimony regarding value properly excluded where there was no evidence that he had knowledge about sales of nondefective properties in his neighborhood and witness characterized testimony about value as "a guess"). Reliance Ins. Co. v. ProTech Conditioning & Heating, Inc., 28 Fla. L. Weekly (Fla. App. 2003) (owner qualified to testify re: property damages and value). See also authorities cited at West's ☞ 157 EVIDENCE, k474(16)(18).

71. See authorities cited at West's ☞ 157 EVIDENCE, k543.5.

72. Hall v. Lovell Regency Homes, L.P., supra note 70.

73. Roanoke Hosp. Ass'n v. Doyle & Russell, Inc., 214 S.E.2d 155, 160 (Va. 1975); see also authorities cited at West's ☞ 115 DAMAGES, k16.

74. Id.

75. Roanoke Hosp., supra note 73 at 160–61; see also authorities cited at West's ☞ 115 DAMAGES, k23.

76. See authorities cited at West's ☞ 115 DAMAGES, k208(1).

circumstances were within the contemplation of the parties is a question of fact.[77] As with so much of the law in this area, the cases applying these principles are confusing and sometimes contradictory. As one author noted, it is sometimes hard to distinguish between the definitions of "direct" damages and "consequential" damages.[78]

In addition to direct damages, owners may also seek consequential damages such as lost profits and higher interest rates resulting from delay in completing the project. These damages may be substantial. As noted above, consequential damages are more difficult to prove and to recover than direct damages because they do not flow naturally from delay. The owner's ability to recover consequential damages may depend on proof of the contractor's knowledge of the owner's intended use of the project.

Parties to design and construction contracts may waive or disclaim liability for consequential damages,[79] and courts have enforced such waivers.[80] Even if there is no contractual bar to recovering consequential damages, owners must prove these damages were reasonably foreseeable[81] at the time of contracting and were within the parties' contemplation. However, this does not mean that the parties were required to discuss the potential damages at the time of contracting.[82]

---

77. *Id.*; *see also* ARTHUR LINTON CORBIN, 11 CORBIN ON CONTRACTS § 1012 at 77 (interim ed. 2002).

78. Lynn R. Axelroth, *Mutual Waiver of Consequential Damages—The Owner's Perspective*, 18:1 CONSTR. LAW. 11, 12 (Jan. 1998).

79. *E.g.*, AIA Document A201, General Conditions of the Contract for Construction ¶ 3.10 (1997 edition), and AIA Document B141, Standard Form of Agreement Between Owner and Architect with Standard Form of Architect's Services ¶ 1.3.6 (1997 Edition); *see generally* Axelroth, *supra* note 78; J. William Ernstrom & Michael F. Dehmler, *Mutual Waiver of Consequential Damages—The Contractor's Perspective*, 18:1 CONSTR. LAW. 4 (Jan. 1998).

80. *E.g.*, Mistry Prabhudas Manji Eng. Pvt. Ltd. v. Raytheon Eng'rs & Constructors, Inc., 213 F. Supp. 2d 20 (D. Mass 2002) (consequential damages waiver was not unconscionable and was enforceable); *see also* authorities cited at West's ☞ 115 DAMAGES, k118.

81. Hadley v. Baxendale, 9 Exch. 341, 156 Eng. Rep. 145 (1854).

82. RESTATEMENT (SECOND) OF CONTRACTS § 348, cmt. a (1981) provides: "Furthermore, the party in breach need not have made a 'tacit agreement' to be liable for the loss. Nor must he have had the loss in mind when making the contract, for the test is an objective one based on what he had reason to foresee."

Owners should be aware that even if they are successful in obtaining a judgment for consequential damages, in some cases the architect and the general contractor may be unable to pay the judgment. Some commentators suggest that to avoid this problem owners should limit waivers of consequential damages and carve out the consequential damages covered by the architect's or the contractor's insurance in these contracts.[83] This would provide the owner with some additional security for recovery of such damages, although the insurers may still raise coverage issues when claims are made.

Lost Profits

Lost profits claims present additional evidentiary issues.

> It is not possible to state the precise degree of approach to certainty required for the recovery of profits as damages for breach of contract. If the mind of the court is certain that profits would have been made if there had been no breach by the defendant, there will be a greater degree of liberality in allowing the jury to bring in a verdict for the plaintiff, even though the amount of profits prevented is scarcely subject to proof at all. In this respect, at least, doubts will generally be resolved in favor of the party who has certainly been injured and against the party committing the breach.[84]

In cases involving an established business, courts have considered past profits a reasonably certain measure by which to calculate a damage award.[85] A new business, however, does not have its own history of profits, which makes these damages more difficult to prove. Thus, in such cases, courts have considered both the profit history of the plaintiff's similar business at a different location, and the profit history from the business in question if it was successfully run by someone else before the plaintiff, to be measures of reasonable

---

83. James D. Weier, Seth D. Lamden, Ric D. Glover, *Preserving Consequential Damages Through Limited Waivers and Insurance Coverage*, 22:3 Constr. Law. 22 (Summer 2002).

84. Arthur Linton Corbin, 11 Corbin on Contracts § 1022 (interim ed. 2002).

85. *See generally* authorities cited at West's ⬥ 115 DAMAGES, k190.

certainty for a damage award when a new business has been injured.[86] In *Guard v. P & R Enterprises*, the Alaska Supreme Court noted that to preclude recovery of lost profits as a matter of law merely because a business was newly established would encourage those contracting with such a business to breach their contracts, and refused to "apply an inflexible rule denying recovery of lost profits to a new business for breach of contract."[87]

In *Perini Corp. v. Greate Bay Hotel & Casino, Inc.*,[88] the New Jersey Supreme Court refused to interfere with an arbitration award to the Sands hotel of $14,500,000 in consequential damages resulting from a seven-month delay in completing renovations of a casino in Atlantic City. Although Perini argued that lost profits were not contemplated by the parties when the contract was entered into, the court held that

> the testimony of Sands's personnel clearly established that Sands intended to increase its profits by attracting more patrons from the boardwalk. Certainly, Perini had to be aware of Sands's motive at the time it entered into the contract. Also, Sands stressed the importance of timely completion of the project. On numerous occasions Sands informed Perini that it wished to have the project completed prior to the beginning of the summer season, the casino industry's busiest season. Perini was well aware of the projected completion date. In an inter-office memorandum, dated September 26, 1983, Perini's project manager wrote: "The projected completion date is June 15, 1984, which is 12 work days beyond the required completion date on May 31, 1984." Furthermore,

---

86. Standard Mach. Co. v. Duncan Shaw Corp., 208 F.2d 61, 64 (1st Cir. 1953) (applying Rhode Island law); Guard v. P & R Enters., 631 P.2d 1068, 1072 (Alaska 1981), *citing* Mech. Wholesale, Inc. v. Universal-Rundle Corp., 432 F.2d 228, 231 (5th Cir. 1970) (applying Texas law); Gerwin v. Southeastern California Ass'n of Seventh Day Adventists, 92 Cal. Rptr. 111, 119 (Cal. Ct. App. 1971); Vickers v. Wichita State Univ., 518 P.2d 512, 517 (Kan.1974); Fera v. Vill. Plaza, Inc., 242 N.W.2d 372, 374 (Mich. 1976); Brenneman v. Auto-Teria, Inc., 491 P.2d 992, 994 n.1 (Or. 1971); Ferrell v. Elrod, 469 S.W.2d 678, 686 (Tenn. Ct. App. 1971); *see also* authorities cited at West's 🔑 115 DAMAGES, k40(2), k190.

87. 631 P.2d 1068, 1072 (Alaska 1981), *citing Vickers v. Wichita State Univ., supra* note 86, 518 P.2d at 517; *see also* authorities cited at West's 🔑 115 DAMAGES, k40(2), k190.

88. 610 A.2d 364 (N.J. 1992).

Perini knew that Sands would delay construction if the project could not be completed by May 1984. Thus, it appears that the arbitrators had more than enough evidence to conclude that Perini was aware that its failure to complete the project in a timely fashion could lead to a significant loss of income.[89]

The damages awarded were measured by the casino's estimated profits during the delay period. Perini argued that the renovation of the casino was akin to a new business, making lost profits speculative; the owner countered by showing that "the casino had a proven track record; the location and nature of the business never changed; and the management team never changed."[90] Further, even had the renovation been considered a "new business," the trend in recent cases has been to award lost profits for a new business when they can be proved with reasonable certainty.[91]

Foreseeability

Because consequential damages must have been contemplated to be recoverable, the question of foreseeability frequently arises in claims for such damages. Comment a to Section 348 of the Restatement (Second) of Contracts provides:

Requirement of foreseeability. A contracting party is generally expected to take account of those risks that are foreseeable at the time he makes the contract. He is not, however, liable in the event of breach for loss that he did not at the time of contracting have reason to foresee as a probable result of such a breach. The mere circumstance that some loss was foreseeable, or even that some loss of the same general kind was foreseeable, will not suffice if the loss that actually occurred was not foreseeable. It is enough, however, that the loss was foreseeable as a probable, as distinguished from a necessary, result of his breach. Furthermore, the party in breach need not have made

---

89. *Id.* at 499.
90. *Id.* at 509.
91. *Id., citing* Robert L. Dunn, Recovery of Damages for Lost Profits 3d § 4.2 (1987).

a "tacit agreement" to be liable for the loss. Nor must he have had the loss in mind when making the contract, for the test is an objective one based on what he had reason to foresee. There is no requirement of foreseeability with respect to the injured party. In spite of these qualifications, the requirement of foreseeability is a more severe limitation of liability than is the requirement of substantial or "proximate" cause in the case of an action in tort or for breach of warranty. Compare Restatement, Second, Torts § 431; Uniform Commercial Code § 2-715(2)(b). Although the recovery that is precluded by the limitation of foreseeability is usually based on the expectation interest and takes the form of lost profits ... the limitation may also preclude recovery based on the reliance interest.[92]

Corbin states that "contemplation" includes what was actually foreseen and what was reasonably foreseeable. If there are special circumstances, it is not even necessary that the defendant knew of them; it is enough that a reasonable person in the same position would have known of them.[93]

Calculation of Owner Delay Damages

Owner delay damages are usually calculated using evidence of the owner's additional financing costs, loss of use, lost profits, additional overhead expenses, and additional management expenses.[94] These need not be proved with exact certainty. The usual rule is that the damages must be supported by sufficient evidence to establish them to a reasonable person.[95] However, a recent case allowed an owner to prove its damages by the "total cost" method. In *United*

---

92. RESTATEMENT (SECOND) OF CONTRACTS §348, cmt. a (1981).

93. ARTHUR LINTON CORBIN, 11 CORBIN ON CONTRACTS § 1010 at 68 (interim ed. 2002); *see also* authorities cited at West's 115 DAMAGES, k163(2).

94. *See* authorities cited at West's 115 DAMAGES, k122; 95 CONTRACTS, k298.

95. *See* authorities cited at West's 115 DAMAGES, k163(4).

States Fidelity & Guaranty Co. v. Braspetro Oil Services Co.,[96] the court stated:

> Frederick Hamilton, the Petrobras Defendants' accounting expert, testified credibly that the total cost overrun on the P-31 Project was $116,209,776. This figure was arrived at by determining what Brasoil spent in excess of the adjusted budget. The adjusted budget was arrived at by taking the initial contract price ($163,000,021), adding the change orders that were actually approved ($16,968,846), and adding other adjustments that the technical expert for the Petrobras Defendants concluded Petrobras should be liable for ($9,043,048), to arrive at a total adjusted budget of $189,011,915. Brasoil had actual costs for the P-31 Project of approximately $306,968,000, but the experts for the Petrobras Defendants subtracted other costs such as overhead and duplicative payroll costs that should not be included in costs, reducing the actual cost figure to approximately $305,221,000. Subtracting the approximate adjusted budget figure from the actual cost leaves a cost overrun of just over $116,209,000.[97]

An owner's delay damages may include damages incurred as a result of the delayed sale of the project and the expenditure of additional administrative costs during the extended construction period. In *McDevitt & Street Co. v. Marriott Corp.,*[98] the completion of a hotel was delayed. The court held that, as a result,

> Marriott (1) was deprived of the use of the sale proceeds for 132 days; (2) did not receive ground lease payments; or (3) lost management fees for that period; and (4) incurred additional administrative costs. The Court concludes that Marriott is entitled to $416,823 as compensation for the delayed receipt of sale proceeds, lost ground lease payments, and certain administrative expenses.[99]

96. 219 F. Supp. 2d 403 (S.D.N.Y. 2002).
97. *Id.* at 455 (citations omitted).
98. 713 F. Supp. 906 (E.D. Va. 1989), *aff'd in part, rev'd in part,* 911 F.2d 723 (4th Cir 1990), *on remand,* 754 F. Supp. 513 (E.D. Va.), *aff'd in part, rev'd in part,* 948 F.2d 1281 (4th Cir. 1991).
99. 713 F. Supp. at 929.

Time of Damages Calculation

One of the more vexing problems in calculating an owner's damages in a construction case is the principle that damages are assessed "as of the date of the breach of contract."[100] Courts routinely state this principle but offer precious little guidance as to how it should be applied. Usually the owner's damages for repairing defective work are incurred months or years after the project is completed. If the breach occurred during construction or as of the date of substantial completion, how does this affect the proof of damages?

In *Centex-Rooney v. Martin County*,[101] the owner sued its construction manager for the cost to repair construction defects. The project was completed in 1988 and the repairs took place over several years thereafter. The case was tried in 1996. The construction manager stipulated that any breach of contract occurred as of the date the project was substantially completed. Consequently, the owner had to present its damages in 1988 dollars. To do this required the owner's damages expert to testify to the total amount of expenditures and then deflate them into a lump sum in 1988 dollars.

> The County's damage expert, Mark Gauthier, testified that he reviewed and analyzed reports received from the County, which detailed the expenses incurred with respect to the sick building issue, and accumulated information from these reports in a computer database. He explained that he examined each expenditure and, upon ascertaining its purpose, determined whether it should be claimed or unclaimed, placing all expenses relating to upgrades, as well as all unresolved and questionable expenses, in the unclaimed category. Gauthier testified that the County did not claim reconstruction expenses for any upgrades or improvements over the original

---

100. Arthur Linton Corbin, 11 Corbin on Contracts § 1005 at 46 (interim ed. 2002) states: "In all cases in which valuation in dollars is required, compensation for the plaintiff's losses is to be made with reference to the conditions existing at the time when performance is due and the contract is broken."

101. 706 So.2d 20 (Fla. Dist. Ct. App. 1997), *rev. den.*, 718 So.2d 1233 (Fla. 1998).

plans and specifications; relocation expenses for furniture cleaning, storage, new furniture, water bottle rentals, lease deposits,
utilities or janitors; or financing expenses for anything other
than the new construction. Over Centex's foundation and rel-
evance objections, the court allowed Gauthier to testify from a
prepared summary report, which was projected on a screen
(but not placed in evidence), that recapitulated the County's
claimed and unclaimed expenses for reconstruction, relocation, and financing. He then deflated the County's claimed
expenses to 1988 dollars and calculated a single present value
as of the date of the breach.[102]

However, in *Anchorage Asphalt Paving v. J.R. Lewis*,[103] the
Alaska Supreme Court noted that because the litigation had
extended over a decade, during which there was extraordinary inflation,

> limiting the plaintiff to the time of breach cost or repair has
> the potential of subverting the remedial purposes of the dam-
> age award. Simply put, where inflation has eroded the time of
> breach monetary valuation of an injury to a fraction of what is
> required to remedy the plaintiff's injury, then the time of breach
> rule may be regarded as inappropriate. Because the circum-
> stances of individual cases differ drastically, it is impractical to
> adopt a definite point in time to value damages. It has been
> found preferable to leave the question to the trial court's
> discretion.[104]

The *Anchorage Asphalt Paving* court further noted:

> The rules of law governing the recovery of damages for breach
> of contract are very flexible. Their application in the infinite
> number of situations that arise is beyond question variable and
> uncertain. Even more than in the case of other rules of law,
> they must be regarded merely as guides to the court, leaving
> much to the individual feeling of the court created by the spe-
> cial circumstances of the particular case.[105]

---

102. 706 So.2d at 27.
103. 629 P.2d 65 (Alaska 1981).
104. *Id.* at 68.
105. *Id.*, citing 5A CORBIN ON CONTRACTS § 1002 at 33 (1964).

Both the *Centex-Rooney*[106] and *Braspetro Oil Services Co.* opinions[107] are instructive, because the damages proof in those cases was presented through fact witnesses as well as through expert witnesses, providing a broad evidentiary basis to support the damages award in the event of an appeal.[108]

MITIGATION OF DAMAGES

It is hornbook law that an injured party must mitigate its damages.[109] In most jurisdictions, mitigation is an affirmative defense, on which the contractor has the burden of proof.[110] However, some courts have required the owner to prove that it attempted to mitigate its damages as part of its proof.[111] Since mitigation of damages and claims of "betterment" are frequently raised in construction cases, it is prudent for the

---

106. Note 101, *supra*.

107. Note 96, *supra*.

108. "At trial, several County witnesses testified about the actual costs incurred for demolition, redesign, and reconstruction of the buildings, relocation and financing. The County introduced several boxes of vouchers and checks relating to its relocation and reconstruction expenses through its budget administrator." *Centex-Rooney, supra* note 101, at 27. In *Braspetro Oil Services Co., supra* note 96, "The testimony by Mr. Hamilton [accounting expert] and by Scott McClure, the naval architecture expert for the Petrobras Defendants, was reasonable and credible, and was supported by contemporaneous documentation and the testimony of the Petrobras managers for the P-19 and P-31 Projects." 219 F. Supp. 2d at 455.

109. Arthur Linton Corbin, 11 Corbin on Contracts § 1039 at 208–09 (interim ed. 2002):

Since the purpose of the rule concerning damages is to put the injured party in as good a position as he would have been put by full performance of the contract at the least necessary cost to the defendant, the plaintiff is never given judgment for damages for losses that he could have avoided by reasonable effort without risk of other substantial loss or injury. It is not infrequently said that it is the "duty" of the injured party to mitigate his damages so far as that can be done by reasonable effort on his part. Since there is no judicial penalty, however, for his failure to make this effort, it is not desirable to say that he is under a "duty." His recovery against the defendant will be exactly the same whether he makes the effort and mitigates his loss, or not; but if he fails to make the reasonable effort, with the result that his injury is greater than it would otherwise have been, he cannot recover judgment for the amount of this avoidable and unnecessary increase. The law does not penalize his inaction; it merely does nothing to compensate him for the loss that he helped to cause by not avoiding it.

See also Restatement (Second) of Contracts § 350 (1) (1981): "Damages are not recoverable for loss that the injured party could have avoided without undue risk, burden or humiliation."

110. *See generally* authorities cited at West's ☞ 115 DAMAGES, k163(2).

111. *See* Nello L. Teer Co. v. Hollywood Golf Estates, Inc., 324 F.2d 669 (5th Cir. 1963), *cert. denied*, 377 U.S. 909 (1964).

owner to include evidence regarding its efforts to mitigate damages, and to reduce its claimed damages for any "betterments," in its damages proof.

LIQUIDATED DAMAGES

Because of the difficulty in calculating owners' damages for delay, many construction contracts provide for liquidated damages in a specific dollar amount to be paid for each day that the contractor is late in completing the project (or a specified portion of it). Liquidated damages provisions usually require payment of a specific sum for each day of delay, although the amount may differ in different phases of the project.[112] Some contracts provide for liquidated damages for breach of some parts of the contract while allowing actual damages for other breaches. In *Hathaway & Co. v. United States*,[113] the contract stated, "The contractor shall pay, in addition to the liquidated damages hereinbefore specified, all expenses for inspection and superintendence."[114] The Supreme Court held that "[t]here is no reason why parties competent to contract may not agree that certain elements of damage difficult to estimate shall be covered by a provision for liquidated damages and that other elements shall be ascertained in the usual manner."[115]

While simplifying damage calculations, liquidated damages provisions create a host of other legal snarls. The first legal issue to be faced is whether the liquidated damages provision is enforceable. Many courts have held that liquidated damages are not collectible if they are in fact a "penalty."[116] Some courts also hold that an owner cannot

---

112. *See* authorities cited at West's ⊕ 115 DAMAGES, k163(3).

113. 249 U.S. 460 (1919).

114. *Id.* at 463.

115. *Id.*; *accord*, Hillsborough County Aviation Auth. v. Cone Bros. Contracting Co., 285 So.2d 619 (Fla. Dist. Ct. App. 1973); *see also* authorities cited at West's ⊕ 115 DAMAGES, k85.

116. RESTATEMENT (SECOND) OF CONTRACTS § 356 (1981); *see also* authorities cited at West's ⊕ 115 DAMAGES, k76, k80(1).

recover liquidated damages unless it suffered some actual damages as a result of the alleged breach.[117]

One commentator has stated:

> The law of liquidated damages embodies the language of dichotomy. The law is characterized by the great divide between enforceable liquidated damages clauses and unenforceable penalties. Parties may agree to stipulated damages but only at an amount that is considered reasonable. An amount above anticipated or actual compensatory damages is presumed to be a penalty, and the common law abhors penalties. The incongruity between freedom of contract principles and the nonenforcement of penalty clauses has generated an extensive body of scholarly commentary.[118]

The Restatement (Second) of Contracts provides:

> Damages for breach by either party may be liquidated in the agreement but only at an amount that is reasonable in the light of the anticipated or actual loss caused by the breach and the difficulties of proof of loss. A term fixing unreasonably large liquidated damages is unenforceable on grounds of public policy as a penalty.[119]

Consequently, owners seeking to enforce liquidated damages provisions against tardy contractors are frequently faced with assertions that the contractual liquidated damages provision is unenforceable because the stipulated amount is unreasonable and, therefore, a penalty. Unfortunately, the Restatement

---

117. In United States v. Bethlehem Steel Co., 205 U.S. 105 (1907), the U.S. Supreme Court upheld imposition of liquidated damages even though the government sustained no actual damages. However, because this case involved a wartime government contract, its application to private commercial contracts should be limited. *Accord*, Bethlehem Steel Co. v. City of Chicago, 350 F.2d 649 (7th Cir. 1965). *Contra*, Massman Constr. Co. v. City Council, 147 F.2d 925 (6th Cir. 1945); Norwalk Door Closer Co. v. Eagle Lock & Screw Co., 220 A.2d 263 (Conn. 1966) (refusing to enforce liquidated damage clause where no actual damage); RESTATEMENT (SECOND) OF CONTRACTS § 356(1), cmt. b (1979): "If ... no loss at all has occurred, a provision fixing a substantial sum as damages is unenforceable." *See* Susan V. Ferris, *Liquidated Damages Recovery under the Restatement (Second) of Contracts*, 67 CORNELL L. REV. 862 (April 1982); *see also* authorities cited at West's ⊕ 115 DAMAGES, k85.

118. Larry A. DiMatteo, *A Theory of Efficient Penalty: Eliminating the Law of Liquidated Damages*, 38 AM. BUS. L.J. 633, 635 (Summer 2001).

119. RESTATEMENT (SECOND) OF CONTRACTS § 356(1) (1981).

provides no guidance as to the applicable time frame for the analysis of the reasonableness of the liquidated damages amount: the time of contracting, the time of breach, or the time of trial.

Courts use two approaches in determining whether a liquidated damages provision is a penalty. The "prospective approach" focuses on the estimation of the potential damages at the time of contract formation. "Under this approach the amount of actual damages at the time of the breach is of little or no significance to the recovery of liquidated damages."[120] The "retrospective approach" not only analyzes the estimation of damages at the time of contract formation but also considers the relationship between the liquidated damages amount and the actual damages caused by the breach. Under this approach, if the liquidated sum greatly exceeds the amount of actual damages, the liquidated damages will be considered a penalty and recovery will be limited to actual damages.[121]

If the owner cannot enforce its liquidated damages agreement, it must prove its actual damages resulting from the delay. Thus, as one commentator has noted,

> Under the current state of the law, however, the provisions do not achieve their potential as effective dispute avoidance mechanisms because parties often turn to the courts to adjudicate validity of the provisions on a case-by-case basis. With no guarantee that their provisions will be enforced, parties may be confronted with the very uncertainty they hoped to avoid.[122]

A possible solution to this problem would be a uniform liquidated damages statute for public contracts, akin to the Uniform Commercial Code.[123] Such a statute would be an

---

120. Brazen v. Bell Atl. Corp., 695 A.2d 43 (Del. 1997); Guiliano v. Cleo, Inc., 995 S.W.2d 88, 98 (Tenn. 1999), *citing* Gaines v. Jones, 486 F.2d 39 (8th Cir. 1972).

121. Kelly v. Marx, 694 N.E. 2d 869 (Mass. App. Ct. 1998); Shallow Brook Assocs. v. Dube, 599 A.2d 132 (N.H. 1991).

122. Scott M. Tyler, *No (Easy) Way Out: "Liquidating" Stipulated Damages for Contractor Delay in Public Construction Contracts*, 44 Duke L.J. 357, 358 (1994) [hereinafter *No Way Out*].

123. *See No Way Out, supra* note 122, at 420.

extension of the current law in some jurisdictions, because some states have enacted statutes requiring liquidated damages provisions in certain public contracts.[124] Other states specifically authorize public owners to withhold payment from contractors in specified circumstances, including delay in performance.[125] California has long had a statute providing that "a sum specified is valid as liquidated damages unless manifestly unreasonable."[126]

A second legal issue in liquidated damages claims is whether an owner can enforce a liquidated damages provision against a contractor if the owner is responsible for part of the delay. Courts have reached varying conclusions on this issue. Some courts refuse to award any liquidated damages where the owner was responsible for part of the delay,[127] while other courts have "apportioned" the liquidated damages based on each party's contribution to the delay.[128] Some commentators suggest that "owners and contractors may wish to avoid the uncertainty in the law by specifically agreeing in their construction contract that per diem liquidated damages shall be apportioned where both parties contribute to late completion of the project, and thus insulate themselves from the archaic and arbitrary bite of the 'all or none' judicial approach."[129]

If a contract provides for liquidated damages for breach, this limits the amount the owner can recover for that breach. A liquidated damages clause precludes the owner from seeking its actual damages, even if the liquidated damages are far

---

124. *E.g.*, Fla. Stat. Ann. § 337.18 (2002).

125. *E.g.*, Ga. Code Ann. § 13-11-5 (2002); Mo. Rev. Stat. § 34.057 (2003).

126. Cal. Civ. Code § 1671 (2003).

127. Grand Rapids Asphalt Paving Co. v. City of Wyoming, 185 N.W. 2d 591 (Mich. Ct. App. 1971); Aetna Cas. & Sur. Co. v. Bd. of Trustees, 35 Cal. Rptr. 765 (Cal. Ct. App. 1963); *see also* authorities cited at West's ☞ 115 DAMAGES, k85.

128. Calumet Constr. Corp. v. Metro. Sanitary Dist., 533 N.E.2d 453 (Ill. App. Ct. 1988); *see also* authorities cited at West's ☞ 115 DAMAGES, k85.

129. David W. James, *Concurrency and Apportioning Liability and Damages in Public Contract Adjudications*, 20 Pub. Cont. L. J. 490 (Summer 1991); Rocky Unruh & John Worden, *Liquidated Damages for Delay in Completion of Commercial Construction Projects: Are They Recoverable by the Owner When the Owner Contributes to the Delay?* 34 Santa Clara L. Rev. 1 (1993).

less than the owner's actual damages.[130] Owners must be careful to review liquidated damages clauses for adequacy.

Enforceability of liquidated damages clauses depends on precision in contract drafting. Listing the damages included in the clause and the calculations done to arrive at it may be helpful in enforcing it later. Also, if the clause is intended only to cover certain types of damages (e.g., the owner's extended overhead) and not others (e.g., the owner's liability to third parties for delay damages), this intent should be stated specifically.[131]

Liquidated damages are normally assessed up to the date of substantial completion, since the owner then has beneficial occupancy of the building. However, where a contract provided for liquidated damages "for any work that shall remain uncompleted," the owner was awarded liquidated damages until the engineer certified the building was finally complete, nearly a year after substantial completion.[132] Some standard form contracts provide for a lesser amount of liquidated damages to be assessed between substantial completion and final completion.[133]

There is a split of authority regarding whether a contractor who abandons a project before completion is liable for liquidated damages.[134] A number of courts have held that an

---

130. Trans World Airlines v. Travelers Ind. Co., 262 F.2d 321 (8th Cir. 1959); X.L.O. Concrete Corp. v. John T. Brady & Co., 482 N.Y.S.2d 476 (App. Div. 1984); *see also* authorities cited at West's ☞ 115 DAMAGES, k80, k85.

131. *See generally* Annotation, *Contractual Provision for Per Diem Payments for Delay in Performance as One for Liquidated Damages or Penalty*, 12 A.L.R. 4th 891 (1982).

132. Sutter Corp. v. Tri-Boro Mun. Auth., 487 A.2d 933 (Pa. Super. Ct. 1985).

133. *E.g.*, EJCDC Document C-250, Standard Form of Agreement Between Owner and Contractor on the Basis of a Stipulated Price ¶ 4.03 (2002 edition) provides, in part:

Owner and Contractor agree that as liquidated damages for delay (but not as a penalty), Contractor shall pay Owner $_____ for each day that expires after the time specified ... for Substantial Completion until the Work is substantially complete. After Substantial Completion, if the Contractor shall neglect, refuse or fail to complete the remaining Work within the Contract Time or any proper extension thereof that shall be granted by the Owner, Contractor shall pay Owner $_____ for each day that expires after the time specified ... for completion and readiness for final payment until the Work is completed and ready for final payment.

134. *See generally* Annotation, *Liability of Contractor Who Abandons Building Project Before Completion for Liquidated Damages*, 15 A.L.R. 5th 376 (1993).

abandoning contractor is liable for liquidated damages, especially where the abandonment occurs after the contract completion date. However, some courts have held contractors not liable for liquidated damages because abandonment was not contemplated as part of the liquidated damages clause. Consequently, to avoid this situation, a liquidated damages clause should specify that it applies to the contractor's abandonment of the project as well as to delays in completion.

Liquidated damages are not limited to delay damages. Design professional contracts frequently limit the owner's damages for breach of contract to the amount of the design professional's fee or the amount of available insurance, a form of liquidated damages. While some states have statutes prohibiting design professionals from limiting their liability,[135] other states allow such limitations,[136] and some courts have held these limitations are enforceable in design professional contracts.[137]

Owner's Damages Recoverable from Performance Bond Surety

If there is a performance bond on the project, the surety may be liable for the damages caused by the contractor's default under its contract with the owner.[138] A surety bond is

---

135. *E.g.*, Wis. Stat. Ann. § 895.49 (2002); Va. Code Ann. §54.1–411 (2003); *see* Paul Bennett Morrow, *The Unconscionability of a Liquidated Damages Clause: A Practical Application of Behavioral Decision Theory*, 22 Pace L. Rev. 27 (Winter 2001).

136. Cal. Civ. Code § 2782.5 (2003).

137. Valhal Corp. v. Sullivan Assocs., Inc., 44 F.3d 195 (3d Cir. 1995) ($50,000 limitation of liability in architectural contract enforceable); Florida Power & Light Co. v. Mid-Valley, Inc., 763 F.2d 1316 (11th Cir. 1985) (limitation of engineer's liability to insurance coverage upheld); Markborough California, Inc. v. Superior Court, 227 Cal. App.3d 705 (Cal. App. 1991); *see generally* Howard W. Ashcraft, Jr., *Limitation of Liability—The View After Markborough*, 11 Constr. Law. 3 (Aug. 1991); Allen Holt Gwyn, *Legislative and Judicial Responses to Limitation of Liability Provisions*, 16 Constr. Law. 61 (Oct. 1996); Robert J. Harris, *Limitation of Liability Clauses: Allocating Risky Business*, 13 Constr. Law. 18 (Oct. 1994); Michael S. Zetlin & Francine M. Chillemi, *Building a Safe Haven: Clauses Imposing Monetary Limits on Designer Liability*, 20 Constr. Law. 5 (Jan. 2000); *see also* authorities cited at West's ☞ 95 CONTRACTS, k114.

138. *See generally* The Law of Performance Bonds (Lawrence R. Moelmann & John T. Harris eds., 1999) [hereinafter Performance Bonds]; *see also* authorities cited at West's ☞ 309 PRINCIPAL AND SURETY, k1, k10.

a "written instrument executed by the principal and surety in which the surety agrees to answer for the debt, default or miscarriage of the principal."[139] The contract of a surety is interpreted according to the standards that govern the interpretation of contracts in general.[140] Therefore, it is important that the owner and its counsel review the bond terms carefully and follow any requirements to perfect a claim on the bond.

Most performance bonds are conditioned upon the contractor's performance of its obligations under the contract. The bond terms may provide that the surety's obligations under the performance bond do not arise until the owner declares the contractor to be in default under the contract.[141] Although the terms "default" and "breach" are sometimes used interchangeably, not every breach of contract constitutes a "default." "To constitute a legal default, there must be (1) a material breach or series of material breaches (2) of such magnitude that the obligee is justified in terminating the contract."[142] Some contracts define events of default; however, the events listed may not be the exclusive grounds for declaring a default under the contract.[143] In declaring a default, the owner must make the declaration in clear, direct, unequivocal language. The declaration must inform the surety that the principal has committed a material breach or material breaches of the contract and that the surety must

---

139. Cates Constr., Inc. v. Talbot Partners, 980 P.2d 407 (Cal. 1999).

140. RESTATEMENT OF SECURITY § 88 (1941).

141. Typical performance bond language provides that the surety's obligations arise "Whenever Principal shall be, and shall be declared by Obligee to be in default under the contract, the Obligee having performed Obligee's obligations thereunder." *See* authorities cited at West's ⊕⇒ 309 PRINCIPAL AND SURETY, k139.

142. L & A Contracting Co. v. S. Concrete Servs., Inc., 17 F.3d 106 (5th Cir. 1994), *citing* James A. Knox, *Representing the Private Owner,* in CONSTRUCTION DEFAULTS: RIGHTS, DUTIES AND LIABILITIES § 9.3 at 201 (Robert F. Cushman & Charles A. Meeker eds., 1989); James A. Knox, *What Constitutes a Default Sufficient to Justify Termination of the Contract: A Surety's Perspective,* 2:1 CONSTR. LAW. 1 (Summer 1981). *See also* authorities cited at West's ⊕⇒ 309 PRINCIPAL AND SURETY, k100(1); ⊕⇒ 95 CONTRACTS, k318.

143. There is a split of authority on whether a default provision that does not provide that it is "exclusive" bars other remedies for terminating the contract. *See* Olin Corp. v. Cent. Indus., Inc., 576 F.2d 642 (5th Cir 1978).

immediately commence performing under the terms of its bond.[144]

Assuming that there is a contractor default under the contract, the owner must act promptly in notifying the contractor and the surety of the default. The owner's failure to declare the contractor in default may waive the default and the owner's right to make a claim for it on the performance bond.[145] For example, in *Bank of Brewton, Inc. v. International Fidelity Insurance Co.*,[146] the owner sent a number of letters to the contractor and the surety complaining about the pace and quality of the contractor's work and threatening to declare a default. The surety asked the owner to clarify the status of the contract. The owner asked the surety what constitutes a contract default and how to send a contractor default notice to the surety. However, the owner never sent a formal declaration of default to the surety and allowed the contractor to continue working on the project through substantial completion.

When the owner sued the contractor and the surety for damages on the performance bond, the trial court entered summary judgment for the surety. The Alabama Supreme Court upheld the judgment, holding that the surety's obligations under the bond were never triggered because the owner never declared the contractor in default or terminated the contract.[147] The court noted, "[A] mere threat is not sufficient to trigger the obligations of a surety."[148] However, depending on the bond's terms, it may not always be necessary for the owner to terminate the contract in order to declare a default under the performance bond.[149]

---

144. *L & A Contracting Co. v. S. Concrete Servs.*, *supra* note 142, at 111; *see also* authorities cited at West's ⟴ 309 PRINCIPAL AND SURETY, k139.

145. *See also* authorities cited at West's ⟴ 309 PRINCIPAL AND SURETY, k141.

146. 827 So.2d 747 (Ala. 2002).

147. The bond required the owner to declare a contractor default and formally terminate the contractor's right to complete the contract. *Id.* at 749.

148. *Id.* at 754.

149. DCC Constructors, Inc. v. Randall Mech., Inc.. 791 So.2d 575 (Fla. Dist. Ct. App. 2001) (contract termination not required under bond terms).

The surety sued on account of a principal's default on the contract may raise all defenses that the defaulting contractor could have raised, as well as defenses specific to the surety such as failure to comply with notice requirements[150] or overpayment.[151]

Performance bond sureties may be liable for liquidated or delay damages owed by their principals, although courts have different views on whether the bond must specify that delay damages are covered in order for the surety to be liable.[152] Also, owners should keep in mind that

> the mere fact that the bonded contractor or the completing surety has failed to complete the project within the original contract time frame, is not of itself a circumstance which permits a liquidated damages assessment against the surety. There are many legal doctrines which provide a surety—particularly a completing surety—with a wide range of defense to an owner's automatic assessment of such damages.[153]

Some courts have allowed sureties to raise the "cardinal change" doctrine as a defense to an owner's performance bond claim:

> A cardinal change "is one which, because it fundamentally alters the contractual undertaking of the contractor, is not compre-

---

150. Sch. Bd. v. TIG Premier Ins. Co., 110 F. Supp. 2d. 1351 (N.D. Fla. 2000) (owner's failure to notify surety of contractor's breach rendered bond null and void); *see also* text associated with notes 122–26 *supra*.

151. The obligee's overpayment to the contractor may constitute an impairment of the surety's collateral (the contract balance) and allow the surety to reduce its performance obligation *pro tanto*. Nat'l Union Ind. Co. v. G.E. Bass & Co., 369 F.2d 75 (5th Cir. 1966); Restatement (Third) of Suretyship and Guaranty § 42 (1996). However, not all owner overpayments provide a *pro tanto* discharge to a surety. *E.g.*, United States Fid. & Guar. Co. v. Braspetro Oil Servs. Co., 219 F. Supp. 2d. 403 (S.D.N.Y. 2002); *see also* authorities cited at West's 309 PRINCIPAL AND SURETY, k115, k117.

152. *Compare* Cates Constr. v. Talbot Partners, *supra* note 139 (delay damages covered by performance bond even if not specifically addressed), *with* American Home Assur. Co. v. Larkin Gen. Hosp., 593 So.2d 195 (Fla. 1992) (surety not liable for delay damages unless such responsibility is specified in bond) *and* Downtown Area Sch. Dist. v. Int'l Fid. Ins. Co., 769 A.2d 560 (Pa. Commw. Ct. 2001) (surety not liable for delay damages where bond was ambiguous); *but see* National Fire Ins. Co. v. Fortune Constr. Co., 320 F.3d 1260 (11th Cir. 2003) (where liquidated damages are part of underlying contract and incorporated by reference into bond, the surety is on notice of the time element of performance and the contractual consequences of failure to timely perform).

153. J. Charles Sheak & Timothy J. Korzun, *Liquidated Damages and the Surety: Are They Defensible?* 9:2 Constr. Law. 19 (April 1989).

hended by the normal changes clause." A surety is discharged where the bonded contract is materially changed without the surety's knowledge or consent and the surety suffers prejudice as result of the changes.[154]

Generally, the surety will be discharged only if there are material changes to the underlying contract that prejudice the surety. In that case, the surety is discharged to the extent it has been prejudiced.[155]

Most performance bonds state that the surety waives notice of any alteration or extension of time by the owner.[156] Changes that are commensurate with the project's size and that are not material or qualitative are insufficient to support a surety's claim of "cardinal change."[157] In deciding whether there has been a "cardinal change," a court may also look at the total number of changes, whether the changes were made early or late in the project, whether the changes unduly interfered with or disrupted ongoing construction work, and the dollar amount of the changes in comparison to the total contract amount.[158]

Because the performance bond incorporates the construction contract, the performance bond surety may be liable for warranty claims and for latent defect claims discovered after substantial completion.[159] As one court stated, the surety's liability for completion of the project according to the terms and conditions of the contract "is not dependent upon whether the defect was discovered before or after substantial completion."[160]

Owners' latent defect claims often face statute of limitations defenses from sureties. Many bonds contain a limitations

---

154. F. Malcolm Cunningham, *Cardinal Change: Discharge of the Surety's Obligation*, 22:4 CONSTR. LAW. 12 (Fall 2002); *see also* RESTATEMENT (THIRD) OF SURETYSHIP AND GUARANTY, § 37 (1996); authorities cited at West's ⊕ 309 PRINCIPAL AND SURETY, k115, k117.

155. RESTATEMENT (THIRD) OF SURETYSHIP AND GUARANTY § 37, cmt. a (1996).

156. *E.g.*, AIA Document A312, Performance Bond ¶ 8 (1984 edition).

157. *United States Fid. & Guar. Co. v. Braspetro Oil Servs.*, *supra* note 96, at 456.

158. *Id.*

159. PERFORMANCE BONDS, *supra* note 138, at 141; Federal Ins. Co. v. Southwest Florida Retirement Ctr., Inc., 707 So.2d 1119 (Fla. 1998).

160. *Federal Ins. Co. v. Southwest Florida Retirement Ctr., Inc.*, *supra* note 159.

period that may be shorter than the applicable statute of limitations. For example, the American Institute of Architects form Performance Bond (A312) provides that suit must be brought within two years from the date final payment to the contractor was due. Some jurisdictions do not permit contracts shortening the statute of limitations,[161] but many jurisdictions allow this. Also, many states have enacted statutes of repose related to latent defects in construction projects that may limit the owner's ability to make defect claims against a performance bond surety. In some instances there are different statutes of limitation applicable to claims against the performance bond surety and the construction contractor.[162]

Sureties may be liable in some states for punitive or exemplary damages if they act in bad faith or violate a state's unfair claims settlement practice law.[163] However, a surety's bond obligation does not include liability for punitive damages awarded against its principal.[164]

Punitive and Enhanced Damages

"Punitive damages serve as a form of punishment and to deter others from conduct which is sufficiently egregious to call for the remedy."[165] Punitive damages[166] are generally not awarded for breach of contract, even if the breach is willful, unless there is also proof of fraud or tortious conduct independent of the contract breach.[167] "A promisor's motive for breaching a contract is generally regarded as irrelevant because the prom-

---

161. *E.g.*, FLA. STAT. ANN. § 95.03 (2002).

162. *E.g.*, *Federal Ins. Co. v. Southwest Florida Retirement Ctr., Inc.*, *supra* note 159 (statute of repose did not apply to owner's claim against surety; owner's claim was barred by contract statute of limitations); *see also* authorities cited at West's ⊕⇒ 309 PRINCIPAL AND SURETY, k149.

163. Unfair claims settlement practice acts are discussed in Chapter 3 of this text.

164. Annotation, *Liability of Surety on Private Bond for Punitive Damages*, 2 A.L.R. 4th 1254, 1255 (1980).

165. McClure v. Walgreen Co., 613 N.W. 2d 225, 230 (Iowa 2000).

166. Punitive damages are also referred to as "exemplary" or "vindictive" damages or "smart money." *See* note 164 *supra*.

167. Hulsey Pool Co. v. Troutman, 306 S.E.2d 83 (Ga. Ct. App. 1983); *see also* authorities cited at West's ⊕⇒ 115 DAMAGES, k151.

isee will be compensated for all damages resulting from the breach."[168] While some jurisdictions allow award of punitive damages for breach of contract if the "evidence shows a culpable state of mind,"[169] this is the minority view.[170]

Evidence of mismanagement and negligence is insufficient to support a punitive damages claim for breach of contract. For example, in *Indiana & Michigan Electric Co. v. Terre Haute Industries*,[171] the contractor sued the owner for wrongful termination of the contract and presented evidence of "negligence and mismanagement ... in the execution of the project; of mistakes in drawings and specifications, of mislabeled and misfabricated materials and supplies; of improper design; of interference and delays caused by other contractors and subcontractors; and of delays caused by weather, all of which caused [the contractor] to be, without its fault, 143 days behind schedule."[172] The contractor also presented evidence that the owner "made demands upon [the contractor] concerning compliance with the contract schedule, extra work without extra pay, an acceleration schedule at [the contractor's] expense and the like," and that the owner negligently failed to investigate to determine if there were adequate grounds for termination before terminating the contract.[173]

Vacating the trial court's award of punitive damages to the contractor for "wrongful breach of contract," the appellate court noted:

> [The contractor] characterizes the acts of [the owner] as malicious and oppressive. We are of the opinion, that, at worst, the

---

168. Indiana & Michigan Elec. Co. v. Terre Haute Indus., Inc., 507 N.E. 2d 588, 610 (Ind. Ct. App. 1987), *citing* Vernon Fire & Cas. Ins. Co. v. Sharp, 349 N.E. 2d 173 (Ind. 1976).

169. Public Serv. Co. v. Diamond D Constr. Co., 33 P.3d 651 (N.M. Ct. App. 2001). "A defendant acts with a culpable state of mind when the evidence shows that the defendant acted with reckless disregard for the rights of the plaintiff or that the defendant knew that its actions could harm the interests of the plaintiff but failed to exercise care to avoid such harm." *Id.* at 663–64.

170. *See generally* Annotation, *Recovery of Punitive Damages for Breach of Building of Construction Contract*, 40 A.L.R. 4th 110 (1985).

171. 507 N.E. 2d 588, 615 (Ind. Ct. App. 1987).

172. *Id.* at 616.

173. *Id.*

complained of conduct was substandard business practice, and arrogance, which ... are not bases for punitive damages. [The contractor's] principal, recurring theme is [the owner's] unsuccessful attempt to exact from [the contractor] what was not due. [The owner's] striving for advantage is neither unusual nor particularly shocking in the give and take of the commercial world. No case is cited which holds that such conduct is a basis for punitive damages. We are equally unpersuaded that the personality defects of [the owner's] officers ... add any weight to the award of punitive damages. We know of no authority that permits the imposition of punitive damages merely because the contracting party or his agents are disagreeable people. We do not believe that such a trait, however annoying, is a quasi-crime.[174]

Many of the construction cases where punitive damages have been allowed for breach of contract are consumer cases where there was evidence that a builder deliberately violated a building code or the plans and specifications, so that the structure was unfit for use.[175]

The United States Supreme Court has held that for a punitive damages award to pass constitutional muster, it must satisfy the following requirements: (1) the punitive damages award must relate to conduct occurring within the state; (2) a defendant must receive fair notice of the conduct that will subject him to punishment; (3) a defendant must receive fair notice of the severity of the penalty the state may impose. As to the third element there are three "guideposts" for courts to consider: (1) the degree of reprehensibility of the conduct; (2) the disparity between the harm or potential harm suffered by the plaintiff and its punitive damages award; and (3) the differences between this remedy and the civil penalties authorized or imposed in comparable cases.[176]

174. *Id.* at 617.
175. *E.g.*, F. D. Borkholder Co. v. Sandock, 413 N.E.2d 567 (Ind. 1980); Sands v. R. G. McKelvey Bldg. Co., 571 S.W.2d 726 (Mo. App. 1978).
176. BMW of N. America, Inc. v. Gore, 517 U.S. 559 (1996).

The Supreme Court recently overturned a $145 million punitive damage award against an insurer, where the compensatory damages were $1 million, holding that the punitive damages were "excessive and in violation of the due process clause of the Fourteenth Amendment to the Constitution of the United States.[177] This decision will likely affect the amount of punitive damages awards in all types of cases, including construction cases.[178] Without fixing bright line limits on punitive damages awards, the Court stated, "Our jurisprudence and the principles it has now established, demonstrate, however, that, in practice, few awards exceeding a single-digit ratio between punitive and compensatory damages, to a significant degree, will satisfy due process."[179]

Many states have enacted "Unfair and Deceptive Trade Practices" acts,[180] which provide for treble damages and attorney's fees for violations. These have been applied in construction cases and may provide an easier route for owners to obtain enhanced damages than a punitive damages claim. Federal or state false claims laws are frequent bases for enhanced damages claims in public contracts, allowing substantial recoveries for public owners.[181]

Emotional Distress

Although an individual owner dealing with a nonperforming contractor will likely suffer mental and emotional distress, generally these damages are not recoverable under a tort theory where there is no physical injury to the plaintiff.[182]

---

177. State Farm Mut. Auto. Ins. Co. v. Campbell, 123 S.Ct. 1513 (2003).

178. *E.g.,* Eden Elec., Ltd. v. Amana Co., L.P., No. C00-80, 2003 WL 1961282 (N.D. Iowa April 21, 2003) (punitive damages award in fraud case reduced from $17,875,000 to $10 million based on State Farm decision).

179. *Id., citing Gore, supra* note 176, and TXO Prod. Corp. v. Alliance Res. Corp. 509 U.S. 443 (1993).

180. Unfair and deceptive trade practices acts and false claims acts are discussed in Chapter 3 of this text.

181. *See generally* authorities cited at West's ⊕═ 393 UNITED STATES, k120–23.

182. The general rule is that where a tortfeasor's negligence causes emotional distress without physical injury, such damages may not be awarded. WILLIAM PROSSER, W. PAGE KEETON, & DAN D. DOBBS,

(continued)

Although Restatement (Second) of Contracts Section 353 makes reference to the possibility of recovery of emotional distress damages in breach of contract cases, the first illustration to that section indicates that breach of a construction contract is not the type of breach that will typically support emotional distress damages.[183]

Even where plaintiffs are allowed to claim that a "negligent" breach of contract caused them emotional distress, courts have been reluctant to allow emotional distress damages. As the California Supreme Court stated:

> While we do not doubt that the Blagroves were justifiably and seriously distressed over the damage to [their home], adopting a rule allowing trial on the issue and recovery if proved would result in unacceptable burdens for both the judicial system and defendants. We therefore hold that emotional distress damages in connection with property damages are not compensable.[184]

Moreover, "typical damages for breach of house construction contracts can appropriately be calculated in terms of monetary loss" whereas "damages in contracts of a more personal nature in which emotional disturbance damages are allowed are usually intangible. Thus, there would ordinarily be only

PROSSER AND KEETON ON THE LAW OF TORTS § 54, at 361 (5th ed. 1984) ("Where the defendant's negligence causes only mental disturbance, without accompanying physical injury, illness, or other physical consequences, and in the absence of some other independent basis for tort liability, the great majority of courts still hold that in the ordinary case there can be no recovery."). *But see* Harrison v. McMillan, 828 So.2d 756 (Miss. 2002) (allowing recovery for emotional distress damages where owner testified that repair work on his house exacerbated his diabetes); Kishmarton v. William Bailey Constr., Inc. 754 N.E.2d 785 (Ohio 2001) (allowing emotional distress damages for breach of construction contract based on OHIO CONSTITUTION Art. I, § 16, and the RESTATEMENT (SECOND) OF CONTRACTS, citing Douglas J. Whaley, *Paying for the Agony: The Recovery of Emotional Distress Damages in Contract Actions*, 26 SUFFOLK U. L. REV. 935, 948 (1992).

183. RESTATEMENT (SECOND) OF CONTRACTS § 353, first illus. (1981): A contracts to construct a house for B. A knows when the contract is made that B is in delicate health and that proper completion of the work is of great importance to him. Because of delays and departures from specifications, B suffers nervousness and emotional distress. In an action by B against A for breach of contract, the element of emotional disturbance will not be included as loss for which damages may be awarded.

184. Erlich v. Menezes, 981 P.2d 978 (Cal. 1999); *see also* Blagrove v. JB Mech., Inc. 934 P.2d 1273 (Wyo. 1997).

a nominal recovery unless emotional disturbance damages were allowed."[185]

CONCLUSION

Because of the flexibility in damages rules and the fact-specific issues unique to each case, the law of owner's damages is a crazy quilt of conflicting rules and decisions attempting to apply those rules. Some ways for owners' counsel to avoid roadblocks to damages recovery are to: (1) review contractual notice requirements for damages claims and default notices to sureties to be sure notices are timely sent; (2) advise clients of the need to document and to separately account for expenditures for repair work and to keep track of any betterments; and (3) utilize fact and technical witnesses regarding construction issues to support accounting expert testimony about damages.

---

185. Hancock v. Northcutt, 808 P.2d 251, 258 (Alaska 1991).

Breach of Contract: Contractor Damages

6

C. ALLEN GIBSON, JR.

The subject of damages is vitally important to a contractor that is affected by an owner's breach of the parties' contract. There are a number of ways in which the contractor can be impacted by an owner's breach, but most theories of recovery are rooted in contract analysis. The general contractor is often in a precarious situation when facing an owner who demands strict performance of the contract while the contractor must rely upon subcontractors to perform much of the actual work. This chapter addresses contractor damages principally from the general contractor's point of view. However, most of the analysis also applies to a subcontractor's breach-of-contract claim against the general contractor. In fact, the general contractor may often find itself in the situation where it must either assert the subcontractor's claim, through the use of a liquidating agreement, or assist the subcontractor in its claim for those damages that are properly attributable to the owner.

The general measure of a contractor's damages as a result of an owner's breach is the reasonable extra cost incurred in performing the contract plus the lost profit on the contract. This general measure of damages attempts to return the parties to the same position they would have been in if there had been no breach.[1] Specific theories of recovery are discussed below.

IMPLIED WARRANTY OF PLANS AND SPECIFICATIONS

The United States Supreme Court does not often render opinions in construction cases. However, in *United States v. Spearin*,[2] the Court established a very significant implied warranty in construction contracts—the owner's implied warranty that the plans, specifications, and other information supplied to the contractor are accurate and suitable for construction of the project. If the contractor constructs the project in accordance with the owner-supplied plans and specifications, then the contractor is generally not liable to the owner for any damages or failures that may result. The *Spearin* case involved the allocation between owner and contractor of damages to a sewer project. However, the decision has spawned a line of cases that provide an opportunity for contractors to recover damages from owners as a result of defective plans.[3] This "Implied Warranty of Plans and Specifications" is the generally accepted rule and applies to both public and private contracts.[4] In most jurisdictions, the warranty will apply even if the owner attempts to disclaim it,

---

1. *See* authorities cited at West's ☞ 115 DAMAGES, k120(3).

2. 248 U.S. 132, 136 (1918).

3. *See* 1, 4 STEVEN G. M. STEIN, CONSTRUCTION LAW ¶¶ 2.01[2][c], 5.03[2][b], 18.02[1] (2002); Annotation, *Construction Contractor's Liability to Contractee for Defects or Insufficiency of Work Attributable to the Latter's Plans and Specifications*, 6 A.L.R. 3rd 1394 (1966); authorities cited at West's ☞ 95 CONTRACTS, k205.15(5).

4. 1 STEIN, *supra* note 3, ¶ 5.03[2](b).

shift an inspection obligation to the contractor, or include some other exculpatory clause.[5]

In order to recover from the owner, the contractor must be able to prove that it was unaware of the inaccuracy or defect in the plans and specifications. If a contractor knows about defects and proceeds to bid for and perform the work, then it will not be allowed recovery for any resulting damages.[6] This limitation is important because the courts hold that if the contractor has not been misled by the error in the plans and specifications, it cannot claim that it has been damaged. Additionally, the contractor must show that it actually followed the plans and specifications in the performance of its work. If it failed to perform in accordance with the plans provided by the owner, or failed to follow the sequence of work set out in the plans and specifications, then no recovery against the owner will be allowed under the implied warranty.[7] Of course, a contractor may nonetheless retain rights to damages if it discloses a perceived defect but is directed by the owner to construct the job as originally specified.

In addition, most courts have held that the contractor has a "duty to investigate or inquire about a patent ambiguity, inconsistency, or mistake when the contractor recognized or should have recognized an error in specifications or drawings."[8] Therefore, any patent ambiguities will require some inquiry from the contractor prior to bidding or performing the work. However, the contractor is not obligated to inquire

---

5. *Spearin, supra* note 2, 248 U.S. at 136–37; *see also* P.T. & L. Constr. Co. v. New Jersey Dep't of Transp., 531 A.2d 1330 (N.J. 1987) and cases reviewed therein; authorities cited at West's ⊕═ 95 CONTRACTS k280(3), ⊕═ 360 STATES k104, ⊕═ 393 UNITED STATES k70(3), ⊕═ 200 HIGHWAYS k113(4).

6. Robins Maint., Inc. v. United States, 265 F.3d 1254, 1257 (Fed. Cir. 2001); authorities cited at West's ⊕═ 393 UNITED STATES, k70(29), k70(30).

7. T.L. James & Co. v. Traylor Bros., Inc., 294 F.3d 743, 752 (5th Cir. 2002); authorities cited at West's ⊕═ 95 CONTRACTS, k199(1). *But see* City of Charlotte v. Skidmore, Owings & Merrill, 407 S.E. 2d 571 (N.C. Ct. App. 1991) (trial court properly submitted to jury the issue of allocation between defective design and defective construction).

8. White v. Edsall Constr. Co., 296 F.3d 1081, 1085 (Fed. Cir. 2002); *see also* authorities cited at West's ⊕═ 393 UNITED STATES, k70(30).

beyond the documents provided by the owner or to perform an independent analysis of the design provided by the owner.[9]

If the contractor can successfully establish all of the prerequisites of the cause of action for breach of the Implied Warranty of Plans and Specifications, then it is entitled to recover as damages the additional costs resulting from those defective plans.[10] All reasonable costs incurred in overcoming the defects or attempting to do so will be recoverable by the contractor.[11] Those reasonable additional costs may include the actual costs of performing, additional expenses incurred in nonproductive work, extended overhead expenses, and, possibly, wage or equipment rental escalation costs.[12]

Depending on the severity of the problem, a contractor may also have the option of stopping work after the defect in the plans or specifications is discovered and recovering the cost of the work performed up to that time. Shortly after the *Spearin* case was decided, the United States Supreme Court decided another construction case in *United States v. Atlantic Dredging Company*,[13] involving misrepresentations by the government regarding the nature of materials that had to be dredged. The Court held that the contractor could cease work upon discovering the misrepresentation in the plans. The Court also held that the contractor was entitled to recover the cost of the work it had performed to that date as compensatory damages.

Finally, if a material error in the design is discovered prior to beginning work, the contractor may have a right to rescind the contract.[14] It is important that this action be taken immediately upon discovery of that material mistake in

---

9. *See, e.g.,* authorities cited at West's ☞ 393 UNITED STATES, k70(30).

10. *See, e.g.,* authorities cited at West's ☞ 393 UNITED STATES, k70(29).

11. *White, supra* note 8, 296 F.3d at 1087.

12. *See P.T.&L. Constr., supra* note 5, 531 A.2d at 1333.

13. 253 U.S.1 (1920).

14. *See, e.g.,* authorities cited at West's ☞ 393 UNITED STATES, k73(24).

the plans and before the contractor incurs significant additional costs.[15] Of course, the contractor that seeks to rescind (or halt performance of) the contract faces a possible counterclaim for any additional costs in performing the work incurred by the owner after the contractor terminates its performance, so these responses to a design defect present considerable risk and should be used only where the contractor is sure of its position.

UNFORESEEN SITE CONDITIONS

A contractor entering into a construction contract that does not include a Differing Site Conditions (DSC) clause typically agrees to perform its scope of work at a particular price, bearing the risk of any conditions that exist at the site, whether known or unforeseen. A prudent contractor, under such circumstances, will add an appropriate contingency to its contract price to compensate it for unexpected conditions that it might experience. Alternatively, the bidding contractors may incur the additional cost of conducting their own extensive site investigations in order to gather more accurate information and reduce the contingent risk. In either circumstance, the owner is likely to pay in the end for the risk of unforeseen conditions, whether or not they are encountered. A DSC clause can alleviate the need for the contractor to build contingencies into its bid for the unknown cost of construction, and it provides a mechanism for the contractor to obtain an equitable adjustment to its contract for the unanticipated costs and schedule delay encountered as a result of unforeseen site conditions.

In the absence of an appropriate contract provision, a contractor must rely on various other theories to recover its additional costs. These theories might include a claim of

---

15. Centex Constr. Co. v. James, 374 F.2d 921 (8th Cir. 1967).

breach of implied warranty or defective specifications (as covered in more detail above), mutual mistake by the parties, failure to disclose superior knowledge, or a common-law claim of misrepresentation that may be very difficult to prove. DSC clauses are now found in most construction contracts, affording the contractor a specified, contractual theory of recovery if it encounters unforeseen site conditions.

The standard DSC clause in federal construction, found in Federal Acquisition Regulation Section 52.236-2, reads as follows:

a. The Contractor shall promptly, and before the conditions are disturbed, give a written notice to the Contracting Officer of (1) subsurface or latent physical conditions at the site which differ materially from those indicated in this contract, or (2) unknown physical conditions at the site, of an unusual nature, which differ materially from those ordinarily encountered and generally recognized as inhering in work of the character provided for in the contract.

b. The Contracting Officer shall investigate the site conditions promptly after receiving the notice. If the conditions do materially so differ and cause an increase or decrease in the Contractor's cost of, or the time required for, performing any part of the work under this contract, whether or not changed as a result of the conditions, an equitable adjustment shall be made under this clause and the contract modified in writing accordingly.

c. No request by the Contractor for an equitable adjustment to the contract under this clause shall be allowed, unless the Contractor has given the written notice required; *provided*, that the time prescribed in (a) [above] for giving written notice may be extended by the Contracting Officer.

d. No request by the Contractor for an equitable adjustment to the contract for differing site conditions shall be allowed if made after final payment under this contract.[16]

---

16. 48 C.F.R. § 52.236-2 (2001). All references to the FAR in this chapter are to the 2001 revision, found generally in Title 48 of the Code of Federal Regulations.

The American Institute of Architects (AIA) also includes a Differing Site Conditions clause in its General Conditions, as follows:

> Claims for Concealed or Unknown Conditions. If conditions are encountered at the site which are (1) subsurface or otherwise concealed physical conditions which differ materially from those indicated in the Contract Documents or (2) unknown physical conditions of an unusual nature, which differ materially from those ordinarily encountered and generally recognized as inherent in construction activities of the character provided for in the Contract Documents, then notice by the observing party shall be given to the other party promptly before conditions are disturbed and in no event later than 21 days after first observance of the conditions. The Architect will promptly investigate such conditions and if they differ materially and cause an increase or decrease in the Contractor's cost of, or time required for, performance of any part of the Work, will recommend an equitable adjustment in the Contract Sum or Contract Time, or both. If the Architect determines that the conditions at the site are not materially different from those indicated in the Contract Documents and that no change in the terms of the Contract is justified, the Architect shall so notify the Owner and Contractor in writing, stating the reasons. Claims by either party in opposition to such determination must be made within 21 days after the Architect has given notice of the decision. If the conditions encountered are materially different, the Contract Sum and Contract Time shall be equitably adjusted.[17]

Other widely used standard form construction contracts have also adopted Differing Site Conditions clauses.[18] This analysis will focus principally on the FAR and AIA provisions.

---

17. AIA Document A201, General Conditions of the Contract for Construction ¶ 4.3.4 (1997 edition).

18. *See* Associated General Contractors of America Document 200, Standard Form of Agreement and General Conditions Between Owner and Contractor ¶ 3.16.2 (2000 edition): Engineers Joint Contract Documents Committee Document C-700, Standard General Conditions of the Construction Contract ¶ 4.03 (2002 edition); Design-Build Institute of America Document 535, Standard Form of General Conditions of Contract Between Owner and Design/Builder § 4.2 (1998 edition).

The language of both of these contract provisions sets forth certain notice requirements and provides that an "equitable adjustment" will be made if the contractual conditions are met. Both the FAR and the AIA also recognize two separate types of differing site condition claims. A Type I condition generally differs from that which is indicated in the contract documents. A Type II condition does not rely upon a difference from the representations made in the contract, but exists where conditions encountered differ materially from those ordinarily encountered in the type of work being undertaken.

A contractor seeking to recover under either type of a DSC claim must carefully follow the notice requirements in the contract clause. There is a distinct difference between the FAR requirement that notice be given "before the conditions are disturbed" and the AIA provision that notice be given "promptly before conditions are disturbed and in no event later than twenty-one days after first observance of the conditions." Both of these provisions are in the contract to give the owner an opportunity to investigate the site conditions before they have been changed by the contractor's activity. While some decisions have found that the failure to provide timely notice of a differing site condition is a complete defense,[19] other decisions recognize the difficulty faced by a contractor in trying to determine exactly when conditions vary sufficiently to justify assertion of a claim.[20] In *Dawco Construction, Inc. v. United States*,[21] the United States Claims Court rejected the government's argument that the notice was untimely. The court recognized the difficulty of identifying a "differing site condition" and acknowledged that a contractor often must work in an area for some period of time before it can be determined that there truly is a

---

19. *See* Fru-Con Constr. Corp. v. United States, 43 Fed. Cl. 306, *modified*, 44 Fed. Cl. 298 (1999); *see also* authorities cited at West's ⊕═ 393 UNITED STATES, k70(36).

20. *See, e.g.*, authorities cited at West's ⊕═ 393 UNITED STATES, k70(22.1).

21. Dawco Constr. Inc. v. United States, 18 Cl. Ct. 682, *aff'd in part, rev'd in part*, 930 F.2d 872 (Fed. Cir. 1991).

difference in the site conditions. As the court succinctly stated, "One aberrant rock or root does not necessarily constitute a differing site condition."[22] Nevertheless, the contractor will be well advised to provide notice to the owner of a potential claim for differing site conditions as soon as it can reasonably determine that such a claim might exist.

In order to establish a Type I Differing Site Condition claim, the contractor must prove each element of the contractual provision, including (1) that the contract documents made an affirmative representation or indication of site conditions; (2) that the actual conditions differed materially from those represented in the contract documents; (3) that the actual conditions could not have been reasonably anticipated from either examination of the site or review of the contract documents and (4) that the contractor relied upon the information provided by the owner.[23] As stated by the court in *Iacobelli Construction, Inc. v. County of Monroe*, "the essential issue in a Type I claim is 'whether the contractor could reasonably have anticipated the conditions encountered from a knowledgeable interpretation of the contract documents, his inspection of the site, and his general experience as a contractor.' "[24] That court actually set forth six elements to establish a Type I Differing Site Conditions claim; other courts and commentators reduce it to three.[25] In any event, the significant difference between Type I and Type II claims is that in a Type I claim the contractor must prove that the contract documents affirmatively indicated some condition,[26] failing which it will not be entitled to an equitable adjustment.[27]

---

22. 18 Cl. Ct at 693.

23. *See, e.g.*, authorities cited at West's ☞ 316A PUBLIC CONTRACTS, k16; ☞ 393 UNITED STATES, k70(22.1)(30).

24. 32 F.3d 19, 24 (2d Cir. 1994) (citations omitted).

25. *See* Jeffrey M. Chu, *Differing Site Conditions: Whose Risk Are They?*, 20:2 Constr. Law. 5 (April 2000).

26. *See* Foster Constr. C.A. & Williams Bros. Co., J.V. v. United States, 435 F.2d 873 (Ct. Cl. 1970); *see also* authorities cited at West's ☞ 316A PUBLIC CONTRACTS k16; ☞ 393 UNITED STATES k70(22.1)(30).

27. Stuyvesant Dredging Co. v. United States, 834 F.2d 1576, 1581 (Fed. Cir. 1987); *see also* authorities cited at West's ☞ 393 UNITED STATES, k70(22.1).

By contrast, a Type II Differing Site Conditions claim does not rely upon any affirmative representation by the owner or the contract documents. As noted above, the contractor must show that the conditions were "unknown" and that they were "of an unusual nature, which differ materially from those ordinarily encountered." Since the owner will not have made any representations with regard to the site conditions, the contractor has a heavier burden to demonstrate that the actual conditions encountered were materially different from those that would ordinarily be expected.[28] One of the leading cases analyzing a Type II DSC claim is *Servidone Construction Corporation v. United States.*[29] The contractor encountered considerable problems with the soils while constructing an earthen embankment. The Claims Court found that the soils encountered by the contractor were "unusual" in that they varied significantly from the soils generally encountered in the region.[30] It concluded that a reasonable contractor performing an adequate site inspection and with knowledge of soils in the area would not have anticipated the actual conditions encountered at the job. Even though Servidone had acted unreasonably in preparing its bid, the court held it was entitled to an equitable adjustment since the actual conditions could not have been anticipated by any contractor bidding the project.[31] The court did reduce the claimed damages in order to adjust for the costs which Servidone should have anticipated if it had reasonably prepared its bid.[32]

Whether the contractor asserts a Type I or a Type II DSC claim, the contract provisions allow for an equitable adjustment in the contract amount. There is considerable federal precedent evaluating the elements of an "equitable adjustment." The primary purpose is to provide compensation to

---

28. *See, e.g.*, authorities cited at West's ⊕═ 393 UNITED STATES, k70(22.1), k74(11).

29. Servidone Constr. Corp. v. United States, 19 Cl. Ct. 346 (1990), *aff'd*, 931 F.2d 860 (Fed. Cir. 1991).

30. 19 Cl. Ct. at 370.

31. *Id.*

32. *Id.* at 389.

the contractor for the reasonable costs incurred in performing the additional, unanticipated work.[33] The courts will not allow a contractor to use a Differing Site Conditions claim to recover for its bid errors. Consequently, a considerable amount of effort usually goes into proving the reasonableness of the contractor's original bid. It is incumbent upon the contractor to maintain reasonably detailed, accurate cost records for the additional work required to address the differing site conditions.[34] Of course, courts can make their own determination of the reasonable costs incurred by a contractor in the performance of its work, regardless of the amount of detail provided in support of the claim.

Frequently, a contractor is unable to calculate accurately the specific damages caused by a differing site condition. In those circumstances the courts may allow either a "jury verdict" approach to damages or a "total cost" method of computing the equitable adjustment.[35] Neither of these methods is favored by the courts.[36]

A "jury verdict" approach involves a court's awarding an amount (like a jury award) that "in the view of the trier of facts is fair in light of all the facts of the case or, put another way, is supported by consideration of the entire record."[37] The Federal Circuit Court of Appeals has explained that the "jury verdict method ... [is] most often employed when damages cannot be ascertained by any reasonable computation from actual figures."[38] The contractor has the burden of

---

33. *See* authorities cited at West's ⊕═ 393 UNITED STATES, k74(12.1).

34. *See* M.J. Paquet, Inc. v. New Jersey Dep't of Transp., 794 A.2d 141 (N.J. 2002) where the court succinctly summarized the measure of the federal government's equitable adjustment as "the difference between what it would have cost to perform the work as originally required and what it cost to perform the work as changed."

35. The same sorts of damage issues arise in connection with other types of claims in addition to differing site conditions claims.

36. See Annotation, *Construction and Effect of "Changed Conditions" Clause in Public Works or Construction Contract with State or its Subdivision*, 56 A.L.R. 4th 1042 (1987) and cases cited therein. The "total cost" and "jury verdict" approaches to proof of damages are discussed at length in Chapter 10 of this text.

37. Dawco Constr. Inc. v. United States, 18 Cl.Ct. 682, 699 (1989), *aff'd in part, rev'd in part*, 930 F.2d 872 (Fed. Cir. 1991).

38. *Id.*, 930 F.2d. at 880.

proving that there is no more reliable method to determine the damages in order to establish an entitlement to the "jury verdict" method.

Although the "total cost" method of calculating damages is also the subject of considerable criticism, it has the advantage of being based upon calculations of the actual costs incurred by the contractor. Under this approach, the contractor proves the actual costs and deducts its original bid costs for the same scope of work to determine the amount by which its the actual costs exceeded the bid.

The Federal Circuit Court of Appeals has stated that "a trial court must use the total cost method with caution and as a last resort. Under this method, bidding inaccuracies can unjustifiably reduce the contractor's estimated costs. Moreover, performance inefficiencies can inflate a contractor's cost."[39] The court noted that it is a "rare case" in which the contractor can justify using the total cost method.

In a more recent decision, the United States Court of Federal Claims reaffirmed the standard for using a total cost method approach to an equitable adjustment in a differing site condition claim. *Baldi Bros. Constructors v. United States*[40] repeated the warning that trial courts use this method with caution because of the potential that bidding inaccuracies and performance inefficiencies will impact the damage calculations. In determining the increased costs of performance incurred by the contractor, the court allowed direct costs, overhead, profit and bonding costs. It is incumbent upon the contractor employing any of these theories to maintain accurate records of actual costs in order to successfully obtain an equitable adjustment for differing site conditions.

Once the contractor has proved entitlement to an equitable adjustment for unforeseen conditions, the amounts will include the costs associated with addressing those conditions,

---

39. *Servidone, supra* note 29, at 861–62; *see also* authorities cited at West's ⊕ 316A PUBLIC CONTRACTS, k23; ⊕ 393 UNITED STATES, k70(22.1), k74(12.1).

40. Baldi Bros. Constructors v. United States, 50 Fed. Cl. 74, 79–80 (2001).

which consist of not only the direct cost of performing the extra work and the additional supervision associated with it, but also the extra costs associated with the extended time of performance.[41] One commentator lists the specific costs for which an owner may be obligated as follows: (1) direct costs of performance, (2) delay costs for labor, equipment, and inefficient operations, (3) increased costs due to disruption of other work, (4) additional supervision services, and (5) increased project and home office overhead including insurance, bond premiums, interest on loans, and a reasonable profit on all costs.[42]

DELAY AND ACCELERATION

Many owners complain that their contractors do not finish projects in a timely manner. Contractors, of course, often assert that the owner has interfered with the contractor's progress or has otherwise delayed completion of the project through its own conduct. There are a number of grounds upon which a contractor can base a claim for owner-caused delay. These include interference with the contractor's work, delayed or restricted access to the site, the owner's failure to coordinate, defective plans and specifications, changes in the work, delays in making changes or in approving shop drawings, and failure to make timely progress payments.[43]

In many instances when a project is late, both the owner and the contractor will assert delay claims against each other. It is rarely the case that all of the delay on any project is caused solely by one party. Therefore, a delay claim analysis often involves the question of concurrent delays. The courts have reached differing conclusions regarding the parties' entitlement to damages in a concurrent delay situation. In some cases one party is allowed to recover despite its contribution

---

41. *See* 1 STEIN, *supra* note 3, ¶ 5.03[1][b][viii].
42. *Id.*
43. 2 STEIN, *supra* note 3, ¶ 6.11.

to the delay; in others neither party is entitled to recover if it contributed to the delay, but the more appropriate trend appears to allow an apportionment of delay and associated damages based upon the relative contributions of each party to critical delays.

> The general rule is that "[w]here both parties contribute to the delay neither can recover damage[s] unless there is in the proof a clear apportionment of the delay and expense attributable to each party. ...." Courts will deny recovery where the delays are concurrent and the contractor has not established its delay apart from that attributable to the government.[44]

The burden is on the contractor claiming delay damages to distinguish the portion of the delay caused by the owner from the portion caused by its own conduct (or by independent, but noncompensable causes). This issue is almost always a question of fact.[45] Although the responsibility for apportioning the cause of various delays may be difficult, the courts recognize that it is not impossible, and through the use of expert analysis the parties should be able to apportion responsibility for delay in most cases.[46]

In addition to actual delays caused by the owner, the contractor may also be affected by the owner's acceleration of the project. Classically, acceleration of its effort costs the contractor in premium labor charges for overtime, often in increased supervision expense, in the cost of additional equipment or crews deployed, and possibly in the increased cost of performance due to inefficiencies resulting from its disrupted work sequencing. The owner may expressly accelerate the project by requiring the contractor to increase the pace of activity so as to complete the project more quickly than it otherwise would be completed. This often happens when the contractor is either actually behind schedule or the

---

44. William F. Klingensmith Inc. v. United States, 731 F.2d 805, 809 (Fed. Cir.1984); *see also* authorities cited at West's ⊕═ 95 CONTRACTS, k300(3).

45. Pathman Constr. Co v. Hi-Way Elec. Co., 382 N.E.2d 453, 460 (Ill. App. 1978).

46. *See* authorities cited at West's ⊕═ 393 UNITED STATES, k70(31), (34).

owner perceives that the contractor is behind schedule. Such directed acceleration is most easily accomplished when the owner has the authority under the contract to direct the contractor to accelerate.[47] In the absence of direct authority to order acceleration, the owner and contractor may nevertheless agree to an acceleration of the contractor's performance and, at the same time, agree to the method for determining the contractor's additional costs associated with the increased activity. This negotiated acceleration should result in a change order which addresses the additional compensation for the contractor in order to induce the acceleration.

A contractor is more often faced with "constructive acceleration," the situation where, without any overt directive to do so, it is compelled to accelerate its performance in order to meet the construction schedule because the owner has failed to approve a justified extension of time. One treatise sets forth the elements of a constructive acceleration claim as follows: (1) excusable delay; (2) notice to the defendant of the excusable delay and a request for an extension of time; (3) refusal or failure to grant the requested extension within a reasonable time; (4) an express or implied order to accelerate; and (5) actual acceleration.[48]

The contractor's damages for acceleration or delay include many of the same elements. In general, the contractor will be entitled to recover the increased costs that are proximately caused by the delay or acceleration, including the costs of extended performance.[49] In both claims, the contractor may recover increased overhead costs, whether it is to increase production or is simply the ordinary overhead costs extended by virtue of the delay. Also, any escalation in labor costs as a result of the extended period of performance will be an element of the contractor's damages. The contractor will also be able to recover for any increases in costs of materials or

---

47. *See* 48 C.F.R. § 52.243-4 (2001).

48. 2 STEIN, *supra* note 3, ¶ 6.12[2]; *see also* Norair Eng'g Corp. v. United States, 666 F.2d 546, 548 (Ct. Cl. 1981); authorities cited at West's ☞ 316A PUBLIC CONTRACTS, k23.

49. *See* authorities cited at West's ☞ 95 CONTRACTS, k299(2).

equipment rental costs. Often, in delay cases, the contractor experiences idle time or "stand-by" time for labor and equipment, and these should be recoverable damages. In an acceleration case, the contractor may also experience additional costs due to labor inefficiencies as a result of the increased level of activity. Loss of productivity, although difficult to measure, is an element of damages in both acceleration and delay claims. In an acceleration case, the cost of increased supervision will be a proper element of damages while the extended costs of supervision in a delay claim becomes the proper measure of that portion of the damages.

One of the more difficult elements of damage for a contractor to quantify is that of extended overhead. While field office overhead can usually be calculated with some certainty, the impact of a delay on home office overhead is much more difficult. Although it has been the subject of much criticism, most courts still use the *Eichleay* formula in calculating home office overhead costs.[50] The *Eichleay* formula attempts to determine the appropriate amount of home office overhead allocable to the contract in dispute and then determine a daily home office overhead figure for that project. Although the formula is somewhat imprecise, it adopts a reasonable approach to estimate the appropriate amount of the contractor's home office overhead to include in the delay claim. Many contractors will argue that the problem-plagued project actually requires much more commitment of time from the home office than the formula accounts for; owners, however, will often argue that the delay did not actually cause damage to the contractor if the contractor was able to obtain other work during the delay period or if the contractor otherwise was able to reduce its home office overhead costs during the delay period. The *Eichleay* formula is discussed more thoroughly in Chapter 2 of this book.

---

50. George Hyman Constr. Co. v. Washington Metro. Area Transit Auth., 816 F.2d 753 (D.C. Cir. 1987); authorities cited at West's ⬭ 115 DAMAGES, k117. The foundation of the doctrine is the decision in Eichleay Corp., 60-2 BCA ¶ 2688 (ASBCA 1960).

FAILURE TO MAKE PAYMENTS

It is a fundamental concept in contract law that if one party breaches the agreement by failing to pay the other party an amount properly due, then the nonbreaching party may recover as damages that amount that will compensate him or her for all losses incurred as a result of the breach.[51] This concept is based on the principle that each person is entitled to the "benefit of the bargain" as if the contract were fully performed. If the owner's failure to pay the contractor is a material breach, then the contractor is entitled to recover all costs of proper performance of the contract plus the antici-pated profit on the balance of the work.[52] If the contractor has properly performed, this will include all pending pay requests, plus additional payment for work performed after the last billing and prior to the breach or termination of the work, plus interest on those amounts that are properly due. In addition, the contractor will generally recover those lost profits on the unperformed portion of the contract that can be proved with reasonable certainty.[53]

A considerable dispute can arise over the determination of the appropriate figure for a contractor's lost profits. The owner will almost certainly argue that the claim for profits is speculative or conjectural and therefore should not be allowed. The nonbreaching contractor will need to prove not only the anticipated (or bid) profit for the job but also that this figure was reasonable and attainable but for the owner's breach. Of course, the contractor cannot recover the cost of the work that it does not perform. If the cost to com-plete the contract is greater than the remaining contract bal-ance, then the contract is demonstrably unprofitable, and the contractor will not be able to recover for lost profits.

The parties may, by contract, specify the damages that are recoverable for breach of that contract. The AIA General

---

51. 25 C.J.S. *Damages* § 108 (2002); authorities cited at West's ⌖ 115 DAMAGES, k117.
52. 1 STEIN, *supra* note 3, § 4.14[2].
53. 25 C.J.S. *Damages* § 60 (2002); *see also* authorities cited at West's ⌖ 115 DAMAGES, k40.

Conditions specifically address remedies available to the contractor for the owner's failure to make timely payment. Paragraph 9.7.1 of the 1997 General Conditions gives the contractor a specific remedy after providing appropriate notice to the owner. Pursuant to those contract terms, the contractor may "stop the work until payment of the amount owing has been received."[54] A contractor may also be entitled to adjustments to the contract time and the contract sum even in the event that the owner subsequently cures its breach by making up the overdue payment to the contractor. The clause provides that the contract sum "shall be increased by the amount of the contractor's reasonable costs of shutdown, delay and start-up, plus interest as provided for in the Contract Documents."[55] If the owner persists in its nonpayment and does not cure the breach, then the contractor may also terminate the contract,[56] and may recover specifically enumerated damages, to include "payment for Work executed and for proven loss with respect to materials, equipment, tools, and construction equipment and machinery, including reasonable overhead, profit and damages."[57] This contract provision parallels the common law in allowing the contractor to recover all of its reasonable losses incurred as a result of the owner's breach.

The AIA General Conditions, however, do limit the contractor's consequential damages. In Paragraph 4.3.10 both the contractor and the owner waive claims for consequential damages against each other. The contractor's damages forfeited by this waiver are stated to include "damages incurred by the contractor for principal office expenses including the compensation of personnel stationed there, for losses of financing, business and reputation, and for loss of profit except

---

54. AIA Document A201, General Conditions of the Contract for Construction ¶ 9.7.1 (1997 edition).
55. *Id.*
56. *Id.* ¶¶ 14.1.1.3, 14.1.3.
57. *Id.* ¶ 14.1.3.

anticipated profit arising directly from the work."[58] This contract provision was new to the 1997 edition of the AIA documents and has been the subject of much discussion.[59] A contractor entering into an AIA form agreement must carefully consider the risks and benefits associated with this contract provision since it might significantly limit the contractor's damages in the event of a breach by the owner.

CHANGES WITHIN THE SCOPE OF THE CONTRACT

As discussed in the next section, the contractor has various options available when the owner requires significant changes to the contract, either in quantity or magnitude, that so alter the work as to drastically change the scope of the original agreement. The contractor may address these situations with cardinal change or abandonment theories. An owner will more frequently request or demand changes to the contract that do not effect a cardinal change and therefore are not a breach of the agreement. This section will consider these less significant changes as "within the scope" of the contract, although technically if work is within the defined scope of the contractor's responsibilities, then the contractor would not be entitled to additional compensation for performing that work. Of course, the parties may agree to the terms of any change they wish to the existing agreement, resulting in either a modification of that contract (i.e., a change order) or there may be a new contract formed by the agreement for additional work. In either event, the contractor's compensation is set forth in the new agreement.

Most of the standard form contracts anticipate that changes in the work will be required and incorporate language to address those changes. The AIA General Conditions of the

---

58. *Id.* ¶ 4.3.10.

59. *See, e.g.,* J. William Ernstrom & Michael F. Dehmler, Mutual Waiver of Consequential Damages: The Contractor's Perspective, 18:1 CONSTR. LAW. 2 (Jan. 1998); Lynn R. Axelroth, Mutual Waiver of Consequential Damages—The Owner's Perspective, *id.* at 11.

Contract for Construction (Document A201) accomplish this in Article 7, which comprises two pages of that form document. The A201 recognizes that the owner and contractor may agree to a change and provides a procedure for establishing written change orders,[60] but also authorizes the owner unilaterally to order a change in the work "within the general scope of the Contract" through the use of a Construction Change Directive.[61] When the owner directs that work be performed pursuant to a Construction Change Directive, the Contract Sum and Contract Time are to be adjusted either through agreement between the parties or through the involvement of the architect.[62] The contractor is allowed, by express contract provisions, to recover its labor costs and labor burden, material and equipment costs, rental costs, bond and insurance premiums, permit fees, additional supervision costs, and a reasonable allowance for overhead and profit.[63] The architect is authorized to determine the reasonable adjustment to the contract based upon information provided by the contractor.

Even if the contract documents do not expressly provide for compensation to the contractor for additional work required by the owner, the contractor may have a recovery at common law. The Seventh Circuit Court of Appeals, applying Illinois law, has held that

> [i]n order for a contractor to recover money for "extra work," it must show by clear and convincing evidence that the work was (1) outside the scope of the original contract; (2) ordered at the direction of the owner; (3) agreed to be paid for by the owner either by words or by conduct; (4) not voluntarily furnished by the contractor; and (5) not rendered necessary by fault of the contractor.[64]

Each of these elements that must be proved by the contractor is subject to great dispute by the owner. An owner will often deny

---

60. *Id.* ¶ 7.2.
61. *Id.* ¶ 7.3.1.
62. *Id.* ¶¶ 7.3.3, 7.3.6.
63. *Id.* ¶ 7.3.6.
64. Brant Constr. Co. v. Metro. Water Reclamation Dist., 967 F.2d 244, 246 (7th Cir. 1992) (citations omitted); *see also* authorities cited at West's ⊕ 95 CONTRACTS, k232(2).

that it ordered the "extra" work or otherwise agreed to pay for it. It may not be sufficient for the contractor to simply show that the owner knew that the work was being performed and acquiesced in the contractor's performance of that work.[65] It is clear that the contractor will have a much stronger argument in favor of compensation for extra work if it can prove that the work was requested, ordered, or authorized by the owner.[66]

Contracts with the federal government generally include a standard changes clause that allows for an equitable adjustment in the contract price when a change in the work is required. This equitable adjustment

> compensates a contractor for increased costs reasonably incurred because the government ... increased the amount or difficulty of work required by the contract, or delayed or accelerated that work ... [including] work added by formal change orders ... [or] from "constructive changes," which occur when the government does something to increase a contractor's costs without issuing a formal change order.[67]

The equitable adjustment usually compensates the contractor for the difference between the cost of performing the work with the change and the cost of performing the work without the change. It is well recognized that a contractor must prove liability, causation, and injury, including the reasonableness of its claimed additional costs, in order to recover an equitable adjustment.[68]

CHANGES BEYOND THE SCOPE OF THE CONTRACT

As noted above, almost every contractor on a construction project will be faced with owner-initiated changes to the requirements of the contract. Those changes may arise as a

---

65. Dave Kolb Grading, Inc. v. Terra Venture Bridgeton Project, 85 F.3d 351, 354 (8th Cir. 1996); *see also* authorities cited at West's ⊕═ 95 CONTRACTS, k232(3).

66. *See* 17A C.J.S. *Contracts* §§ 400, 401, 403 (1999).

67. Morrison Knudsen Corp. v. Fireman's Fund Ins. Co., 175 F.3d 1221, 1243–44 (10th Cir. 1999) (citations omitted); *see also* authorities cited at West's ⊕═ 393 UNITED STATES, 70(20).

68. *Morrison Knudsen, supra* note 67, at 1244; *see also* authorities cited at West's ⊕═ 393 UNITED STATES, k74(10).

result of conscious decisions by the owner, omissions or deficiencies in the plans or specifications, unforeseen conditions (discussed above), weather events, or a myriad of other causes. Since most contract documents attempt to anticipate and address the need for changes to the requirements of the contract, as discussed in the preceding section, changes that are within the scope of the contract can usually be addressed by using the mechanisms set forth in the parties' contract. Occasionally, a contractor will encounter a situation in which the owner either makes a single, fundamental change in the scope of work or instigates a series of smaller changes, the accumulation of which causes a significant impact to the contractor even though no single change was crucial. The owner almost certainly believes that the individual changes are all properly and fully addressed by the change order procedure in the contract documents. In fact, the contractor may agree at the time the individual changes are presented. However, upon reflection the contractor may realize that the impact of the sum of the changes could not be fully understood until the end of the project and was thus not adequately addressed during performance.

A contractor may find that the limitations of the contract prevent it from fully recovering for the impact of these scope changes. Although any one change may have only a minimal impact on price and no significant impact on time, hundreds (or thousands) of those changes spread across the life of the project may have a significant impact on the contractor. When the contractual remedies to address these changes are insufficient, contractors will often turn to the cardinal change theory as a means for relief. "It is well-settled that a cardinal change 'occurs when the government [or owner] effects an alteration in the work so drastic that it effectively requires the contractor to perform duties materially different from those originally bargained for.'"[69] It is fundamental to the

---

69. PCL Constr. Servs., Inc. v. United States, 47 Fed. Cl. 745, 804 (2000); *see also* authorities cited at West's ⊕═ 393 UNITED STATES, k73(17).

cardinal change concept that the contractor be directed "to perform work which is not within the general scope of the contract" and that it is beyond the contractor's expectation that such a change would be permitted by the changes clause of the contract.[70] It is the "drastic modification" by which the owner attempts to "impose obligations on a contractor far exceeding any contemplated by their contract" that establishes the cardinal change.[71] If the change falls within the contemplation of the parties, then it is authorized by and can be addressed through the changes provisions of the contract. Therefore, it is critical to the proof of a cardinal change claim that the contractor establish that the change *fundamentally* alters its obligations.

It has been repeatedly stated that "each case must be analyzed on its own facts and in light of its own circumstances, giving just consideration to the magnitude and quality of the changes ordered and their cumulative effect upon the project as a whole."[72] A cardinal change dispute necessarily requires a fact-intensive inquiry and one in which the contractor undertakes a significant burden to prove its entitlement.[73] It is fundamental to the analysis that the changes imposed by the owner are so significant that they cannot be adequately addressed by the contract and thus cause a breach of the contract.[74] If the remedies set forth in the contract for changes are adequate, then a cardinal change will not exist. This proposition is significant to the contractor because the remedy that exists for breach of the contract due to a cardinal change may be significantly different from the contractual remedies for additional work. Of course, one remedy available to the contractor for breach of the agreement is the

---

70. *PCL Constr. Servs.*, *supra* note 69.

71. Becho, Inc. v. United States, 47 Fed. Cl. 595, 600 (2000).

72. *E.g.*, Wunderlich Contracting Co. v. United States, 351 F.2d 956, 966 (Ct. Cl. 1965); *see also* Saddler v. United States, 287 F.2d 411 (Ct. Cl. 1961); authorities cited at West's ☞ 95 CONTRACTS, k296; ☞ 393 UNITED STATES, k70(22.1), (27), (30), k73(17).

73. *Becho*, *supra* note 71, at 601; *PCL Constr. Servs.*, *supra* note 69, at 804.

74. Allied Materials & Equip. Co. v. United States, 569 F.2d 562, 564 (Ct. Cl. 1978); *see also* authorities cited at West's ☞ 393 UNITED STATES, k73(17), k74(11).

right to refuse to perform the requested change. This opportunity will be available only in those circumstances in which
the contractor is faced with a single, obvious, substantial
change to the scope of its work.[75] However, the choice to
refuse performance has the attendant risk that the contractor
may be found to have wrongfully abandoned the contract if a
court later concludes that the disputed change was, in fact,
within the scope anticipated by the parties. As astutely stated
by the United States Court of Claims, "Undoubtedly, the
cautious contractor might often proceed under the revised
contract because of doubt whether he could invoke the cardinal change doctrine."[76]

Although the analysis in each case is both fact-intensive
and case specific, the United States Court of Federal Claims
recently provided succinct guidance on factors to consider.

> Indeed, while there is no precise calculus for determining
> whether a cardinal change has occurred, the courts have con-
> sidered, inter alia, the following factors: (i) whether there is a
> significant change in the magnitude of work to be performed;
> (ii) whether the change is designed to procure a totally differ-
> ently item or drastically alter the quality, character, nature or
> type of work contemplated by the original contract; and
> (iii) whether the cost of the work ordered greatly exceeds the
> original contract cost.[77]

Each of these factors is crucial to the contractor's ability to
recover under a cardinal change theory. While there are no
"bright line" tests for the magnitude required to constitute a
drastic change, past decisions will provide some guidance.

In *Saddler v. United States*, one of the earliest cases endorsing the cardinal change theory, the contractor provided a unit
price bid for construction of a levee embankment. The government proposed a change order that doubled the amount of

---

75. *See, e.g.,* authorities cited at West's ☞ 393 UNITED STATES, k73(17), k74(15).

76. *Allied Materials, supra* note 74.

77. *Becho, supra* note 71, at 601 (citations omitted); *see also* authorities cited at West's ☞ 393 UNITED STATES, k73(17).

earth to be placed in the levee and required the contractor to supply additional equipment. Under those circumstances the court held that a cardinal change had occurred.[78] Similarly, the Eighth Circuit Court of Appeals held that scope changes that required a contractor to significantly increase its costs of backfilling a pipeline, from $600,000 to approximately $2 million, would constitute a cardinal change.[79] That court noted that tripling the cost of that portion of the work caused a 50 percent increase in the overall cost of performance of the contract.[80] In both of these cases, the *nature* of the work being requested was the same as that under the original contract; it was the *magnitude* of that work that caused the cardinal change.

A much more difficult analysis is required when individual changes are not significant but the accumulation of changes causes the contract to be drastically altered. In *PCL Construction*, the court stated that "courts must look beyond simple arithmetic when assessing a cardinal change claim."[81] Although the contractor there asserted that 356 owner changes in effect changed the contractor's "means and methods" and resulted in a cardinal change, the court held that this evidence was insufficient. [82]

If a cardinal change by the owner has resulted in a material breach of the contract and the contractor justifiably elects to refuse further performance of the contract, it is entitled to recover its anticipatory profits on the contract just as in any other breach of contract case.[83] In those circumstances where the contractor continues performance,

---

78. *Saddler, supra* note 72.

79. Peter Kiewit Sons' Co. v. Summit Constr. Co., 422 F.2d 242, 255 (8th Cir. 1969); *see also* authorities cited at West's 95 CONTRACTS, k312(1).

80. 422 F.2d at 255.

81. *PCL Constr., supra* note 69, at 806, *citing* S.J. Groves & Sons Co. v. United States, 661 F.2d 170 (Ct. Cl. 1981), in which a $6 million change to a $2 million contract was held not to be a cardinal change.

82. *Id.; but see* Hensel Phelps Constr. Co. v. GSA, 01-1 BCA ¶ 31,249 at p. 154,313 (GSBCA 2001) (claim based on cumulative changes allowed).

83. *Allied Materials, supra* note 74, at 564; *see also* authorities cited at West's 115 DAMAGES, k124(3).

but subsequently proves that a cardinal change occurred, it is entitled to recover all of the reasonable costs of its services including a reasonable markup for overhead and profit.[84]

As noted above, a contractor that is faced with a single, drastic change to the scope of its work or that realizes that an excessive number of changes have had a drastic impact may choose to refuse to perform the changes in the scope of work. Instead of a cardinal change theory, however, the contractor may choose to assert the abandonment doctrine, under which the contractor asserts not that the work has been abandoned, but that the contract provisions have. Although some cases treat abandonment and cardinal change as synonymous,[85] many courts recognize them as fundamentally different.[86] It is important to note that the intent of the parties to abandon the contract is essential to this analysis, although that intent can be implied by the parties' conduct.[87] Since abandonment of the contract must be mutual, the contractor must refuse to continue performance after it determines that the owner has expressed its intent to abandon.[88] If the contractor continues to perform, then the courts may well conclude that the changes ordered by the owner were within the scope of the contract and within the contemplation of the parties, thereby eviscerating the contractor's cardinal change claim as well.

Finally, it should be noted that the California Supreme Court, in *Amelco Electric v. City of Thousand Oaks*, held that the abandonment theory of liability does not apply against a

84. *Peter Kiewit Sons' Co.*, *supra* note 79, at 265; *Saddler*, *supra* note 72, at 415–16; *see also* authorities cited at West's ⊕ 115 DAMAGES, k124(3).

85. *See* Aaron P. Silberman, *Beyond Changes: Abandonment and Cardinal Change*, 22:4 Constr. Law. 5 (Fall 2002).

86. Amelco Elec. v. City of Thousand Oaks, 38 P.3d 1120, 1126 (Cal. 2002). *But see* Justin Sweet, *The Amelco Case: California Bars Abandonment Claims in Public Contracts*, 32:2 Pub. Cont. L. J. 285, 324 (Winter 2003), arguing that "post-completion, inefficiency claims" such as the *Amelco* court considered should be treated as neither abandonment nor cardinal change claims, but as claims for breach of the owner's implied obligation to allow the contractor to perform the work in a logical, orderly, and efficient manner.

87. R.M. Taylor, Inc. v. Gen. Motors Corp., 187 F.3d 809, 813 (8th Cir. 1999), *cert. den.*, 528 U.S. 1159 (2000); *see also* authorities cited at West's ⊕ 95 CONTRACTS, k256.

88. *R.M. Taylor, Inc.*, *supra* note 87, at 813.

public entity since the theory is "fundamentally inconsistent with the purpose of the competitive bidding statute."[89] Although it discussed the cardinal change doctrine, the court was not faced with and did not decide the issue of whether that theory would apply to contract disputes in California.

WRONGFUL TERMINATION

An owner's wrongful termination of a contractor is a material breach of the contract. Upon proof of the wrongful termination, the contractor is entitled to exercise several options, unless otherwise limited by the contract documents. Those options include (1) accepting the termination, rescinding the contract, and recovering under a *quantum meruit* theory; (2) challenging the termination, continuing performance, and pursuing damages in addition to the contract price; or (3) accepting the wrongful termination as a breach and pursuing a claim for all payments due and lost profits.[90] The contractor will have to give careful consideration to the choice of remedy to determine which method provides the best protection. While it may be impractical for a terminated contractor to actually continue performance, its willingness and ability to continue to perform may be a significant factor. Ordinarily, however, the contractor will be required to remove its forces from the project and pursue the other damage remedies.

Most construction contracts incorporate termination provisions. An owner may not only have the right to terminate a contractor for cause, but it may also have a contractual right to terminate the contractor for convenience. The AIA's 1997 General Conditions of the Contract for Construction provide detailed language regarding terminations for cause and for convenience.[91] If the contractor is terminated for cause, it is

---

89. *Amelco, supra* note 86, at 1127.

90. 1 STEIN, *supra* note 3, ¶ 4.15[5].

91. *See* AIA Document A201, General Conditions of the Contract for Construction ¶¶ 14.2, 14.4 (1997 edition).

only entitled to recover any balance of the contract sum that remains after the owner has paid for completion of the work.[92] However, the contractor's entitlement to compensation is significantly different if the owner has terminated for convenience. The AIA General Conditions specifically provide that "in case of such termination for the owner's convenience, the contractor shall be entitled to receive payment for Work executed, and costs incurred by reason of such termination, along with reasonable overhead and profit on the Work not executed."[93] Therefore, a contractor who is terminated for convenience has a contractual measure of damages that is substantially similar to the damages that would be recoverable for wrongful termination. The contractor will rarely challenge a termination for convenience under these provisions unless there is some other material breach by the owner.

The assertion of a wrongful termination claim necessarily implies a breach of the agreement between the parties. If the owner has terminated the contract for cause, then it is claiming a breach by the contractor. The wrongful termination claim by the contractor is based upon its assertion that the owner's termination was not proper, and is, therefore, a breach of the agreement. Of course, in order to recover for wrongful termination, the contractor must necessarily prove that the owner's action in terminating the contract was not proper. However, the contractor has another alternative. It may accept the termination, rescind the contract, and pursue a claim based on *quantum meruit* to "recover the full value of his services independent of the contract price."[94] As long as the contractor does not continue to perform, it can waive the contract and any limits of recovery associated with the contract, and pursue only the reasonable value of the work performed.[95] This provides the contractor a unique opportunity

---

92. *Id.* ¶ 14.2.4.

93. *Id.* ¶ 14.4.3.

94. Paul Hardeman, Inc. v. Arkansas Power & Light Co., 380 F. Supp. 298, 337–38 (E.D. Ark. 1974); *see also* authorities cited at West's ⊕ 205H IMPLIED AND CONSTRUCTIVE CONTRACTS, k67.

95. *Paul Hardeman, Inc., supra* note 94, at 337–38.

to evaluate whether it is better served by bringing suit for damages due to breach of the contract or for the reasonable value of the work actually performed. Selecting the appropriate theory may well depend on whether the contract would be profitable for the contractor if fully performed or whether the contractor would be better served to simply recover for the work already in place.

Of course, with any *quantum meruit* claim, there will be considerable disagreement over the appropriate value to be assigned to the work actually performed. The owner will certainly argue that it should not be responsible for excess costs resulting from the contractor's inefficiencies, so the actual expenditures by the contractor may not be the appropriate measure of damages. An Arkansas federal district court utilized the competing bids for the work to help determine the appropriate amount of damages. It was "convinced that the proper method for determining the fair and reasonable value of the work performed in this case requires [the court] to take into consideration ... evidence of the actual expenditures of [the contractor] as well as evidence of the second, third and fourth bid figures."[96] That court further stated: "No one standard of fair value leads to as just a solution as does a proper consideration of all of the factors involved."[97] In applying "all of the factors," the court found a fair and reasonable value of the work and services actually performed by the contractor and awarded that amount.

If the contractor chooses to assert a breach of contract claim for wrongful termination, rather than the *quantum meruit* claim, some courts recognize the measure of damages as "the amount already spent in performance of the contract plus lost profit and overhead on the entire contract amount."[98] Since the owner's wrongful termination of the contract has prevented the contractor's performance, if the

---

96. *Id.* at 341.

97. *Id.*

98. United States o/b/o Taylor & Polk Constr., Inc. v. Mill Valley Constr., Inc., 29 F.3d 154, 160 (4th Cir. 1994); *see also* United States v. Behan, 110 U.S. 338, 344 (1884); authorities cited at West's ⊕⇒ 393 UNITED STATES, k67(19.1).

contractor can show that it was without fault and willing to perform then it should be entitled to the amounts previously expended plus its reasonably anticipated overhead and profit on the entire contract. Of course, the contractor must still provide adequate evidence of the amounts appropriately spent in performance of the contract and the reasonable overhead and profit that would have been earned if the contract had been fully performed. The owner may also raise a defense based on the contractor's failure to mitigate its damages if the contractor does not make an effort to secure additional work to cover its claimed overhead expenses.

In a government contract setting there is a slightly different analysis. Although a contractor pursuing a claim for wrongful termination will ordinarily have the burden of proof of its claim, the United States Court of Appeals for the Federal Circuit has stated that "the government should bear the burden of proof with respect to the issue of whether termination for default was justified, regardless of the forum and regardless of whose 'claim' is being asserted."[99] The government bears this burden because a default termination "is a drastic sanction ... which should be imposed (or sustained) only for good grounds and on solid evidence."[100] If the court concludes that the default decision "was arbitrary or capricious, or that it represents an abuse of [the contracting officer's] discretion," then it will set aside the decision.[101] If the court concludes that the government's default termination was improper, then the termination is converted to a termination for the convenience of the government.[102] The nature of the termination is significant since a convenience termination allows the contractor to recover additional termination expenses that are not recoverable in a default termination.

---

99. Lisbon Contractors, Inc. v. United States, 828 F.2d 759, 765 (Fed. Cir. 1987); *see also* authorities cited at West's ⊕═ 393 UNITED STATES, k74(10).

100. 828 F.2d at 765.

101. Darwin Constr. Co. v. United States, 811 F.2d 593, 597 (Fed. Cir. 1987).

102. *Id.* at 598; see also *Lisbon, supra* note 99, at 767.

A contractor may also challenge the government's termination for convenience, although the burden is on the contractor to show that the government acted in bad faith or abused its discretion. Considerable case law states that there is an assumption that the government acts in good faith when making decisions about its contracts. "A contractor can overcome this presumption only if it shows through 'well-nigh irrefragable[103] proof' that the government has a specific intent to injure it."[104] The cases discussing this measure of proof require evidence that the government had a specific intent to injure, that the government was "motivated alone by malice," that a conspiracy existed to remove the contractor, or that the government otherwise engaged in conduct which was "designedly oppressive."[105]

The contractor still has the burden of proving the costs or equitable adjustment to which it is entitled if a wrongful default termination is converted to a termination for convenience, as contracts commonly permit. If a contractor either fails to mitigate its damages or does not present adequate proof of the amount of damages, then it will not be entitled to recover.[106] It is important to note that the contractor must present its damage evidence through witnesses with direct knowledge of the project and the causation of the damages being claimed. The Tenth Circuit Court of Appeals succinctly stated: "A contractor must present more than general, unsubstantiated pronouncements from its own witnesses that various acts of the government caused ... overruns."[107]

---

103. BLACK'S LAW DICTIONARY (7th ed.) defines "irrefragable" as "Unanswerable; not to be controverted; impossible to refute."

104. Caldwell & Santmyer Inc. v. Glickman, 55 F.3d 1578, 1581 (Fed. Cir. 1995); *see also* authorities cited at West's ⌖ 393 UNITED STATES, k74(10).

105. Torncello v. United States, 681 F.2d 756, 770–71 (Ct. Cl. 1982); *see also* authorities cited at West's ⌖ 393 UNITED STATES, k63.

106. *Lisbon Contractors, supra* note 99, at 767–68.

107. *Morrison Knudsen, supra* note 67, at 1248 (citations omitted); *see also* authorities cited at West's ⌖ 393 UNITED STATES, k74.2.

IMPOSSIBILITY OR IMPRACTICABILITY

A contractor faced with a difficult job and experiencing time and cost overruns might believe that it is impossible to accomplish performance under the contract. The courts have recognized the doctrine of "impossibility of performance," which is usually used as a defense to a breach of contract claim. A closely related, but distinct, doctrine is that of "commercial impracticability" or "commercial frustration." While both doctrines are primarily used as defenses to excuse non-performance, they remain important considerations for any contractor asserting a damage claim against an owner.

As stated by the Missouri Court of Appeals, "the doctrine of impossibility of performance excuses a party to a contract from performance when an Act of God, the law, or other party renders performance impossible."[108] An important element of the defense is that the event creating impossibility of performance must be unexpected.[109] The Missouri court found that a change order deleting a portion of the contract was not an unexpected event and therefore the doctrine did not apply. If the parties are aware that an event may occur and do not contractually address the risk of that event, then the party required to perform will nevertheless have the obligation to continue performance. However, if both parties contemplate the continued existence of some particular circumstance, then the unexpected absence of that circumstance without the fault of either party will support the doctrine of impossibility.[110]

The mere fact that it may be difficult to accomplish a task, or even that a particular contractor is unable to accomplish the task, will not support an impossibility of performance

108. Werner v. Ashcraft Bloomquist, Inc., 10 S.W.3d 575, 577 (Mo. Ct. App. 2000); *see also* authorities cited at West's ⊕═ 95 CONTRACTS, k309(1).

109. *See* authorities cited at West's ⊕═ 95 CONTRACTS, k309(1).

110. Chase Precast Corp. v. John J. Paonessa Co., 566 N.E.2d 603 (Mass. 1991); *see* authorities cited at West's ⊕═ 95 CONTRACTS, k309(2).

claim. "It is generally well settled that subjective impossibility, that is, impossibility which is personal to the promissor and does not inhere in the nature of the acts to be performed, does not excuse nonperformance of a contractual obligation."[111] In *The B's Co. v. BP Barber & Associates, Inc.*, the trial judge found that a pipeline project was "a most difficult job requiring an experienced crew and proper equipment. ... It appeared most difficult or perhaps impossible for [the claimant] but apparently a routine operation for an experienced operator in the field."[112] Since the job was not objectively impossible, the claimant was not allowed to recover on that basis. Therefore, the contractor must prove objective impossibility, i.e., that the job cannot be done, in order to prevail on the defense of impossibility of performance.

Impracticability of performance or commercial frustration provides another legal theory for the contractor to excuse performance. Under some circumstances, it may also provide an opportunity for an equitable adjustment in the contract price. The United States Court of Appeals for the Federal Circuit recently addressed a claim based on commercial impracticability and stated that

> a contract is commercially impracticable when performance would cause "extreme and unreasonable difficulty, expense, injury, or loss to one of the parties."... A contract is said to be commercially impracticable when, because of unforeseen events, "it can be performed only at an excessive and unreasonable cost," or when "all means of performance are commercially senseless."[113]

Under this theory, although performance of the contract remains possible, the expected value of the performance is destroyed by the supervening circumstances.[114] The event

---

111. The B's Co. v. BP Barber & Assocs., Inc., 391 F.2d 130, 137 (4th Cir. 1968); *see* authorities cited at West's ⊕⇒ 95 CONTRACTS, k309(1).

112. *The B's Co., supra* note 111, at 137.

113. Raytheon Co. v. White, 305 F.3d 1354, 1367 (Fed. Cir. 2002); *see* authorities cited at West's ⊕⇒ 95 CONTRACTS, k309(1), k323(1).

that renders the performance of the contract impracticable must affect some basic assumption on which the contract was made.[115] Thus, even if the contract is still capable of performance, a party will not be required to perform if the commercial purpose is frustrated by a change in one of the principal considerations of the contract.

Ordinarily, the consequence of impracticability or commercial frustration is that the parties are excused from further performance, so it may serve the contractor as a shield against claims or counterclaims by an owner for default or delay damages. However, the doctrines may also on occasion be wielded as swords. If the contractor can prove impracticability in a government contract, then the facilitating event or circumstances may be treated as a constructive change and provide the contractor an opportunity for an equitable adjustment.[116]

The doctrine of commercial frustration or impracticability is subject, like the doctrine of impossibility, to the caveat that "if the event was reasonably foreseeable ... the parties should have provided for its occurrence in the contract and the absence of such provision indicates an assumption of risk by the promissor."[117] Moreover, the mere fact that the contractor has experienced a significant cost overrun (57 percent in the quoted case) is not sufficient to render a contract commercially impracticable. Contractors will be well served to remember the admonition of the Missouri Court of Appeals that "the doctrines of commercial frustration and of impossibility of performance are limited in application so as to preserve the certainty of contracts."[118]

---

114. *Chase, supra* note 110, at 605–06.
115. *Paquet, supra* note 34, at 148; *see also* RESTATEMENT (SECOND) OF CONTRACTS § 261 (1981).
116. *Raytheon, supra* note 113, *id.*
117. *Werner, supra* note 108, at 577; *Raytheon, supra* note 113, at 1367.
118. *Werner, supra* note 108, at 578.

Design Professional Liability to the Client 7

ALLEN HOLT GWYN

INTRODUCTION

The design professional is the high priest of the construction process. He is involved at the birth of a project—before permits, bids, turned earth. Projects may be conceived by need, but the vitality of a project begins with its design. Memorable buildings are described first by reference to the vision and depth of the designer, and second to the craft of the builder.

The relationship between design professionals and owner clients is unique in the construction industry. It is a professional relationship, one in which trust and confidence are reposed. Design professionals are required to subordinate their interests to those of their clients.[1]

The design professional's job is in many ways the most difficult in the construction industry. Construction is a collaborative process. It requires

---

1. Justin Sweet, Sweet on Construction Law § 2.1 (1997).

cooperation from all participants. But collaboration must have a nucleus, and that nucleus is the project design. The design professional's plan must be clear enough for the other participants to understand, estimate, and properly sequence so that the desired product is achieved within the allocated time for completion.

Design professionals must use skill and attention to ensure proper communication concerning the design and its implementation. This communication may be by drawing or sketch, as well as by letter, email, or project web site. The manner and form of project communication are limited only by the creativity of those in charge of the process.

Design professionals are most effective in communicating their design plans when they understand their audience and comprehend its point of view. Design professionals must be cognizant of the economic pressures a project imposes upon the owner and the project's contractors. They must use these economic levers in a positive way for the project's benefit. This is an acquired expertise—it is not regularly taught as part of the professional school curriculum.

Design professionals tend to have a different economic outlook about a project from that held by other project participants, including the client owner. Alone among the project participants, the design professional owns property rights in the intellectual property created for a project. Design professionals are often granted independent evaluative powers over the conduct of various parties and the effect of various events upon the prosecution of the project work. Because design professionals do not normally benefit financially from project cost savings, their project outlook can be quite different from that of bidding contractors. This is especially true when design professionals are called upon to evaluate the effect of a delay upon a project's progress schedule caused by their or the owner's actions.

On many projects, the design professional alone approves contractor submittals and substitutions, certifies progress payments, recommends time extensions (compensable and noncompensable), and passes upon the acceptability and completion of contractor work. When this power to rule upon the scope and acceptability of the work of others is coupled with the owner's power of the purse, the design professional's role can approach that of the project sovereign. As observed by one court, the design professional in such a situation assumes the power of economic life over contractors and subcontractors working at the project.[2] It is no wonder that many contractors treat the design professional solicitously. Even when benevolent, "he must be praised, decorated, tolerated."[3]

As American construction law has developed, it has recognized the design professional's unique status within the construction process. Courts have acknowledged the professional relationship binding, and the standard of care owed by, design professionals to their client owners. Because design professionals are held to a professional standard, expert testimony is normally required in order to show that the design professional did not satisfy the standard of care that other professionals similarly situated would have exercised.[4]

Courts have also acknowledged that the professional negligence standard imposed by law may be modified by contract.[5] In the absence of express contractual provisions to the

---

2. *See* United States v. Rogers & Rogers, 161 F. Supp. 132, 136 (S.D. Cal. 1958).

3. Marcus Tullius Cicero, commenting upon the proper decorum to be observed around Octavian (in Latin: *laudandus, ornandus, tollendus*).

4. *See* Noble v. Worthy, 378 A.2d 674, 676–77 (D.C. 1977); Seaman Unified Sch. Dist. No. 345, Shawnee County v. Casson Constr. Co., 594 P.2d 241 (Kan. Ct. App. 1979); Hotel Utica, Inc. v. Ronald G. Armstrong Eng'g Co., 404 N.Y.S.2d 455 (App. Div. 1978); Annotation, *Expert Testimony—Architect's Malpractice*, 3 A.L.R. 4th 1023 (1981); *see also* authorities cited at West's ⚿ 272 NEGLIGENCE, k1672; ⚿ 95 CONTRACTS, k349(1). *But see* M.J. Womack, Inc., v. State House of Representatives, 509 So.2d 62 (La. Ct. App. 1987) (expert testimony was unnecessary to establish that an architect was negligent in failing to check existing blueprints of the state capitol before designing renovations to the building, since the nature and existence of the architect's negligence was within the commonsense grasp of lay jurors).

5. *See, e.g.*, Town of Breckenridge v. Golforce, Inc., 851 P.2d 214 (Colo. Ct. App. 1992) (higher USGA design standards within design professional contract upheld); *see also* authorities cited at West's ⚿ 95 CONTRACTS, k349(1). In discussing the design professional's role, courts have noted that there is a difference between design professionals' responsibilities to client owners and the duties they owe to other construction participants. *See e.g.*, the discussion concerning design professionals' tort responsibilities in Chapter 8 of this text.

contrary, liability and responsibility are not imputed to the design professional merely by the existence of a construction design defect.[6] Likewise, absent specific contract language, a design professional does not impliedly warrant, to his client or anyone else, a perfect design or a satisfactory result.[7] On the other hand, design professionals owe a duty to the public (as well as to their clients) to exercise due professional care to design safe buildings.[8]

This chapter examines the design professionals' contractual and professional responsibility to their clients and the damages that may be recovered by the client/promissee for

---

6. *See, e.g.*, Mounds View v. Walijarvi, 263 N.W.2d 420, 424 (Minn. 1978):

Architects, doctors, engineers, attorneys, and others deal in somewhat inexact sciences and are continually called upon to exercise their skilled judgment in order to anticipate and provide for random factors which are incapable of precise measurement. The indeterminable nature of these factors makes it impossible for professional service people to gauge them with complete accuracy in every instance. ... Because of the inescapable possibility of error which inheres in these services, the law had traditionally required not perfect results, but rather the exercise of that skill and judgment which can be reasonably expected from similarly situated professionals.

See also authorities cited at West's ☞ 95 CONTRACTS, k205.25.

7. The vast majority of courts hold that without a specific agreement, no claim exists against a design professional for breach of an implied warranty relating to the designer's work or services. Gravely v. Providence P'ship, 549 F.2d 958 (4th Cir. 1977) (Virginia law); K-Mart Corp. v. Midcom Realty Group of Connecticut, 489 F. Supp. 813 (D.C. Conn. 1980) (Connecticut law); Palmer v. Brown, 273 P.2d 306 (Cal. Ct. App. 1954); Johnson-Valand-Archuleta, Inc. v. Roark Assocs., 572 P.2d 1220 (Colo. Ct. App. 1977); Audlane Lumber & Builders Supply, Inc. v. D.E. Britt Assocs., Inc., 168 So.2d 333 (Fla. Dist. Ct. App. 1964), *cert. denied*, 173 So.2d 146 (Fla. 1965); Mississippi Meadows, Inc. v. Hodson, 299 N.E.2d 359 (Ill. App. Ct. 1973); Klein v. Catalano, 437 N.E.2d 514 (Mass. 1982); Iborman's Inc. v. Lake State Dev. Co., 230 N.W.2d 363 (Mich. Ct. App. 1975); City of Mounds View v. Walijarvi, 263 N.W.2d 420 (Minn. 1978); Bd. of Trustees v. Kennerly, Slomanson & Smith, 400 A.2d 850 (N. J. Super. Ct. 1979); State v. Gathman-Matotan Architects & Planners, Inc., 653 P.2d 166 (N.M. 1982); Rochester Fund Muns. v. Amsterdam Mun. Leasing Corp., 746 N.Y.S.2d 512 (App. Div. 2002); Sears, Roebuck & Co. v. Enco Assocs., 370 N.Y.S.2d 338 (Sup. Ct. 1975), *aff'd*, 385 N.Y.S.2d 613 (App. Div. 1976); Ressler v. Nielsen, 76 N.W.2d 157 (N.D. 1956); Smith v. Goff, 325 P.2d 1061 (Okla. 1985); Scott v. Potomac Ins. Co., 341 P.2d 1083 (Or. 1959); Ryan v. Morgan Spear Ass'n, Inc., 546 S.W.2d 678 (Tex. Ct. App. 1977); *see also* authorities cited at West's ☞ 272 NEGLIGENCE, k1205(4); ☞ 95 CONTRACTS, k205.25. *But see* Broyles v. Brown Eng'g Co., 151 So. 2d 767 (Ala. 1963) (holding that an engineer engaged to perform drainage design should expect to be charged with a "guaranty as to the sufficiency and adequacy of the plans and specifications"); Tamarac Dev. Co. v. Delamater, Freund & Assocs., P.A., 675 P.2d 361 (Kan. 1984) (upholding claim against architect for implied warranty of workmanlike result).

8. JUSTIN SWEET, LEGAL ASPECTS OF ARCHITECTURE, ENGINEERING AND THE CONSTRUCTION PROCESS § 15.10B (4th Ed. 1989); *see also* Greenhaven Corp. v. Hutchcraft & Assocs., Inc., 463 N.E.2d 283 (Ind. Ct. App. 1984); authorities cited at West's ☞ 95 CONTRACTS, k196.

breach of a design professional's standard of care or contractual undertaking.[9] The contractual scope of the design professional's undertaking, married to the standard of care of design professionals similarly situated in the community where services are provided, defines the design professional's liability yardstick.[10]

LIABILITY FOR COST ESTIMATES

Owners commonly want their design professionals to provide a budgetary estimate of the cost of the construction work. Many design professionals are reluctant to do so. Design professionals argue that they cannot provide accurate cost estimates because they lack control over most of the cost components, including cost of equipment, materials and labor, timing of commencement of the work, level of contractor skill, and most construction delays. Design professionals often view cost estimates as mere guesses because many project events that affect project cost are beyond the design professionals' control.

A design professional who does provide an estimate of construction costs may be held to have agreed to an additional contractual obligation, called a cost condition. If that condition is not met, i.e., if the construction bids exceed the design professional's estimate, or the actual cost of construction exceeds the estimate, the design professional may be

---

9. The "default" setting for the "client" of the design professional discussed in this chapter is the owner, consistent with the traditional owner/architect or owner/engineer contractual model. The obligations and damages described herein, however, follow the contractual relationship. The design professional may have a "client" arrangement with other promisee/recipients of his or her professional services, and the rules discussed in this chapter would also apply to that arrangement.

10. *See* C. ALLEN FOSTER, RICHARD D. CONNER, ET AL., CONSTRUCTION AND DESIGN LAW § 4.6(a) 2 (1991): "The classic statement of the professional standard of care is that a design professional must possess that degree of skill and learning ordinarily exercised by other professionals of good standing in the community and must apply that knowledge with the diligence ordinarily exercised by reputable designers under similar circumstances." *See also* authorities cited at West's 95 CONTRACTS, k280(4).

exposed to liability to the project owner for damages, including loss of fee.[11]

Whether the arrangement between the owner/client and the design professional contains a cost condition is a question of fact. If the design professional provides the owner with something less than a true cost estimate, courts have held that a cost condition is not created.[12] When the design professional's engagement does not include an obligation to design a structure within a specified budget or to estimate the construction costs of a proposed project, construction at a cost greater than anticipated by or acceptable to the owner is no defense to the design professional's action to recover the contracted fee.[13]

A true cost condition is normally created only by an express agreement establishing a maximum cost of the project. In *Kahn v. Terry*,[14] the owner terminated the architect for the architect's alleged failure to furnish plans for a portion of an improvement within an allegedly agreed-upon fixed construction budget. The design contract, however, provided that a fixed limit of construction cost would not be established merely by the architect's furnishing a project budget, unless such fixed limit was agreed to in writing and signed by the parties.[15] The court held that the absence of a specific agreement to a fixed construction cost nullified the owner's defense, entitling the architect to compensation for its services.

A cost condition may be implied. In *Sea Ledge Properties, Inc. v. Dodge*,[16] the design professional promised, then failed,

---

11. Rosenthal v. Gauthier, 69 So.2d 367 (La. 1953); Durand Assocs. v. Guardian Inv. Co., 183 N.W.2d 246 (Neb. 1971); *see also* authorities cited at West's ⊕ 95 CONTRACTS, k280(1), k321(1).

12. *See, e.g.*, White v. Kanrich, 20 Cal. Rptr. 37 (Ct. App. 1962); Jay Dee Shoes, Inc. v. Ostroff, 59 A.2d 738 (Md. 1948); Griswold & Rauma, Architects, Inc. v. Aesculapius Corp., 221 N.W.2d 556 (Minn. 1974).

13. Getzschman v. Miller Chem. Co., 443 N.W.2d 260, 270 (Neb. 1989); *see also* authorities cited at West's ⊕ 95 CONTRACTS, k312(1).

14. 628 So. 2d 390 (Ala. 1993).

15. *Id.*

16. 283 So. 2d 55 (Fla. Dist. Ct. App. 1973).

to procure for the owner a contractor that would construct the project for the stipulated sum. The owner hired a contractor that completed the work at a higher price. The owner was entitled to enforce the promise as a cost condition and to recover from the design professional the difference between the stipulated sum and the reasonable cost to complete the work.[17]

In an unusual twist to this situation, a design builder was treated as if it were an owner. In C. L. Maddox Inc. v. Benham Group, Inc.,[18] the design builder sought several million dollars of damages against its subcontractor/ design professional on the project. The design professional was held liable for the completeness and accuracy of the preparation of certain design information that was submitted to the design-build contractor for use in bidding. The appellate court affirmed verdicts based not only on express contracts for professional services, but also on an implied warranty sufficient to impose liability on the design professional for bidding errors.[19]

A design professional's liability to the project owner arising from cost-estimating is not limited to the initial estimate. In *Williams Engineering, Inc. v. Goodyear*,[20] the design professional's liability arose from its failure to monitor costs going forward from the initial estimate to the remaining costs of construction during the course of the project. The owners were unaware of the escalation of the project cost until after the work had been completed. The court noted that on cost-plus, fast-track projects (such as the one at issue), owners are more in need of reliable estimates of construction costs than on projects that use the traditional design-bid-build delivery method.[21]

The American Institute of Architects' standard form owner-architect contract documents address the issue of the

---

17. *Id.*
18. 88 F.3d 592 (8th Cir. 1996).
19. *Id.*
20. 496 So.2d 1012 (La. 1986).
21. *Id.*

design professional's estimate of the project construction cost.[22] Under the AIA contract language, if a project must be designed within a specified maximum construction cost, the architect is given some control over the materials, equipment, component systems, and types of construction used in the project. If the lowest bid exceeds the fixed limit, the owner has several options. The owner could increase the fixed budget limit, authorize re-bidding, negotiate with bidders, or allow and permit the architect with owner cooperation to revise the project scope and quality to reduce the project's cost.[23] If the owner chooses the last option, the architect is to modify the contract documents at no additional charge to the owner. After redesigning the project, the architect will be entitled to his or her fee, regardless of whether the project is constructed.[24]

Loss of the Design Professional's Fee

Where a maximum cost condition has been established, a majority rule and a minority rule have evolved to govern the payment of the design professional's fee in the event the actual construction cost exceeds the stated limit.[25] The majority rule provides that the design professional cannot recover a fee if the actual cost substantially exceeds the estimated cost.[26] The minority rule holds that the design professional cannot recover a fee if the actual costs exceed the estimated cost in any way.[27]

---

22. AIA Document B141, Standard Form of Agreement between Architect and Owner (1987 edition) provided in ¶ 5.2.2 that if a fixed limit of cost condition were established as a condition of the contract, it had to be expressed in a signed written agreement. In the 1997 edition of the B141, the express requirement of a written agreement in order to create a cost condition was deleted, but otherwise the framework of the 1987 edition remains.

23. AIA Document B141, Standard Form of Agreement Between Owner and Architect with Standard Form of Architect's Services ¶ 5.2.4 (1997 edition).

24. *Id.* at ¶ 5.2.5.

25. Annotation, *Effect on Compensation of Architect or Building Contractor of Express Provision in Private Building Contract Limiting the Cost of the Building*, 20 A.L.R.3D 778 (1968).

26. *See* authorities cited at West's 95 CONTRACTS, k321(1), k280(4).

27. *See* authorities cited at notes 25 and 26, *supra*.

A design professional's responsibility for a cost condition may be excused if the owner contributes to the cost overrun by changing the design.[28] The owner may also be deemed to have waived the cost condition by its conduct, for example, by proceeding with construction in the face of anticipated cost overruns without making changes to reduce such overruns, or by limiting the bidding to certain favored contractors.[29]

Other Damages

Losing a fee because of a failure to meet a cost condition is but one risk the design professional faces when cost-estimating for the owner. The design professional may also be found liable to the owner for losses incurred by the owner arising from the design professional's failure to perform to a professional standard of care in estimating construction costs.[30]

The proper measure of damages for underestimating construction costs varies among jurisdictions.[31] The design professional may be held liable for the difference between the estimate and the actual cost of the work.[32] The Colorado Supreme Court has awarded an owner a similar recovery, less 10 percent of the estimate, which the court deemed to be a normal, not unexpected overrun.[33] In *Kostohryz v. McGuire*,[34] the Minnesota Supreme Court awarded an owner a more limited damages recovery—the excess of the structure's

---

28. Anshen & Allen v. Marin Land Co., 17 Cal. Rptr. 42 (Ct. App. 1961); Griswold & Rauma, Architects, Inc. v. Aesculapius Corp., 221 N.W.2d 556 (Minn. 1974); *see also* authorities cited at West's ⬧ 95 CONTRACTS, k280(4).

29. *See* Jacquin-Florida Distilling Co. v. Reynolds, Smith & Hills, Architects-Engineers-Planners, Inc., 319 So.2d 604 (Fla. Dist. Ct. App. 1975); *see also* authorities cited at West's ⬧ 95 CONTRACTS, k305(2), k280(4).

30. Kellogg v. Pizza Oven, Inc., 402 P.2d 633 (Colo. 1965) (the architect made no attempt to re-check his original estimate; there was sufficient testimony that if had done so, he would have discovered a 40 percent error); Kostohryz v. McGuire, 212 N.W.2d 850 (Minn. 1973); *see also* authorities cited at West's ⬧ 272 NEGLIGENCE, k1205(4), k1672.

31. *See* authorities cited at West's ⬧ 115 DAMAGES, k120(2)(3), k123.

32. *See* Kaufman v. Leard, 248 N.E.2d 480 (Mass. 1969).

33. Kellogg v. Pizza Oven, Inc., 402 P.2d 633 (Colo. 1965).

34. Kostohryz v. McGuire, 212 N.W.2d 850 (Minn. 1973).

cost over its market value—rather than the difference between the estimate and the actual cost.

Unless waived or limited by the owner-design professional contract (as in AIA Document B141 ¶ 1.3.6, 1997 edition), consequential damages arising from the design professional's failure to accurately estimate costs may also be recovered by the owner. Such damages may include delay damages incurred during the project-redesign period or expenses incurred by the owner in reliance on the original cost estimate.[35]

COSTS OF CORRECTING DEFECTIVE DESIGN

A design professional may be liable to the client owner for any foreseeable damages arising from defective drawings and specifications.[36] Actionable defective performance by design professionals generates claims arising from:

- Inaccurate site plans
- Inadequate or insufficient details
- Failure to design to owner's purpose
- Ambiguous sketches that cause extra work
- Selection of unsuitable materials
- Violation of building codes

The design professional has a duty to correct design errors, both before and during the construction stage.[37] In *State v.*

---

35. Peteet v. Fogarty, 375 S.E.2d 527 (S.C. Ct. App. 1988); *see also* authorities cited at West's ☞ 95 CONTRACTS, k321(4); ☞ 115 DAMAGES, k120(2)(3), k123.

36. *See, e.g.,* Grossman v. Sea Air Towers, Ltd., 513 So.2d 686 (Fla. Dist. Ct. App. 1987); State v. Wolfenbarger & McCulley, 690 P.2d 380 (Kan. 1984); City of Charlotte v. Skidmore, Owings & Merrill, 407 S.E.2d 571 (N.C. Ct. App. 1991); Campbell County Bd. of Educ. v. Brownlee-Kesterson, Inc., 677 S.W.2d 457 (Tenn. Ct. App. 1984); *see also* authorities cited at West's ☞ 272 NEGLIGENCE, k1672; ☞ 360 STATES, k109.

37. *See* authorities cited at West's ☞ 241 LIMITATION OF ACTIONS, k46(6), k55(3)(5); ☞ 95 CONTRACTS, k196.

Lundin,[38] a New York court held: "The architect's duty to design a proper building is a continuous one that does not end until the building is completed."[39] Design professionals are obligated to report any serious problems with the design before construction is completed if they reasonably should have known of the design problem.[40]

An owner's cost overruns arising from undisclosed or inaccurately described soil or subsurface conditions may expose the design professional to further liability.[41] The design professional's liability to the project owner may arise from a failure to properly discover the nature and condition of the site or from the failure of the design to accommodate the actual site conditions.[42]

A design professional may also be liable if the design is incomplete. Although the design professional does not impliedly warrant a complete set of drawings free from all mistakes,[43] most design professionals (and courts) acknowledge that an incomplete design is not the norm, and can be expensive to rectify once construction has commenced.[44] A design professional who fails to adequately or sufficiently detail the materials to be used in the improvement or structure designed

---

38. 459 N.Y.S.2d 904, 906 (App. Div.), *aff'd*, 459 N.E. 2d 486 (N.Y. 1983).

39. *Id.*

40. Comptroller ex. rel. VMI v. King, 232 S.E.2d 895, 901 (Va. 1977); *see also* authorities cited at West's 95 CONTRACTS, k196.

41. *See* Housing Vermont v. Goldsmith & Morris, 685 A.2d 1086 (Vt. 1996) (project architect was liable to a developer for malpractice in the creation of a site grading plan that proved insufficient for construction purposes and that resulted in significant cost overruns. The site plan had to be redesigned and the work corrected at substantial additional cost); *see also* authorities cited at West's 272 NEGLIGENCE, k1672.

42. Zontelli & Sons, Inc. v. City of Nashwauk, 373 N.W.2d 744 (Minn. 1985) (engineer negligently underestimated the amount of unsuitable material to be removed from the project site); Nat'l Cash Register Co. v. Haak, 335 A.2d 407 (Pa. Super. 1975); A.E. Inv. Corp. v. Link Bldrs., Inc., 214 N.W.2d 764 (Wis. 1974) (plaintiff was a tenant of the building designed by the defendant architect); Reiman Constr. Co. v. Jerry Hiller Co., 709 P.2d 1271 (Wyo. 1985) (architect failed to design the building to accommodate the findings of the soils engineer's report).

43. *See* discussion at notes 6, 7, and 10, *supra*. "As a general rule, an architect's efficiency in preparing plans and specifications is tested by the rules of ordinary and reasonable skill usually exercised by one of that profession." Klein v. Catalano, 437 N.E.2d 514, 525 (Mass. 1982).

44. *See* Gen. Trading Corp. v. Burnup & Sims, 523 F.2d 98 (3d Cir. 1975); *see also* authorities cited at West's 272 NEGLIGENCE, k1205(4), k1672.

may be liable to the owner for the costs to correct the resulting mistake or deficiency.[45]

A design professional may be held liable to the owner if the work, completed in accordance with the design professional's plans, fails to satisfy the owner's purpose.[46] In *Bloomsburg Mills, Inc. v. Sordoni Construction Co.*,[47] an architect was hired to design a building that would maintain a constant and specific temperature and humidity. To accomplish this required a built-up roof with a vapor seal, which would prevent leakage of moisture from the outside and condensation from the inside. The architect's roof design specified an improper vapor seal plus fiberglass material inadequate for the intended use. The building would not maintain the constant temperature and humidity required, and the owner ultimately had to install a new roof. The architect was found liable for the cost of the new roof, less credit for the remaining useful life of the original roof.[48]

Many courts hold that a design professional's contract with an owner contains an implied obligation that the completed improvement will be suitable and capable of being used by the owner for the purpose for which it was designed.[49] If the design is unsuitable, the architect will be charged with the cost of redesign, and some portion of the retrofit costs.[50] If the improvement cannot be economically retrofitted, the design professional will be responsible for any diminution in value.[51] The design professional may also be held responsi-

---

45. *See* Pearce & Pearce, Inc. v. Kroh Bros. Dev. Co., 474 So.2d 369 (Fla. Dist. Ct. App. 1985); *see also* authorities cited at West's ⊕═ 272 NEGLIGENCE, k1205(4), k1672; ⊕═ 95 CONTRACTS, k284(4).

46. *See* authorities cited at West's ⊕═ 95 CONTRACTS, k196.

47. 164 A.2d 201 (Pa. 1960).

48. *Id.*

49. St. Joseph Hosp. v. Corbetta Constr. Co., 316 N.E.2d 51, 64 (Ill. App. Ct. 1974); Greenhaven Corp. v. Hutchcraft & Assocs., 463 N.E.2d 283, 285 (Ind. Ct. App. 1984); *see also* authorities cited at West's ⊕═ 95 CONTRACTS, k196. *But see* Strauss Veal Feeds, Inc. v. Mead & Hunt, Inc., 538 N.E.2d 299 (Ind. Ct. App. 1989) (the scope of the implied duty is limited by the express terms of the design professional-owner contract).

50. *See* authorities cited at West's ⊕═ 115 DAMAGES, k120(2)(3), k123.

51. *See* authorities cited at note 49, *supra.*

ble for the cost of replacing defective materials unsuitable for their intended purpose, so long as the design professional had a role in the selection of the materials.[52]

Design professionals are expected to know the location of the structures they are designing and are obligated to design in accordance with applicable building codes.[53] The implied suitability obligation discussed above includes the design professional's duty to prepare drawings and specifications that conform to applicable building codes and other local ordinances. But the design professional's duty to prepare drawings and specifications in conformance with building codes can be modified by express provisions of the design professional's contract with the project owner.[54] If the design professional and the owner agree that the plans prepared by the design professional need not necessarily conform to applicable codes or ordinances, this express agreement trumps the design professional's implied duty to provide conforming plans.[55]

The damage the project owner incurs as a result of the design professional's defective performance depends on the specific type of defective performance and the circumstances of the particular project. Generally, however, the damages recoverable from the design professional[56] include the costs of redesign,[57] cost to repair defective or noncomplying

---

52. *See* Brushton-Moira Cent. Sch. Dist. v. Alliance Wall Corp., 600 N.Y.S.2d 511 (A.D. 1993) (insulated wall panels recommended by the architect were inappropriate for owner's building); St. Joseph Hosp. v. Corbetta Constr. Co., 316 N.E.2d 51 (Ill. App. Ct. 1974); Scott v. Potomac Ins. Co., 341 P.2d 1083 (Or. 1959) (architect was liable when he did not have sufficient knowledge of the material he approved for use in the building and made no independent effort to ascertain the suitability of the material for its intended use or purpose); authorities cited at West's ⊕═ 115 DAMAGES, k45, k123.

53. St. Joseph Hosp. v. Corbetta Constr. Co., 316 N.E.2d 51 (Ill. App. Ct. 1974); *see also* authorities cited at West's ⊕═ 95 CONTRACTS, k196.

54. *See* authorities cited at West's ⊕═ 95 CONTRACTS, k280(4).

55. *Id.;* Greenhaven Corp. v. Hutchcraft & Assocs., 463 N.E.2d 283, 285 (Ind. Ct. App. 1984) (architect's original plans conformed to fire code's requirement of two remote exits, but owner requested the plan be changed to provide only one exit).

56. *See* authorities cited at West's ⊕═ 115 DAMAGES, k120(2), k123.

57. Housing Vermont v. Goldsmith & Morris, 685 A.2d 1086 (Vt. 1996).

work,[58] diminution in value of the improvement,[59] and consequential damages.[60] These damages may be recoverable in various combinations as the facts dictate.

LIABILITY FOR ERRORS, OMISSIONS, OR DELAYS DURING CONTRACT ADMINISTRATION

The design professional's contract administration duties are often as important to a successful project as the design duties, and carry comparable potential for liability. The design professional's contract administration obligations commonly fall into three broad categories: construction review, claim/dispute resolution, and payment certification. The particular duties and obligations the design professional assumes within these broad tasks may expose the designer to liability to the project owner for damages arising from breach of the particular duty or obligation at issue. And, as discussed in

---

58. Grossman v. Sea Air Towers, Ltd., 513 So.2d 686 (Fla. Dist. Ct. App. 1987) (the proper measure of damages was the amount necessary to restore a parking deck to its original condition. Costs incurred by the owner to increase the load capacity of the deck were not properly chargeable to the design professionals because those costs would have been the owner's responsibility even in the absence of any fault of the designers); City of Charlotte v. Skidmore, Owings & Merrill, 407 S.E.2d 571 (N.C. Ct. App. 1991) (trial court did not err in instructing jury on "cost of repair" measure of damages without reference to "diminution in value" measure of damages where the defects were so significant that the work did not substantially conform to the contract and the decreased value of the improvement erected justified the high cost of the repairs); Brushton-Moira Cent. Sch. Dist. v. Alliance Wall Corp., 600 N.Y.S.2d 511 (A.D. 1993); Campbell County Bd. of Educ. v. Brownlee-Kesterson, Inc., 677 S.W.2d 457 (Tenn. Ct. App. 1984); see also Reiman Constr. Co. v. Jerry Hiller Co., 709 P.2d 1271 (Wyo. 1985) (case contains good discussion of damages, but was remanded for additional findings of fact as to trial court's computation of owner's cost-of-repair damages); D & O Contractors, Inc. v. Terrebonne Parish Sch. Bd., 545 So.2d 588 (La. Ct. App. 1989). But see State v. Wolfenbarger & McCulley, 690 P.2d 380 (Kan. 1984) (award of cost for post-construction modification to structure was not a windfall to the project owner because the modification would not have been made but for the original design error).

59. Italian Econ. Corp. v. Cmty. Eng'rs, Inc., 514 N.Y.S.2d 630 (Sup. Ct. 1987) (owner was entitled to recover both the cost of repairs necessary to bring the building into code compliance and diminution in value of the building subsequent to making the repairs, where the structural repairs made necessary because of the defective design resulted in loss of floor space and windows).

60. Grossman v. Sea Air Towers, Ltd., 513 So.2d 686 (Fla. Dist. Ct. App. 1987) (owner of apartment building was awarded loss of rental income resulting from repair work necessitated by architect's defective design); Mercy Hosp. v. Hansen, Lind & Meyer, P.C., 456 N.W.2d 666 (Iowa 1990).

Chapter 8, in some jurisdictions the design professional also assumes a direct tort responsibility to prime and trade contractors for negligent or deliberate conduct outside of the design professional's standard of care that damages the project contractors.

The designer who has contracted with the project owner to provide the project drawings and specifications is not necessarily obligated to provide construction administration services as well. The designer often does provide these services as the next step in the project process, but the obligation is neither implied nor inherent in the owner-design professional relationship. The scope of project supervision duties and obligations the design professional undertakes is a matter of contract between the designer and the project owner.[61]

The most common complaint against design professionals based on improper contract administration occurs when defective work gets past the administering design professional. "The design professional should have caught the nonconforming work. It's his fault this happened" is a familiar refrain. But the design professional's contractual obligations usually do not mirror the owner's expectations.

The AIA standard form documents do not require the architect to inspect the contractor's work.[62] AIA Document B141, Standard Form of Agreement Between Owner and Architect with Standard Form of Services ¶ 2.6.2.1 (1997 edition) provides:

> The Architect, as a representative of the Owner, shall visit the site at intervals appropriate to that stage of the Contractor's operations, or as otherwise agreed by the Owner and the Architect in Article 2.8: (1) to become generally familiar with and to keep the Owner informed about the progress and quality of the portion of the Work completed, (2) to endeavor to guard the Owner against defects and deficiencies in the Work,

---

61. *See* authorities cited at West's ⊕ 95 CONTRACTS, k280(4).

62. This has not always been the case. *See* C. Sapers, *Special Commentary: Ruminations on Architectural Practice*, West Group Annual Construction Contracts, January 20, 2001, Washington, D.C.

and (3) to determine in general if the Work is being performed in a manner indicating that the Work, when fully completed, will be in accordance with the Contract Documents. However, the Architect shall not be required to make exhaustive or continuous on-site inspections to check the quality or quantity of the Work.

A substantially similar provision is found in AIA Document A201, General Conditions of the Contract for Construction ¶ 4.2.2 (1997 edition). Likewise, a similar provision is found in the Engineers Joint Contract Documents Committee ("EJCDC") Document 1910-8, Standard General Conditions of the Construction Contract (1990 edition) at ¶ 9.2.

These contract provisions attempt to allocate between the design professional and the contractor the project review or "supervision" responsibilities. Under all the standard form contracts, the design professional's role is akin to a "general supervisor," with no control over or charge of construction means, methods, or techniques. Under the standard form contracts, it is the contractor who is tagged as the "supervisor" responsible for construction means, methods, and techniques.[63] As to the design professionals, the primary object of these provisions is to impose the duty or obligation upon the architect or engineer to assure the owner that before final acceptance the project will be completed substantially in accordance with the plans and specifications.[64]

Even in the absence of a written contract between the design professional and the client that limits the design pro-

---

63. *See, e.g.,* AIA Document A201, General Conditions of the Contract for Construction ¶ 3.3.1 (1997 edition). There are, however, a number of situations where means and methods are bound up within the design. For instance, owners often desire to have their projects built with specific types or brands of materials. When the owner specifies a sole-source product, means and methods attendant to such product become part of the specifications. *See, e.g.,* Edward M. Crough, Inc. v. Dep't of Gen. Servs., 572 A.2d 457 (D.C. App. 1990) (sole-source roofing materials). Owners and designers also frequently prepare specifications containing both design details and performance requirements. If the two are not properly coordinated, the responsibility for the same will be placed upon the owner and designer. W.H. Lyman Constr. Co. v. Vill. of Gurnee, 403 N.E.2d 1325 (Ill. App. Ct. 1980).

64. Diocese v. R-Monde Contractors, 562 N.Y.S.2d 593, 596 (Sup. Ct. 1989).

fessional's obligation to supervise the contractor's work, the design professional has only limited exposure arising from a contractor's defective or deficient work. Without an express contractual obligation, the design professional is not required to monitor the contractor's work closely enough so as to be held responsible for the contractor's defective work.[65] The design professional's responsibilities do, however, normally extend to construction defects so serious or obvious that they should have been detected by the design professional even upon minimal inspection.[66]

As the "general supervisor," the design professional is intended to have minimal exposure to liability for damages caused by contractor-controlled construction methods or techniques. But courts struggle with the obvious conflict between the architect's clear responsibility for design and the contractually disclaimed responsibility for observing that the design is accomplished, especially if the design professional undertakes and gets paid for site visits. Courts, like owners, often assume that architects are doing more than just taking in the air when they conduct a compensated site visit. Although design professionals, pursuant to this type of limited "visitation" obligation,[67] are required contractually only to make periodic visits to the construction site and determine in general if the work is proceeding in accordance with the contract, they nevertheless assume a duty (1) to exercise reasonable care to determine whether the contractor's work was properly performed and (2) to order repair or correction of defects or deficiencies they discover in the contractor's work.[68]

---

65. *See* authorities cited at West's 🔑 95 CONTRACTS, k280(4), k284(1).

66. ESO, Inc. v. Kasparian, 594 N.E.2d 557 (Mass. App. Ct. 1992); *see also* authorities cited at West's 🔑 95 CONTRACTS, k196, k280(4), k312(1).

67. *See* AIA Document A201, General Conditions of the Contract for Construction ¶ 4.2.2 (1997 edition).

68. Roland A. Wilson & Assocs. v. Forty-O-Four Grand Corp., 246 N.W.2d 922 (Iowa 1976); Diocese of Rochester v. R-Monde Contractors, 562 N.Y.S.2d 593 (Sup. Ct. 1989); Equitable Life Assurance Soc'y v. Nico Constr. Co., 666 N.Y.S.2d 602 (App. Div. 1997) (structural engineer failed to make adequate inspections of the work; defective work performed by the contractor during the period when the engineer failed to inspect the work was chargeable against the engineer); *see also* authorities cited at West's 🔑 95 CONTRACTS, k280(4).

In proper cases, courts do not hesitate to impose responsibility and liability upon design professionals for the cost of repairs to defective work. The fact that exhaustive, repeated on-site inspections are not required[69] does not allow design professionals to close their eyes on the construction site, refrain from engaging in any inspection procedure whatsoever, and then disclaim liability for construction defects that monitoring would have prevented.[70] Contract provisions limiting design professionals' inspection duties do not absolve them from all possible liability or relieve them of the duty to perform reasonably the limited contractual duties they agreed to undertake. While an agreement may absolve design professionals of liability for the contractor's breaches, negligent acts, and omissions, the standard contract terms do not absolve them of liability arising out of their own failure to inspect reasonably consistent with their contract and their professional standard of care.[71]

Defining the extent of the duty to administer a project's construction by listing particular tasks is practically impossible. Projects vary greatly, in scope, cost, and complexity. Even the minimal supervisory power a design professional assumes under the standard form contracts ordinarily requires the design professional to assure that the completed work conforms to the drawings and specifications. If a designer has the responsibility to assure the owner that the contractor's work so conforms, the designer also has the corresponding duty to inform the owner of nonconforming work.

In *Board of Education v. Sargent, Webster, Crenshaw & Folley*,[72] the AIA owner-architect contract disclaimers did not absolve the architect from liability for failing to alert the

---

69. *See* authorities cited at West's ⊕ 95 CONTRACTS, k284(1).

70. First Nat'l Bank v. Cann, 503 F. Supp. 419, 436 (N.D. Ohio 1980); *see also* authorities cited at note 4, *supra*, and West's ⊕ 95 CONTRACTS, k196; ⊕ 272 NEGLIGENCE, k1205(4).

71. Watson, Watson, Rutland/Architects, Inc. v. Montgomery County Bd. of Educ., 559 So.2d 168, 173 (Ala. 1990); U.R.S. Co. v. Gulfport-Biloxi Reg'l Airport Auth., 544 So.2d 824 (Miss. 1989); *see also* authorities cited at West's ⊕ 95 CONTRACTS, k196, k312(1).

72. 539 N.Y.S.2d 814 (A.D. 1989).

owner of defects known to the architect during performance of the construction work. When, as a result of a periodic site visit, the architect discovers defects in the work that the owner, if notified, could take steps to ameliorate, the imposition of liability upon the architect for failure to notify the owner is based on breach of the architect's contractual duty, and not as guarantor of the contractor's performance.[73]

Similarly, in *Diocese of Rochester v. R-Monde Contractors*,[74] a New York court held that an architect could not rely on the exculpatory language in the owner-architect agreement (similar to AIA Document B141 ¶ 2.6.2.1, quoted above) to immunize itself from liability to the owner for failure to discover and correct defects in the contractor's work. The architect prepared plans for a church renovation. The architect was required to make periodic inspections and determine whether the work conformed to the plans. On the architect's motion for summary judgment, the court rejected the architect's reliance on language excusing the architect from responsibility for defective construction methods or for acts or omissions of the contractor. The architect had the contractual responsibility to inspect the work and guard against defective work. Factual issues precluded finding that there was no failure by the architect to exercise the degree of care required.[75]

The design professional's approval of a contractor's use of materials not in accordance with the project specifications may expose the design professional to liability if the use of the substitute materials damaged the owner in some way, as by reducing the value of the owner's project.[76] And, when

---

73. *Id; see also* Hunt v. Ellisor & Tanner, Inc., 739 S.W.2d 933 (Tex. Ct. App. 1987) (the exculpatory provisions are nothing more than an agreement that the architect is not the insurer or guarantor of the contractor's obligation to carry out the work in accordance with the contract documents).

74. 562 N.Y.S.2d 593 (Sup. Ct.1989).

75. *Id.; see also* Gables CVF, Inc. v. Bahr, Vermeer & Haeker Architect, Ltd., 506 N.W.2d 706 (Neb. 1993); authorities cited at West's ☞ 95 CONTRACTS, k312(1).

76. *See, e.g.,* Bechtold Paving, Inc. v. City of Kenmare, 446 N.W.2d 19 (N.D. 1989); South Union, Ltd. v. George Parker & Assocs., AIA, 504 N.E.2d 1131 (Ohio Ct. App. 1985); *see also* authorities cited at West's ☞ 95 CONTRACTS, k312(1).

particular construction techniques are specified in the plans, the contractor is not responsible when such procedures do not work.[77] In *C.J. Langenfelder & Son, Inc. v. Commonwealth*,[78] the owner and its in-house design staff were held to have impliedly warranted that the contractor's concrete was adequate for the owner's intended purposes, even though the concrete mix design was prepared and submitted by the contractor's concrete supplier. In inspecting and approving the concrete mix design and ingredients and in testing the concrete prior to placement, the owner had exercised such close control that it could not avoid responsibility for any later nonconformity and delay.[79]

Where the design professional's breach of contract or failure to satisfy a professional standard of care allows the contractor to perform defective or deficient work, or work not in compliance with the project specifications, and the owner is injured as a result, the proper measure of damages recoverable by the owner is commonly the reasonable cost of labor and materials necessary to place the affected work in the condition contemplated by the parties at the time they entered into the owner-designer contract.[80]

To establish liability, an owner must offer proof of damages caused by a contractor's defective or nonconforming work, as well as the scope of the design professional's supervisory responsibilities. Courts also require the owner to present expert testimony as to the design professional's failure to exercise due care in performing supervisory duties and

---

77. Midwest Dredging Co. v. McAninch Corp., 424 N.W.2d 216 (Iowa 1988) (contractor not liable for delay resulting from using specified dredging and piping technique); *see also* Natus Corp. v. United States, 371 F.2d 450, 455 (Ct. Cl. 1967); authorities cited at West's ⬥ 95 CONTRACTS, k312(1); ⬥ 393 UNITED STATES, k70(30), k73(22), k74(4).

78. 404 A.2d 745 (Pa. 1979).

79. *Id.* at 751.

80. *E.g.*, U.R.S. Co. v. Gulfport-Biloxi Reg'l Airport Auth., 544 So.2d 824 (Miss. 1989); Bechtold Paving, Inc. v. City of Kenmare, 446 N.W.2d 19 (N.D. 1989) (trial court improperly ordered the engineer to pay the owner whatever amount was necessary for the owner to redo the defective work performed by the contractor rather than a specified amount of damages to make the owner whole based on expert testimony); South Union, Ltd. v. George Parker & Assocs., AIA, 504 N.E.2d 1131 (Ohio Ct. App. 1985); *see also* authorities cited at West's ⬥ 115 DAMAGES, k111, k120(2)(3), k123.

obligations.[81] In *Annen v. Trump*,[82] the project owner claimed that it incurred damages as the result of the engineer's failure to inspect the roof installation for defects and to verify that the work was properly performed. The owner argued that because the contractor's installation was improperly performed, it followed that the engineer had negligently supervised the construction of the roof. The court held that expert testimony was required. The supervisory duties of the engineer, the extent of those duties, and the expertise to determine whether there was compliance with the specifications and plans were outside of the common knowledge and experience of laymen.[83]

A second basis for design professional liability to the owner during project administration is for acts taken by the design professional to resolve claims by and between the owner and the contractor. Contracts often contain detailed procedures for the design professional to rule upon claims between the owner and contractors.[84] The design professional may be liable to the owner for breach of contract for failing to follow the claim resolution procedures set forth in the parties' contract or for failing to act impartially in performing his or her duties.[85]

A third basis for the design professional's liability during contract administration is approval of progress payments and final payment to contractors. If the design professional's contract with the owner requires the design professional to issue a statement certifying the progress or completion of the work, the general rule is that the designer must exercise

---

81. Watson, Watson, Rutland/Architects, Inc. v. Montgomery County Bd. of Educ., 559 So.2d 168 (Ala. 1990); Annen v. Trump, 913 S.W.2d 16 (Mo. Ct. App. 1995); *see also* authorities cited at West's ⊕ 272 NEGLIGENCE, k1672; ⊕ 157 EVIDENCE, k571(3).

82. 913 S.W.2d 16 (Mo. Ct. App. 1995).

83. *Id*; *see also* discussion at notes 4, 5, and 6, *supra*.

84. *See, e.g.*, AIA Document A201, General Conditions of the Contract for Construction, Articles 4.3 and 4.4 (1997 edition).

85. *See* Meco Sys., Inc. v. Dancing Bear Entm't, Inc., 948 S.W.2d 185 (Mo. Ct. App. 1997); *see also* authorities cited at West's ⊕ 272 NEGLIGENCE, k1205(4); ⊕ 308 PRINCIPAL AND AGENT, k61(1); ⊕ 95 CONTRACTS, k196.

this duty in reasonable accordance with the standards of the profession. The design professional is charged with the duty of using the reasonable care of one skilled in the profession when issuing payment certificates and can be held liable for damages resulting from his failure to act accordingly.[86]

Contracts commonly include limitations on exactly what the design professional is certifying in issuing certificates for payment. For example, AIA Document A201, General Conditions of the Contract for Construction ¶ 9.4.2 (1997 edition), provides that:

> [T]he issuance of a Certificate for Payment will not be a representation that the Architect has (1) made exhaustive or continuous on-site inspections to check the quality or quantity of the Work, (2) reviewed construction means, methods, techniques, sequences or procedures, (3) reviewed copies of requisitions received from Subcontractors and material suppliers and other data requested by the Owner to substantiate the Contractor's right to payment, or (4) made examination to ascertain how or for what purpose the Contractor has used money previously paid on account of the Contract Sum.

A breach of the design professional's duty to reasonably inspect the work and to issue a certificate representing the accuracy of the contractor's request may result in liability to the owner.[87] A design professional who fails to recognize defects that would have been detected through the exercise of ordinary care, and who certifies to the owner that the work is in conformance with the contract documents, may be held liable for damages. Liability arises from the

---

86. *See, e.g.,* Roland A. Wilson & Assocs. v. Forty-O-Four Grand Corp., 246 N.W.2d 922 (Iowa 1976); Newton Inv. Co. v. Barnard & Burk, Inc., 220 So.2d 822 (Miss. 1969); *see also* authorities cited at West's ☞ 272 NEGLIGENCE, k1205(4); ☞ 308 PRINCIPAL AND AGENT, k61(1); ☞ 95 CONTRACTS, k196.

87. *See generally* Annotation, *Liability of Architect or Engineer for Improper Issuance of Certificate,* 43 A.L.R.2D 1227 (1955); *see also* Palmer v. Brown, 273 P.2d 306 (Cal. Ct. App. 1954); Browning v. Maurice B. Levien & Co., 262 S.E.2d 355 (N.C. Ct. App. 1980); authorities cited at West's ☞ 272 NEGLIGENCE, k1205(4); ☞ 308 PRINCIPAL AND AGENT, k61(1); ☞ 95 CONTRACTS, k196.

improper issuance of certificates for progress payments and final payment.

In addition to certifying that the progress of the work matches the contractor's claims in the pay applications, the design professional may be contractually required to determine that the contractor has paid all of its subcontractors and suppliers and any other person with inchoate lien rights. The design professional who undertakes this duty to the owner may be liable to the owner for negligence in authorizing final payment to the contractor before all potential lien claimants have been properly paid by the contractor.

In *Palmer v. Brown*,[88] the owner sued the project architect asserting that the architect breached its contract by issuing certificates of payment without first determining whether the contractor had paid its subcontractors or suppliers. At the time the architect issued the certificate for payment, the contractor had outstanding debts to subcontractors and suppliers. Following payment to the contractor pursuant to the architect's certificate of payment, the contractor still failed to pay its subcontractors, resulting in liability of the owner to these creditors. The court held that the owner's complaint stated a cause of action against the architect b ased on the architect's duty to protect the owner by verifying that the contractor had paid all outstanding debts on the project or by obtaining partial or final lien waivers from the contractor's subcontractors and suppliers.[89]

In a more recent case, an architect was found not to have owed or breached a duty to the owner to assure that the contractor paid its subcontractors. In *Fabe v. WVP Corp.*,[90] the court found for the architect, based on a provision in the owner-architect contract similar to that of AIA A201 stated above. In *Fabe*, the architect reviewed the contractor's payment applications and the work performed, and certified

---

88. 273 P.2d 306 (Cal. Ct. App. 1954).

89. *Id.*

90. 760 S.W.2d 490 (Mo. App 1988).

payment to the contractor. It was later discovered that the contractor had not paid its subcontractors, laborers, or materialmen. The owner sought damages alleging that the architect negligently failed to discover that the contractor had submitted fraudulent lien waivers and certificates for payment. The court rejected the owner's argument that the architect's act of examining the lien waivers gave rise to the concomitant duty to determine the authenticity of those documents.[91]

---

91. *Id.*

Tort Damages

8

ALLEN HOLT GWYN

INTRODUCTION

At common law, there were bright line distinctions between civil actions brought in contract and those brought in tort. Elements of proof were different, as were recoverable damages. Proof of a tort was generally more burdensome—requiring proof of a duty of care, foreseeability, "but for" and proximate causation, rather than simply a contract and a breach. At common law, contracting parties were free to assign various risks between them, and such assignments were generally upheld. If one commercial party was damaged by a contractual partner's act, the remedy was *ex contractu*. There was no tort recovery. This separateness survives today in Article 2 of the Uniform Commercial Code.[1] But in many

---

1. For buyers and sellers of goods, Article 2 of the Uniform Commercial Code codifies the rules for contract formation, acceptance, rejection, cover, disclaimers, damages, and consequential and incidental damage waivers.

245

other areas of commerce the distinctions and barriers between contract and tort law can be as blurred as the colored glass in a kaleidoscope.

A construction project is a monumental mix of goods and services combined to create a new and functioning edifice. Whether a building, a water-retaining structure, or a system to generate or distribute power, today's projects are complex, requiring coordination among numerous participants who have different expertise. Specialization in the furnishing of construction goods and services permeates the construction industry. We still build with bricks and mortar, but we rely upon sophisticated components installed by specialists using delivery systems with ever-more-complex risk allocations. Amenities found in today's starter houses make them complex structures in comparison to the multistory office buildings of the 1930s.

As construction projects become more complex, they cost more. Owners, like all consumers, don't want to pay more.[2] This puts pressure on construction design, especially the design of components. Cost concerns now filter the design of every construction material. And because speed of installation is a function of overall cost, price also affects components' means and methods of application. Designers of construction components continually look for ways to make products that cost less, are quicker and easier to install, have a more desirable appearance, and perform better than last year's models. A quantifiable improvement in any of these characteristics will increase market share. But as construction component design is revisited and revised in the name of cost, performance characteristics are affected. When the performance criteria of components are materially altered, the performance of major building systems may be compromised. The redundancies of conservative design that were

---

2. Many off-the-shelf consumer goods decrease in price as availability increases. Consumers of many goods—especially newer technology goods—have become accustomed to getting more for the same price as last year, or even more for a lesser price.

de rigueur for buildings in decades past too often play second fiddle to the latest bells and whistles of convenience.

Then, too, the increasing complexity of buildings has challenged the architect's role. Architects formerly were the arbiters of component design and selection. This has changed. Product design and, recently, system design have devolved to component manufacturers. No longer is the architect the project's most knowledgeable leader. As observed by a leading Columbia University professor, by the end of the 1970s architects came to know less and less about more and more until some were said "to know nothing about everything."[3]

The construction design landscape is evolving, and the designers in the manufacturing sector are on the leading edge. Selection and coordination of building components, long the province of design professionals, are in today's world being usurped by contractors and component manufacturers. Through "value engineering" or outright design delegation,[4] architects defer to component designers. Contractor-led design/build arrangements often relegate the architect to backroom subcontractor status. With the right of component selection comes the responsibility to coordinate the chosen products with the building's structure and complementing systems. In this area, design professionals hand off much of their former role, if not all of their responsibility.[5] To a larger and larger degree, construction services have become coordinated deliveries of products.

---

3. Mario Salvadore, Why Buildings Stand Up: The Strength of Architecture 24 (1980). No longer is the architect capable of the expertise required by the court in Hubert v. Aiken, 2 N.Y.S. 711 (C.P. 1888), aff'd, 25 N.E. 954 (N.Y. 1890) ("he is an expert in carpentry, cements, mortar, in the strength of materials ... new conveniences...").

4. The American Institute of Architects' standard general conditions of the contract between owner and contractor now explicitly allow the delegation of the architect's design responsibility to the contractor and its subcontractors. See AIA Document A201, General Conditions of the Contract for Construction ¶ 3.12.10 (1997 edition).

5. Design professionals "of record" retain liability, especially to their clients, for adequate and code compliant design, whether the design professional performs the work or delegates it to others. Justin Sweet, Legal Aspects of Architecture, Engineering and the Construction Process § 15.10B (4th ed. 1989); see also Johnson v. Salem Title Co., 425 P.2d 519 (Or. 1967) (structural

(continued)

Specialization in the construction industry has also morphed the contractual process. Virtually all projects have dozens of contractual arrangements. Specialized equipment must be furnished and installed by ever-more-specialized subcontractors and suppliers. The traditional design-bid-build project delivery method is but one of many available contractual vehicles. Owners can choose among construction managers, multi-prime contractors, design-builders, joint ventures, and so on—the ability to customize the process grows every year.[6] But there is one industry constant—there are more and more entities providing specialized goods and services. Subcontractors, suppliers, and subconsultants abound, in ever-deepening Dante-esque circles.

The specialization of construction goods and services, and the reliance upon newly designed, prefabricated construction products,[7] have strained the law of contracts. When something goes wrong on a construction site, or when the completed edifice doesn't meet expectations, there are usually a number of entities with a hand in the cause. Products that perform well in one setting may, for instance, lack the robustness to weather ambient conditions in another place.

As product diversification expands, the importance of selecting complementary construction components has increased. It is now as significant to select and coordinate as it is to install properly. When problems occur, are they the fault of the design professional, the installer, the manufacturer, the maintenance team, or all of the above? Getting to the bottom of a construction problem often requires a detailed investigation, and a good deal of finger-pointing

---

engineering requirements were nondelegable, even to a professional engineer). The result is different if the design professional never had the responsibility as part of its scope of services. *See* Aleutian Constructors v. United States, 24 Cl. Ct. 372 (1991) (specifications required contractor to design and build roof); Mudgett v. Marshall, 574 A.2d 867 (Me. 1990) (error of structural engineer hired by design-build contractor not imputed to owner's design professional not hired to design building).

6. The American Institute of Architects' Standard Form of Agreement Between Owner and Architect, AIA Document B141 (1997 edition), provides owners a menu of architectural services from which to choose.

7. Many of these products are designed to meet a specific price point to achieve market share.

regrettably ensues. Major responsibility may lie far down, or even outside, the contractual chain.

Contract law has adapted in several areas to market conditions. Warranties from manufacturers of certain goods (typically finished goods, specially designed equipment, and appliances) allow affected parties to leapfrog broken links in the contractual chain.[8] There is also a federal statutory remedy for defective consumer household goods.[9] Under the common law of contracts, however, privity reigned. Further, providers of services and labor were often immune from responsibility once their work was accomplished and accepted.[10]

In prior decades, a contractor would directly employ different types of skilled labor for a job (carpenters, masons, ironworkers, concrete finishers, etc.). Today's builder hires separate subcontractors and suppliers. When problems develop today, claims may be passed among multiple entities, with multiple contractual arrangements. For many issues, the common law contract causes of action can be cumbersome in the extreme. If a problem takes several years to manifest itself, if contractual responsibilities for the work are not the same up and down the chain of specialization, or if there are gaps in the scope of and responsibilities for the work,

---

8. *See, e.g.,* Groppel Co. v. United States Gypsum Co., 616 S.W.2d 49 (Mo. Ct. App. 1981); *see also* authorities cited at West's ⊕⇒ 343 SALES, k255, k427.

9. The Magnuson-Moss Act, 15 U.S.C.A. § 2301 *et seq.* (2002), provides consumers with statutory remedies for breach of a manufacturer's or vendor's written or implied warranty of a consumer product. The Act also provides certain minimum requirements for written warranties. Upon establishing that the warranty was breached, the consumer may elect the remedy of refund, repair, or replacement, and may recover attorney's fees if he prevails. The Act applies to personal, family, or household products, but may include "building materials" such as paneling, siding, or storm windows, when purchased in connection with remodeling a home. *See* authorities cited at West's ⊕⇒ 92H CONSUMER PROTECTION, k6. In one of the leading cases, the Act was applied to roofing materials. Muchisky v. Frederic Roofing Co., 838 S.W.2d 74 (Mo. Ct. App. 1992) (affirming verdict, and award of attorney's fees, in favor of homeowner on a re-roofing project).

10. *See, e.g.,* U-Haul Int'l, Inc. v. Mike Madrid Co., 734 N.E.2d 1048 (Ind. Ct. App. 2002). As with many other judicially created defenses, exceptions to this doctrine have swallowed the rule. *See* Suneson v. Holloway Constr. Co., 992 S.W.2d 79 (Ark. 1999), and the discussion below as to the erosion of this judicially created defense. One year after *Suneson,* however, the Arkansas state legislature reinstated the doctrine as it relates to public projects. *See* Ark. Code Ann. § 16-56-112(h) (2001 Supp.).

damages may occur for which there is no common law contract remedy.[11] This is a fertile field for the seeds of tort law to take root.

In other areas of commerce, tort law's responsibilities and remedies have continuously insinuated themselves. Beginning with Judge Cardozo's opinion in *MacPherson v. Buick Motor Co.*,[12] courts have imposed the duty to act reasonably as an objective standard of acceptable conduct. This duty exists independently of any agreement between parties, and applies to conduct both inside and outside a contractual relationship.[13] Tort law imposes upon all members of society certain minimum standards of behavior—including the obligation to take reasonable steps to protect others from being injured or having their possessions destroyed or damaged. If these standards are violated, tort law compensates without serious regard to risk allocation, so long as the injury is foreseeable and proximately caused by the defendant's wrong.

Tort law is more about compensation and less about risk allocation. This emphasis is reflected in the liberal rules of tort damages. A negligence victim is entitled to recover for both direct and consequential losses proximately caused by a tortfeasor's breach of duty.[14] In contrast, the general rule of contract damages is that consequential damages are not recoverable unless they were within the contemplation of the parties at the time of contracting and became a basis for the parties' bargain.[15]

As discussed in Chapter 9 of this text, there are certain limitations on tort damages, especially purely economic damages. In the construction industry, this chiefly manifests itself

---

11. *See* Chapter 1 of this text.

12. 111 N.E. 1050 (N.Y. 1916).

13. *See* Morse/Diesel, Inc. v. Trinity Indus., Inc., 655 F. Supp. 346, 355 (S.D.N.Y. 1987); *see also* authorities cited at West's ⊕══ 184 FRAUD, k45.

14. *See* authorities cited at West's ⊕══ 115 DAMAGES, k20.

15. *See* Hadley v. Baxendale, 156 Eng. Rep. 145 (Ex. 1854); discussion in Chapter 1 of this text; *see also* authorities cited at West's ⊕══ 115 DAMAGES, k23.

in the judge-made "economic loss rule," prohibiting economic damages, direct or consequential, when there is no concurrent physical injury or property damage.[16] In a way, the economic loss rule is a judicial response to what some commentators have characterized as an assault on privity and a cancerlike invasion by torts into the contractual setting.[17] But the economic loss rule has hardly been applied uniformly. Each year new opinions put a new spin on the rule, making its application and exceptions a matter of locality.[18]

Particularly invasive of the construction setting have been the torts of negligent construction and negligent misrepresentation. Negligence in performing construction-related duties can support a cause of action independent from contract breach.[19] The separate tort of negligent misrepresentation (normally also alleging economic damages) may be asserted against owners, design professionals, specialty contractors, and suppliers—any project participant who disseminates information.[20] Although these economic torts have been bemoaned by a number of commentators,[21] they have not afflicted the construction industry alone. Many states have adopted the Restatement (Second) of Torts, allowing negligence-based causes of action for economic damages in business transactions involving appraisers,[22] building

---

16. *See* discussion in Chapter 9 of this text at 330; *see also* authorities cited at West's ⊕⇒ 272 NEGLIGENCE, k463.

17. *See, e.g.,* Murray H. Wright & Edward E. Nicholas, *The Collision of Tort and Contract in the Construction Industry,* 21:3 U. RICH. L. REV. 457 (1987).

18. *See* discussion in Chapter 9 of this text.

19. *See* Olympic Prods. Co. v. Roof Sys., Inc., 363 S.E.2d 367 (N.C. Ct. App.), *cert. denied,* 366 S.E.2d 862 (N.C. 1988); *see also* authorities cited at West's ⊕⇒ 313A PRODUCTS LIABILITY, k42.

20. RESTATEMENT (SECOND) OF TORTS § 552 (1977) [hereinafter RESTATEMENT], entitled "Information Negligently Supplied for the Guidance of Others;" *see also* authorities cited at West's ⊕⇒ 184 FRAUD, k45.

21. *See, e.g.,* JUSTIN SWEET, SWEET ON CONSTRUCTION LAW §§ 4.10, 11.13 (1997); Steven G. M. Stein, Paul Cottrell & Mark C. Friedlander, *A Blueprint for the Duties and Liabilities of Design Professionals after Moorman,* 60 CHI.-KENT L. REV. 163 (1984).

22. Private Mortgage Inv. Servs., Inc. v. Hotel & Club Assocs., Inc., 296 F.3d 308 (4th Cir. 2002).

inspectors,[23] and construction managers,[24] as well as lawyers[25] and accountants,[26] despite lack of privity.

Because this text concerns construction damages for construction participants, more emphasis is placed upon recovery of economic damages, as opposed to personal injuries or even property damages.[27] This chapter will also discuss fraud, strict liability for construction accidents, interference with contractual relations, and new uses for the traditional torts of trespass and nuisance. Finally, this chapter will comment on the state of the law relating to the liability of sureties for independent tortious actions in responding to bond claims by obligees and third-party beneficiaries.

NEGLIGENT MISREPRESENTATION BY OWNERS: ECONOMIC DAMAGES

Because owners are generally not participants in the actual construction work, tortious acts by an owner in the construction process most often take the form of negligent misrepresentation.[28] The tort of negligent misrepresentation is

---

23. Thompson v. Waters, 526 S.E.2d 650 (N.C. 2000).

24. EH Constr. LLC v. Delor Design Group, Inc., No. 1998-CA-001476-NR, 2000 WL 339939 (Ky. Ct. App. March 31, 2000).

25. See Mozzochi v. Beck, 529 A.2d 171, 175 (Conn. 1987) ("courts generally now permit actions for professional malpractice without reference to privity, so long as the plaintiff is the intended or foreseeable beneficiary of the professional's [here, a lawyer's] undertaking"); Rozny v. Marnul, 250 N.E.2d 656 (Ill. 1969); Orshoski v. Krieger, No. OT-01-009, 2001 WL 1388037 (Ohio Ct. App. Nov. 9, 2001), appeal denied, 763 N.E.2d 1185 (Ohio 2002) ("The requirement of privity in a legal malpractice action [for negligent misrepresentation] should be put to a well-deserved burial"); Bradford Sec. Processing Services, Inc. v. Plaza Bank & Trust, 653 P.2d 188 (Okla. 1982). But see Bovee v. Gravel, No. 2001-347, 2002 WL 1940968 (Vt. Aug. 13, 2002).

26. United States v. Natelli, 527 F.2d 311 (2d Cir. 1975), cert. denied, 425 U.S. 934 (1976); Fisher v. Katz, 266 F. Supp. 180 (S.D.N.Y. 1976); Sharp v. Coopers & Lybrand, 83 F.R.D. 343 (E.D. Pa. 1974); Credit Alliance Corp. v. Arthur Andersen & Co., 483 N.E.2d 110 (N.Y. 1985) (accountants were liable in negligence to "noncontractual parties" who relied to their detriment on inaccurate, negligently prepared reports). But see Semida v. Rice, 863 F.2d 1156, 1160 (4th Cir. 1988); Smullian & Blumenthal, P.A. v. Futz, 762 A.2d 582 (Md. 2000).

27. For an excellent treatise on the law governing personal injuries on construction projects, see MARC M. SCHNEIER, CONSTRUCTION ACCIDENT LAW (1999); see also the discussion of the economic loss rule in Chapter 9 of this text.

28. An owner's acts toward a contractor, otherwise tortious, may also (and more readily) be termed breaches of contract, as the jurisprudential history of construction law reflects. Many tortious

articulated in Section 552 of the Restatement (Second) of Torts. Entitled "Information Negligently Supplied for the Guidance of Others," it states:

> [O]ne who, in the course of his business, profession or employment, or in any other transaction in which he has a pecuniary interest, supplies false information for the guidance of others in business transactions, is subject to liability for pecuniary loss caused to them by their justifiable reliance upon the information, if he fails to exercise reasonable care or competence in obtaining or communicating the information.

These claims were first fully articulated in American jurisprudence by a troika of opinions from the United States Supreme Court in the second decade of the twentieth century.[29] Although the facts involved the government owners' acts of "concealment" and "misrepresentation," accepted American tort law was not sufficiently developed to sanction a separate extracontractual cause of action.[30] And, as the parties were in privity, contract law was sufficient to allow compensatory damages for the misrepresentations.[31]

Many states today recognize both contract and tort remedies for business misrepresentations.[32] Many injured contractors opt to pursue contract rather than tort remedies for misrepresentations, especially in jurisdictions slow to accept tort concepts that parallel traditional contract remedies.[33] So long as there are no limiting contract provisions,[34] if the

---

acts within contractual relationships were redressed *ex contractu* until the acceptance of expanded tort responsibility with or without privity as espoused by the Restatement. *See* notes 29, 30, and 31, *infra*.

29. United States v. Atl. Dredging Co., 253 U.S. 1 (1920); Christie v. United States, 237 U.S. 234 (1915); Hollerbach v. United States, 233 U.S. 165 (1914). For an excellent description of the effect of these three cases in the development of American construction law, *see* PHILIP L. BRUNER & PATRICK J. O'CONNOR, JR., BRUNER AND O'CONNOR ON CONSTRUCTION LAW § 14:20 (2002).

30. *See, e.g., Christie v. United States, supra* note 29, where the Court stated: "There was a deceptive representation of the material, and it misled." The recovery awarded by the Court was, however, based in contract.

31. *Id.*

32. *See* authorities cited at West's ⊕══ 13 ACTION, k27(1).

33. *See, e.g.,* Morris, Inc. v. State, 598 N.W.2d 520 (S.D. 1999) (contract disclaimers are void when the DOT makes material representations; contract recovery allowed); *see also* authorities cited at West's ⊕══ 316A PUBLIC CONTRACTS, k16.

34. For instance, a specified, reduced overhead and profit percentage for changed or extra work.

contractor is in privity with the owner, there should be little if any difference in recoverable damages for an owner's negligent misrepresentation under tort or contract theories.

To state a tort claim for negligent misrepresentation by an owner, a contractor must prove that the owner supplied false information to the contractor for its use and upon which the contractor reasonably relied, and that the contractor suffered damages at the owner's project as a result.[35] Unlike negligent misrepresentation claims against design professionals and construction managers discussed below, the defense of lack of privity of contract is generally inapplicable in claims against owners. Most project participants who could receive and rely on owner-disseminated information are in privity of contract (or in the chain of privity) with the owner.

Contractors' negligent misrepresentation claims against owners (and the pass-through claims of their subcontractors) arise most often in the context of representations made by the owner or by the owner's agent about anticipated site conditions. A negligent misrepresentation made by an owner may be in the form of a positive representation or the omission of a material fact.[36]

To state a claim of negligent misrepresentation, the contractor must have reasonably relied upon the information provided by the owner and been misled by that information.[37] A contractor is entitled to rely on the owner's representations

---

35. *See, e.g.,* D.A. Elia Constr. Corp. v. N.Y. State Thruway Auth., 734 N.Y.S.2d 295 (App. Div. 2001); *see generally* RESTATEMENT § 552; *see also* authorities cited at West's ⊕⇒ 184 FRAUD, k64(1), ⊕⇒ 316A PUBLIC CONTRACTS, k16, ⊕⇒ 268 MUNICIPAL CORPORATIONS, k360(3), ⊕⇒ 200 HIGHWAYS, k113(4), ⊕⇒ 360 STATES, k104.

36. *See, e.g.,* Sanders Co. Plumbing & Heating, Inc. v. City of Independence, 694 S.W.2d 841 (Mo. Ct. App. 1985) (city provided contractor with inaccurate soil condition data upon which contractor relied in formulating its bid). *But see* Panamint, Inc., 87-2 BCA ¶ 19,927 (ENG BCA1987) (the government's failure to warn of high concentrations of poison oak and ivy in an area to be cleared by the contractor was not actionable misrepresentation because this undisclosed information was not information that the contractor could not otherwise obtain from other accessible sources).

37. D. Federico Co. v. New Bedford Redevelopment Auth., 723 F.2d 122 (1st Cir. 1983); Umpqua River Navigation Co. v. Crescent City Harbor Dist., 618 F.2d 588 (9th Cir. 1980); *see* authorities cited at West's ⊕⇒ 184 FRAUD, k13(3).

unless inaccuracy of the representation is subjectively known or obvious to the contractor.[38] A contractor cannot be said to have detrimentally relied upon a misrepresentation by an owner where the contractor either knows the true facts or has a reasonable opportunity to ascertain the truth of the representation.[39] This is true whether the contractor pursues a contract or tort damage theory.

Reliance is a thorny issue for contractors asserting negligent misrepresentation claims. Courts recognize that owners generally are not in the business of construction, and contractors are. Contractors are often required by courts to anticipate site and other construction problems, and to ask questions. A contractor's reliance will be acknowledged judicially where circumstances dictate that the contractor was not in a position to assume responsibility for investigation of site conditions or to verify the owner's representations. Such circumstances commonly occur when project time constraints do not allow the contractor sufficient time to make an independent investigation[40] or where a pre-bid inspection would not have revealed the inaccuracy of the owner's representations.[41]

To limit a contractor's ability to rely on alleged representations made by the owner, owners often include in their contracts provisions exculpating themselves from responsibility for erroneous information.[42] The owner may include,

---

38. Chris Berg, Inc. v. Acme Min. Co., 893 F.2d 1235 (11th Cir. 1990); *see also* authorities cited at West's ⊕═ 184 FRAUD, k20.

39. McDevitt & Street Co. v. Marriott Corp., 713 F. Supp. 906 (E.D.Va. 1989), *aff'd in part, rev'd in part*, 911 F.2d 723 (4th Cir. 1990), *on remand*, 754 F. Supp. 513 (E.D.Va. 1991) (contractor's reliance on owner's soils reports held insufficient to support extra work claim where contractor did not perform pre-bid investigation); *see also* authorities cited at West's ⊕═ 95 CONTRACTS, k232.

40. *See* Thomas M. Durkin & Sons v. Dep't of Transp., 742 A.2d 233 (Pa. Commw. Ct. 1999) (no reasonable way for contractor to perform pre-bid test, which would have revealed errors); *see also* authorities cited at West's ⊕═ 316A PUBLIC CONTRACTS, k21.

41. *See* Sherman R. Smoot Co. v. Ohio Dep't of Admin. Servs., 736 N.E.2d 69 (Ohio Ct. App. 2000) (the court allowed contractor to recover although he failed to conduct a pre-bid investigation because such investigation would not have revealed conditions encountered); *see also* Stanford v. Owens, 332 S.E.2d 730 (N.C. Ct. App.), *cert. denied*, 336 S.E. 2d 402 (N.C. 1985); authorities cited at West's ⊕═ 360 STATES, k108.

42. Such clauses tend (1) to make reports of site conditions available but not a part of the contract documents, (2) to have the contractor acknowledge that there will be errors and variations

(continued)

in its bid documents or in the contract, a provision that attempts to shift site liability by obligating the contractor to investigate site conditions. The success of exculpatory clauses depends largely on the specificity of the clause and the type of problem encountered.[43] Where a reasonable inspection by the contractor would not have disclosed the inaccuracy of the owner's representation, an exculpatory clause may not effectively prevent the contractor's claims based on the representation.[44] In at least one instance, a finding of an "industry practice" of contractors' relying on soil condition data from project owners has been held to trump an owner's disclaimer of accuracy of data provided in bid documents.[45] Contractor damages flowing from an owner's misrepresentation include the increased cost to perform the affected work, delay damages, and lost profits.[46]

Negligent Misrepresentation by Design Professionals and Other Project Participants: Economic Damages

Design professionals are subject to liability under Restatement Section 552 for negligent communication of inaccurate information. One of the more analytical discussions of the policy concerns underlying this tort in the construction setting is found in the *Lansdowne* decision from the United States District Court for the Eastern District of Pennsylvania.[47]

---

between the information in the report and actual conditions, and (3) to have the contractor agree that no claim for extras will be made (at least against the owner) due to an inaccuracy within the report.

43. *See* P.T. & L. Constr. Co. v. State, 531 A.2d 1330, 1335–36 (N.J. 1987); *see also* Ruby-Collins, Inc. v. City of Charlotte, 740 F. Supp. 1159 (W.D.N.C. 1990).

44. Grow Constr. Co. v. State, 391 N.Y.S.2d 726 (App. Div. 1977).

45. Sanders Co. Plumbing & Heating, Inc. v. City of Independence, 694 S.W.2d 841 (Mo. Ct. App. 1985).

46. *See* State Rd. Dep't v. Houdaille Ind., 237 So.2d 270 (Fla. Dist. Ct. App. 1970) (method changed from bulldozers to draglines on mats); P. T. & L. Constr. Co. v. State, 531 A.2d 1330 (N.J. 1987). *But see* Green Constr. Co. v. Kansas Power & Light Co., 732 F. Supp. 1550 (D. Kan. 1990) (equitable relief only was recoverable under contractor's negligent misrepresentation claim; to recover more than equitable relief, the contractor had to prove that the owner had committed fraud upon the contractor).

47. Borough of Lansdowne, Pa. v. Sevenson Envt'l Servs., Inc., No. 99-3781, 2000 WL 1886578 (E.D. Pa., December 12, 2000).

In *Lansdowne*, the excavation subcontractor successfully maintained a Section 552 negligent misrepresentation claim against the owner's engineer. Inaccurate plans failed to show the proper location of utility lines, and when the subcontractor was held accountable by the municipality for damage to the lines, the subcontractor impleaded the engineer. The court brushed aside the engineer's lack-of-privity defense, stating that contractual privity had no place in a Section 552 negligent misrepresentation case. The tort limitation on the class of potential plaintiffs—those who were intended to use the engineer's information and who reasonably relied upon such information—was sufficient for the court. The court concluded that this result did not undermine legal policy considerations that support the privity requirement in contract actions.[48]

There are several hidden legal and factual obstacles to making a negligent misrepresentation case against a design professional. The first is the requirement to prove the element of false or inaccurate information. A design professional's erroneous prediction or opinion may not be sufficient to support the tort. Specifications prepared by design professionals, unless they contain specific measurements or other facts susceptible of actual knowledge, will often not support a claim of negligent misrepresentation.[49] When courts

---

48. *See also* Aliberti, LaRochelle & Hodson Eng'g Corp. v. FDIC, 844 F. Supp. 832 (D. Me. 1994); Hewett-Kier Constr., Inc. v. Lemuel Ramos & Assocs., Inc., 775 So. 2d 373 (Fla. Dist. Ct. App. 2000) (defective plans prepared by a design professional for an owner were known to be for use by bidding contractors). *But see* Tolan & Son, Inc. v. KLLM Architects, Inc., 719 N.E.2d 288 (Ill. App. Ct. 1999) (the job of a design professional is to design a structure rather than to provide information; providing information was incidental to the designer's business and therefore outside RESTATEMENT § 552).

49. *See* Guardian Constr. Co. v. Tetra Tech Richardson, Inc., 583 A.2d 1378 (Del. Super. Ct. 1990); *see also* authorities cited at West's ☞ 184 FRAUD, k11(1). Some jurisdictions hold that erroneous information in plans and specifications is incidental to the primary purpose of the architect's work, and therefore outside the scope of § 552 of the Restatement. This is especially important in Illinois and states following Illinois in recognizing an exception to the economic loss rule for the tort of negligent misrepresentation. Rankow v. First Chicago Corp., 870 F.2d 356 (7th Cir. 1989); Moorman Mfg. Co. v. Nat'l Tank Co., 435 N.E.2d 443 (Ill. App. Ct. 1982); *see also* authorities cited at West's ☞ 184 FRAUD, k25.

hold design professionals liable, it is most often when the design professional knew or should have known that the information was inaccurate at the time it was communicated.[50]

Second, as with other claims of negligence against a design professional, expert testimony is required to establish the applicable standard of care in communicating information. In *Dickerson Int'l, Inc. v. Klockner*,[51] a developer claimed that the engineer was professionally negligent in failing to make an adequate investigation with respect to the true location of the hundred-year flood plain, and that the engineer had negligently misrepresented the number of lots that would require flood insurance. The court held that the plaintiff developer's failure to present expert testimony as to what test or investigation a civil engineer should have performed was fatal to both the negligence count and the negligent misrepresentation count.[52]

Third, it is important to look to the duties undertaken by the design professional in its contract. If it was not within the design professional's scope of services to provide information, then the fact that the information was inaccurate may be irrelevant.[53] Proving this tort against design professionals involves mixed and complex questions of law and fact. Many courts are sensitive to the argument that the design professional's standard of care must be commensurate with the duties assumed.[54]

If the communication of information was material, was within the scope of the design professional's services, was related to a present or pre-existing fact, and was reasonably relied upon,[55] the design professional can be liable. Thus,

---

50. *See* Nota Constr. Corp. v. Keyes Assocs., 694 N.E.2d 401 (Mass. App. Ct. 1998).

51. 743 N.E.2d 984 (Ohio Ct. App. 2000).

52. *Id.; see also* authorities cited at West's ⊕══ 184 FRAUD, k58(2).

53. *See* Tolan & Son, Inc. v. KLLM Architects, Inc., 719 N.E.2d 288 (Ill. App. Ct. 1999).

54. *See, e.g.,* Williams & Sons Erectors v. S. C. Steel, 983 F.2d 1176 (2d Cir. 1993) (architect owed no duty to contractor); *see also* authorities cited at West's ⊕══ 184 FRAUD, k25.

55. *See, e.g.,* Technologies, Inc. v. Sverdrup & Parcel, Inc., 739 P.2d 1318 (Ariz. Ct. App. 1986) (no reliance).

where an engineering company falsely represented a new construction budget to a bank, knowing it was wrong at the time,[56] or where a consultant falsely indicated that extra work would be paid for pursuant to the contract,[57] or when an engineer failed to adequately perform soil compaction tests,[58] courts have held design professionals liable, notwithstanding lack of privity.[59]

The tort of negligent misrepresentation can lie whether or not the injured party has a contract with the information-disseminating party.[60] The Restatement of Torts also makes it clear that direct communication of the information is not necessary.[61] Potential liability for nondirected communication is particularly significant within the construction setting, where subcontractors routinely receive information generated by a design professional but delivered through the owner and general contractor. Likewise, manufacturers may deliver information to design professionals that may later be relied upon by owners. And it is not necessary for the party providing the information to know the identity of its recipient; the identity of the class of those who were intended to receive and use the information is normally sufficient.[62]

Construction managers have proven to be attractive targets for negligent misrepresentation claims. One of the earlier opinions allowing the cause of action in the construction setting concerned a construction manager. In *John Martin*

---

56. Aliberti, LaRochelle & Hodson Eng'g Corp. v. FDIC., 844 F. Supp. 832 (D. Me. 1994).

57. Foster Wheeler Enviresponse, Inc. v. Franklin County Convention Facilities Auth., 623 N.E2d 134 (Ohio Ct. App. 1993).

58. AAA Excavating, Inc. v. Francis Constr., Inc., 678 S.W.2d 889 (Mo. Ct. App. 1984).

59. *See also* Jim's Excavating Service, Inc. v. HKM Assocs., 878 P.2d 248 (Mont. 1994); John Martin Co. v. Morse/Diesel, Inc., 819 S.W.2d 438 (Tenn. 1991).

60. *See* authorities cited at West's ⚖ 184 FRAUD, k13(3). If the party who receives and relies upon the information contracted directly with the person providing the information, the recipient could sue under the contract or for negligent misrepresentation.

61. RESTATEMENT § 552, cmt. g.

62. *Id.* cmt. h provides:
> It is enough that the maker of the representation intends it to reach and influence either a particular person or persons, known to him, or a group or class of persons, distinct from the much larger class, who might reasonably be expected sooner or later to have access to the information and foreseeably to take some action in reliance upon it.

Company v. Morse/Diesel, Inc.,[63] a subcontractor successfully maintained a negligent misrepresentation action against the construction manager arising from his actions in administering the project. This case is particularly noteworthy because there was no privity between the subcontractor and the construction manager, and the subcontractor had sustained only economic damages. The appellate court held that the economic loss rule did not apply. In Tennessee, at least, these two pillars of liability avoidance (lack of privity and the economic loss rule) are apparently unavailable to construction managers.[64]

The liability of other construction participants who provide inaccurate information will depend upon the circumstances. Manufacturers and suppliers who provide information touting their products may well be subject to liability in tort if their products don't deliver or are inappropriate for a particular application.[65] In some cases, the UCC disclaimers routinely used by manufacturers and distributors will not protect them. Of course, plaintiffs must still prove actual, reasonable reliance,[66] and that the products were properly installed in accordance with the manufacturers' instructions.[67] Further, a number of courts hold that if the recipient of information has the opportunity to make pertinent inquiries but fails to do so through no artifice or inducement of the provider, an action for negligent misrepresentation will not lie.[68]

63. 819 S.W.2d 428 (Tenn. 1991).

64. *Id; see also* EH Constr. LLC v. Delor Design Group, Inc., No. 1998-CA-001476-MR, 2000 WL 339939 (Ky. Ct. App. Mar. 31, 2000).

65. *See, e.g.,* Miller v. Big River Concrete, LLC, 14 S.W.3d 129 (Mo. Ct. App. 2000). This liability for negligent misrepresentation is separate from a products liability claim based on negligent manufacture, discussed below.

66. *See* Gawara v. United States Brass Corp., 74 Cal. Rptr. 2d 663, 669–70 (Cal. Ct. App. 1998) (homeowners and developers failed to show they relied, directly or indirectly, on the alleged misrepresentations of polybutylene plumbing sellers and manufacturers).

67. *See* Village of Cross Keys, Inc. v. United States Gypsum, 556 A.2d 1126, 1132 (Md. 1989) (plaintiffs could not recover for negligent misrepresentations in defendant's promotional publications when they did not follow specifications for product use in construction).

68. *See* Bloomsburg Mills, Inc. v. Sordoni Constr. Co., 164 A.2d 201 (Pa. 1960) (design professional should have tested and ascertained knowledge of performance characteristics of materials); *see also* Simms v. Prudential Life Ins. Co, 537 S.E.2d 237 (N.C. Ct. App. 2000); Libby Hill Seafood

Restatement Section 552 recognizes that a duty to be accurate in one's business information is a separate and independent duty outside of the contractual undertaking. Courts that recognize this independent tort duty typically give short shrift to the argument that the risk of tort liability was not part of or bargained for in the supplier/manufacturer's contract.[69]

NEGLIGENT DESIGN: ECONOMIC, PERSONAL INJURY AND PROPERTY DAMAGE

A design professional's liability in tort extends to project owners, other project participants, and certain other third parties. Although the focus here is on tort and negligence issues, the design professional's contract under which it performed the relevant work must also be examined. The scope of the design professional's contractual duties and responsibilities often plays a large role in determining the extent of the design professional's tort liability.[70]

Design professionals practice an inexact science. They are not required to perform to perfection, nor do they warrant that their drawings and specifications will be free from all defects.[71] Although a design professional may accept a higher

---

Restaurants, Inc. v. Owens, 303 S.E.2d 565 (N.C. Ct. App.), *review denied*, 307 S.E.2d 164 (N.C. 1983); authorities cited at West's 🔑 184 FRAUD, k22(1).

69. *See, e.g.*, State v. United States Steel Corp., 919 P.2d 294 (Haw. 1996) (manufacturer's letters to the architect touting its product, which proved defective when incorporated into the structure, were sufficient to support a negligent misrepresentation claim, with damages arising from the opinions and recommendations regarding the product. The economic loss rule did not apply. Conversely, the court noted that the economic loss rule would bar a claim based on negligent design or manufacture of the product). *But see* Wausau Tile, Inc. v. County Concrete Corp., 593 N.W. 2d 445 (Wis. 1999) (purchasing manufacturer has no claim in tort against supplier of defective goods for purely economic losses); Marvin Lumber and Cedar Company v. PPG Industries, Inc., 223 F.3d 873 (8th Cir. 2000) (applying Minnesota law, if the alleged tort violation concerns the subject of the contract, no independent tort remedy will be for economic damages).

70. *See generally* the discussion in Chapter 7 of this text., and authorities cited at West's 🔑 184 FRAUD, k25. The design professional's scope of services is also important in the design/build situation. *See* C.L. Maddox, Inc. v. Benham Group, Inc., 88 F.3d 592 (8th Cir. 1996) (engaged to keep contractor informed of the progress and quality of the work, the architect assumed no liability or responsibility for the quality of the design/build contractor's work; held, no recovery).

71. *See, e.g.*, Nelson v. Commonwealth, 368 S.E.2d 239 (Va. 1988); *see also* Chapter 7 of this text. *But see* Broyles v. Brown Eng'g Co., 151 So.2d 767, 770 (Ala. 1963) (opining that engineer's

(continued)

standard of care or responsibility by contract,[72] the usual standard of performance is equal to that expected generally from design professionals similarly situated in the particular community where the services are provided.[73] Performance below this standard of care is likely to expose the design professional to liability.[74] Proof of conduct failing to meet the standard of care, however, generally requires expert testimony from one of the design professional's peers.[75]

This standard applies to all to whom the design professional may owe a duty of care. Many courts hold that the duty of care extends beyond those entities with which the design professional is in privity of contract.[76] The duty of care extends to entities or persons who may foreseeably be injured by the design professional's negligence. That class

---

design agreement created an implied warranty of "sufficiency and adequacy of the plans and specifications to reasonably accomplish the purpose for which they were intended"); Tamarac Dev. Co. v. Delamater, Freund & Assocs., P.A., 675 P.2d 361 (Kan. 1984) (upholding claim against architect for implied warranty of workmanlike result).

72. *See, e.g.,* Chesapeake Paper Prods. Co. v. Stone & Webster Eng'g Corp., 51 F.3d 1229 (4th Cir. 1995); Town of Breckenridge v. Golforce, 851 P.2d 214 (Colo. Ct. App. 1992).

73. *See* City of Eveleth v. Ruble, 225 N.W.2d 521 (Minn. 1974), authorities cited at West's ☞ 272 NEGLIGENCE, k322, k1205; *see also* C. A. FOSTER, RICHARD D. CONNER, ET AL., CONSTRUCTION AND DESIGN LAW § 4.6(a)2 (1991): "The classic statement of the professional standard of care is that a design professional must possess that degree of skill and learning ordinarily exercised by other professionals of good standing in the community and must apply that knowledge with the diligence ordinarily exercised by reputable designers under similar circumstances."

74. *See* Reiman Constr. Co. v. Jerry Hiller Co., 709 P.2d 1271 (Wyo. 1985) (architect and structural engineer breached duty to owner of new building and were negligent in failing to design the building to account for the soil conditions made known to them by the soils engineer).

75. *See* Annotation, *Expert Testimony—Architect's Malpractice,* 3 A.L.R. 4th 1023 (1981); *see also* Hernandez v. Flor, No. 01-0183 (PAM/RLE), 2003 U.S. Dist. LEXIS 1782 (D. Minn. Jan. 16, 2003) (proponents of expert witness must prove admissibility by a preponderance of evidence and demonstrate to the court that the evidence is "grounded in the methods and procedures of science." *Daubert* provides six nonexclusive factors for courts to consider in determining admissibility; if the court determines that some or all of the factors are absent, but that the expert should be permitted to testify, the absence of some factors goes to the weight of the expert testimony); Walker v. Bluffs Apartments, 477 S.E.2d 472 (S.C. 1996) (testimony from a licensed residential builder and licensed building inspector was insufficient to establish breach of professional standard of care against architect); authorities cited at West's ☞ 272 NEGLIGENCE, k1662, k1672, k1675.

76. *See, e.g.,* Duncan v. Missouri Bd. for Architects, Prof'l Eng'rs & Land Surveyors, 744 S.W.2d 524 (Mo. Ct. App. 1988) (*in dicta*); Ralph L. Kaskell, Jr., *A Post Mortem of a Post Mortem: The Hyatt Collapse—A Post Mortem,* 12:1 CONSTR. LAW. 9 (Jan. 1992); Michael S. Zetlin, *Contractor v. Design Professional Lawsuits: Unnecessary for Contractors and Perilous for Design Professionals,* 12:3 CONSTR. LAW. 14 (Aug. 1992); *see also* BRUNER & O'CONNOR, *supra* note 29, § 17:19, and cases cited therein.

includes entities or persons involved with the actual construction of the project—the contractor or subcontractor who relied on the design professional's negligent design, and workers who are injured while performing work based on the negligent design. [77]

It is foreseeable that the contractor or subcontractor who performs in accordance with the design professional's drawings and specifications will be harmed economically if the drawings or specifications are defective.[78] Whether the contractor can recover against the design professional is another matter. Some courts allow professional negligence claims by project participants where privity is lacking and where only economic damages are alleged.[79] Other courts do not, based on either lack of privity[80] or the bar of the economic loss rule.[81]

It is likewise foreseeable that if the architect undertakes to review and certify monthly pay applications, the architect's overcertifications may harm the owner,[82] and the architect's

---

77. If a design professional has accepted a higher standard of care by contract, however, courts generally do not apply that increased responsibility to those not in privity with the design professional. *See* Peter Kiewit Sons' Co. v. Iowa S. Utils. Co., 355 F. Supp. 376, 379 (S.D. Iowa 1973).

78. The contractor's cost to perform the work within the scope of its contract will generally increase, as may the time required to perform the work.

79. *See, e.g.*, Affholder, Inc. v. Preston Carroll Co., 27 F.3d 232 (6th Cir. 1994); S.K. Whitty & Co. v. Laurence L. Lambert & Assocs., 576 So.2d 599 (La. Ct. App. 1991); Waldor Pump & Equip. Co. v. Orr-Schelen-Mayeron & Assocs., 386 N.W.2d 375 (Minn. Ct. App. 1986); Shoffner Indus., Inc. v. W.B. Lloyd Constr. Co., 257 S.E.2d 50 (N.C. Ct. App.), *cert. denied*, 259 S.E. 2d 301 (N.C. 1979); *see also* authorities cited at West's ⬥ 272 NEGLIGENCE k1205(4)(5), k1524(5); ⬥ 208 INDEMNITY, k67.

80. *See* Bryant Elec. Co. v. City of Fredericksburg, 762 F.2d 1192 (4th Cir. 1985) (court affirmed dismissal of contractor's suit against architect alleging negligent design, applying Virginia law requiring privity of contract between contractor and architect); Blake Constr. Co. v. Alley, 353 S.E.2d 724 (Va. 1987); *see also* authorities cited at West's ⬥ 272 NEGLIGENCE, k481; ⬥ 379 TORTS, k20, 272.

81. *See, e.g.*, 2314 Lincoln Park W. Condo. Ass'n v. Mann, Gin, Ebel & Frazier, Ltd., 555 N.E.2d 346 (Ill. 1990); *see also* authorities cited at West's ⬥ 272 NEGLIGENCE, k463, k1205(4)(5). Interestingly, Illinois allows a negligent misrepresentation claim by those not in privity with a design professional where only economic losses are alleged. *See* Moorman Mfg. Co. v. National Tank Co., 435 N.E.2d 443 (Ill. 1982) (permitting recovery for pecuniary losses based upon negligent and intentional misrepresentation). A more thorough discussion of the economic loss rule is found in Chapter 9 of this text.

82. *See* the discussion in Chapter 7 of this text concerning the design professional's contract liability to the owner.

undercertifications may harm contractors, subcontractors, and their sureties.[83] The architect's negligent approval of payment applications has been the basis of successful claims, despite the lack of privity between the architect and the claimant.[84] In a recent case, a subcontractor successfully stated a cause of action against the project architect who was aware that the general contractor had failed to furnish the payment bond required by Oklahoma's Little Miller Act.[85] Other areas of contract administration also present risks for design professionals. Negligent inspection or supervision of the work can be a source of liability.[86]

Germane to all forms of designer negligence is the scope of work undertaken by the design professional. This is especially true in actions involving allegedly negligent contract administration.[87] The current versions of the American Institute of Architects (AIA) form contract documents, specifically the contracts between owner and architect and between owner and general contractor, expressly limit the role and responsibilities of the project architect during contract administration.[88] Revisions to the AIA standard form documents over the years have continually narrowed the scope of the architect's responsibilities during construction. "Construction administration" became "contract administration." The architect's role "to supervise" at the site became "to inspect"

---

83. *See, e.g.*, RPR & Assocs. v. O'Brien/Atkins Assocs., P.A., 921 F. Supp. 1457 (M.D.N.C. 1995), *aff'd*, 103 F.3d 120 (4th Cir. 1996), 24 F. Supp. 2d 515, 524 (M.D.N.C. 1998) (architect liable to contractor for erroneous refusal to issue certificates of completion or payment).

84. *Id; see also* In re Designed Ventures, Inc., 132 B.R. 677 (Bankr. R. I. 1991); Westerhold v. Carroll, 419 S.W.2d 73 (Mo. 1967); authorities cited at West's 🔑 272 NEGLIGENCE, k1205(4); 🔑 95 CONTRACTS, k186(1).

85. Boren v. Thompson & Assocs., 999 P.3d 438 (Okla. 2000).

86. *See, e.g.*, Aetna Ins. Co. v. Hellmuth, Obata & Kassabaum, 392 F.2d 472 (8th Cir. 1968); U.R.S. Co. v. Gulfport-Biloxi Reg'l Airport Auth., 544 So.2d 824 (Miss. 1989); Davidson & Jones, Inc. v. County of New Hanover, 255 S.E.2d 580 (N.C. Ct. App.), *cert. denied*, 259 S.E.2d 911 (N.C. 1979); *see also* authorities cited at West's 🔑 272 NEGLIGENCE, k1205(4)(5).

87. *See, e.g.*, Ins. Co. of N. Am. v. Town of Manchester, 17 F. Supp. 2d 81 (D. Conn. 1998).

88. *See, e.g.*, AIA Document B141, Standard Form of Agreement Between Owner and Architect (1997 edition); AIA Document A201, General Conditions of the Contract for Construction (1997 edition).

and, later still, "to visit."[89] The risk allocation scheme within the AIA family of documents places the responsibility for quality and quantity of the work during construction squarely upon the contractor. The role of the architect during construction, as the owner's representative, is "not to make exhaustive or continuous on-site inspections to check the quality or quantity of the Work" but to "visit the site."[90] Nevertheless, where an engineer's duties on a unit-price sewer line project included a review of the amount of work for payment, and such review allowed overbilling by the contractor, the engineer was liable for the overcertification.[91]

Design professionals also have a duty to correct their design during the construction phase. This duty does not end until the building is completed and accepted.[92] On many projects, this issue arises during a communication exchange known as a request for information (RFI). Initiated by the contractor, an RFI results from a perceived need for a contractor to clarify or correct something about the design.[93] RFIs are a necessary component of today's construction process, especially given the design services being provided by multiple entities. Bifurcated design responsibility necessitates design coordination, and the RFI process, used properly, permits proper and timely attention to coordination issues. Design professionals are obligated to clarify and correct their design, and it typically makes no difference that their errors may derive from information provided by third parties.[94] The

---

89. See AIA Document B141, ¶ 2.6.2.1 (1997 edition); AIA Document A201, ¶ 4.2.2 (1997 edition).

90. *Id.*

91. American Fid. Fire Ins. Co. v. Pavia-Byrne Eng'g Corp., 393 So.2d 820 (La. Ct. App. 1981).

92. State v. Lundin, 459 N.Y.S.2d 904, 906 (App. Div.), *aff'd*, 459 N.E.2d 486 (N.Y. 1983); *see also* authorities cited at West's ☞ 241 LIMITATION OF ACTIONS, k46(6), k55(5).

93. RFIs are also a tool that may be used offensively by contractors to build a case for claimed extras. Many design professionals are suspicious of RFIs, especially those requesting seemingly obvious clarifications. Some cynically refer to these RFIs as "requests for income."

94. London Borough of Merton v. Low, 18 B.L.R. 130 (Ct. App. 1981). American Fid. Fire Ins. Co. v. Pavia-Byrne Eng'g Corp., 393 So.2d 820 (La. Ct. App. 1981).

rationale for the design professional's duty to correct is akin to the responsibility of accountants to correct errors in financial statements.[95]

The principal duty of design professionals, to correct their mistakes and coordinate design, runs to the owner. The duty also, however, runs to the public. An owner may decide that it is not worth the cost to provide the extra structural support required to protect against a twenty-year snowstorm, as opposed to a five-year snowstorm. As between the owner and architect, if the owner knowingly refuses to follow the architect's recommendation to correct the design, the owner releases the architect from responsibility.[96] Unknowing third persons, however, killed or injured when a roof loaded with a twenty-year storm collapses upon them, are not bound by the owner's release. Design professionals have an independent obligation to exercise due care in designing a structure.[97] This obligation is generally nondelegable by design professionals-of-record.[98] In the hypothetical posed above, the architect may have a duty to notify the appropriate authorities.

Actions by construction workers against design professionals for personal injuries incurred as a result of negligent design are often less successful than contractors' economic damage actions against design professionals.[99] There are two reasons for this difference. The first is that a worker's personal injury is often found not to be a foreseeable occurrence. The second, and probably more common, reason is

---

95. *See, e.g.*, United States v. Natelli, 527 F.2d 311, 319 (2d Cir. 1975), *cert. denied*, 425 U.S. 934 (1976); Fisher v. Katz, 266 F. Supp. 180, 184–89 (S.D.N.Y. 1976).

96. *See* Greenhaven Corp. v. Hutchcraft & Assocs., Inc., 463 N.E.2d 283 (Ind. Ct. App. 1984); Bowman v. Coursey, 433 So.2d 251 (La. Ct. App. 1983); *see also* authorities cited at West's ⟠ 95 CONTRACTS, k280(4).

97. SWEET, *supra* note 5, §§ 7.03C, 17.09D; *see also* Duncan v. Mo. Bd. for Architects, Prof. Eng'rs & Land Surveyors, 744 S.W.2d 524 (Mo. Ct. App. 1988); authorities cited at West's ⟠ 95 CONTRACTS, k280(4), k322(4).

98. SWEET, *supra* note 5, § 15.10B.

99. Assuming, of course, that the contractor's economic damage action is asserted in a jurisdiction that does not apply the economic loss rule in favor of design professionals. *See* Chapter 9 of this text.

that the purported design error or deficiency is found to involve services beyond the scope of the design professional's contract. That is, a construction worker is more likely to be injured as a result of breach by a contractor or subcontractor, usually of a duty within the scope of construction means or methods. Design professionals commonly have no responsibility for contractor means and methods.[100]

A third group of potential plaintiffs who may also have sustainable claims against a design professional for damages caused by the design professional's negligent design are collectively referred to as nonparticipants. This group includes visitors, tenants, and occupants of the completed improvement as well as adjacent landowners. Nonparticipants may bring claims against the design professional for the recovery of damages for personal injuries, property damage, and economic losses, including delay damages, cost to repair defective design, or lost profits. The same standard of care and foreseeability-of-injury analysis discussed at the outset of this chapter is applicable to claims brought by nonparticipants.[101]

The scope of the design professional's contractual undertaking is also relevant in determining the scope of the design professional's duty to nonparticipants. A design professional

---

100. *See, e.g.*, Nat'l Found. Co. v. Post, Buckley, Schuh & Jernigan, Inc., 465 S.E.2d 726 (Ga. Ct. App. 1995) (a contractor's employee, injured in a fall from a shoring wall, was owed no duty by the engineer who approved the shop drawing for the wall with regard to the placement of temporary handrails or barricades; the placement of temporary safety measure was the responsibility of the contractor while the design of the permanent structure was the responsibility of the engineer); McAninch v. Robinson, 942 S.W.2d 452 (Mo. Ct. App. 1997) (architect's scope of work did not include specifying a safe and proper method for excavation of a trench); Nicholson v. Turner/Cargile, 669 N.E.2d 529 (Ohio Ct. App. 1995); Rodriguez v. Universal Fastenings Corp., 777 S.W.2d 513 (Tex. App. 1989) (engineer was not charged with duty to determine whether the design and construction of forms were adequate to brace the work under construction). *But see* Caldwell v. Bechtel, Inc., 631 F2d 989 (D.C. Cir. 1980); Rian v. Imperial Mun. Servs. Group, Inc. 768 P.2d 1260 (Colo. Ct. App. 1988) (where architect had obligation to design stairs on which contractor's employee was injured, architect's negligent design could be actionable); Bennett v. Bank of Montreal, 590 N.Y.S.2d 98 (App. Div. 1992); *see also* authorities cited at West's ☞ 272 NEGLIGENCE, k1205(4)(5).

101. *See, e.g.*, Brown v. McBro Planning & Dev. Co., 660 F. Supp. 1333 (D.V.I. 1987) (hospital employee's personal injury claim arising from fall at hospital); Robert & Co. Assocs. v. Tigner, 351 S.E.2d 82 (Ga. Ct. App. 1986) (claim by motorist against engineer for defectively designed intersection); Bridgman v. Sanitary Dist., 517 N.E.2d 309 (Ill. App. Ct. 1987) (adjacent landowner's property damage claim for damage to landowner's water supply during sewer project); Francisco v. Manson,

(continued)

cannot be held liable for injuries resulting from design defects for which the design professional had no responsibility.[102] In *Title v. Giattina, Fisher & Co., Architects, Inc.*,[103] the estate of a prisoner sued the jail architect following the prisoner's suicide in the jail. The court held the architect owed no duty to the prisoner to design a suicide-proof jail. The architect's duty was to design a building (the jail) for its intended use.[104]

NEGLIGENT CONSTRUCTION: ECONOMIC DAMAGES

In any discussion of tort damages arising from negligent construction, situations where the project owner is the plaintiff should be considered separately from those where a third party is the plaintiff. This section will first discuss claims of negligence brought by the project owner, and follow that with a discussion of claims brought by third parties. Liability for personal injuries arising from negligent construction will be discussed later in this chapter in the section on site safety.

Negligence Claims Brought by Project Owner

In many cases, project owners will pursue tort claims against contractors and subcontractors for economic damages in addition to breach of contract and breach of warranty claims.[105] The elements of a negligent construction claim are the same

---

Jackson & Kane, Inc., 377 N.W.2d 313 (Mich. App. 1985) (architect that designed swim facility was liable to estate of diver injured in a fall from the diving platform. Although the diving platform design may have been proper for a competitive swimming facility, it was not proper for this recreational facility). *But see* Tahoe-Vinings v. Vinings Partners, 424 S.E.2d 30 (Ga. Ct. App. 1992) (purchasers of improved real property could not state negligence claim against project architect because the architect owed no duty to the purchasers).

102. *See, e.g.,* Hanselka v. Lummus Crest, Inc., 800 S.W.2d 665 (Tex. Ct. App. 1990); *see also* authorities cited at West's ⊕ 272 NEGLIGENCE, k1205(4)(5); ⊕ 95 CONTRACTS, k280(4).

103. 597 So.2d 679 (Ala. 1992).

104. *Id.; see also* La Bombarbe v. Phillips Swager Assocs., 474 N.E.2d 942 (Ill. App. Ct. 1985); authorities cited at West's ⊕ 95 CONTRACTS, k196.

105. *See* discussion in John W. Hays, *Construction Defect Claims Against Design Professionals and Contractors*, 22:2 CONSTR. LAW. 9 (Spring 2003).

as negligence claims in most contexts. The plaintiff must prove the existence of a duty of care owed to it by the defendant contractor or subcontractor, the breach of that duty of care, actual loss suffered by the plaintiff proximately caused by that breach, and foreseeability of injury to the plaintiff.[106]

For various reasons, an owner may decide to pursue a negligence action rather than a breach of contract or breach of warranty action. First may be the lack of privity of contract between the plaintiff and the defendant.[107] Second, the contractor with whom the owner is in privity may be judgment proof, and pursuing other defendants may be the only practical alternative. The presence of strict contractual notice provisions or liability limitations may also make a contract action either unfavorable or untenable.

The plaintiff owner must be careful not to confuse a potential negligence claim for economic damages with a claim for breach of contract or breach of warranty. Simple failure to perform one's contract, even carelessness, may not support a negligence action. Breach of a separate duty is generally required.[108] A plaintiff may bring both a claim for negligence and a breach of warranty claim arising from the same operative facts and injuries, but the pleadings should recognize and incorporate different elements.[109]

---

106. *See, e.g.,* Chenango County Ind. Dev. Agency v. Lockwood Greene Eng'rs, Inc., 494 N.Y.S.2d 832 (App. Div. 1985).

107. *See* Briggs v. Riversound Ltd. P'ship., 942 S.W.2d 529 (Tenn. Ct. App. 1996) (subsequent purchaser of house stated negligence claim against builder of house despite prior decisions barring subsequent purchasers from bringing breach of implied warranty claims against builders with whom they lacked privity).

108. *See* N.C. State Ports Auth. v. Lloyd A. Fry Roofing Co., 232 S.E.2d 846 (N.C. Ct. App. 1977), *aff'd,* 240 S.E.2d 345 (N.C. 1978), where the court declared that the negligent performance of a contract does not, as between contracting parties, generally give rise to a negligence action. The court went on to list four exceptions to this rule, including situations where personal injury or property damage occurred. *See also* authorities cited at West's ☞ 379 TORTS, k1, k3.

109. *See* Woodward v. Chirco Constr. Co., 687 P.2d 1269 (Ariz. 1984); Cosmopolitan Homes, Inc. v. Weller, 663 P.2d 1041 (Colo. 1983); Seely v. Loyd H. Johnson Constr. Co., 470 S.E.2d 283 (Ga. Ct. App. 1996); Keyes v. Guy Bailey Homes, Inc., 439 So. 2d 670 (Miss. 1983); Terlinde v. Neely, 271 S.E.2d 768 (S.C. 1980); *see also* authorities cited at West's ☞ 272 NEGLIGENCE, k219; West's ☞ 13 ACTION, k27(1).

Actionable common law breaches of tort duty in the construction setting have included the following: (a) a general contractor's failure to supervise,[110] (b) an owner's or contractor's failure to use due care in securing or recommending a competent consultant or subcontractor,[111] (c) a general contractor's failure to adequately hire competent subcontractors or to supervise them,[112] the failure of a contractor or subcontractor to follow applicable code requirements or perform the work in a workmanlike manner,[113] and the failure of a contractor or subcontractor to warn of the effects of its work or to select proper materials.[114]

Potential tort liability is especially important in the relationship between the project owner and subcontractors due to the absence of privity of contract between them. A subcontractor's deficient performance may elicit a breach of contract claim by the contractor. The same deficient performance may also give rise to a claim of negligence by the owner directly against the subcontractor.

The general contractor is liable in contract to the owner for the deficient or negligent work performed by its subcontractors.[115] The contractor may also be liable in tort, if a separate duty can be shown.[116] The contractor cannot escape liability to the owner under either theory by claiming

110. Hartrick Erectors, Inc. v. Maxson-Bets, Inc., 389 S.E.2d 607 (N.C. Ct. App. 1990).

111. See Kreekside Partners v. Nord Bitumi U.S., Inc., 963 F. Supp. 968 (D. Kan. 1997) (incompetent roofing contractor); Olympic Prods. Co. v. Roof Sys., Inc., 363 S.E.2d 367 (N.C. Ct. App.), cert. denied, 366 S.E.2d 862 (N.C. 1988); Deitz v. Jackson, 291 S.E.2d 282 (N.C. Ct. App. 1982).

112. Rainer Steel Erection v. York Constr. Co., 351 S.E.2d 136 (N.C. Ct. App. 1986); Sullivan v. Smith, 289 S.E.2d 870 (N.C. Ct. App.), review denied, 294 S.E. 2d 220 (N.C. 1982).

113. Oates v. JAG, Inc., 333 S.E.2d 222 (N.C.1985).

114. Edwards v. Hamill, 138 S.E.2d 151 (N.C. 1964); see also N.C. State Ports Auth. v. Lloyd A. Fry Roofing Co., 232 S.E.2d 846 (N.C. Ct. App. 1977), aff'd, 240 S.E.2d 345 (N.C. 1978), discussed at note 108, supra.

115. Point East Condo. Owners' Ass'n, Inc. v. Cedar House Assocs. Co., 663 N.E.2d 343 (Ohio Ct. App. 1995); accord, United States Fid. & Guar. Co. v. Jacksonville State Univ., 357 So. 2d 952 (Ala. 1978); see also authorities cited at West's 95 CONTRACTS, k189.

116. See Seely v. Loyd H. Johnson Constr. Co., 470 S.E.2d 283 (Ga. Ct. App. 1996) (jury question as to whether the contractor negligently failed to exercise reasonable degree of skill, care, and ability in directing and controlling the work of its subcontractors); see also authorities cited at West's 272 NEGLIGENCE, k1032, k1205(7).

that the work at issue was performed by an independent subcontractor.[117]

Historically, the contractor's completion of its work and the owner's acceptance of the work (absent contract terms providing otherwise) generally constituted a waiver of claims for damages resulting from negligent construction.[118] Numerous judicial exceptions to this rule have virtually negated its validity. The most commonly found exceptions to this rule are situations where:

- The completed work creates a condition that is inherently or imminently dangerous.[119]

- The completed work creates a condition that is reasonably certain to endanger third persons.[120]

- The contractor creates a latent defect that is either deliberately concealed by the contractor or not reasonably discoverable by the owner.[121]

- The work results in a public nuisance.[122]

Inasmuch as these exceptions have effectively nullified the rule, several jurisdictions have essentially abandoned it altogether and have adopted a rule of tort liability based on latency of defects and foreseeability of injury.[123] Under this

---

117. *Id.; see also* Brooks v. Hayes, 395 N.W.2d 167 (Wis. 1986); authorities cited at West's ⊕ 255 MASTER AND SERVANT, k318(1); ⊕ 95 CONTRACTS, k280(2).

118. *See, e.g.,* Counts v. MK-Ferguson Co., 680 F. Supp. 1343 (E.D. Mo. 1988); El Shorafa v. Ruprecht, 345 So. 2d 763 (Fla. Dist. Ct. App. 1977); PPG Indus., Inc. v. Genson, 217 S.E.2d 479 (Ga. Ct. App. 1975); *see also* authorities cited at West's ⊕ 272 NEGLIGENCE, k1205(8). This doctrine may be, and often is, altered by specific contract terms.

119. Bush v. SECO Elec. Co., 118 F.3d 519 (7th Cir. 1997); Price v. Wright Contracting Co., 359 S.E.2d 406 (Ga. Ct. App. 1987); Coleman v. City of Kansas City, 859 S.W.2d 141 (Mo. Ct. App. 1993); *see also* authorities cited at West's ⊕ 272 NEGLIGENCE, k1205(8).

120. Kristek v. Catron, 644 P.2d 480 (Kan. Ct. App. 1982); *see also* authorities cited at West's ⊕ 272 NEGLIGENCE, k1205(8).

121. Sanchez v. Swinerton & Walberg Co., 55 Cal. Rptr. 2d 415 (Cal. Ct. App. 1996); Pennington v. Cecil N. Brown Co., 371 S.E.2d 106 (Ga. Ct. App. 1988); *see also* authorities cited at West's ⊕ 272 NEGLIGENCE, k1205(8).

122. Chesser v. King, 428 S.W.2d 633 (Ark. 1968), *abrogated by* Suneson v. Holloway Constr. Co., 992 S.W.2d 79 (Ark. 1999); *see also* authorities cited at West's ⊕ 272 NEGLIGENCE, k1205(8); ⊕ 279 NUISANCE, k3(1).

123. *See, e.g.,* Suneson v. Holloway Constr. Co., 992 S.W.2d 79 (Ark. 1999) (but former rule reinstated as to public projects by ARK. CODE ANN. § 16-56-112(h) (2001 Supp)); Minton v. Krish,

(continued)

rule, a contractor may be liable for injuries and other damages arising after completion of its work and acceptance of the work by the owner to all who may foreseeably be harmed by the contractor's negligent performance.[124]

Negligence Claims Brought by Third Parties

A claim by a third party against a contractor or subcontractor for negligent construction not resulting in personal injury is subject to more limitations than negligent construction claims brought by the project owner. The primary difference between claims brought by the owner and claims brought by third parties is the greater burden of proof on the third party, and the application in many jurisdictions of the economic loss rule.[125]

The third party must first prove that its injury was a reasonably foreseeable consequence of the contractor's negligent conduct. In addition, the third party often has a more difficult time proving proximate causation than does the project owner. And as discussed above, even in jurisdictions where the economic loss rule does not apply,[126] where a negligent construction claim is brought against a contractor or subcontractor by a subsequent owner of the improved property, the subsequent owner will usually have to prove not only that

---

642 A.2d 18 (Conn. App. Ct. 1994); W.P. Johnson Props., Inc. v. Miller, 549 So.2d 213 (Fla. Dist. Ct. App. 1989) (contractor was not liable to third party for injuries occurring after the contractor has completed the work as long as the defective condition is patent); Jordan Demolition Corp. v. Jackson, 657 N.E.2d 450 (Ind. Ct. App. 1995); Lynch v. Norton Constr. Inc., 861 P.2d 1095 (Wyo. 1993). *But see* Coleman v. City of Kansas City, 859 S.W.2d 141 (Mo. Ct. App. 1993) (a contractor's liability to third parties extends beyond the date of the owner's acceptance of the work only when the work is so defective as to be imminently dangerous); *see also* authorities cited at West's ☞ 272 NEGLIGENCE, k1205(8).

124. *See, e.g.*, Council of Co-Owners Atlantis Condo., Inc. v. Whiting-Turner Contracting Co., 517 A.2d 336 (Md. 1986); Honey v. Barnes Hosp., 708 S.W.2d 686 (Mo. Ct. App. 1986); Oates v. JAG, Inc., 333 S.E.2d 222 (N.C. 1985); *see also* authorities cited at West's ☞ 272 NEGLIGENCE, k213, k1205, k1672.

125. *See* Aas v. Superior Court, 12 P.3d 1125 (Cal. 2000) (a landmark case holding that the economic loss rule prevents recovery in negligence for the cost of correcting construction defects that have not caused property damage). For discussions of the economic loss rule generally, see authorities cited at West's ☞ 272 NEGLIGENCE, k463.

126. See generally the discussion in Chapter 9 of this text.

the contractor caused the defects but also that the defects were latent or concealed in some manner.[127]

NEGLIGENCE AND STRICT LIABILITY IN THE MANUFACTURE OR SALE OF GOODS: PERSONAL INJURIES AND PROPERTY DAMAGES

Manufacturers and suppliers of goods intended for use in an improvement to real property are potentially liable to all those persons or entities foreseeably injured as a result of the manufacturers' or suppliers' actions or inactions.[128] The incorporation of the goods into the improvement prior to discovery of the defect generally does not affect the defendant's liability.[129]

There are several sources for this potential liability. The first is simple negligence in the manufacture or sale of the subject product. The second is strict product liability. Plaintiffs commonly allege causes of action based on both theories. Whereas liability in negligence requires proof of fault by the defendant, liability under a strict product liability claim does not. A manufacturer or seller is negligent when its product does not meet the manufacturer's specifications.[130] A manufacturer or seller is also negligent when it has knowledge of a latent defect rendering a product unsafe and fails to provide an adequate warning of such defect.[131]

---

127. *See* Cosmopolitan Homes, Inc. v. Weller, 663 P.2d 1041 (Colo. 1983); Briggs v. Riversound Ltd. P'ship, 942 S.W.2d 529 (Tenn. Ct.. App. 1996) (subsequent purchasers not barred from asserting negligence claim against builder for latent defects); *see also* authorities cited at West's ☞ 272 NEGLIGENCE, k1205(2).

128. *See* authorities cited at West's ☞ 313A PRODUCTS LIABILITY, k42.

129. *See* Philadelphia Nat'l Bank v. Dow Chem. Co., 605 F. Supp. 60 (E.D. Pa. 1985) (owner sued manufacturer of additive incorporated into mortar used by contractor on the masonry of the building).

130. *See* MacPherson v. Buick Motor Co., 111 N.E. 1050 (N.Y. 1916) (wheel failure tied to defective manufacture), and its progeny; *see also* authorities cited at West's ☞ 313A PRODUCTS LIABILITY, k8.

131. *See* Honey v. Barnes Hosp., 708 S.W.2d 686 (Mo. Ct. App. 1986) (window manufacturer was negligent in failing to manufacture windows with stops in them as required in the project specifications, and in failing to warn).

A manufacturer has a duty to give adequate warning of unreasonable danger involved in the normal use of its product where the manufacturer knows or should have known of the danger.[132] To recover on a strict liability claim, the plaintiff need only show the presence of a defect that was present when the product left the defendant's possession and that the defect was the proximate cause of the plaintiff's bodily injury or property damage.[133]

> Pursuant to Section 402A of the Restatement (Second) of Torts,
>
> (1) One who sells any product in a defective condition unreasonably dangerous to the user or consumer or to his property is subject to liability for physical harm thereby caused to the ultimate user or consumer, or to his property, if (a) the seller is engaged in the business of selling such a product, and (b) it is expected to and does reach the user or consumer without substantial change in the condition in which it is sold.
>
> (2) The rule stated in Subsection (1) applies although (a) the seller has exercised all possible care in the preparation and sale of his product, and (b) the user or consumer has not bought the product from or entered into any contractual relation with the seller.[134]

This form of liability applies only where the defendant has sold the alleged defective product in the ordinary course of its business, and does not extend liability to the occasional seller.[135]

In actions alleging a manufacturer's negligence that causes personal injury or property damage, defendants often rely on the lack of proximate causation and foreseeability to defeat claims. In actions where economic damages are alleged, man-

---

132. *See* Williams v. Airport Appliance & Floor Covering, Inc., 445 So.2d 764 (La. Ct. App. 1984); *see also* authorities cited at West's ⬤══ 313A PRODUCTS LIABILITY, k14.

133. *See* Zehring v. Wick Agri-Buildings, 590 F. Supp. 138 (N.D. Ohio 1984); *see also* authorities cited at West's ⬤══ 313A PRODUCTS LIABILITY, k42.

134. RESTATEMENT § 402A.

135. *See* Counts v. MK-Ferguson Co., 680 F. Supp. 1343 (E.D. Mo. 1988); *see also* authorities cited at West's ⬤══ 313A PRODUCTS LIABILITY, k62.

ufacturers need not search for flaws in a plaintiff's case. Instead, manufacturers can aggressively raise the shield of the economic loss rule. Stated simply, under this rule a party is not allowed to recover in tort or in strict liability for purely economic damages.[136] The rule is easiest to apply in product liability cases, where the rule originated,[137] but in a number of jurisdictions the rule has been extended to pure negligence actions against construction service providers, including design professionals,[138] contractors, and subcontractors.[139]

STRICT LIABILITY OF OWNERS, DESIGN PROFESSIONALS, CONTRACTORS AND SUBCONTRACTORS, AND LIABILITY IN NEGLIGENCE FOR SITE SAFETY

This chapter has previously discussed strict liability in tort for manufacturers and sellers of goods arising from Section 402A of the Restatement. Owners, design professionals, contractors, and subcontractors can also be strictly liable in the construction setting in cases of personal injury and property damage where the construction activities are abnormally dangerous[140] or the facts of the situation impose a specific duty upon a construction participant to provide a safe work environment for a specific class of individuals.

---

136. *See, e.g.,* Pulte Home Corp. v. Osmose Wood Preserving, Inc., 60 F.3d 734 (11th Cir. 1995) (builder's claim for defective fire retardant chemical as applied to plywood sheathing barred by rule); Livermore Amador Valley Wastewater Mgmt. Agency v. Northwest Pipe & Casing Co., 915 F. Supp. 1066 (N.D. Cal. 1995); Morris v. Osmose Wood Preserving, Inc., 667 A. 2d 624 (Md. 1995); *see also* authorities cited at West's ⬅ 272 NEGLIGENCE, k463.

137. Commentators mostly agree that today's economic loss rule was laid down in Seely v. White Motor Co., 403 P.2d 145 (Cal. 1965) (en banc), which involved the sale of a truck. At least one court has refused to apply the economic loss rule except in products cases. *See* State v. United States Steel Corp., 919 P.2d 294 (Haw. 1996).

138. *See, e.g.,* Rissler & McMurray Co. v. Sheridan Area Water Supply Joint Powers Bd., 929 P.2d 1228 (Wyo. 1996); *see also* Chapter 9 of this text.

139. *See* Aas v. Superior Court, 12 P.3d 1125 (Cal. 2000) (landmark case).

140. *See* RESTATEMENT § 520.

Owners and, to a lesser extent, contractors may insulate themselves from strict liability damages by contractual indemnity provisions, and except for ultrahazardous activities, by employing independent contractors who control the work environment for their employees.[141] Design professionals can position themselves still further from strict liability damages by requiring careful articulation (in the owner/design professional agreement and in the owner/contractor agreement) that others (generally contractors) are responsible for means and methods of the work, including the safety of those performing the work.[142]

Strict liability is imposed upon owners and contractors when the work involves ultrahazardous activities.[143] Owners and contractors sometimes select construction methods that are highly dangerous—to employees, adjoining landowners, and other third parties. The use of explosives is a notable example. Pile driving and certain demolition activities are others.[144] Liability for injuries caused by these ultrahazardous activities is often imposed even if the work is carried on with reasonable care.[145]

Excavation is another area where strict liability may be imposed. At common law, an excavating owner was liable, irrespective of negligence, for damages proximately caused by the excavation.[146] This was so even if an experienced inde-

---

141. See RESTATEMENT § 409; see also authorities cited at West's ⊕═ 255 MASTER AND SERVANT, k318(1).

142. In the 1997 revisions to the AIA family of standard form contracts, the architect is relieved of responsibility for safety and for construction means and methods by no less than a dozen provisions. See, e.g., AIA Document A201, General Conditions of the Contract for Construction Article 10 (all paragraphs), ¶¶ 3.18.1, 3.18.2, 4.22, 4.23 (1997 edition).

143. See also authorities cited at West's ⊕═ 272 NEGLIGENCE, k305, k1555.

144. Caporale v. C.W. Blakeslee & Sons, 175 A.2d 561 (Conn. 1961); Annotation, Liability for Property Damage by a Concussion from Blasting, 20 A.L.R.2D 1372 (1951).

145. The doctrine of strict liability for abnormally dangerous activities springs from an English case decided in 1868. In Rylands v. Fletcher, [1868] L.R. 3 H.L. 330, an owner's reservoir collapsed, filling up the shafts of an adjoining coal mine. Although the reservoir owners were not aware of the coal mining activities and were not found to be negligent, strict liability was imposed, similar to liability for trespassing cattle and dangerous animals. See also Walker F. Rucker, Jr., Liability of Owners and Contractors for Strict Liability Offenses During Construction, CONSTRUCTION LAW ADVISOR (Nov. 1985); authorities cited at West's ⊕═ 272 NEGLIGENCE, k305, k1555.

146. See also authorities cited at West's ⊕═ 15 ADJOINING LANDOWNERS, k3.

pendent contractor performed the work.[147] The Restatement modifies this strict liability slightly, so that both the owner and the "possessor" (typically, the contractor) of a construction site may be liable for failure to exercise reasonable care to warn people of the excavation and its possible consequences. The duty to warn carries increased significance in excavation situations if there are buildings or other improvements on the adjacent property.[148] Many courts today do not regard typical construction excavating as an ultrahazardous activity. Many modern cases apply a negligence standard for recovery of damages to adjacent property caused by excavation. Negligence may be based on a deviation from commonly accepted engineering practices.[149]

Construction owners may in some situations be subject by statute to additional safety obligations, whose violation can lead to strict liability in certain circumstances. Some statutes impose a general requirement to provide a safe workplace; others require compliance with specific safety regulations. Many states, and the U.S. Congress, have enacted statutes that require both.[150]

Generally, every employer owes a duty of reasonable care to protect its employees from recognized hazards likely to cause bodily injury, regardless of whether it controls a workplace, and to compensate an injured employee for work-related injury or illness.[151] Specific duty provisions (such as provided in 29 U.S.C. § 654(a)(2)) govern employers subject to OSHA regulations. These employers are those who

147. *See* Crnkovich v. Scaletta, 277 N.W.2d 416 (Neb. 1979).

148. RESTATEMENT § 370; *see also* authorities cited at West's 🔑 15 ADJOINING LANDOWNERS, k4(1).

149. *See, e.g.,* Spall v. Janota, 406 N.E.2d 378 (Ind. Ct. App. 1980); Hermanson v. Morrell, 252 N.W.2d 884 (N.D. 1977); *see also* authorities cited at West's 🔑 15 ADJOINING LANDOWNERS, k4(3).

150. *See, e.g.,* 29 U.S.C.A. § 654(a) (2000); CAL. LAB. CODE § 6400 *et seq.* (2003); MD. CODE ANN., LAB. & EMPL. § 5-104 (2002).

151. Of course, the dollar amount of an employer's liability is, for ordinary negligence, set by a state's workers' compensation acts. It takes an exceptional case, with intentional or reckless conduct, to create nonstatutory liability of an employer to its employee that exceeds workers' compensation recovery. *See, e.g.,* Woodson v. Rowland, 373 S.E.2d 674 (N.C. Ct. App. 1988) and cases cited therein; *see also* authorities cited at West's 🔑 413 WORKERS' COMPENSATION, k2084.

control the workplace, and their duty extends to all employees at the workplace, including those of an independent contractor who performs work there.[152]

If the only alleged violation by the owner or general contractor is its failure to provide a safe workplace, liability generally does not extend beyond injuries to the defendant's own employees. A subcontractor's employee is generally not entitled to recover for personal injuries against either the owner or the general contractor for the breach of a general duty to provide a safe workplace.[153]

The standards of the federal Occupational Safety and Health Administration permeate the construction industry. These standards are codified in Volume 29 of the Code of Federal Regulations (CFR). The list of required practices and safety devices contained within the CFR is meant to be illustrative only—it is by no means complete. States are free to promulgate their own statutes and regulations affecting construction work. Still, the violation of a safety standard does not necessarily give an injured worker the keys to a contractor's pickup truck. A plaintiff seeking recovery for violation of a safety statute generally must establish that (1) the statute was intended to protect the plaintiff, (2) the statute was intended to prevent the harm that actually occurred,[154] and (3) the violation proximately caused the injury.[155]

An owner who undertakes a construction project often has little or no experience with the construction process. Likewise, general contractors (and even construction man-

---

152. *See, e.g.,* Teal v. E.I. DuPont de Nemours & Co., 728 F.2d 799, 804–05 (6th Cir. 1984); *see also* authorities cited at West's ⬤➞ 272 NEGLIGENCE, k1037.

153. Adkins v. Aluminum Co. of Am., 750 P.2d 1257 (Wash. 1988); Bozung v. Condo. Builders, Inc., 711 P.2d 1090 (Wash. Ct. App. 1985); *see also* authorities cited at West's ⬤➞ 255 MASTER AND SERVANT, k316(1).

154. Schwartz v. Foley, 530 N.Y.S.2d 281 (App. Div. 1988) (owner of one- or two-family dwelling exempt from statute); Copertino v. Ward, 473 N.Y.S.2d 494 (App. Div. 1984) (owner not liable under New York labor law to workers for deficiency in independent contractor's plant tools and method of work).

155. *See* Buxton v. Amoco Oil Co., 676 F. Supp. 722 (W.D. La. 1987); Antunes v. 950 Park Ave. Corp., 539 N.Y.S.2d 909 (App. Div. 1989); *see also* authorities cited at West's ⬤➞ 272 NEGLIGENCE, k1204(5).

agers) are in some instances not particularly familiar with the intricacies of sophisticated building systems, such as fire alarm systems, fire sprinkler systems, and security systems. In each instance, the owner of the site, or the general contractor or construction manager as possessor of the site for the duration of the project, contracts with another party who has a specific expertise and the independence to carry out the specialty work. Where the owner or possessor of a site engages an independent entity to perform sophisticated work, the owner/possessor logically looks to the independent entity to be responsible for dangers associated with such work.

The "independent contractor rule," as judicially fashioned in the eighteenth and nineteenth centuries, and acknowledged in Restatement (Second) of Torts Section 409, holds that the employer of an independent contractor is not liable in tort for the physical harm (personal injury or property damage) caused to another by an act or omission of the independent contractor.[156] The rationale for the rule is based on control and expertise. Because the independent contractor has both control and expertise, it, rather than its customer, is the proper party to be charged with the responsibility of preventing harm.[157]

There are significant exceptions to this rule. The first exception is based on the responsibility of the owner or possessor (construction manager or general contractor) to select a competent independent contractor.[158] Allegations that the duty to select a competent contractor was breached generally take two forms. The breach of duty may be framed either as an end run around the independent contractor defense, or as a separate affirmative claim of actionable negligence.[159]

---

156. *See also* authorities cited at West's ⊕═ 255 MASTER AND SERVANT, k315.

157. RESTATEMENT § 409.

158. *See* RESTATEMENT §§ 411, 412; *see also* authorities cited at West's ⊕═ 255 MASTER AND SERVANT, k315.

159. *See, e.g.,* Olympic Prods. Co. v. Roof Sys., Inc., 363 S.E.2d 367 (N.C. Ct. App.), *cert. denied,* 366 S.E.2d 862 (N.C. 1988) (negligence of owner); Deitz v. Jackson, 291 S.E.2d 282 (N.C. Ct. App. 1982) (negligence of general contractor).

Proving negligent selection can be difficult, as few owners or general contractors desire, or willingly provide evidence that they recklessly hired, incompetent contractors or subcontractors. More importantly, there must be a causal connection between the lack of competence complained of and the injury.[160]

The second general exception to the independent contractor rule is that some activities, generally referred to as ultrahazardous activities or activities with extraordinary risk, carry risks that impose a higher standard of care. The risks of such activities are deemed to be nondelegable to an independent contractor.[161] Blasting,[162] the use of fire, and pile driving[163] are routinely considered ultrahazardous activities.

Restatement Section 520 lists six factors to be considered in determining whether an activity is abnormally dangerous. These factors are

1. Existence of high degree of risk of some harm to the person, land, or chattel of others

2. Likelihood that the harm that results will be great

3. Inability to eliminate the risk by the exercise of reasonable care

4. Extent to which the activity is not a matter of common usage

5. Inappropriateness of the activity to the place where it is carried on

6. Extent to which the value to the community is outweighed by its dangerous attributes[164]

---

160. *See* RESTATEMENT § 411, cmt. b; *see also* Levy v. Currier, 587 A.2d 205 (D.C. 1991); authorities cited at West's 255 MASTER AND SERVANT, k315.

161. *See* RESTATEMENT § 423; *see also* authorities cited at West's 255 MASTER AND SERVANT, k319.

162. Correa v. Curbey, 605 P.2d 458 (Ariz. 1979) ("blasting is the paradigm case of an abnormally dangerous activity…"). *But see* RESTATEMENT § 520, which makes a distinction between blasting on an uninhabited mountainside and blasting in the midst of a city.

163. Caporale v. C.W. Blakeslee & Sons, 175 A.2d 561 (Conn. 1961).

164. RESTATEMENT § 520.

The issue whether the activity is to be classified as abnormally dangerous or not is one for the court.[165] The reasonable and prudent person standard, normally resolved by the jury, does not apply; an ultrahazardous activity is one whose risk cannot be eliminated by the exercise of reasonable care.[166] The characterization of an activity as ultrahazardous makes it nondelegable.[167] The activity's intrinsic risk, rather than an individual or entity's conduct in connection with such activity, is the test.[168]

Beyond explosives, fire, and pile driving, jurisdictions are split over the characterization of other construction work as an ultrahazardous activity. Many courts are reluctant to find that regular construction activities are abnormally dangerous. Trenching is a prime example. Some courts hold that the duty to avoid the risk of a cave-in during trenching is a nondelegable duty;[169] others disagree.[170]

The Restatement also recognizes a separate type of nondelegable duty for activities creating "peculiar" risks.[171] This sort of risk arises where the usual and ordinary risk associated with the general type of work has been increased into a special danger. For instance, work on a scaffold does not necessarily involve a special risk,[172] but painting on a scaffold above a public sidewalk might.[173] The "peculiar" risk doctrine of the Restatement has been applied most liberally in California.[174]

---

165. *Id.* cmt. l; *see also* authorities cited at West's 🖙 255 MASTER AND SERVANT, k332(1.1).

166. *See also* authorities cited at West's 🖙 272 NEGLIGENCE, k305, k1555.

167. *See also* authorities cited at West's 🖙 255 MASTER AND SERVANT, k319.

168. *See* Clark-Aiken Co. v. Cromwell-Wright Co., 323 N.E.2d 876 (Mass. 1975).

169. Griesel v. Dart Indus., Inc., 591 P.2d 503 (Cal. 1979).

170. *See, e.g.*, Robinson v. Poured Walls of Iowa, Inc., 553 N.W.2d 873 (Iowa 1996) (trench excavation does not involve an abnormal risk); Woodson v. Rowland, 373 S.E.2d 674 (N.C. Ct. App. 1988).

171. RESTATEMENT § 416; *see also* BRUNER & O'CONNOR, *supra* note 29 § 7:20.

172. *See* Ortiz v. Ra-El Dev. Corp., 528 A.2d 1355 (Pa. Super. Ct. 1987).

173. Richman Bros. Co. v. Miller, 3 N.E.2d 360 (Ohio 1936). *But see* Sievers v. McClure, 746 P.2d 885 (Alaska 1987) (roofer's employee fell from icy roof; held, no peculiar risk).

174. Even in California, however, the peculiar risk doctrine is not applied to injuries sustained by employees of an independent contractor, normally covered by workers' compensation statutes. *See, e.g.*, Privette v. Superior Court, 854 P.2d 721 (Cal. 1993); *see also* Zueck v. Oppenheimer Gateway

(continued)

The third, and most common, exception to the independent contractor rule derives from the control retained by the employer over the delegated work.[175] Control of the work will make the owner liable for contractor torts.[176] Control includes negligent direction of the independent contractor. If defective plans and specifications supplied to the general contractor cause physical harm, the owner will often be liable, and the independent contractor defense will not apply.[177]

Cases considering whether or not an owner (or contractor or construction manager) has retained sufficient control over the delegated work to avoid the independent contractor rule are legion.[178] Support for either side of many similar reoccurring fact disputes can be found.[179] The better-reasoned cases look closely at the means and methods of the actual construction work from which the injury arose, and at the employer's control over those means and methods.[180] The degree of an owner's involvement in site safety issues can also be key. The "retained control" at issue is not control for

---

Props., Inc., 809 S.W.2d 384 (Mo. 1991); Fleck v. ANG Coal Gasification Co., 522 N.W.2d 445 (N.D. 1994).

175. Much of the case law concerning the retained control doctrine arises from disputes between the owner and an injured employee of the general contractor or a subcontractor. Most construction contracts, and all of the industry standard form contracts, place an affirmative duty upon general contractors to provide for a safe project. E.g., AIA Document A201, General Conditions of the Contract for Construction, Article 10 (1997 edition). These agreements are sufficient for most courts to impose liability on general contractors, even if the general contractors do not exercise control. See, e.g., Smith v. United States, 497 F.2d 500 (5th Cir. 1974).

176. RESTATEMENT § 414. See authorities cited at West's ⊕⟹ 255 MASTER AND SERVANT, k318.

177. Moloso v. State, 644 P.2d 205 (Alaska 1982); see also Bd. of Comm'rs v. Vickers, 61 P. 891 (Kan. 1900) (owner was liable for the death of a construction worker during the collapse of a bridge under construction, especially when the general contractor had warned the owner before construction began that if the bridge was built as designed, it would not stand).

178. See authorities cited at West's ⊕⟹ 272 NEGLIGENCE, k1205(7); ⊕⟹ 255 MASTER AND SERVANT, k318.

179. For an excellent and comprehensive treatment of this subject, see SCHNEIER, supra note 27, ch. 3.

180. See, e.g., Durham v. Warner Elevator Mfg. Co., 139 N.E.2d 10 (Ohio 1956); Dow Chem. Co. v. Bright, 89 S.W.3d 601 (Tex. 2002) (injured carpenter had no claim against the owner, which had no contractual control over the independent contractor's means and methods or actual control over the carpenter's work, notwithstanding safety rules and directions as to results).

the purposes of agency; it is control that is more akin to supervision.[181]

An owner's rights to inspect,[182] to stop work, or to perform other ordinary owner contract rights will generally not constitute exceptions to the independent contractor rule.[183] Even the right of general oversight for safety normally does not constitute retained control by an owner.[184] But owners can step outside the protection of the independent contractor rule when they seek to perform a part of the work, by retaining either design or operational responsibility for the project.[185]

Similarly, general contractors and construction managers who do not have contractual responsibility for project safety,[186] or who do not have the right to control the manner and methods of an independent subcontractor's work, should not be held liable for the acts of the independent subcontractor.[187] However, should the contractor or construction

---

181. RESTATEMENT § 414, cmt. a. An employer's liability under the retained control exception has been said to require a three-step analysis: (1) Did the employer's principal exercise control over the independent contractor? (2) Was the exercise of that control negligent? (3) Did such negligent control cause the plaintiff's injury?

182. Thresher v. Gerken, 309 N.W.2d 488 (Iowa 1981) (right to inspect for contract conformity did not rise to the level of control).

183. Martinez v. United States, 661 F. Supp. 762 (W.D. Tex. 1987) (owner's right to stop work insufficient to constitute control of work); Plummer v. Bechtel Constr. Co., 451 N.W.2d 631 (Mich. Ct. App. 1990) (owner's right of general inspection over safety procedures did not constitute control of work).

184. Valentia v. Giusto, 581 N.Y.S.2d 939 (App. Div. 1992) (owner's inspection and demands for correction of defects did not make owner a supervisor); see Adams v. Inland Steel Co., 611 N.E.2d 141 (Ind. Ct. App. 1993) (owner who required compliance with safety rules but did not control the means and methods or direct safety measures was not liable under an exception to the independent contractor rule).

185. Deville v. Budd Constr. Co., 617 So.2d 570 (La. Ct. App. 1993) (DOT's contractual retention of the right to control the type and placement of construction warning signs and barricades meant the State was liable to an injured motorist); Chura v. Baruzzi, 596 N.Y.S.2d 592 (App. Div. 1993) (where owner received bids, negotiated contracts, and was present at the site daily self-performing work and overseeing the project, owner was held to retain control over the work).

186. See, e.g., Foley v. Rust Int'l, 901 F.2d 183 (1st Cir. 1990); Abraham v. Andrews Trucking Co., 893 P.2d 1156 (Wyo. 1995).

187. RESTATEMENT § 409, cmt. b; see Chesin Constr. Co. v. Epstein, 446 P.2d 11 (Ariz. Ct. App. 1968); Kelly v. Howard S. Wright Constr. Co., 582 P.2d 500 (Wash. 1978); Bozung v. Condo. Builders, Inc., 711 P.2d 1090 (Wash. Ct. App. 1985) (where the subcontractor was an expert, the

(continued)

manager have the right to control the work of the independent subcontractor, then it has a duty, within the scope of its control, to exercise reasonable care for the protection of those who may be injured by the independent subcontractor's actions.[188] The responsibility that accompanies control also extends to gratuitous services.[189]

The scope of the retained control doctrine is not unlimited. A general contractor's "retained control" does not extend to hazards that are peculiar to a specialty subcontractor's activities and that the general contractor cannot be expected to supervise.[190] Likewise, a contractor will not be held liable under the retained control doctrine for the acts of a professional engineer hired by the contractor.[191]

Modern day risk assessment and avoidance in the construction process, especially for the risks of personal injury and property damage, are most often concerned with the types, costs, and availability and policy limits of insurance. During a "buyer's" or "soft" insurance market, many construction participants are lulled into placing increased emphasis on

---

general contractor who visited the site sporadically to ensure compliance with plan and specs was held not to have retained control); see also authorities cited at West's ⊕═ 272 NEGLIGENCE, k1205(7).

188. Lee Lewis Constr., Inc. v. Harrison, 70 S.W.3d 778 (Tex. 2001) (general contractor that required all subcontractors to follow a voluminous, detailed safety manual, and assigned a superintendent the responsibility of inspecting the job site to see that subcontractor employees were properly utilizing fall-protection equipment, was held to have retained a right to control subcontractor safety measures, and was therefore liable for the fatal fall of a subcontractor employee); Corsetti v. Stone Co., 483 N.E.2d 793 (Mass. 1985). But see Bond v. Howard Corp., 650 N.E.2d 416 (Ohio 1995) (contractor retained control over part of the work of the independent subcontractor but because contractor did not exercise control over means and methods of the work which injured the employee, no exception to the independent contractor rule). General supervisory capacity, without active participation in the activity which caused the injury, is insufficient to create control.

189. See Nelson v. Union Wire Rope Corp., 199 N.E.2d 769 (Ill. 1964) (contractor's commercial general liability insurer's periodic site safety inspections imposed duty to perform even gratuitous safety services nonnegligently).

190. Rogers v. West Constr. Co., 623 N.E.2d 799 (Ill. Ct. App. 1993) (pile-driving subcontractor employee could not recover against general contractor under retained control doctrine where project site was cleared of all other personnel, including contractor's safety supervisor, at the beginning of pile-driving activities).

191. See Mudgett v. Marshall, 574 A.2d 867 (Me. 1990) (employees of the erection contractor could not impose liability upon the steel fabricator that had hired the engineer who performed the mathematical calculations, which contained errors).

insurance products rather than on proper construction practices and contractual risk allocation. This is perhaps understandable, given the many variations of insurance products that are thrown at owners, contractors, subcontractors, and design professionals during soft insurance markets.

The decade of the 1990s, for instance, saw the maturity of wrap-up policies, which combined workers' compensation, commercial general liability, professional liability, contractor's pollution liability, builder's risk (including consequential loss), and vehicle insurance. Wrap-up coverage could be owner-controlled (OCIP) or contractor-controlled (CCIP). The majority of these policies and programs, however, seem to be price-competitive only when the project budget exceeds around $40 million. Also, OCIPs and CCIPs provide completed operations coverage for only a specified period of time after the project is completed.[192] During soft insurance markets, owners can also procure, for larger construction projects, increased professional liability coverage limits to afford umbrella or excess coverage above the errors and omissions coverage of the project's design professional.

Perhaps the most controversial type of insurance that blossomed in the soft market of the 1990s was the subcontractor default insurance policy. These policies, marketed as a better alternative to traditional subcontractor performance bonds, caused a good deal of controversy in the construction industry, especially with those involved in the sale of surety products.[193] An analysis of subcontractor default insurance policies is beyond the scope of this text. But such a policy can be more flexible and more cost efficient than a subcontractor

---

192. *See* James D. O'Connor & Jacqueline P. Sirany, *Controlled Insurance Programs in the Industry: Putting a Ribbon on Wrap-Ups*, STADIUMS, ARENAS, MALLS, AND MORE: THE COMMUNITY IMPACT PROJECT Tab III (ABA Forum on the Construction Industry Annual Meeting April, 2001) (program materials).

193. *See, e.g.,* the animated debate between two recent articles in the ABA's construction law journal: Terry Gray, *Point/Counterpoint: Default Insurance—An Alternative to Traditional Surety Bonds*, 22:1 CONSTR. LAW. 17 (Winter 2002); Lynn M. Schubert & Robert J. Duke, *Point/Counterpoint: Surety Bonds—The Best Protection Against Contractor or Subcontractor Default, id.* at 22.

performance bond. Such policies, though, typically include a significant deductible amount. They are also self-correcting— that is, the cost of such subcontractor default insurance is heavily dependent on the policyholder's performance history with its subcontractors.

In "hard" insurance markets, many of the more aggressive insurance products are likely to become more difficult to obtain, or nonexistent. They will surely become more expensive. When premium investment yields fall and insurance company claim reserves climb, insurance claims managers tend to increase the power of their magnifying glass on the facts of newly asserted claims. The circumstances of each claimed loss are analyzed to determine the carrier's duty to defend and extent of coverage. In hard markets, this analysis becomes more strict.[194] Hard insurance markets are known for the increased number of outright claim denials, refusals to defend, and declaratory judgment actions to deny coverage.

Seasoned construction practitioners and their counsel therefore emphasize best management practices for construction administration and contractor and subcontractor selection, in good economic times and in bad. Contractual risk allocation works best when the risk in the field is placed upon the entity best able to control and manage the risk. Pure insurance products are more likely (without delay) to compensate for or indemnify against an unexpected event rather than a preventable one.

FRAUD

Fraud is as old as time and as versatile as human ingenuity. Fraud is a generic term—it embraces many dastardly acts. Courts are reluctant to define fraud for fear that the craft of

---

194. In the recent hard market, insurance claims representatives have begun directly contacting plaintiffs and their counsel, without the knowledge or participation of the insured or the insured's regular counsel, to discuss the event of loss and damages claimed. This sort of conduct is controversial, as it tends to allow a carrier to hear what it wants to hear about the claim, and put its version of the loss, often a "no coverage" or "nonoccurrence" spin, on the circumstances of the claim.

humankind would find a way to commit fraud while evading the definition.[195] Suffice it to say that fraud takes place in the construction industry, just as it does in every other commercial activity.

Although definitively listing areas of potentially fraudulent activity in the construction industry would be futile, examples of both actual and constructive fraud are not uncommon. Actual fraud is an active misrepresentation or the concealment of a material fact that conveys a false impression, to the unfair advantage of the maker and to the detriment of the person who acts upon the false information.[196] Actual fraud can be fraud in the inducement to make an agreement[197] or fraud in executing or obtaining the benefits of the agreement.[198] Constructive fraud arises from a breach of duty by one in a confidential or fiduciary relationship with another that induces justifiable reliance by the other to his prejudice.[199]

The elements of actual fraud or deceit are (1) the false representation of a material fact, which is (2) reasonably calculated to deceive, (3) made with the intent to deceive, and (4) does in fact deceive, (5) resulting in damages to the injured party.[200] Some courts also add the requirement of reasonable reliance upon the misrepresentation.[201]

---

195. *See* Furst v. Merritt, 130 S.E. 40 (N.C. 1925).

196. *See* Roberson v. Williams, 83 S.E.2d 811 (N.C. 1954); Archer v. Griffith, 390 S.W.2d 735 (Tex. 1964); *see also* authorities cited at West's ⊕═ 184 FRAUD, k3.

197. *See* Odom v. Little Rock & I-85 Corp., 261 S.E.2d 99 (N.C. 1980) (fraud claim withstood motion for summary judgment where lender mislabeled land acquisition loan as "construction loan," thereby obtaining subordination of purchase money mortgage); ABM Farms, Inc. v. Woods, 692 N.E.2d 574 (Ohio 1998).

198. Also called fraud in the *factum*. *See* Bangert Bros. Constr. Co. v. Kiewit Western Co., 310 F.3d 1278 (10th Cir. 2002) (under Colorado law, a testing laboratory was held liable for fraud in modifying and falsifying concrete mix test results); Vela v. Marywood, 17 S.W.3d 750 (Tex. App. 2000), *petition for review denied*, 53 S.W.3d 684 (Tex. 2001).

199. *See* Assilzadeh v. Cal. Fed. Bank, 98 Cal. Rptr. 2d 176 (Cal. Ct. App. 2000); *see also* authorities cited at West's ⊕═ 184 FRAUD, k6.

200. *See* Whitlock v. Duke Univ., 829 F.2d 1340 (4th Cir. 1987); C.F.R. Foods, Inc. v. Randolph Dev. Co., 421 S.E.2d 386, 388–89 (N.C. Ct. App.) *review denied*, 424 S.E.2d 906 (N.C. 1992) (citations omitted); *see also* authorities cited at West's ⊕═ 184 FRAUD, k3.

201. *Id; see also* Gawara v. United States Brass Corp., 74 Cal. Rptr. 2d 663 (Cal. Ct. App. 1988) (judgment for defendants affirmed where a homeowner and developer failed to show they actually *(continued)*

Actual fraud allegations can arise where suppliers and manufacturers have overstated the qualities and performance characteristics of their products,[202] where owners have misrepresented the existence of a bond or other security,[203] and where contractors conceal construction defects. In *Allen v. Roberts Construction Co.*,[204] the owners of approximately thirty houses sued the builders alleging various causes of action, including fraud. On appeal from an adverse verdict, the builders argued there was no evidence that they had actual knowledge of structural defects in the plaintiffs' houses at the time they were sold. But as there was evidence of similar cracks in previous houses built by the defendants in the same subdivision using the same slab-on-grade method (which, incidentally, failed to meet building code standards for thickness and compaction), the appellate court held the defendant builders' knowledge of undisclosed structural defects could be inferred.[205] Each repetitive problem became a badge of fraud.

Although most cases of actual fraud or deceit involve the misrepresentation of an existing fact, in a rare case, an actionable misrepresentation may be inferred from a statement that is in the form of a promise.[206] Although more difficult to

---

relied, either directly or indirectly, on the alleged misrepresentations of sellers and manufacturers of polybutylene plumbing products); Smith v. Remodeling Serv., Inc., 648 So.2d 995 (La. Ct. App. 1994) (fraud must be more than mistake, even unilateral mistake); *see also* authorities cited at West's ⬦ 184 FRAUD, k20.

202. *See* City of Richmond v. Madison Mgmt. Group, Inc., 918 F.2d 438, 443–44 (4th Cir. 1990) (evidence that concrete pipe's internal supporting wires were insufficient to meet the project specifications despite supplier's misrepresentations of acceptability supported jury award); Rowan County Bd. of Ed. v. United States Gypsum Co., 418 S.E.2d 648 (N.C. 1992) (manufacturer's touting of product as suitable for schools when it knew there were potential health and dust hazards was sufficient to support fraud verdict).

203. J.M. Westfall & Co. v. Windswept View of Asheville, Inc., 387 S.E.2d 67 (N.C. Ct. App.), *cert. denied*, 394 S.E.2d 175 (N.C. 1990) (owner's misrepresentation to supplier that contractor had issued payment bond as part of owner's request to supplier to continue to provide materials constituted fraud).

204. 532 S.E.2d 534 (N.C. Ct. App. 2000).

205. *Id.*

206. RESTATEMENT § 525, cmt. f, which provides in pertinent part:

A statement that is in form a prediction or promise as to the future course of events may justifiably be interpreted as a statement that the maker knows of nothing which will make

prove, the misrepresentation of an intention can support an action for deceit.[207] And it bears repeating that in virtually all jurisdictions, fraud must be pleaded with particularity.[208]

The distinguishing element of actual fraud is the element of *scienter*, a knowing, intentional misstatement or conceal-ment. Some jurisdictions, and the Federal False Claims Act,[209] have a fairly liberal *scienter* requirement, satisfied by proof of "reckless disregard" or "deliberate indifference," as well as proof of a knowing intent to deceive.[210] States that impose a more stringent *scienter* standard, however, often have more liberal consumer protection statutes or unfair and deceptive trade practices statutes that do not require a strict intent to deceive.[211] Where there is a higher *scienter* requirement, proof of fraud by promises of future events or conse-quences[212] can be problematical. Situations where the intent to deceive is unclear are often dismissed.[213]

Constructive fraud can also occur in the construction setting. Constructive fraud requires a special confidence reposed in one party who is bound to act in good faith and

---

the fulfillment of his prediction or promise impossible or improbable. Thus a statement that a second-hand car will run 15 miles on a gallon of gasoline is an implied assertion that the condition of the car makes it capable of so doing, and is an actionable misrepresentation if the speaker knows that it has never run more than 7 miles per gallon of gasoline.
See authorities cited at West's ☞ 184 FRAUD, k12.

207. Leake v. Sunbelt Ltd., 377 S.E.2d 285 (N.C. Ct. App.), *cert. denied*, 381 S.E.2d 774 (N.C. 1989) (representation by owner's agent to purchaser that trees would remain at site to buffer highway construction was sufficient to constitute fraud when trees were bulldozed).

208. *See* Fed. R. Civ. P. 9(b); *see also* authorities cited at West's ☞ 184 FRAUD, k41.

209. 31 U.S.C.A. §§ 3729 *et seq.* (2000).

210. *See* 31 U.S.C.A. § 3729 (b) (2000); United States v. TDC Mgmt. Corp., 24 F.3d 292, 297–98 (D.C. Cir. 1994).

211. *See, e.g.*, N.C. Gen. Stat. § 75-1.1 *et seq.* (1977); Chapter 3 of this text. In states where unfair and deceptive trade practices do not require proof of intent to deceive, many practitioners allege fraud as an extra count but focus upon the elements of the unfair and deceptive trade practices statute. Then, too, damages are routinely trebled under such statutes.

212. Warfield v. Hicks, 370 S.E.2d 689 (N.C. Ct. App.), *cert. denied*, 374 S.E. 2d 602 (N.C. 1998) (unspecific statement by general contractor to owner about future consequences of using beetle-infested beams in house construction did not constitute fraud).

213. Myers & Chapman, Inc. v. Thomas G. Evans, Inc., 374 S.E. 2d 385 (N.C. 1988) (subcon-tractor's payment application which contained false statement was insufficient to support scienter requirement).

with due regard to the interests of the party reposing confidence.[214] There are generally two requirements: one party having (1) control over another, or another's property, and (2) the authority to act for another.[215] Courts generally have declined to define special and fiduciary relationships. The function performed by the party in whom the confidence is reposed is more important to the issue than any particular title held.[216] Thus, courts generally regard the determination whether an entity owes a fiduciary responsibility as a question of fact.[217]

Constructive fraud occurs when the party in whom confidence is reposed or who occupies the superior position has taken advantage of its position and harmed the other party by failing to act in the interest of the person to whom the fiduciary obligation is owed.[218] This can take the form of remaining silent when speaking up is necessary to put the interests of the subordinate party first. In constructive fraud cases, there is normally no requirement that the plaintiff establish the defendant's *scienter*—that is, actual knowledge of the falsity of the representation.[219]

Architects are often appointed by contract documents as arbiters of disputes arising between owner and contractor. In rendering such decisions, architects are required ethically not to show partiality to either owner or contractor.[220] So

---

214. *See also* authorities cited at West's ⊕⇒ 184 FRAUD, k6.

215. Tin Originals, Inc. v. Colonial Tin Works, Inc., 391 S.E.2d 831 (N.C. Ct. App. 1990) (parties in equal bargaining positions, even if in an interdependent relationship such as that between manufacturer and exclusive distributor, do not occupy a fiduciary relationship); *see also* authorities cited at West's ⊕⇒ 184 FRAUD, k7.

216. *See, e.g.,* Anderson v. Ciba-Geigy Corp., 759 F.2d 1518 (11th Cir.), *cert. denied*, 474 U.S. 995 (1985).

217. *Id.*

218. *See* Stephenson v. Warren, 525 S.E.2d 809 (N.C. Ct. App.), *review denied*, 543 S.E.2d 883 (N.C. 2000).

219. *See* Schweizer v. Mulvehill, 93 F. Supp. 2d 376 (S.D.N.Y. 2000); F. McConnell & Sons, Inc. v. Target Data Sys., Inc., 84 F. Supp. 2d 980 (N.D. Ind. 2000).

220. *See* AIA Document A201, General Conditions of the Contract for Construction ¶ 4.2.12 (1997 edition).

long as the architect/arbiter acts in good faith toward both, there is an arbitral immunity for the architect's decisions, even incorrect decisions.

Design professionals with this arbitral responsibility have both the superior position and the influence in the arbitral situation to create an opportunity for constructive fraud. If the contractor claims that the owner should pay for extra work caused by defective plans and specifications, the architect is placed in a quandary. If he believes that his design (or the design of a subconsultant for which he is responsible) was inaccurate or incomplete and he rules in favor of the contractor, the architect may be obligated to indemnify the owner. Likewise, if the architect erroneously rules in favor of the owner (finding no defect in the plans) has he placed his own interests above that of the contractor, to whom he owes a special duty as an impartial arbiter?[221]

The preceding hypothetical points up a dicey situation for an arbiter/architect. Architects and other design professionals who are involved in project administration face similar decisions daily, concerning which products to approve, which work to reject, whether to certify payment applications, and the like. A number of jurisdictions hold that in carrying out these tasks, the architect has no arbitral immunity and can be liable for negligent acts.[222] And in some situations, arbitrary conduct on the part of a certifying architect can constitute constructive fraud.[223]

There have been a few cases where constructive fraud is alleged in the cost-plus owner/contractor relationship. Cost-plus contracts, even the standard form cost-plus contracts, set forth contractor duties that are different from those in

---

221. *See* Paschen Contractors, Inc. v. John J. Calnan Co., 300 N.E.2d 795 (Ill. App. Ct. 1973) (architect could not decide whether his design work contained errors to detriment of subcontractor).

222. *See RPR & Assocs., supra* note 83; *see also* A.R. Moyer, Inc. v. Graham, 285 So.2d 397 (Fla. 1973); Cerny Pickas & Co. v. Dallach, 249 Ill. App. 424 (Ill. App. Ct. 1928); authorities cited at West's ☞ 272 NEGLIGENCE, k1205(4).

223. *See* Edward Edinger Co. v. Willis, 260 Ill. App. 106 (Ill. App. Ct.1931).

lump-sum contracts. AIA Documents A111 and A117 are cost-plus forms. Each provides, in paragraph 3.1:

> Contractor accepts the relationship of trust and confidence established by the Agreement and covenants with the Owner to cooperate with the Architect and utilize the Contractor's best skill, efforts and judgment in furthering the interests of the Owner.[224]

In *Eastover Ridge, L.L.C. v. Metric Constructors, Inc.,*[225] the owner contended that paragraph 3.1 of its contract imposed a fiduciary duty upon the contractor. The court looked behind the language to the facts of the relationship, and found evidence the owner also had retained an architect to render opinions as to acceptability of the work. The court held as a matter of law that no fiduciary relationship existed between the contractor and owner, in light of the involvement in the project of the architect as the owner's agent.[226]

TRESPASS AND NUISANCE: ECONOMIC AND PROPERTY DAMAGES

Construction participants can also be held liable in tort for trespass and nuisance. Whenever construction activity harms adjacent property, either or both of these causes of action may be asserted.[227] Historically, these causes of action have been brought when one's land or building is damaged by a contractor's work,[228] but other project participants, including design professionals, can be joined in the liability mix.[229]

Normally, a trespass will result in some property damage, so the economic loss rule generally does not come into play. In a recent case from the New York Court of Appeals, however, the owner and managing agent of a building under

---

224. AIA Document A111, Standard Form of Agreement Between Owner and Contractor when the basis for payment is the cost of the work plus a fee with a negotiated guaranteed maximum price, ¶ 3.1 (1997 edition).

225. 533 S.E.2d 827 (N.C. Ct. App. 2000).

226. *Id.*

227. *See, e.g.,* Concannon v. Horley Dev. Corp., 769 S.W.2d 183 (Mo. Ct. App. 1989).

228. *See also* RESTATEMENT § 370.

229. *See* BRUNER & O'CONNOR, *supra* note 29, §§ 17:34, 17:36.

construction were held to be immune from liability for purely economic damages to neighboring businesses when the streets around Times Square were closed following the collapse of a section of wall.[230] The court's application of the rule extended to, and rejected, the plaintiffs' claim alleging a public nuisance.[231]

Causes of action alleging trespass and nuisance are particularly attractive in situations where construction law and environmental law overlap. As land-disturbing activities become more and more regulated,[232] upstream property developers may be liable in trespass or nuisance for sedimentation of streams, increased turbidity, and other contaminants.[233] In *Whiteside Estates, Inc. v. Highlands Co.*,[234] the owners of property downstream from a developer successfully maintained nuisance and trespass actions after the developer's land-disturbing activities caused sediment to flow into and damage the downstream owners' creek and lake. The nuisance claim was upheld because the interference with the downstream owners' property had been repeated, substantial, and unreasonable.

The developer argued that suspended solids in the water course continued downstream, and therefore there could not be a trespass. Because there was evidence to show that the suspended solids were deposited in the plaintiffs' lake, however, the court rejected this argument. Damages were awarded in an amount sufficient to repair and restore the downstream owners' property.[235]

---

230. 532 Madison Ave. Gourmet Foods, Inc. v. Finlandia Ctr., Inc., 750 N.E.2d 1097 (N.Y. 2001).

231. *Id.*

232. *See, e.g.,* Clean Water Act, 33 U.S.C.A. §§ 1251–1387 (2002).

233. Unfortunately for developers and contractors, these injuries may be excluded from coverage from most commercial general liability policies. *See, e.g.,* Penn. Nat. Mut. Cas. Ins. Co. v. Triangle Paving, Inc., 121 F.3d 699 (4th Cir. 1997) (because sedimentation was held to be a pollutant due to extensive regulatory control, coverage was precluded by the pollution exclusion); *see also* authorities cited at West's ⬦ 405 WATERS AND WATER COURSES, k119.

234. 553 S.E.2d 431 (N.C. Ct. App. 2001); *see also* Brister v. Gulf Cent. Pipeline Co., 684 F. Supp. 1373 (W.D. La. 1988) (ruptured pipeline).

235. *Whiteside Estates, supra* note 234; *see also* City of Bloomington v. Westinghouse Elec. Corp., 891 F.2d 611 (7th Cir. 1989).

TORTIOUS INTERFERENCE WITH CONTRACTUAL RELATIONSHIP

Tortious interference with contractual relations is the intentional act by a defendant that causes a third party to terminate, refuse to renew, fail, or refuse to perform a contract with the plaintiff. The essential elements are

1. A valid contract between the plaintiff and a third party, conferring contract rights upon the plaintiff against the third party;

2. Knowledge by the defendant of the plaintiff's contract with such third party;

3. Intentional inducement of the third party by the defendant to not perform, renew, or terminate the third party's contract with the plaintiff;

4. Which causes plaintiff actual damages; and

5. For which there is no justification.[236]

A construction project creates a number of situations that, if there is spite or ill will involved, can satisfy the elements of tortious interference. For instance, improper rejection of work by a design professional, when coupled with bad purpose, will be actionable.[237] The interruption of progress payments can bring a project to a halt. If the interruption is caused by someone other than the owner, and can be shown to have been done with an improper purpose, it will constitute an actionable tort.

---

236. RESTATEMENT § 766; *see also* Embree Constr. Group, Inc. v. Rafcor, Inc., 411 S.E.2d 916 (N.C. 1992) (officers of corporate owner, who personally guaranteed corporate owner's construction loan, then intentionally induced corporate owner not to pay contractor and not to request lender to pay progress payments, held to have tortuously interfered); United Labs., Inc. v. Kuykendall, 370 S.E.2d 375 (N.C. 1988); Childress v. Abeles, 84 S.E.2d 176 (N.C. 1954); authorities cited at West's ☞ 379 TORTS, k12.

237. Tortious interference with contract should be distinguished from mere interference by a contract party, which constitutes a breach of contract. For instance, an owner who interferes with a contractor's work plan, fails to cooperate, or otherwise interferes with contractor's progress is liable for the contractor's extra costs. While this constitutes a compensable event, it is not tortious interference with contract. No matter the motivation, a party to a contract cannot commit the tort of interfering with that contract. *See, e.g.*, Colonial Bank v. Patterson, 788 So.2d 134, 137 (Ala. 2000); *see also* authorities cited at West's ☞ 379 TORTS, k12.

In *Lexington Homes, Inc. v. W. E. Tyson Builders,*[238] a building supplier persuaded the project lender to dishonor a progress payment by falsely representing that the contractor did not intend to pay the supplier with loan funds. Other subcontractors and suppliers filed liens on the property, and the completion of the project was seriously delayed while the legal mess was sorted out. The contractor incurred substantial extra costs. The supplier's conduct was held to constitute tortious interference with contract.[239]

Allegations of tortious interference with contract also can arise out of the relationship on a project among design professionals, contractors, and subcontractors. Design professionals have traditionally been employed as owners' agents during construction, with the ability and power to open bids, certify low bidders, reject defective work, certify work for payment, and determine substantial and final completion. Many general contracts also require certification by the design professional before default termination can be declared. Default terminations of contractors and subcontractors are often highly charged, emotional situations and are ripe for allegations of tortious conduct.[240] These situations provide the potential for actionable cases of tortious interference with contractual relations.[241]

In the contractor or subcontractor versus design professional situation, interference with contract is often easy to prove. What is not so easy, generally, is the indispensable proof that the design professional had some animus or bad purpose in connection with his actions (the third element), and that the design professional was unjustified in his action

---

238. 331 S.E.2d 318 (N.C. Ct. App. 1985).

239. *Id.*

240. *See* R.P. Russo Contractors & Eng'rs, Inc. v. C.J. Pettinato Realty & Dev. Inc., 482 A.2d 1086 (Pa. Super. Ct. 1984); Lincor Contractors, Ltd. v. Hyskell, 692 P.2d 903 (Wash. Ct. App. 1984).

241. Tortious interference with contract is more difficult to establish in the bidding context, because at the time of the bid opening there is not yet a contract. For those jurisdictions that allow the tort of intentional interference with prospective business advantage as a sister cause of action to tortious interference with contract, the claim may still be allowed. *See* Marc M. Schneier, *Tortious Interference with Contract Claims against Architects and Engineers*, 10:2 CONSTR. LAW. 3 (May 1990).

(the fifth element). Professor Justin Sweet concludes that the owner/architect agreement clothes with a qualified privilege the architect's decisions relating to rejection of work and to certification of an event of default on the part of the contractor. As Professor Sweet observes, "Interference is not wrongful if it is privileged."[242]

Many courts, cognizant of the unique role of the design professional, require conduct on the part of the design professional unrelated to protecting the owner's interest in contract performance to constitute tortious interference.[243] In this situation the design professional is often viewed similarly to the corporate officer who induces the company to sever its relations with a contractual party. Absent other evidence, the corporate officer's actions are presumed to have been taken in the interest of the corporation.[244]

BAD FAITH CLAIMS AGAINST SURETIES

Performance and payment bonds have long been utilized in the construction industry. Bonds are purchased to provide to the obligee (typically the owner or prime contractor) and intended beneficiaries' a third party to look to financially in the event of default by the bond's principal (the prime contractor or a subcontractor). Suretyship is a financial credit relationship, not an indemnity relationship.[245] Suretyship in the construction setting is a tripartite arrangement among principal, obligee, and surety. Payment bonds also identify a class of intended beneficiaries (referred to as claimants), typically subcontractors and suppliers of a tier inferior to the

---

242. JUSTIN SWEET, LEGAL ASPECTS OF ARCHITECTURE, ENGINEERING AND THE CONSTRUCTION PROCESS §§ 17.08(C), (D) (4th ed. 1989).

243. *See, e.g.,* Waldinger Corp. v. CRS Group Eng'rs, Inc., 775 F.2d 781 (7th Cir. 1985); Hanzel Constr., Inc. v. Wehde & Southwick, Inc., 474 N.E.2d 38 (Ill. App. Ct. 1985); Fleischer v. Hellmuth, Obata & Kassabaum, Inc., 870 S.W.2d 832 (Mo. Ct. App. 1993) (construction manager failed to show that architect was motivated by malice or ill will toward construction manager in reporting manager's performance); *see also* authorities cited at West's ◈═ 379 TORTS, k12, k27.

244. *See* Wilson v. McClenny, 136 S.E.2d 569, 578 (N.C. 1964).

245. *See, e.g.,* Angelo v. Prop. Dev. Corp., 306 S.E.2d 162 (N.C. Ct. App. 1983); *see also* authorities cited at West's ◈═ 309 PRINCIPAL AND SURETY, k185.

bond principal. Performance bonds have a penal sum, which in most situations constitutes the maximum amount for which the surety may be liable.[246] As discussed above, tort law has, in the last quarter century especially, insinuated itself into commercial transactions of most every type. The same is true of the law of suretyship. Some courts have determined that sureties can be liable separately to obligees and third-party beneficiaries for bad faith.[247]

Courts that have allowed obligees or claimants to maintain actions for bad faith against sureties have followed one of two theoretical bases. Some have found a "special relationship" between a performance bond surety and its obligee similar to that between an insurance carrier and its insured.[248] Other jurisdictions that have allowed the tort of bad faith have done so because of egregious conduct on the part of the bonding company, typically the surety's failure to investigate a claim.[249]

Other courts have refused to apply tort law to suretyship relations at all, limiting all obligee claims to those based in contract.[250] And a significant number of jurisdictions either

---

246. The penal sum limit applies to monetary damages that the performance bond surety must pay its obligee. *See* South Carolina Pub. Serv. Comm'n v. Colonial Constr. Co., 266 S.E.2d 76 (S.C. 1980). If the surety takes over the work of its defaulted principal, however, the surety will be liable for all of the costs to complete the work, whether within the penal sum or not. Int'l Fid. Ins. Co. v. City of Rockland, 98 F. Supp. 2d 400, 428 (S.D.N.Y. 2000) ("long established case law holds that a surety's takeover of its principal's contract pursuant to a performance bond always subjects the surety to liability beyond the penal limit of the bond"); *see also* Cont'l Realty Corp. v. Andrew J. Crevolin Co., 380 F. Supp. 246 (S.D.W.Va. 1974) (surety held liable beyond the penal sum due to surety's breach of its own bond obligations after the principal's default).

247. *See, e.g.,* United States ex rel. Don Siegel Constr. Co. v. Atul Constr. Co., 85 F. Supp. 2d 414 (D.N.J. 2000) (surety may be liable for bad faith to subcontractor claimant under payment bond); Loyal Order of Moose Lodge 1392 v. Int'l Fid. Ins. Co., 797 P.2d 622 (Alaska 1990) (surety may be liable for bad faith to owner/obligee on performance bond); Dodge v. Fid. & Deposit Co., 778 P.2d 1240 (Ariz.1989); *see also* authorities cited at West's 🔑 309 PRINCIPAL AND SURETY, k131.

248. *See* Transamerica Premier Ins. Co. v. Brighton Sch. Dist., 940 P.2d 348 (Colo. 1997); *see also* authorities cited at West's 🔑 309 PRINCIPAL AND SURETY, k52.

249. *See* Loyal Order of Moose Lodge 1392 v. Int'l Fid. Ins. Co., 797 P.2d 622 (Alaska 1990) (failure of performance bond surety to "minimally" investigate claim of principal's default); *see also* Miracle Mile Shopping Center v. Nat'l Union Indem. Co., 299 F.2d 780 (7th Cir. 1962); authorities cited at West's 🔑 309 PRINCIPAL AND SURETY, k52.

250. *See* Norwood Co. v. RLI Ins. Co., No. 01-6153, 2002 WL 485694 (E.D. Pa., Apr. 4, 2002) (bad faith action against a surety is not available in Pennsylvania, distinguishing a bond from an

(continued)

are silent or have sided with the bonding companies on the issue of a "special relationship" between surety and obligee on a performance bond sufficient to support a bad faith claim in tort.[251]

In contrast, the general agreement of indemnity between the surety and its principal is almost universally acknowledged to create a "special relationship," obligating the surety to act in good faith toward its principal in handling claims on the bond. Because the principal agrees to indemnify the surety for amounts paid under the bond, at least one court has determined that a surety may be liable in bad faith for unreasonably failing to assert the principal's defenses to bond claims and for making unwarranted payments under the bond.[252] Other courts have disallowed a surety's indemnity claim against its principal and guarantors when it improperly settled a bond claim.[253]

If a court determines that a "special relationship" exists between the performance bond surety and its obligee, the injured obligee may be able to assert bad faith claims similar to those allowed by an insured against its insurance carrier, such as for the carrier's failure to pay claims within the policy limits, and for failure to act in good faith in handling

---

insurance policy); *accord,* Inst. of Mission Helpers v. Reliance Ins. Co., 812 F. Supp. 72 (D. Md. 1992) (construing Maryland law not to allow a bad faith claim by an obligee); Cates Constr., Inc. v. Talbot Partners, 980 P.2d 407 (Cal. 1999); Masterclean, Inc. v. Star Ins. Co., 556 S.E.2d 371 (S.C. 2001) (answering certified question; South Carolina does not allow performance bond obligee to sue surety in tort for bad faith). *But see* Cont'l Realty Corp. v. Andrew J. Crevolin Co., 380 F. Supp. 246 (S.D.W.Va. 1974) (performance bond surety that failed to take over or pay was required to pay the penal sum for the principal's default and the obligee's additional costs due to the surety's breach of the bond); *see also* authorities cited at West's 🔑 309 PRINCIPAL AND SURETY, k59, k82(2), k142.

251. Many jurisdictions are silent on this issue. Of those that have sided with the bonding companies, the more thoughtful opinions include Great Am. Ins. Co. v. N. Austin Mun. Util. Dist., 908 S.W.2d 415 (Tex. 1995) (no "special relationship" between performance bonding company and obligee); Republic Ins. Co. v. Board of County Comm'rs, 511 A.2d 1136 (Md. Ct. Spec. App. 1986); *Cates Constr., Inc., supra* note 250 (California does not extend tort remedies against insurers to other commercial relationships).

252. City of Portland v. George D. Ward & Assocs., Inc., 750 P.2d 171 (Or. Ct. App.), *review denied,* 757 P.2d 422 (Or. 1988).

253. *See* Associated Arntz Contracting Co. v. St. Paul Fire & Marine Ins. Co., 54 Cal. Rptr. 2d 888 (Cal. Ct. App. 1996); Masterclean, Inc. v. Star Ins. Co., 556 S.E.2d 371 (S.C. 2001) (dicta); Associated Indem. Corp. v. CAT Contracting, Inc., 964 S.W.2d 276 (Tex. 1998).

first-party insurance claims.[254] As a number of commentators and courts have noted, this analysis flies in the face of the large volume of decisional law rejecting any attempt to equate the relationship between insurance and suretyship.[255] Despite this precedent, some courts recognize that surety bonds are purchased with premiums, and that certain minimum standards of conduct should be required. This is consistent with the development of tort law elsewhere in contractual settings—a minimum standard of conduct regardless of the existence of a contractual undertaking.[256]

Because a surety occupies a tripartite relationship, it has dual obligations—to its bond principal and to its obligee (and, under payment bonds, to the claimants/intended beneficiaries). The surety's primary duty, other than to pay legitimate claims, is to investigate and act reasonably and seasonably based on the knowledge gleaned from an independent investigation.[257] When a principal is terminated, a performance bond surety may complete the project and pay damages up to the penal sum, or challenge the propriety of the termination and deny

---

254. The much ballyhooed June 2001 jury verdict for mold damages in the Melinda Ballard case in Austin, Texas, arose from claims asserted not against a contractor, but against the Ballards' homeowners' insurance company. Ballard's $32.1 million award was made up of $6.2 million for replacement of the home and contents, $5.0 million for mental anguish, $12.0 million in punitive damages, and $8.9 million in legal fees. This verdict was due to a determination by the jury of bad faith on the part of the first-party, homeowners insurance company, which allegedly stonewalled the Ballards for two years. See generally discussions of the case at sites such as http://www.breatheasier.com/Press_Mold_Best's_Reviews.htm. The Ballard verdict has now been reduced on appeal to $4 million plus undetermined attorney's fees. See Allison v. Fire Ins. Exchange, No. 03-01-00717CV, 2002 Tex. App. LEXIS 8957 (Tex. App. Dec. 19, 2002).

255. See Henry Angelo & Sons, Inc. v. Prop. Dev. Corp., 306 S.E.2d 162, 165 (N.C. Ct. App. 1983) (the "ABCs of insurance and suretyship law … [demonstrate that] insurance and suretyship are not synonymous terms, and if any appellate court anywhere has ever so held, our research has failed to disclose it.") (citing cases); Masterclean, Inc. v. Star Ins. Co., 556 S.E.2d 371 (S.C. 2001).

256. See United States ex rel. Don Siegel Constr. Co. v. Atul Constr. Co., 85 F. Supp. 2d 414 (D.N.J. 2000). But see Morse/Diesel, Inc. v. Fid. & Deposit Co., 763 F. Supp. 23 (S.D.N.Y. 1991) (as obligee was not a signatory to the bond, surety owed no implied duty of good faith and fair dealing to obligee).

257. See Loyal Order of Moose Lodge, supra note 249, 778 P.2d at 628; see also Farmer's Union Cent. Exch., Inc. v. Reliance Ins. Co., 675 F. Supp. 1534, 1542 (D.N.D. 1987) ("The duty to investigate is measured by the standard of reasonableness in any given fact situation"; however, no duty existed to investigate undocumented payment bond claims); authorities cited at West's ⊕ 309 PRINCIPAL AND SURETY, k66(1).

liability. Sureties that properly and timely investigate and then make a reasoned, documented decision will be prepared to respond to a bad faith claim. As stated by the Arizona Supreme Court in *Dodge v. Fidelity and Deposit Co. of Maryland,* "the duty imposed on a surety to deal in good faith with its obligee does not require it to act in bad faith with its principal."[258]

---

258. 778 P.2d 1240, 1243 (Ariz. 1989).

Limitations on Contract and Tort Damages

9

ALLEN HOLT GWYN
and CHARLES M. SINK

INTRODUCTION

As demonstrated throughout this text, owners, design professionals, general and trade contractors, and construction managers can all be held responsible in damages to other construction project participants. Damages may be assessed as an extra to the amount of the initial contract, because of breach of express or implied warranties, and, in tort, separate from contractual remedies. While no one enjoys paying extra or receiving less, the most difficult construction damages to accept are those that are unexpected and for which no funds have been budgeted. Surprising project costs, even if valid, can sour the payor's attitude about an otherwise acceptable project.

It is human nature to not gladly accept responsibility for the perceived folly of others.[1] It is often difficult, especially for owners, to understand why, if they are not at fault, they must pay extra. After all, many owners reason, that was the point of hiring construction "professionals"—contractors and designers—to control costs so that the project would be built without breaking the budget.

When confronted with unexpected overruns or other claims for extras, owners, especially those for whom construction is an irregular event, can feel that unfair advantage has been taken of them. It follows that those who are in the crosshairs for construction damages often seek by contract to limit surprising and unbudgeted damages. And, where the ones who desire to limit their exposure also control the work, they can make the acceptance of limited expectations for unforeseen damages a requirement to obtain the job.

In a hard-dollar, lump-sum contract, bidders often must accept damages-limitation clauses or forgo participation. Partly because of the inequality of bargaining power inherent in such an arrangement, courts have been asked to interpret the meaning and scope of the more onerous limitation clauses.[2] Even though contractors are experienced and certainly ought to know the effect of such provisions at the time the agreement is executed, there are many examples of courts refusing to enforce particularly onerous clauses.[3] Coursing through the law is the ubiquitous rule of reasonableness. An owner's fair advantage over a contractor may be allowed; an unfair advantage may not be. An onerous provision that places the bidder at risk of incurring owner-caused (but nonrecoverable) costs may be acknowledged as (and held to be) part of the contractor's bargain. If, however, an owner abuses the power

---

1. This adage generates a resounding "Amen" when considered from inside the construction industry, where budget-busting problems regularly have many parents.

2. If, for instance, the contractor's damages are significant, caused directly by the owner or its agents, and recoverable but for a damage limitation clause, the contractor may have little to lose and much to gain by asking for judicial relief from the effects of the limiting clause.

3. *See, e.g.,* the discussion of no-damage-for-delay clauses in the next section of this chapter.

of his position and during construction deliberately or carelessly increases the contractor's expenses, a court may find that many foreseeable losses are not barred by the owner's damage limitation clause.

Legislatures have shown that they are not averse to determining what can and cannot be "bargained away" at bid time by contractors. Employing their power to declare a provision "void as against public policy," various state legislatures have sought to level the playing field between those who control construction work and those who perform it.[4] Especially in the public setting, a trend has developed to limit the imposition, by onerous contract provisions, of risks outside of the control of the participants.

On the other side of the economic coin, courts and some legislatures have promulgated rules that limit the recovery of otherwise valid damages against various construction participants. One of the most significant and widely discussed among the judge-made doctrines is the "economic loss rule," which precludes a party's recovery in negligence or strict liability for purely economic damages.[5]

The willingness of courts and legislatures to restrict recoverable damages is a somewhat recent phenomenon. Because such enactions spring from a desire to correct injustice, it may be that the tenor of a proposed rule or statute is determined by the issue's location on the arc created by the pendulum of public opinion. If public opinion favors the contractor or subcontractor who must accept a public owner's one-sided contract, a legislature may void an onerous clause as against public policy. If the body politic believes that damages

---

4. State courts also sometimes divine the existence of an unlegislated "public policy" negating exculpatory agreements as well.

5. *See* Christopher Scott D'Angelo, *The Economic Loss Doctrine: Saving Contract Warranty from Drowning in a Sea of Tort*, 26 U. Tol. Rev. 591, 609 (1995), for a survey of jurisdictions that have adopted the economic loss rule; *see also* Pulte Home Corp. v. Osmose Wood Preserving, Inc., 60 F.3d 734 (11th Cir. 1995) (builder's claim for defective fire retardant chemical as applied to plywood sheathing barred by rule); Morris v. Osmose Wood Preserving, Inc., 667 A.2d 624 (Md. 1995) (same).

recovered by "trial lawyers" have run amok,[6] or if a court concludes that asserted losses are not the foreseeable result of a participant's conduct, damages can be limited, legislatively or judicially.

This chapter will explore specific contractual clauses that some owners,[7] general contractors, and design professionals employ to limit their exposure to certain losses, or to wholesale categories of damages. This chapter will also examine circumstances where legislatures have voided damages-limiting clauses and where judges have refused to enforce such language. In examining these judicial policies, the chapter will attempt to make sense of the often bewildering economic loss rule.[8]

CONTRACTUAL DAMAGE LIMITATIONS

No-Damage-for-Delay Clauses

Owners employ many forms of exculpatory provisions in an effort to reduce damages incurred by their own actions, or by events outside of the contractor's control.[9] Many such clauses restrict a contractor's recovery of time-related damages, even for delays outside the contractor's control such as those caused by conduct of the owner or its representatives. Generally referred to as no-damage-for-delay clauses, these clauses often prohibit a price increase and limit the contrac-

---

6. *See, e.g.*, the current arguments presented to state legislatures and Congress in support of personal injury damage caps for pain and suffering—arguments made and often financed, cynical commentators note, by insurance companies and other typically defense interests.

7. Damage limitation clauses are employed by private and public owners, within manuscript or modified standard form contract documents. Language within many subcontracts (including standard form subcontracts) provides that the provisions of the owner/contractor agreement (including the limiting clauses) "flow down" from the owner through the general contractor to the trade contractors. Whether the trade contractors are limited by these limiting clauses in their rights against general contractors will depend upon the precise language coordinating the provisions of each agreement.

8. For a discussion of several of the defenses treated in this chapter, *see* L. Franklin Elmore and John T. Crawford, Jr., *Defenses in Construction Defect Cases*, 24:2 CONSTR. LAW. 27 (Spring 2003).

9. For a general discussion of "no damage for delay" provisions, see FIFTY STATE MONOGRAPH ON THE ENFORCEABILITY OF "NO DAMAGES FOR DELAY" CLAUSES, AMERICAN BAR ASSOCIATION, SECTION OF LITIGATION (Dennis A. Estis and John S. Morris III eds. 1998); Annotation, *Validity and Construction of "No Damage" Clauses with Respect to Delay in Building or Construction Contract*, 74 A.L.R.3d 187 (1976).

tor's recovery for construction delays to an extension of the contract time.

Such limiting clauses have been much criticized, in part because it is difficult if not impossible for contractors to calculate bid contingencies for future delays outside their control. No-damage-for-delay clauses have also generally not been accepted in the standard construction industry form contracts. For example, the American Institute of Architects (AIA) Document A201, General Conditions of the Contract of Construction, allows the contractor not only more time for owner-caused interference but also monetary damages for increased costs caused by the interruption.[10] Many owners insert no-damage-for-delay clauses to circumvent liability for hindrances they cause, or for foreseeable but unquantifiable delays.[11]

One commentator has argued that no-damage-for-delay clauses should be denied enforcement under the same principle that invalidates liquidated damages clauses that are not based on a reasonable forecast of just compensation.[12] This analogy highlights the equitable problems of enforcing a clause that effectively fixes the monetary liability for any owner's breach (of its duty not to hinder or delay) at zero, a provision that seems particularly one-sided in a contract that carefully protects the owner against potential contractor delays by prescribing generous actual or liquidated delay damages.

In most states, however, no-damage-for-delay provisions are generally enforceable in both public and private construction contracts.[13] Such clauses are distinguished as slightly

---

10. AIA Document A201, General Conditions of the Contract for Construction ¶ 8.3 (1997 edition) [hereinafter the A201].

11. *See* David A. Senter, *The Role of the Subcontractor, in* Fundamentals of Construction Law 128 (2001).

12. Douglas Oles, No Damages Clauses in Construction Contracts: A Critique, 53 Wash. L. Rev. 471 (1978).

13. *See* Daniel E. Terreri & Sons, Inc. v. Mahoning City Bd. of Comm'rs, 786 N.E.2d 921 (Ohio. Ct. App. 2003) ("a 'no damages for delay' clause is a valid and *enforceable* contract provision. ... The reason for enforcing such clauses is to protect the public"); Williams Elec. Co. v. Metric Constructors, Inc. 480 S.E.2d 447 (S.C. 1997); cases cited at West's ⊕═ 316A PUBLIC CONTRACTS, k22; *see also* cases cited at West's ⊕═ 200 HIGHWAYS, k113(4).

less onerous than other exculpatory terms, such as a release or indemnity, since a "no damage" clause relates to foreseeable economic losses resulting from a breach of contract. Because a "no damage" clause at least allows a contract time extension, it does not fully exculpate a contract owner from its own future negligence, and it does not completely shift the risk for tort and negligence damages. On that basis, some courts hold that such provisions need not be conspicuous and unambiguous.[14]

Like most exculpatory clauses, no-damage provisions are strictly and narrowly construed.[15] For example, the following language in a subcontract overrode the contract's no-damage clause:

> Should the Subcontractor be obstructed or delayed in the commencement, prosecution or completion of the work, without fault on his part, by action or inaction on the part of the Owner, Architect, Engineer or Contractor, or by changes in the work, the Subcontractor shall be entitled to include as cost the cost of labor, materials, equipment, supplies and other resultant costs occasioned by such delays and changes *notwithstanding any other provision contained in this agreement*.[16]

Aside from the narrow construction given to no-damage provisions, courts also impose certain exceptions to lessen their effect.[17] The most common exceptions include situations where: (1) the delay was not contemplated by the parties at the time of contracting;[18] (2) the interruption is tantamount to an abandonment of the contract;[19] (3) the delay was caused

---

14. *See, e.g.,* Green Intern., Inc. v. Solis, 951 S.W.2d 384, 386–88 (Tex. 1997).

15. *See* J & B Steel Contractors, Inc. v. C. Iber & Sons, Inc., 642 N.E.2d 1215, 1221 (Ill. 1994); Port Chester Elec. Constr. Corp. v. HBE Corp., 894 F.2d 47 (2d Cir. 1990); cases cited at West's ⊕➡ 95 CONTRACTS, k189.

16. Morse/Diesel, Inc. v. Trinity Indus., Inc., 67 F.3d 435, 438 (2d Cir. 1995) (emphasis in original).

17. *See* cases cited at West's ⊕➡ 95 CONTRACTS k299(2).

18. *See id; see also* JWP/Hyre Elec. Co. v. Mentor Vill. Sch. Dist., 968 F. Supp. 356, 360 (N.D. Ohio 1996).

19. Abandonment of contract has been defined as giving up the right to benefits due under an agreement from the other party. Abandonment may be express or inferred from the circumstances and the conduct of the parties. *See* discussion of abandonment in Chapter 6 of this text at note 86; cases cited at West's ⊕➡ 95 CONTRACTS, k256.

by fraud, misrepresentation, or bad faith;[20] and (4) the delay arose from active, willful interference with the work of the contractor.[21]

Some courts do not recognize the exceptions, holding that when a contract is clear, unambiguous, and explicit, it should be enforced according to the terms the parties have used.[22] Other courts have found evidence insufficient to support invoking an exception to the no-damage clause, for example finding that bad administration of a contract did not fit into any of the enumerated exceptions.[23] At least one court has refused to enforce an exception as a matter of precedent.[24]

If the judiciary refuses to cooperate, affected parties can go to the legislature. Beyond the judicially created exceptions listed above, some state legislatures have statutorily limited the enforceability of no-damage-for-delay clauses.[25] At least twelve states have enacted legislation curtailing this

---

20. *See, e.g.*, Ragan Enters., Inc. v. L & B Constr Co., 492 S.E.2d 671, 672 (Ga. Ct. App. 1997) (clause prohibited delay damages except those "due *solely* to fraud or bad faith on the part of the owner or his agents."). This exemption has been called the "most widely recognized exception to the enforceability of a no-damage-for-delay clause." *See also* United States *ex rel.* Williams Elec. Co. v. Metric Constructors, Inc., 480 S.E.2d 447, 449 (S.C. 1997) (adopting the exception and collecting cases).

21. *See* Langevin v. United States, 100 Ct. Cl. 15 (1943) (failure to pass on shop drawings or make seasonable inspections); Newberry Square Dev. Corp. v. S. Landmark, Inc., 578 So.2d 750, 752 (Fla. Dist. Ct. App. 1991) (owner's failure to provide approved plans and to promptly execute change orders); S. Gulf Utils., Inc. v. Boca Ciega Sanitary Dist., 238 So.2d 458 (Fla. Dist. Ct. App.), *cert. denied*, 240 So.2d 813 (Fla. 1970) (failure to provide right-of-way. "No party can unreasonably rely upon the no damages clause"); cases cited at West's ⬤═ 95 CONTRACTS, k231(1).

22. *See, e.g.*, *United States ex rel. Williams Elec. Co.*, *supra* note 13, 480 S.E.2d at 450 (rejecting the "delays not contemplated by the parties" exception); John E. Gregory & Son, Inc. v. A. Guenther & Sons Co., 432 N.W.2d 584, 587 (Wis. 1988) ("parties can mutually assent to such a clause without contemplating in particularity all of the potential causes of delay. Indeed, the adoption of a 'no damage for delay' clause shows that the parties realize that some delays cannot be contemplated at the time of the drafting of the contract").

23. *See* Martin Mech. Corp. v. P.J. Carlin Constr. Co., 518 N.Y.S.2d 166, 168 (App. Div. 1987). *But see* Triple R Paving, Inc. v. Broward County, 774 So.2d 50 (Fla. Dist. Ct. App. 2000) (evidence of engineer's early knowledge and nondisclosure of design flaw sufficient to support claim of active interference, and not "mere lethargy or bureaucratic bungling").

24. *See* Pellerin Constr., Inc. v. Witco Corp., 169 F. Supp. 2d 568, 584 (E.D. La. 2001) (refusing to adopt the "active interference" exception).

25. See Cheri Turnage Gatlin, *Contractual Limitations on the Right to Recover Delay Damages and Judicial Enforcement of those Limitations*, 22:4 CONSTR. LAW. 32, Fall 2002.

risk-shifting provision:[26] Arizona,[27] California,[28] Colorado,[29] Massachusetts,[30] Missouri,[31] New Jersey,[32] North Carolina,[33] Ohio,[34] Oregon,[35] Rhode Island,[36] Virginia,[37] and Washington.[38] Many of these statutes limit the application of such clauses in the context of public projects. In California a contractor on a public works project may recover delay damages, provided the "delay is unreasonable, and not within the con-

---

26. See Alain Lecusay, Comment, *The Collapsing "No Damages For Delay" Clause in Florida Public Contracts: A Call For Legislative Change*, 15 St. Thomas L. Rev. 425, 446 (2002).

27. Ariz. Rev. Stat. § 34-221 (2003) (applicable to public contracts).

28. Cal. Pub. Cont. Code § 7102 (2003).

29. Colo. Rev. Stat. Ann. § 24-91-103.5 (West 2003) (making no damage for delay clauses unenforceable in public contracts).

30. Mass. Gen. Laws Ann. Ch. 30 § 39O (2003).

31. Mo. Rev. Stat. § 34.058 (2003).

32. N.J. Stat. Ann. § 18A:18A-41 (2003) (limited to public school district contracts):
I[I]t shall be void, unenforceable and against public policy for a provision in a contract entered into under Chapter 18A of Title 18A of the New Jersey Statutes to limit a contractor's remedy for the contracting unit's negligence, bad faith, active interference, tortious conduct, or other reasons uncontemplated by the parties that delay the contractor's performance, to giving the contractor an extension of time for performance under the contract. For the purposes of this section, "contractor" means a person, his assignees or legal representatives with whom a contract with a contracting unit is made.

33. N.C. Gen. Stat. § 143-134.3 (2003) (limited to public projects).

34. Ohio Rev. Code Ann. § 4113.62 (2003) makes "no damage for delay" clauses void and unenforceable:
(C)(1) Any provision of a construction contract, agreement, or understanding, or specification or other documentation that is made a part of a construction contract, agreement, or understanding, that waives or precludes liability for delay during the course of a construction contract when the cause of the delay is a proximate result of the owner's act or failure to act, or that waives any other remedy for a construction contract when the cause of the delay is a proximate result of the owner's act or failure to act, is void and unenforceable as against public policy.

35. Or. Rev. Stat. § 279.063 (2001):
Any clause in a public contract for a public improvement that purports to waive, release or extinguish the rights of a contractor to damages or an equitable adjustment arising out of unreasonable delay in performing the contract, if the delay is caused by acts or omissions of the public contracting agency or persons acting therefor, is against public policy and is void and unenforceable.

36. R.I. Gen. Laws § 37-2-42 (2002) (limiting, but not invalidating, no damage for delay clauses).

37. Va. Code Ann. § 2.2-4335 (2003) (declaring public construction contract provisions barring damages for unreasonable delays void).

38. Wash. Rev. Code Ann. § 4.24.360 (2003) (making no-damage-for-delay clauses void and unenforceable as against public policy).

templation of the parties."[39] Such laws can effectively nullify no-damage-for-delay clauses, particularly in public contracts.[40]

Faced with hostility from the courts and legislatures to no-damage-for-delay provisions, owners may turn to other contractual approaches to limit their liability for their own delays. For instance, liquidated damages for delay allow the contractor to recover a predetermined rate for suspensions that exceed a prescribed length of time. Similarly, requirements for prompt written notice of delays may help owners to budget for resulting cost overruns as they occur.[41]

The interplay over no-damage-for-delay clauses among owners, contractors, courts, and legislatures was summed up nicely by Professor Justin Sweet:

> It's like the volleying I have spoken of: Contractors, through their associations or lawyers, become sensitized to the losses they face when the owner delays or disrupts their work. They bring impact or delay and disruption claims. Owners respond by using "no damage" clauses or invoke as a defense the common law requirement that the amount of damages be proven with reasonable certainty. The contractors hit back by fighting "no damage" clauses in the courts or legislatures and by developing total cost and jury verdict formulas that get them by the certainty requirement. Owner then begins to liquidate. Like a tennis match.[42]

Waivers of Consequential Damages

Another modern trend in limiting recoverable damages is to exclude whole categories of potential losses. Few owners, contractors, or designers, however, want to tacitly encourage a breach of their agreement by relieving the other party's

---

39. *See* CAL. PUB. CONT. CODE § 7102 (2003); *see also* N.C. GEN. STAT. § 143-134.3 (2003).

40. *See* Howard Contracting, Inc. v. G.A. MacDonald Constr. Co., 83 Cal. Rptr. 2d 590, 595–96 (Cal. Ct. App. 1998); cases cited at West's ☞ 268 MUNICIPAL CORPORATIONS, k70, k374(5).

41. *See* Gatlin, *supra* note 25.

42. JUSTIN SWEET, SWEET ON CONSTRUCTION LAW 342 (1997).

responsibility for direct or proximate damages. Because the scope of direct damages often pales in comparison with the panoply of possible consequential damages arising from a construction project gone bad, however, construction participants, especially owners and contractors, have focused upon consequential damage waiver clauses.

In 1997, "mutual waiver of consequential damages" clauses were included in the AIA's new owner-contractor general conditions document, the A201, and its new owner-architect agreement.[43] Both documents are widely used, and the A201 represents today's most common form of general conditions in the construction industry. This new clause has been described as "one of the single most important changes in A201."[44] Paragraph 4.3.10 of A201, states, in pertinent part:

> The Contractor and Owner waive Claims[45] against each other for consequential damages arising out of or relating to this Contract. This mutual waiver includes:
>
> damages incurred by the Owner for rental expenses, for losses of use, income, profit, financing, business and reputation, and for loss of management or employee productivity or of the services of such persons; and
>
> damages incurred by the Contractor for principal office expenses including the compensation of personnel stationed there, for losses of financing, business and reputation, and for loss of profit except anticipated profit arising directly from the Work.
>
> This mutual waiver is applicable, without limitation, to all consequential damages due to either party's termination in

---

43. AIA Document B141, Standard Form of Agreement Between Owner and Architect with Standard Form of Architect's Services (1997 edition) [hereinafter the B141].

44. Kevin Peartree et al., *The New A201—What's in It for the Contractor? An Overview and Analysis*, CONSTRUCTOR 12 (Aug. 1997). A201's consequential damages waiver clause is reputed to have been advanced in response to an arbitration award, upheld by the courts in Perini Corp. v. Greate Bay Hotel & Casino, Inc., 610 A.2d 364 (N.J. 1992), under which the owner recovered $14.5 million for lost profits against its construction manager for a late-delivered casino renovation, more than twenty times the amount of the construction manager's $600,000 fee. *See also* CHARLES M. SINK & MARK D. PETERSEN, THE A201 DESKBOOK: UNDERSTANDING THE REVISED GENERAL CONDITIONS 75 (1998).

45. The A201 defines "Claim" as a "demand or assertion by one of the parties seeking, as a matter of right, adjustment or interpretation of Contract terms, payment of money, extension of time or other relief with respect to the terms of the Contract." A201 ¶ 4.3.10.

accordance with Article 14 [Termination or Suspension of the Contract]. Nothing contained in this Subparagraph 4.3.10 shall be deemed to preclude an award of liquidated direct damages, when applicable, in accordance with the requirements of the contract documents.

This particular clause combines general language in the initial sentence with a portfolio of examples "included" in the waiver. In contrast, the exclusion of consequential damages in the B141 eschews a list of particular losses: "The Architect and Owner waive consequential damages for claims, disputes or other matters in question."[46] The A201 and the B141 thus illustrate two of the most common drafting approaches to excluding consequential damages.

A distinct feature of the AIA standard form documents is that they provide for mediation and arbitration of disputes.[47] The enforceability of consequential damage waivers thus is frequently not interpreted by courts, but more likely construed by the parties in mediation or by a panel of arbitrators. The laudable objective of these new mutual waiver provisions is to promote predictability by relieving breaching owners, contractors, and designers from liability for losses that are abnormally large because of unexpected events arising after formation of the construction contract.[48] Despite this popular goal, such clauses raise concerns.

An ambiguity in A201 and many other such waivers is whether any list of specifically disclaimed consequential damages is intended to be exhaustive. A201 is typical because the catalog of excluded losses is introduced with the following language: "This mutual waiver includes. ..." Debates over the drafters' intent are common, and results predictably inconsistent. Courts generally enforce broad consequential damages waivers, and therefore the parties' expectations need to be

---

46. B141 ¶ 1.3.6.

47. *See* A201 ¶¶ 4.5 (Mediation), 4.6 (Arbitration).

48. *See* Charles M. Sink & Mark D. Petersen, *Indirect, Consequential, and Punitive Damages, in* 2 CONSTRUCTION LAW HANDBOOK § 31.05, at 1158 (1999).

clear.[49] Problems over whether the list is to be treated as complete by the parties should be addressed through clarifying language.

Even without a list of unequivocally excluded losses, a mutual waiver of consequential damages still suffers from some doubt including the lack of consensus over the meaning of the term "consequential damages." The Restatement (Second) of Contracts uses the concept of foreseeability to define "consequential damages."[50] More foreseeable still is the likelihood of debate, and eventual litigation, over the phrase. Lost profits may be the quintessential form of consequential damages, but other categories of damages, such as those listed in A201, paragraph 4.3.10, may feature in disputes over whether they should be characterized as direct or consequential. An owner may believe that any loss of use of the completed construction work (such as through delayed completion) is not consequential, but rather flows directly from the contractor's breach. Conversely, from the contractor's perspective, owner-caused delays lead directly to the contractor's increased overhead, and inability to undertake new work.

Paragraph 4.3.10 of A201 also illustrates another major dilemma: how an indemnity clause operates in conjunction with the waiver. A201's Paragraph 6.2.3 provides:

> The Owner shall be reimbursed by the Contractor for costs incurred by the Owner which are payable to a separate contractor because of delays, improperly timed activities or defective construction of the Contractor. The Owner shall be responsible to the Contractor for costs incurred by the Contractor

---

49. *See, e.g.,* Canal Elec. Co. v. Westinghouse Elec. Corp., 548 N.E.2d 182, 186 (Mass. 1990) (although this case was decided under the Uniform Commercial Code, the court followed the principle that private parties are free to allocate risk as they choose, subject to narrow limitations).

50. RESTATEMENT (SECOND) OF CONTRACTS § 351 (1981) ("Damages are not recoverable for loss that the party in breach did not have reason to foresee as a probable result of the breach when the contract was made"). The foreseeability test perhaps narrows the traditional rule requiring that consequential damages be within the "contemplation" of the parties as a prerequisite to recovery. *See* Hadley v. Baxendale, 9 Ex. 341, 354 156 Eng. Rep. 145, 151 (1854).

because of delays, improperly timed activities, damage to the Work or defective construction of a separate Contractor.[51]

When read in conjunction with the consequential damages waiver of Paragraph 4.3.10, does the A201 indemnity obligation still include reimbursement for consequential damages . if they arise from liability to third parties? It is incumbent upon the parties to both understand and, if necessary, contract around precisely what might be released by a mutual consequential damages waiver.

While it remains unlikely that many courts will become involved in interpreting the AIA's mutual consequential damage waiver provision (because of A201's mandatory arbitration clause), the temptation for owners, contractors, and designers may be to treat any item of damages left out of a list of exclusions as recoverable "direct damages."[52] A clearer approach, preferable to relying on a form contract's concept of "consequential damages," would be to substitute a customized and mutually initialed list of waived damages. The owner, contractor, or designer also should consider including specific costs to be compensated under any "liquidated damages" provision, thus establishing what are consequential losses that are *not* waived. Finally, the owner and contractor need to make sure that their consequential damages waiver is consistent with the subcontracts and supply contracts.[53]

Contractually Capped Damages Clauses

Instead of, or in addition to, eliminating categories of potential damages, design professionals and some contractors try

---

51. A201 ¶ 6.2.3.

52. "Direct damages," universally recoverable by the injured party, "may fairly and reasonably be considered [as] arising naturally, i.e., according to the usual course of things, from such breach of contract itself." *Hadley v. Baxendale, supra* note 50, 156 Eng. Rep. at 151.

53. AIA Document A401, Standard Form of Agreement between Contractor and Subcontractor ¶ 15.4 (1997 edition) waives "consequential damages arising out of or related to this Subcontract," without any list of waived damages. While this provision still contains the undefined "consequential damages," A401 may offer greater protection than A201.

to negotiate a limitation of damages based on a percentage of the contract amount, an absolute number, or an objectively determined figure.[54] So long as the parties are sophisticated, and the limit either was negotiated or could have been bargained for (and the agreement itself is otherwise enforceable), courts generally uphold such provisions as between the contracting parties. In *Markborough California, Inc. v. Superior Court,*[55] the court refused to strike down a clause limiting an architect's liability to the amount of its fee.[56] To be enforced, however, such a clause must clearly and unequivocally express an intent to limit liability.[57]

Design-builders are often presented with contracts containing performance guarantees. To avoid open-ended liability, design-builders frequently limit their exposure to a prescribed percentage of the total contract amount, or to a maximum figure (again, such as the design-builder's fee). Similarly, experienced contractors may bargain for limits on the number of days of liquidated damages, or on the total amount of recoverable liquidated damages. Major equipment manufacturers regularly seek comparable financial constraints on liquidated or other delay damages that may be assessed against them by a general contractor. Counsel for the general contractor therefore must be sure that its exposure to the owner for delay or performance damages is matched by recoverable damages clauses within purchase orders and subcontracts issued for key areas of the project.

54. The last measure could be the amount of the fee or the limits of the designer or contractor liability coverage.

55. 277 Cal. Rptr. 919 (Cal. Ct. App. 1991).

56. *See id.* at 925–27; *see also* cases cited at West's ⊕⟹ 208 INDEMNITY, k27; k30(5).

57. *Compare* Nolde v. Hamm Asphalt, Inc., 202 F. Supp. 2d 1257, 1269 (D. Kan. 2002) (subcontractor need not indemnify construction company for its own negligence where subcontractor agreed to indemnify construction company for claims "on account of any act or omission of the Subcontractor, or any of his officers, agents, employees or servants."); *and* Martin & Pitz Assocs., Inc. v. Hudson Constr. Servs., Inc., 602 N.W.2d 805 (Iowa 1999) (general contractor and subcontractor were not required to indemnify architect where parties' agreements did not provide indemnification for firm's own negligence in clear and unequivocal language) *with* Hagerman Constr. Corp. v. Long Elec. Co., 741 N.E.2d 390, 393 (Ind. Ct. App. 2000) ("the clause speaks of claims, damages, losses and expenses attributable to bodily injury, sickness, disease or death, and injury to or destruction of

Site Investigation Disclaimers

On a fixed-price construction project, the contractor is normally concerned with unforeseen risks that can delay a project and/or increase the cost of construction.[58] Paragraph 4.3.4 of A201 is somewhat typical and allocates risk for unforeseen or concealed conditions:

> If conditions are encountered at the site which are (1) subsurface or otherwise concealed physical conditions which differ materially from those indicated in the Contract Document or (2) unknown physical conditions of an unusual nature, which differ materially from those ordinarily found to exist and generally recognized as inherent in construction activities of the character provided for in the Contract Documents, then notice by the observing party shall be given to the other party promptly before conditions are disturbed and in no event later than 21 days after first observance of the conditions. ... If the conditions encountered are materially different, the Contract Sum and Contract Time shall be equitably adjusted, but if the Owner and Contractor cannot agree on an adjustment in the Contract Sum or Contract Time, the adjustment shall be referred to the Architect for initial determination, subject to further proceedings pursuant to Paragraph 4.4.[59]

Under this approach, recoverable damages depend on the nature of the difficulty encountered. Thus, the contractor bears the risk of added costs for adverse conditions that are outside the relatively narrowly defined circumstances, including those that are above the surface; not concealed (e.g., disclosed on a utility map of buried lines); subsurface or concealed, but not materially different from the drawings, soil reports, or specifications; unknown but not uncommon in

---

property, as well as negligent acts or omissions. These words, taken in this context, are the language of negligence, and, as such, clearly and unequivocally demonstrate that the indemnification clause applies to negligence."). *See* cases cited at West's ☞ 208 INDEMNITY, k33(5); ☞ 115 DAMAGES, k118.

58. Cost-reimbursable agreements effectively leave such risks with the owner; they usually do not oblige the contractor to investigate the site and thus accept the risk of observable conditions.

59. A201 ¶ 4.3.4.

the area; or unknown, uncommon conditions that nevertheless do not differ materially from the ordinary. Accordingly, what are commonly called Type I and Type II differing site conditions, from the (1) and (2) descriptions within Paragraph 4.3.4 of A201 and as developed in the Federal Acquisition Regulation,[60] allocate to owner and to contractor various contingencies and risks by their limitations. From this rough balance, the parties may each, by contract clause or disclaimer, strive to shift to the other still more risk, thus potentially setting new horizons of damages.

Contractors often seek to limit the impact of a site investigation clause by negotiating language that imposes on the contractor a duty only to be "reasonable." Where a site investigation clause does not disclaim owner responsibility for differing site conditions, but merely charges the contractor with knowledge of "reasonably ascertainable" conditions, the contractor may state a claim for extra work for conditions unknown to either party.[61] A contractor may not necessarily be able to

---

60. Differing site conditions clauses are discussed at length in Chapter 6 of this text following note 15.

61. *See* SMC Corp. v. New Jersey Water Supply Auth., 759 A.2d 1223, 1226 (N.J. Super. Ct. App. Div. 2000). The site investigation clause at issue in *SMC* stated:

> 9. *Site Investigation and Representation:*
> The contractor acknowledges that he has satisfied himself as to the nature and location of the work, the general and local conditions particularly those bearing upon transportation, disposal, handling and storage of materials, availability of labor, water, electric power, roads and uncertainties of weather, floods or similar physical conditions at the site, the topography and conditions of the ground, the character of equipment and facilities needed preliminary to and during the execution of the work, *and all other matters upon which information is reasonably obtainable* and which can in any way affect the work or the cost thereof under this Contract. The Contractor further acknowledges that he has satisfied himself as to the character, quality and quantity of information regarding the above *that is reasonably ascertainable from an inspection of the site,* including all exploratory work done by the Authority or the Engineer, as well as information contained in the Drawings and Specifications forming a part of this Contract. The Contractor further acknowledges that he has satisfied himself as to the availability of timber, stone, fill material, etc. both as to quality and quantity required to execute the work. Any failure by the Contractor to acquaint himself *with all the available information* will not relieve him from the responsibility for estimating properly the difficulty or cost to successfully perform the work. The Contractor's attention is drawn to the fact that As-Built Drawings of existing work do not exist and some dimensions shown on the Contract Drawings have been estimated. All dimensions shall be field checked by the Contractor.

Id. at 1225–26; *see also* cases cited at West's ⊕═ 405 WATERS AND WATER COURSES, k193.

turn to the design professional for damages not covered under the differing site conditions clause. Designers often disclaim liability for soil conditions.[62]

On the other hand, owners often seek to modify standard form contracts to (1) disclaim any responsibility for subsurface conditions, (2) provide that subsurface data included in the bidding documents is for information only, and (3) require contractors to make whatever additional subsurface investigation they may deem necessary for a proper elevation of the site.[63] Generally speaking, courts have taken three approaches to the enforceability of subsurface disclaimers:

1. **The "plain language" approach.**[64] Courts applying this approach enforce the unambiguous disclaimer according to its plain meaning.[65] When an owner or contractor makes clear that site data is not part of the contract documents, and no one has warranted the accuracy of test borings, the disclaimer will often be strictly enforced.[66] This approach is commonly premised upon the fact that the data is not part of the Contract Documents. If the inaccurate data is not part of the Contract Documents, then the fact that

---

62. *See* Joseph F. Trionfo & Sons, Inc. v. Bd. of Ed., 395 A.2d 1207 (Md. App. 1979) (refusing contractor's claim for extra work where contractor executed specific release as a prerequisite to obtaining the information and despite the contract provisions excluding such information from the specifications and a strong disclaimer of any guarantee of the report's accuracy); *see also* cases cited at West's ☞ 345 SCHOOLS, k86(2).

63. 1 Steven G.M. Stein, Construction Law ¶ 3.05[3][a] (2002).

64. *See* cases cited at West's ☞ 95 CONTRACTS, k143(2), k232(1); ☞ 316A PUBLIC CONTRACTS, k16.

65. *See* Millgard Corp. v. McKee/Mays, 49 F.3d 1070, 1073 (5th Cir. 1995) ("In short, the disclaimers and the language of the project manual show that the parties placed the risk of underground water on Millgard. Millgard took its chances by not boring its own hole and instead relying on the soil reports. The bargain struck by the parties allocated the risk and there it ends. We enforce the contract"); Frontier Founds., Inc. v. Layton Constr. Co., 818 P.2d 1040, 1042 (Utah Ct. App. 1991) (the contractor was denied extra compensation where soil borings of a "representative area near the building site" were taken, but the contract stated: "The soil report was obtained only for the engineer's use in the design and is not a part of the contract documents. The log of borings is provided for contractor's information but is not a warrant of subsurface conditions").

66. *See* Air Cooling & Energy, Inc. v. Midwestern Constr. Co., 602 S.W.2d 926, 931 (Mo. Ct. App. 1980).

the contractor relied upon the data to his detriment does not mean that the scope of work changed, or that the contractor performed "extra work." Likewise, if the inaccurate data is not part of the Contract Documents, it cannot be used to create a "conflict" with other provisions of the Contract Documents.[67]

2. **The "opportunity to verify" approach.** Some courts will not hold bidding contractors liable for differing site conditions unless the contractors had a meaningful opportunity to verify those conditions. The rationale underlying this approach is that bidders often have a short amount of time to prepare their bids and must rely upon owner representations concerning subsurface and other site conditions.[68] Where the owner's agent has provided site information to a contractor, and the contractor is not reasonably able to discover the true facts for itself before submitting a bid, the contractor is entitled to rely on representations made by the owner and its agent.[69] Other courts reject this approach and enforce the disclaimer despite the contractor's lack of a meaningful opportunity to verify the site conditions.[70] These courts typically apply at the bidding stage the "plain language" approach, described above, despite the fact that the data was provided for the contractor's use in formulating its bid.

---

67. *Id.*

68. *See, e.g.,* Clark Bros. Contractors v. State, 710 P.2d 41, 45 (Mont. 1985) (contract's exculpatory language did not relieve state from liability where the contractor had no opportunity to conduct independent investigation); *see also* cases cited at West's ⊕ 200 HIGHWAYS, k113(4).

69. *See* Raymond Int'l, Inc. v. Baltimore County, 412 A.2d 1296, 1302 (Md. Ct. Spec. App. 1980); cases cited at West's ⊕ 64 BRIDGES, k21(6).

70. *See* Jahncke Serv., Inc. v. Dep't of Transp., 322 S.E.2d 505 (Ga. Ct. App. 1984):

It is undisputed, moreover, that appellants were on notice as to the possibility of errors or discrepancies in the boring report and as to the necessity, before submitting a bid, of making an independent investigation rather than contenting themselves with relying on the boring report. The cited provisions of the contractual documents make it clear that problems of the sort appellant complained of were anticipated and were expressly provided for in the contract.

See also cases cited in Chapter 8 of this text at notes 43–45.

3. **The "superior knowledge" approach.** Some courts hold that general exculpatory clauses disclaiming responsibility for the accuracy of subsurface soil data are of no effect when the positive representations made by the owner plainly are intended to be used by bidding contractors for formulating their bids.[71] For example, contract language requiring the bidder to "satisfy himself as to the character ... of surface and subsurface materials or obstacles to be encountered" cannot negate express statements of fact, upon which the contractor justifiably relied, as to the nonexistence of materials and obstacles.[72] An intentional misrepresentation is not necessarily required to overcome a disclaimer so long as the owner makes positive statements of material fact concerning the work in question and those statements are false.[73] If the contractor has a right to rely upon an owner's affirmative representations, a disclaimer will be ineffective unless it specifically disclaims responsibility *for the contested information.*[74]

According to the Supreme Court of South Dakota in *Morris*, the reason for holding the government liable for certain material misrepresentations is simple:

> Certain jobsite investigations are not expected to be performed by each and every bidder; rather, the government performs

---

71. *See* R.J. Wilder Contracting Co. v. Ohio Turnpike Comm'n, 913 F. Supp. 1031 (N.D. Ohio 1996); Horton Indus., Inc. v. Vill. of Moweaqua, 492 N.E.2d 220 (Ill. App. Ct. 1986); City of Indianapolis v. Twin Lakes Enters., Inc., 568 N.E. 2d 1073 (Ind. Ct. App. 1991); *see also* discussion relating to negligent misrepresentation by owners in Chapter 8 of this text at notes 28–41.

72. *See* E.H. Morrill Co. v. State, 423 P.2d 551 (Cal. 1967); cases cited at West's ☞ 316A PUBLIC CONTRACTS, k21; ☞ 360 STATES, k104.

73. *See* Robert E. McKee, Inc. v. City of Atlanta, 414 F. Supp. 957, 959 (N.D. Ga. 1976); Morris, Inc. v. State, 598 N.W.2d 520 (S.D. 1999); *see also* United States v. Spearin, 248 U.S. 132 (1918); Christie v. United States, 237 U.S. 234 (1016); Hollerbach v. United States, 233 U.S. 165 (1914).

74. *See* W. States Mech. Contractors, Inc. v. Sandia Corp., 798 P.2d 1062, 1065 (N.M. Ct. App. 1990); *Morris, supra* note 73; *see also* Tonkin Constr. Co. v. County of Humboldt, 233 Cal. Rptr. 583 (Cal. Ct. App. 1987); Midwest Dredging Co. v. McAninch Corp., 424 N.W. 2d 216, 222 (Iowa 1988); Jack B. Parson Constr. v. State, 725 P.2d 614, 617 (Utah 1986).

certain basic tests in order to provide each bidder with some information on which he may make his bid. If every bidder were required to perform all the investigations, even though the chance of receiving the bid was remote, the number of bids would decrease and the dollar amount of the bids would increase.[75]

In negotiating a site investigation clause, the owner, contractor, and design professional should all understand the applicable approach to disclaimers of liability for differing site conditions in their jurisdiction. Such knowledge is particularly important for the contractor to accurately allocate risk, since it is the contractor that typically has the least knowledge when it prepares its bid.

Disclaimers of Warranties

Several express and implied warranties are regularly created by the traditional construction process. Parties sometimes attempt to limit or disclaim at least the implied warranties. Contractors especially may be inclined to disclaim implied warranties concerning the work when the owner's remedies for breach are expansive.

Liability for warranty is grounded in sales law and generally governed by the Uniform Commercial Code. Most courts will not apply the U.C.C. to the design professional[76] or others who provide pure services. Thus, disputes over warranty liability and disclaimers generally arise between owner and contractor.

In contracts utilizing A201, the contractor agrees to several express warranties with respect to its construction services:

> The Contractor warrants to the Owner and Architect that materials and equipment furnished under the Contract will be of good quality and new unless otherwise required or permitted by the Contract Documents, that the Work will be free from

---

75. *Morris, supra* note 73, 598 N.W.2d at 523.
76. *See* cases cited at West's ⌖ 95 CONTRACTS, k205.25.

defects not inherent in the quality required or permitted, and that the Work will conform to the requirements of the Contract Documents. Work not conforming to these requirements, including substitutions not properly approved and authorized, may be considered defective. The Contractor's warranty excludes remedy for damage or defect caused by abuse, modifications not executed by the Contractor, improper or insufficient maintenance, improper operation, or normal wear and tear and normal usage. If required by the Architect, the Contractor shall furnish satisfactory evidence as to the kind and quality of materials and equipment.[77]

This clause, which is familiar to most construction industry professionals,[78] contains three separate express warranties: (1) materials and equipment furnished under the contract will be of good quality and new unless otherwise required or permitted by the Contract Documents; (2) the work will be free from defects not inherent in the quality required or permitted; and (3) the work will conform to the requirements of the Contract Documents. Express warranties generally are not subject to disclaimer.

Implied warranties are judicially created doctrines designed to avoid unjust results flowing from the caveat emptor rule and the doctrine of merger.[79] Professor Prosser has labeled the implied warranty "a freak hybrid born of the illicit intercourse of tort and contract."[80] There are several implied warranties applicable to construction projects. Some run from the owner to the contractor, including the owner's implied warranty of the accuracy of representations in the contract[81] and

---

77. A201 ¶ 3.5.1.

78. See Patrick J. O'Connor, Jr., Warranties, Guarantees, and Correction Remedies Under the AIA Document A201 (1997), 18:1 CONSTR. LAW. 19 (Jan. 1998).

79. *See, e.g.*, Bd. of Directors of Bloomfield Club Recreation Ass'n v. Hoffman Group, Inc., 692 N.E.2d 825 (Ill. Ct. App. 1998).

80. William L. Prosser, The Fall of the Citadel (Strict Liability to the Consumer), 50 MINN. L. REV. 791, 800 (1966).

81. *See* United States v. Atlantic Dredging Co., 253 U.S. 1, 11 (1920) (holding that the contractor "ought to be relieved if he was misled by erroneous statements in the specifications"); cases cited at West's 🔑 393 UNITED STATES, k70(30).

the owner's implied warranty of design adequacy and completeness.[82] These are discussed in depth in Chapter 6. Implied warranties are also imposed upon contractors, principally contractor/vendor's implied warranty of habitability, and the contractor's implied warranty of "workmanlike performance." Such warranties are discussed at length in Chapter 3.

Contractors and owners are generally free to contract in writing to limit the warranty of habitability to specific terms, conditions, and remedies, and in certain circumstances to expressly disclaim this implied warranty.[83] This rule is not absolute; a recent decision by the Massachusetts Supreme Court, *Albrecht v. Clifford*,[84] held that the implied warranty of habitability cannot be waived or disclaimed, because to permit the disclaimer of a warranty protecting a purchaser from the consequences of latent defects would defeat the very purpose of the warranty. Boilerplate habitability disclaimers may not be enforced; a more effective disclaimer not only must show a conspicuous provision that fully discloses the consequences of its inclusion, but also that such was a bargained-for term of the agreement. Where the parties clearly and unambiguously express their intention to disclaim implied warranties, the provision will generally be upheld.[85] Even when the disclaimer is clear, however, it will still be strictly construed against the contractor.[86]

---

82. *See* United States v. Spearin, 248 U.S. 132 (1918) ("if the contractor is bound to build according to plans and specifications prepared by the Owner, the contractor will not be responsible for the consequences of defects in the plans and specifications"); cases cited at West's ☞ 95 CONTRACTS, k280(3).

83. *See* cases cited at West's ☞ 95 CONTRACTS, k205.35(4); *see also* Bravorka v. Wolfe Constr., Inc., 573 S.E.2d 656 (N.C. Ct. App. 2002) (separate express warranty supported by insurance was sufficient to uphold disclaimer).

84. 767 N.E.2d 42, 47 (Mass. 2002).

85. Arthur Rutenberg Homes, Inc. v. Norris, 804 So.2d 180, 185 (Ala. 2001).

86. *See, e.g.,* Belt v. Spencer, 585 P.2d 922 (Colo. Ct. App. 1978) (where builder vendor disclaimed liability for cracking of concrete flatwork but did not disclaim liability for heaving, disclaimer clause did not limit liability of builder vendor in implied warranty for defects accompanying heaving of concrete slabs in basement and driveway of new home); Petersen v. Hubschman Constr. Co., 389 N.E.2d 1154 (Ill. 1979) (knowing disclaimer is not against public policy).

The same rules apply to the implied warranty of good workmanship, and most courts do not analyze them separately. This implied warranty requires the builder to construct a home in the same manner as would a generally proficient builder engaged in similar work and performing under similar circumstances. Like the implied warranty of habitability, this implied warranty of good workmanship applies as a matter of law unless the parties clearly and unequivocally express a bargained-for contrary intention.

The owner's implied warranties may also be disclaimed. The owner's warranty that the plans are sufficient or the owner's implied duty to coordinate the work of multiple prime contractors or the owner's many consultants are typical. If the warranties are not expressly disclaimed in the contract, most courts recognize their existence and enforceability.[87]

Waivers of Lien Rights

Lien rights are created by statute,[88] and a contractor's right to enforce them may sometimes be waived, either by express agreement[89] or implied through conduct.[90] Such waivers may be justified and benign (partial lien waivers in exchange for interim payment, for instance),[91] or they may become more assertive (an attempt to waive all lien rights throughout the

---

87. *See* Lynn Axelroth, *The Owner's Perspective, in* FUNDAMENTALS OF CONSTRUCTION LAW 38–39 (2001); *see also* discussion at Chapter 4, note 1 *et seq.*

88. See discussion of lien rights in Chapter 3 of this text, following note 117.

89. *See* cases cited at West's 257 MECHANICS' LIENS, k207–08.

90. For example, under the "joint check rule," when a general contractor makes a materialman and subcontractor joint payees on a check for materials, the materialman, by endorsing the check, is deemed to have been paid the amount of the joint check; there is a presumption that, by endorsing the check, the materialman has received all sums then owed to him and, even if the amount is not collected, he may not assert a mechanic's lien (or payment bond claim). *See* United Metro Materials, Inc. v. Pena Blanca Props., LLC, 4 P.3d 1022, 1028 (Ariz. Ct. App. 2000); Post Bros. Constr. Co. v. Yoder, 569 P.2d 133 (Cal. 1977); cases cited at West's 257 MECHANICS' LIENS, k209, k240.

91. *See, e.g.,* Lyons Fed. Trust & Sav. Bank v. Moline Nat'l Bank, 549 N.E.2d 933, 936 (Ill. App. Ct. 1990) ("The execution of lien waivers does not bar any claim for additional payments because the evidence supports the circuit court's findings that these waivers were necessarily executed ... in order to receive partial payment and were intended to be partial lien waivers as to particular work").

course of construction).[92] Some jurisdictions uphold these "no lien" clauses; other courts only permit objections to be made to the lien's validity.[93] Still other jurisdictions have held that assertive preconstruction waivers are against public policy and unenforceable.[94]

Any agreement to waive lien rights must be certain in its terms and must be clearly and unequivocally established.[95] The owner and contractor generally cannot waive the lien rights of subcontractors, unless the jurisdiction does not grant independent lien rights to subcontractors.[96]

Waivers of lien rights, in conjunction with interim and final pay applications, routinely form an integral part of the contractor's payment on a project, and the project's completion. A201 makes explicit that neither final payment nor any remaining retained percentage shall become due until the contractor provides an affidavit that all indebtedness that could result in an encumbrance on the property has been paid or otherwise satisfied.[97] Subparagraph 9.10.2 continues:

> If a Subcontractor refuses to furnish a release or waiver required by the Owner, the Contractor may furnish a bond satisfactory to the Owner to indemnify the Owner against such lien. If such lien remains unsatisfied after payments are made, the

---

92. *See, e.g.,* Snydergeneral Corp. v. Lee Parcel 6 Assocs. L.P., 681 A.2d 1008 (Conn. App. Ct. 1996) (upholding clear and unambiguous provision where subcontractor released and relinquished right to any and all liens or claim of lien rights).

93. *See, e.g.,* John B. Kelly, Inc. v. Phoenix Plaza, Inc., 378 A.2d 363 (Pa. Super. Ct. 1977).

94. *See, e.g.,* DEL. CODE ANN. tit. 25, § 2706(b) (2002); FLA. STAT. § 713.20(2) (2002); GA. CODE ANN. § 44-14-366(a) (2002); GA. CODE ANN. § 44-14-366(a) (2002) (applies only to subcontracts); N.C. GEN. STAT. § 44A-12(f) (2003); N.Y. LIEN LAW § 34 (2003); and VT. STAT. ANN. tit. 9, § 1921(f) (2003). For a general discussion, *see* Annotation, *Validity and Effect of Provision in Contract Against Mechanic's Lien,* 76 A.L.R.2d 1087 (1961).

95. *See, e.g.,* Benner-Williams, Inc. v. Romine, 437 P.2d 312, 314 (Kan. 1968).

96. *See* Torres v. Meyer Paving Co., 423 N.E.2d 692, 694 (Ind. Ct. App. 1981) ("Pursuant to Ind. Code 32-8-3-1, a subcontractor's mechanic's lien may be waived by a provision in the contract between the contractor and owner."); 53 AM. JUR. 2D *Mechanics' Liens* § 293 (1996); *see also* Annotation, *Release or Waiver of Mechanic's Lien by General Contractor as Affecting Rights of Subcontractor or Materialman,* 75 A.L.R.3D 505 (1977).

97. A201 ¶ 9.10.2.

> Contractor shall refund to the Owner all money that the Owner may be compelled to pay in discharging such lien, including all costs and reasonable attorneys' fees.[98]

Other issues arise when a contractor agrees to a clear and unambiguous waiver of lien rights before receiving payment. Prior to substantial performance, some jurisdictions hold that an unambiguous waiver will release the contractor's lien rights against the property as of the date of the waiver, but not for claims arising subsequent to that date.[99] Other jurisdictions look at the plain meaning of the unconditional waiver and enforce it according to its terms.

A collateral issue for contractors concerns whether an action to enforce rights under a mechanic's lien will waive the contractor's right to arbitration.[100] For instance, in 1997, A201 added a provision allowing a claim related to a lien to be handled similarly to all other claims:

> If a Claim relates to or is the subject of a mechanic's lien, the party asserting such Claim may proceed in accordance with applicable law to comply with the lien notice or filing deadlines prior to resolution of the Claim by the Architect, by mediation or by arbitration.[101]

Paragraph 4.4.8 accords with the statutory or decisional law in many jurisdictions, to the effect that the filing of a necessary lien notice or the taking of other mandatory steps does not by itself waive a contract right of arbitration.[102]

---

98. *Id.*

99. *See, e.g.*, Baker v. Boren, 934 P.2d 951, 962 (Idaho 1997); *see also* statutory prohibitions against prospective lien waivers discussed at note 94, *supra*.

100. *See* Kaneko Ford Design v. Citipark, Inc., 249 Cal. Rptr. 544, 548–49 (Cal. Ct. App. 1988) (right to arbitrate can be waived "based on various factors, including (1) whether the party seeking arbitration previously had taken steps inconsistent with an intent to arbitrate; (2) whether that party had unreasonably delayed in seeking arbitration; and (3) whether that party had acted in 'bad faith' or with 'wilful misconduct.' In addition, a finding of prejudice is necessary"); Ed Loshbaugh & Sons, Inc. v. Ossewarde, 42 P.3d 696 (Idaho 2002); cases cited at West's ⌖ 33 ARBITRATION, k23.3.

101. A201 ¶ 4.4.8.

102. *See* SINK & PETERSEN, *supra* note 48, at 79.

Releases

A release is an agreement in which one or more parties agree to abandon a claim or right.[103] Releases, like other exculpatory agreements, are contractual in nature and interpreted according to the state's contract law. In construing a release, courts consider the intention and understanding of the parties, and whether the language is clear and unambiguous.[104]

As with waivers of lien rights, discussed above, owners often seek to require a contractor's release as a condition to final payment. Such provisions are routine under most construction agreements, including A201.[105] Typically, in exchange for receipt of the final contract payment, the contractor will execute a release extinguishing its rights against the owner. The execution by a contractor of a release that is complete on its face reflects the contractor's unqualified acceptance and agreement with its terms and is binding on both parties.[106] Where a contractor releases "any and all claims" or executes another broad form of release, courts normally hold that this bars a subsequent action. If a broad release is coerced by threatening not to pay the contractor uncontested sums, it is more likely to be held unenforceable.[107] Because releases are strictly construed, a limited release will not bar a contractor from bringing an action that is outside the specific released terms.[108]

As indicated above, exceptionally broad releases are often upheld, even if the contractor believes payments are still

---

103. *See* Peplinski v. Constr. Contractors Bd., 52 P.3d 1129, 1132 (Or. Ct. App. 2002); cases cited at West's ☞ 331 RELEASE, k1.

104. *See, e.g.,* M&A Constr. Corp. v. Akzo Nobel Coatings, Inc., 936 P.2d 451, 456–57 (Wyo. 1997). An example of an ambiguous release can be found in Depot Constr. Co. v. State, 502 N.Y.S.2d 833 (App. Div. 1986) (supplemental agreement that merely stated that item was removed from scope of construction contract was not final, unambiguous release of contractor's claim for pumping work allegedly performed by subcontractor under such item).

105. *See* A201 ¶ 9.10.2.

106. *See* C&H Commercial Contractors, Inc. v. United States, 35 Fed. Cl. 246, 252 (1996); cases cited at West's ☞ 331 RELEASE, k6.

107. *See, e.g.,* Rich & Whillock, Inc. v. Ashton Dev., Inc., 204 Cal. Rptr. 86 (Cal. Ct. App. 1984).

108. *See* cases cited at West's ☞ 331 RELEASE, k30.

due.[109] Some jurisdictions, however, will not enforce a release according to its terms if the parties' course of conduct demonstrates a contrary intent.

In *West End Interiors, Ltd. v. Aim Construction & Contracting Corp.*,[110] the New York Appellate Division refused to bar a subcontractor's claims for additional compensation where the subcontractor was required to sign a release to obtain progress payments. The court stated: "Where a waiver form purports to acknowledge that no further payments are owed, but the parties' conduct indicates otherwise, the instrument shall not be construed as a release."[111] This result likely could have been avoided if the owner had structured the release as a partial waiver of lien rights limited to the work covered by the progress payment.[112]

On federal projects, final payment by the government bars consideration of any claims for damages under the contract that are submitted subsequent to the final payment.[113] Under the terms of these contracts, the government releases final amounts due under the contract only upon execution of a release by the contractor of all claims against the government, except those specifically excepted. The burden is on the contractor to identify and specify such claims clearly in the release,[114] and exceptions to releases are strictly construed against the government contractor. The rationale behind construing exceptions in releases narrowly is that the purpose of a release is to put an end to the matter in controversy.

STATUTORY DAMAGE LIMITATIONS

Damages Limited to Appropriated Funds

The liability of the government under a public works contract normally is the same as that of a party to a private

---

109. *See* cases cited at West's ⊕⇒ 331 RELEASE, k33.

110. 729 N.Y.S.2d 112 (App. Div. 2001).

111. *Id.* at 114–15.

112. CONSTRUCTION CLAIMS MONTHLY, Vol. 23, No. 11, at 2 (Nov. 2001).

113. *See* Mingus Constructors, Inc. v. United States, 812 F.2d 1387, 1391 (Fed. Cir. 1987); cases cited at West's ⊕⇒ 331 RELEASE, k74(6) .

114. *See* cases cited at West's ⊕⇒ 331 RELEASE, k74(10).

contract.[115] Exculpatory contractual terms are often inserted by the federal government, and some states, in order to limit a public owner's liability to the amount of funds appropriated.[116] A typical provision restricts the government's responsibility for the contract price to a special fund.[117] Contractors are charged with notice of the authorized amount that can be expended for a project. Many courts will not hold a federal or state agency liable for any sum above the appropriated amount, if the contract was entered into pursuant to such a statute.[118]

Notwithstanding these provisions, some courts permit recovery in excess of the funds appropriated for the contract. For instance, judges have avoided this limitation by distinguishing between claims under a contract, and damages for a wrongful breach of that contract.[119] And, in *Bates & Rodgers Construction Co. v. Board of Commissioners*,[120] the court permitted the contractor to recover (despite an appropriated limit) because it was damaged by a breach of duty by specific public officials, the county commissioners.

The enforceability of a government's attempt to limit its liability to funds appropriated often depends on the exact language of the applicable statute. Also, some jurisdictions require a formal ordinance or resolution to establish a ceiling for a municipality's contractual liability.[121] In *R.L. Atkins*,

---

115. *See* Phelps v. Logan Natural Gas & Fuel Co., 128 N.E. 58 (Ohio 1920); 64 AM. JUR. 2D, *Public Works and Contracts* § 139 (2001). The same is true when the United States enters into a contract. *See* Mobil Oil Exploration & Producing Southeast, Inc. v. United States, 530 U.S. 604 (2000); cases cited at West's ⬅ 393 UNITED STATES, k70(1).

116. *See* 1 WITKIN SUMMARY OF CALIFORNIA LAW § 898; cases cited at West's ⬅ 268 MUNICIPAL CORPORATIONS, k250. A number of jurisdictions have statutes discussing this subject, and it is necessary to consult specific state rules.

117. *See* Bilardi Constr. v. Spencer, 86 Cal. Rptr. 406, 408 (Cal. Ct. App. 1970) (refusing to enforce such a provision even though there were insufficient funds in the special fund to pay damages awarded to a contractor for breach of contract).

118. See Annotation, Amount of Appropriation as Limitation on Damages for Breach of Contract Recoverable by One Contracting with Government Agency, 40 A.L.R. 4th 998 (1985).

119. *See, e.g.,* Thomas O'Connor & Co. v. City of Medford, 448 N.E. 2d 1276 (Mass. App. Ct. 1983).

120. 274 F. 659 (N.D. Ohio 1920); *see* cases cited at West's ⬅ 104 COUNTIES, k128.

121. *See* R.L. Atkins, Inc. v. Arix, 675 P.2d 336, 337 (Colo. Ct. App. 1983).

Inc. v. Arix, the town's board of trustees passed an ordinance appropriating $865,599 to a sewer fund, and the town's officers designated $400,000 of that fund for a specific project. The court found that because the only applicable ordinance referred to a fund of $865,599, that amount, instead of the $400,000, represented the appropriation ceiling.[122]

Statutory Restrictions on Damages Amounts

As part of comprehensive tort reform legislation, many states have restricted the amount of damages recoverable for non-economic losses.[123] These statutory caps originally arose in the context of medical malpractice, but they often have been extended to all personal injury actions. One of the major goals of such tort reform efforts was to increase the affordability and availability of insurance by making the risks to insured entities more predictable.[124] Judicial decisions have been less predictable, however, as some courts have declared unconstitutional statutory caps on compensatory damages for noneconomic injuries in common law actions for death, bodily injury, and property damage.[125] Other courts uphold the validity of these statutes.

Where applicable to construction claims, these statutory caps complicate the already complex rules for determining compensatory damages.[126] One issue is whether a court should first reduce an award for comparative fault before applying the cap.[127] Such a method can cause a significant difference

---

122. *Id.* ("Once such an ordinance is enacted, it is a complete protection to the taxpaying public, and is formal record notice to all those contracting with a town or a city").

123. *See, e.g.*, ALASKA STAT. § 09.17.010 (2003) (limiting damages to $400,000 for a single injury or death); COLO. REV. STAT. ANN. § 13-21-102.5 (2002); KANSAS STAT. ANN. § 75-6105(a) (2002) (for damages against government employees and entities under the Kansas Tort Claims Act, imposes a $500,000 per occurrence limit); *see also* cases cited at West's 🔑 115 DAMAGES, k127.

124. *See* General Elec. Co. v. Niemet, 866 P.2d 1361, 1364 (Colo. 1994).

125. *See, e.g.*, Best v. Taylor Machine Works 689 N.E.2d 1057, 1076 (Ill. 1997).

126. *See* William E. Westerbeke & Stephen R. McAllister, *Survey of Kansas Tort Law: Part I*, 49 KAN. L. REV. 1037, 1107 (2001).

127. *See* Bright v. Cargill, Inc., 837 P.2d 348, 369 (Kan. 1992) (the statute "clearly instructs the trial court to apply comparative fault principles before entering judgment for $250,000 for pain and

(continued)

in recovery; applying the cap before determining comparative fault generally will ensure that a plaintiff's award will be
substantially less than the applicable statutory cap.[128]

Statutory restrictions on recoverable damages normally
protect public owners, and occasionally the limited waiver of
sovereign immunity has been coupled with limits on
damages.[129] Such tort reform has not been applied to limit
contract recoveries, but often represents a key issue in any
job site injury claim.

JUDICIALLY CREATED DAMAGE LIMITATIONS

Economic Loss Rule

The economic loss rule, stated simply, provides that in an
action alleging negligence[130] or strict liability,[131] a plaintiff
cannot recover its purely economic damages caused by a
defective product that injures only itself. Economic damages
represent "inadequate value, costs of repair and replacement

---

suffering"); *see also Niemet, supra* note 124, 866 P.2d at 1366 (the cap on noneconomic damages refers
to the individual defendants, and not the plaintiff).

128. *See* Westerbeke & McAllister, *supra* note 126, at 1107.

129. *See, e.g.,* TENN. CODE ANN. §§ 9-8-301, -307 (2002) (containing a waiver of state immunity
and caps on recoverable damages); *Id.* §§ 29-20-101, -131 (containing a waiver of municipal immunity and caps on recoverable damages); *see also id.* § 29-20-403(b)(2)(A); Brian P. Dunigan & Jerry J.
Phillips, *Comparative Fault in Tennessee: Where Are We Going, and Why Are We in This Handbasket?,*
67 TENN. L. REV. 765, 881–82 (2000).

130. Because many more negligence situations tend to occur in the construction industry—a
simple negligence claim may exist against a trade contractor or builder, when a strict liability (or negligence per se) claim does not—this chapter will focus primarily upon the application of the economic
loss rule in negligence-based actions. *See* authorities cited at West's ☞ 115 DAMAGES, k136;
West's ☞ 313A PRODUCTS LIABILITY, k17.1.

131. The economic loss rule is generally also applied in actions alleging strict liability. *See*
Stearman v. Centex Homes, 92 Cal. Rptr. 2d 761 (Cal. Ct. App. 2000) (citing cases); Fieldstone Co. v.
Briggs Plumbing Prods., Inc., 62 Cal. Rptr. 2d 701 (Cal. Ct. App. 1997) (prematurely rusted sinks
damaged only themselves, strict liability claim dismissed); Seely v. White Motor Co., 403 P.2d 145
(Cal. 1965). Strict liability actions under § 402 of the RESTATEMENT (SECOND) OF TORTS (1979)
generally involve manufactured products. Those supplying services are generally not strictly liable. *See*
Murphy v. E.R. Squibb & Sons, Inc., 710 P.2d 247 (Cal. 1985) (strict products liability law does not
apply to services); RESTATEMENT (THIRD) OF TORTS: PRODUCTS LIABILITY, § 19, subd. (b) (1998) ("services, even when provided commercially, are not products" and are governed by the law of negligence).

of the defective product or consequent loss of profits without any claim of personal injury or damage to other property."[132] Economic loss also includes the "diminution in value
of the product because it is inferior in quality and [because
it] does not work for the general purpose for which it was
manufactured and sold."[133]

The principle of the economic loss rule is easiest to apply
in product liability cases, where the rule originated.[134] In
many jurisdictions, the economic loss rule has been extended
to claims against all construction service providers, including
design professionals, contractors, subcontractors, and suppliers, regardless of privity and regardless of whether the claims
allege pure negligence, professional negligence, or negligent
misrepresentation. A number of courts have held that consumer homeowners are barred from asserting negligence actions
against manufacturers to recover economic damages—either
to repair defective construction or for the diminution in
value of their home—unless there is property damage to
some other part of the home.[135] A few courts have held that
once incorporated into the structure, the entire structure

---

132. Note, *Economic Loss in Products Liability Jurisprudence*, 66 COLUM. L. REV. 917, 918 (1966).

133. Comment, *Manufacturers' Liability to Remote Purchasers for "Economic Loss" Damages—Tort or Contract?*, 114 U. PA. L. REV. 539, 541 (1966).

134. Commentators mostly agree that today's economic loss rule was first articulated in Seely v. White Motor Co., 403 P.2d 145 (Cal. 1965) (en banc), which involved the sale, repair, and loss of income from a defective truck. There the court stated:

> The distinction that the law has drawn between tort recovery for physical injuries and war-
> ranty recovery for economic loss is not arbitrary and does not rest on the "luck" of one
> plaintiff in having an accident causing physical injury. The distinction rests, rather, on an
> understanding of the nature of the responsibility a manufacturer must undertake in distribut-
> ing his products.

403 P.2d at 151; *see also* East River S.S. Corp. v. Transamerica Delaval, Inc., 476 U.S. 858 (1986). In each of these cases, the product (a truck and a ship's turbines) damaged itself, causing repair costs and lost profits, but no bodily injury or physical damage to other property or product.

135. While this has long been the position taken by general liability insurers—that if there is no property damage to other property, there is no coverage—recent opinions from the Supreme Courts of California, Nevada, and Alabama prohibit any economic loss claim against construction component suppliers other than a direct contract or warranty claim. These opinions foretell the upcoming battle as to the meaning of property "other than the product itself." *See* Keck v. Dryvit Sys., Inc., 830 So. 2d 1 (Ala. 2002); Aas v. Superior Court, 12 P.3d 1125 (Cal. 2000); Calloway v. City of Reno, 993 P. 2d 1259 (Nev. 2000).

itself becomes the "product."[136] As this result would effectively bar all negligence claims for most economic construction defects, at least one commentator has warned of increased personal injury claims by homeowners to avoid the rule.[137]

The traditional inquiry concerns the type of damage caused by the defective product: Was there injury to a person or other property, or was the damage only to the product? In *Seely v. White Motor Co.*,[138] a consumer's action against a truck manufacturer, the only losses were the cost of repairing the truck and loss of income due to the truck's unserviceable state. These damages were not allowed under negligence or strict liability counts, and, because they represented the plaintiff's only damages, the negligence and strict liability causes of action were dismissed.[139] Viewed thusly, the economic loss rule forms a damages restriction only—barring recovery of certain losses under an otherwise viable negligence or strict liability cause of action.[140]

A proper application of the rule occurs when there are only economic damages. If a plaintiff has sustained bodily injury or physical harm to "other property," then in both cases he or she may recover any economic losses together with those physical damages,[141] assuming, of course, the damages are foreseeable and proximately caused by the defendant's conduct.

---

136. *See* Wilson v. Dryvit Sys., Inc., 206 F. Supp. 2d 749 (E.D.N.C. 2002). *But see* Jimenez v. Superior Court, 58 P.3d 450 (Cal. 2002) (defective windows were a distinct product even after installation due to the ease with which they could be removed from one house and installed in another).

137. *See* Mark D. Boynton, *The Wild West Down East: New Economic Law in Construction Defect Claims*, THE CHANGE ORDER, Vol. 17, No. 2 (N.C. Bar. Assn, Feb. 2003).

138. 403 P.2d 145 (Cal. 1965).

139. The Supreme Court of California (Traynor, C.J.) upheld the plaintiff's claims for breach of express warranty, sustaining the jury award to the plaintiff of the purchase price of the truck and plaintiff's lost profits.

140. *See* Casey v. Overhead Door Corp., 87 Cal. Rptr. 2d 603, 610–11 (Cal. Ct. App. 1999) (plaintiffs were not prejudiced by the trial court ruling *in limine* excluding economic damages, since they could have introduced other evidence to support their negligence count, if they had any).

141. *See* Held v. Mitsubishi Aircraft Int'l, Inc., 672 F. Supp. 369, 376–77 (D. Minn. 1987) (applying Texas law); *see also* authorities cited at West's ⬤➠ 313A PRODUCTS LIABILITY, k17.1. Daanen & Janssen, Inc. v. Cedarapids, Inc., 573 N.W.2d 842, 845 (Wis. 1998) ("The economic loss doctrine, however, does not bar ... economic loss claims that are alleged in combination with noneconomic losses") (citing cases). *But see* World Trade Co. v. WestinghouseElec. Corp., 682 N.Y.S.2d 385, 387 (App. Div. 1998) (fact that two injured workers had negligence claims against product manufac-

The legal and policy considerations that underpin the rule in the products liability context rest upon a manufacturer's responsibility for its goods. Defects that cause physical harm are deemed to be properly chargeable to the manufacturer. Those that affect the product's "level of performance" are not, unless the manufacturer agrees to be so charged (e.g., by giving a warranty).[142] These considerations are said to be based in the different common law concepts dividing tort and contract law. To recover in tort, there must be some showing of harm above and beyond disappointed expectations. [143]

As discussed in Chapter 8, tort remedies began in the twentieth century to insinuate themselves into commercial transactions, including construction-related activities. In the decades following *Seely*, some courts became enamored of the economic loss rule's predictability—so enamored that they began applying the rule in negligence actions outside the manufactured products arena.[144] The eagerness of such courts to expand the rule may be due to the discomfort those same jurists feel about the encroachment of tort duties and remedies into commercial transactions. A close reading of many of these decisions tends to show that to these judges, the

---

turer does not inure to the project owner's benefit when owner's only losses are replacement of defective product and consequential damages thereto).

142. *Seely, supra* note 134, 403 P.2d at 195.

143. *Id.; see* East River S.S Corp. v. Transamerica Delaval, 476 U.S. 858, 871 (1986); Nat'l Union Fire Ins. Co. v. Pratt & Whitney, 815 P.2d 601, 604 (Nev. 1991); *see also* 1 A.R. Frumer & M. I. Friedman, Products Liability § 3.01(2)(f) (1991); authorities cited at West's ☞ 379 TORTS, k5, 11; West's ☞ 313A PRODUCTS LIABILITY, k8, 17.1.

144. Courts generally agree that the economic loss rule does not apply to intentional torts. *See* United Int'l Holdings, Inc. v. Wharf (Holdings) Ltd., 210 F.3d 1207 (10th Cir. 2000) (the breaching party is also a tort feasor); Pulte Home Corp. v. Osmose Wood Preserving, Inc., 60 F.3d 734, 739 (11th Cir. 1995) (builder's negligence claim for defective fire retardant chemical as applied to plywood sheathing barred by rule; fraud claim not barred although not proved); Woodson v. Martin, 685 So.2d 1240 (Fla. 1996) (rule does not apply to fraud claims); Moorman Mfg. Co. v. National Tank Co., 435 N.E.2d 443, 449 (Ill. 1982) (economic damage caused by an intentional tort including fraud is the second of the three *Moorman* exceptions to the economic loss rule); Morris v. Osmose Wood Preserving, Inc., 667 A. 2d 624 (Md. 1995) (in accord with *Pulte*); *see also* William Prosser, W. Page Keeton & Dan B. Dobbs, Prosser and Keeton on the Law of Torts § 101, at 708 (5th Ed. 1984); *but see* Marvin Lumber and Cedar Company v. PPG Indus., Inc., 223 F.3d 873 (8th Cir. 2000) (actionable economic loss claims, even fraud claims, must be based on a representation that was outside of or independent to the content); authorities cited at West's ☞ 115 DAMAGES, k36.

economic loss rule does more than exclude specific damages. Rather, it forms an "anti-tort-in-commercial-transactions" principle, and for some a method to revive more predictable privity-of-contract results.[145]

Most jurisdictions have adopted the economic loss rule in actions involving manufacturers of defective products.[146] In this context, the principle applies regardless of whether the parties are or are not in privity.[147] The concept, however, has not been limited to claims arising from defective products. Many negligence claims must now run the rule's gauntlet.[148] Some states apply the precept to professional services; others

---

145. See, e.g., Calloway v. City of Reno, 993 P.2d 1259, 1266, 1274 (Nev. 2000) ("As stated previously, the economic loss doctrine arose, in large part, from the development of products liability, *but its application is broader and serves to maintain a distinction between contract and tort principles.*" " ... the fundamental policy behind [the economic loss] rule is *to restrict parties to commercial transactions to contractual remedies based simply upon the foreseeability of loss of financial expectancies*") (emphasis added). A number of courts have observed, however, that in applying the economic loss rule in the manufactured products context, privity has no role to play. See, e.g., Sullivan Indus., Inc. v. Double Seal Glass Co., 480 N.W. 2d 623, 629 (Mich. Ct. App. 1991) ("The reliance on privity notions to ascertain whether tort or commercial law applies serves only to blur the distinction between, and the applicability of, commercial law and tort law to economic losses"); see also Bowling Green Mun. Utils. v. Thomasson Lumber Co., 902 F. Supp. 134, 136 (W.D. Ky. 1996) (the underlying rationale is that the rights and duties of the parties should be bargained for at arms' length with the parties negotiating the contract as to the allocation of risk).

146. See authorities cited at West's ⊕═ 313A PRODUCTS LIABILITY, k17.1; see generally 4A AMERICAN LAW OF PRODUCTS LIABILITY §§ 60:36–60:60 (3d ed. 1991, Supp. 1995) and Christopher Scott D'Angelo, The Economic Loss Doctrine: Saving Contract Warranty from Drowning in a Sea of Tort, 26 U. TOL. REV. 591, 609 (1995), for a survey of jurisdictions that have adopted the economic loss rule.

147. See, e.g., Seely, supra note 134, 403 P.2d at 147 (rule applied without privity); Town of Alma v. Azco Constr., Inc., 10 P.3d 1256, 1262–63 (Colo. 2000) (en banc) (discussing workable economic loss rule as an "independent duty rule," which applies to all contractual settings regardless of privity); Sullivan Indus., Inc. v. Double Seal Glass Co., 480 N.W.2d 623, 628–29 (Mich. Ct. App. 1991) (court applied rule to parties not in privity—previous state court opinions applied rule only to parties in privity); National Union Fire Ins. Co. v. Pratt & Whitney Canada, Inc., 815 P.2d 601 (Nev. 1991) (rule applied without privity); Daanen & Janssen, supra note 141, 573 N.W.2d at 846 (economic loss rule applies in the manufactured products context, regardless of privity). See also authorities cited at West's ⊕═ 313A PRODUCTS LIABILITY, k17.1.

148. See Ramerth v. Hart, 983 P.2d 848, 851 (Idaho 1999) (economic loss doctrine "applies to negligence cases in general; its application is not restricted to products liability cases"). See also Local Joint Executive Bd. v. Stern, 651 P.2d 637 (Nev. 1982) (where former employees of the MGM Grand Hotel sought to recover lost salaries and employment benefits while the resort was closed following a fire allegedly caused by defendant, economic loss rule applied to prevent recovery); 532 Madison Ave. Gourmet Foods, Inc. v. Finlandia Ctr., Inc., 750 N.E.2d 1097 (N.Y. 2001) (construction-related disasters in midtown Manhattan caused business closures and loss of income, but no recovery allowed without bodily injury or other property damage). See also authorities cited at West's ⊕═ 272 NEGLIGENCE, k463.

demur.[149] The more broadly the principle is applied, the more opportunity for distinctions, subtle and obvious, in its application and effect.

The nuances of the economic loss rule make it a doctrine that is in some jurisdictions riddled with exceptions, and in others honored mainly in the breach.[150] A decade ago, one court lamented that the concept is "stated with ease, but applied with great difficulty."[151] The same may be said today. Legal commentators and jurists cannot agree upon the reasons courts distinguish between proper and improper applications of the rule.[152] At the end of the twentieth century, an astute Florida jurist observed that in his jurisdiction there were three distinct, but often overlapping, economic loss rules:

> First, there is the products liability economic loss rule: If the defendant's product physically damages only itself, causing additional economic loss, no recovery is permitted in "tort."
>
> Second, there is the contract economic loss rule: If the parties have entered into a contract, the obligations of the contract cannot be relied upon to establish a cause of action in

---

149. *See* the discussion in the next sections of this chapter relating to the application of the rule to construction and design services, and to other professional services.

150. *See, e.g.,* Mark C. & Andrea B. Friedlander, Malpractice and the Moorman Doctrine's "Exception of the Month," 86 ILL. BAR J. 600 (Nov. 1998).

151. Sandarac Assoc. v. W.R. Frizzell Architects, 609 So. 2d 1349, 1352 (Fla. Dist. Ct. App. 1992), *overruled by* Moransais v. Heathman, 744 So.2d 973 (Fla. 1973).

152. *Compare* the discussion and analyses of the rule in three articles within *The Construction Lawyer:* (1) Luther P. House, Jr., and Hubert J. Bell, Jr., *The Economic Loss Rule: A Fair Balancing of Interests,* 11:2 CONSTR. LAW. 1 (April 1991) (rule is correctly applied in the construction industry based upon the presence or lack of a duty of those sought to be held liable); (2) G. Anthony Smith, *The Continuing Decline of the "Economic Loss Rule" in Construction Litigation,* 10:4 CONSTR. LAW. 1 (November 1990) (rule should not be applied in construction setting because of the foreseeability of damage to a limited class of users); (3) Steven B. Lesser, *Economic Loss Doctrine and Its Impact Upon Construction Claims,* 14:3 CONSTR. LAW. 21–26 (August 1994) (injured parties too often have no way to affect the hiring or contractual responsibility of, and have no contractual remedy against, project participants. To deny relief to those so harmed violates the protection and the tenets of *Marbury v. Madison*). *Compare* the analyses of the rule by the court in Casa Clara Condo. Ass'n, Inc. v. Charley Toppino & Sons, Inc., 620 So.2d 1244 (Fla. 1993) (high salt concrete caused rebar to rust and balconies to crumble; mere economic damage to "product") *with* that by the court in Borough of Lansdowne, Pa., v. Sevenson Envtl. Servs., Inc., No. 99–3781, WL 1886578 (E.D. Pa. December 12, 2000) (economic loss rule blocks negligence action against construction professional only when parties are in privity).

tort for the recovery of purely economic damages. ... There must be a separate, "independent tort."

Finally, there is the negligence economic loss rule. Common law negligence generally has not been expanded to protect economic interests in the absence of personal injury or property damage.[153]

How a jurisdiction will apply or refuse to apply these differently stated rules may depend upon how the appellate judiciary of that jurisdiction regards the "collision" at the intersection of tort and contract law. In the absence of binding precedent applicable to a particular set of facts, the timbre of the language used by an appellate court in similar cases can be instructive. Courts that seek to "maintain a distinction between contract and tort principles" are likely to agree with the court that held: "Economic losses from a defective building are just as *offensive* to tort law as damages sought for economic losses stemming from a defective product."[154]

In contrast, if the judiciary acknowledges that a "unique relationship" exists among contractors, subcontractors, and design professionals that creates "an interdependence" among project participants, then the court may be more inclined to hold noncontracting parties accountable for economic losses that foreseeably arise from the failure of a project participant to discharge his contractual duties in a nonnegligent manner.[155] If the appellate opinion goes on to emphasize that the economic loss rule "may have some genuine, but limited, value in our damages law," and that "if the doctrine were generally applied to bar all tort claims for economic losses

153. Woodson v. Martin, 663 So.2d 1327, 1331 (Fla. Dist. Ct. App. 1995) (Altenbernd, J. dissenting), *rev'd*, 685 So.2d 1240 (Fla. 1996).

154. Calloway v. City of Reno, 993 P.2d 1259, 1265–66 (Nev. 2000) (emphasis added); *see also* East River S.S. Corp. v. TransAmerica Delaval, 476 U.S. 858, 866 (1986), setting forth the often-quoted reason for the rule—to protect contract law from "drown[ing] in a sea of tort."

155. *See* Caldwell v. Bechtel, 631 F.2d 989, 1000 (D.C. Cir. 1980); United States *ex rel.* Los Angeles Testing Laboratory v. Rogers & Rogers, 161 F. Supp. 132, 135–36 (S.D. Cal. 1958); Davidson & Jones, Inc. v. New Hanover County, 255 S.E.2d 580 (N.C. Ct. App. 1979).

without accompanying personal injury or property damage, the rule would *wreak havoc on the common law of torts,*[156] one can deduce at least where the court will begin its analysis.

The impact of the economic loss limitation is immense. In the construction arena, the rule eliminates many claims for what would otherwise be categorized as property damage.[157] Because of the concept's draconian effect, many courts have struggled with its application to realty improved by the construction process.[158] A number of jurisdictions do not honor the economic loss rule in special situations involving defective construction products and services that create realty improvements, but these courts have been less than uniform in their approach.[159]

Suffice it to say that there are strong feelings in the bar and the judiciary on the subject of the economic loss rule. Meanwhile, its application continues to be dynamic; courts have changed and may continue to change their minds about its proper scope and breadth.[160]

The Economic Loss Rule Relating to Defective Construction Products

As a child of manufactured products liability law, the economic loss rule first was used in the construction context by courts considering allegations of defective construction

---

156. Moransais v. Heathman, 744 So.2d 973, 983 (Fla. 1999) (emphasis added) (professional engineer's negligent inspection failed to disclose defects that caused economic loss, but had not caused property damage or personal injury).

157. *See* Sidney R. Barrett, Recovery of Economic Loss in Tort for Construction Defects: A Critical Analysis, 40 S.C.L. Rev. 891 (1989); see also Janis K. Cheezem, Economic Loss in the Construction Setting: Toward an Appropriate Definition of "Other Property," 12:2 Constr. Law. 21, 22 (April 1992).

158. *See, e.g.,* dialogue between majority and dissenting opinions in Aas v. Superior Court, 12 P.3d 1125, 1132–35, 1143–50 (Cal. 2000).

159. *See* the discussion in the next section of the text regarding construction services and professional services.

160. *Compare* the analysis by the Florida Supreme Court in *Moransais, supra* note 156, and that by the same court in *Casa Clara, supra* note 152, and by an intermediate Florida appellate court in Sandarac Ass'n Inc. v. W.R. Frizzell Architects, Inc., 609 So.2d 1349 (Fla. Dist. Ct. App. 1992), *overruled* by *Moransais.*

products or equipment.[161] Of the many ways a construction project or its participants could be economically harmed, unlooked-for repair costs, lost profits, and other economic damage due to defective equipment or to a negligently manufactured product stand the closest factually to the *Seely* model and constitute the scenario where the economic loss rule ought to be most uniformly applied. Such has proved to be the case, especially when the product has injured "only itself."[162]

Beyond the simplest of facts, however, the analytical landscape for damage caused by defective construction products becomes cluttered. During the construction process, products and equipment are incorporated into systems, and many hands are laid upon them. Not all products remain in their original form once incorporated into a structure. Incorporated products may be identifiable, but to remove or repair them often injures or destroys still other products. Economic losses to the project owner and project participants can also occur when a product is improperly installed.[163] Structures may diminish in value under the stigma of nascent but unrealized injury due to defective components. And, economic damage can be visited upon the owner or upon various project participants due to improper component-related professional services, including defective design, selection, or coordination of construction components.

---

161. *See* Sacramento Reg'l Transit Dist. v. Grumman Flexible, 204 Cal. Rptr. 736 (Cal. Ct. App. 1984) (repair of defective bus parts was not actionable where defect had not caused further damage); Sunnyslope Grading, Inc. v. Bradford, Miller, & Risberg, Inc., 437 N.W.2d 213 (Wis. 1989) (backhoe's defective parts were covered by manufacturer's warranty, but plaintiff's economic damages in the form of additional repair cost, downtime, and lost profits were denied in a tort action where the defective backhoe caused no injury to another person or other property).

162. *See* William K. Jones, Product Defects Causing Commercial Loss, The Ascendancy of Contract Over Tort, 44 U. MIAMI L. REV. 731 (1990); Annotation, Strict Products Liability: Recovery for Damage to Product Alone, 72 A.L.R. 4th 12 (1985 and Supp. 1995); see also Mid Continent Aircraft Corp. v. Curry County Spraying Service, Inc., 572 S.W.2d 308, 312 (Tex. 1978) (quoting Dean Page Keeton on the difference between a dangerous condition that harms only the product and a condition that is dangerous to other persons or property).

163. Those providing construction services may be liable in negligence or implied warranty, but are generally not strictly liable, for their work or for the components they install. *See* discussion at note 131, *supra;* RESTATEMENT (THIRD) OF TORTS: PRODUCTS LIABILITY, § 19, subd. (b) (1998) ("services, even when provided commercially, are not products" and are governed by the law of negligence).

In many construction situations, those economically damaged by a defectively designed or manufactured product, or by negligent professional conduct or defective construction work relating to such a product, are not in privity of contract with (or do not have a contractual remedy against) the provider of the defective product, work, or service. Often, owners or buyers of construction services cannot influence the selection of construction materials, competently judge the quality of a professional's design selection, or evaluate the work of a trade contractor who installs the product. Nor can they bargain for a warranty from any or all of them.[164]

Losses sustained by owners and participants due to the negligent conduct of others in the process are foreseeable. Under a strict application of the economic loss rule, however, these injuries are not recoverable in a negligence action. A party that lacks contractual remedies against the entity causing the loss,[165] or at least the ability either to close or to leap gaps in the contractual chain, will be denied recovery.[166]

To the extent that the economic loss rule is premised upon the type of damages suffered, it is properly applied in the manufactured products context whether the parties are in privity of contract or not.[167] When employed more as an anti-tort-in-commercial-transactions rule, courts have denied

---

164. *See* Steven B. Lesser, Economic Loss Doctrine and Its Impact upon Construction Claims, 14:3 Constr. Law. 21, 22 (August 1994).

165. As shown by discussions of the various clauses within this chapter, sophisticated parties to the construction process can be very creative in crafting contract clauses that limit contractual liabilities.

166. *See* discussion in Richard E. Speidel, *Warranty Theory, Economic Loss, and the Privity Requirement, Once More Into the Void*, 67 B.U.L. Rev. 9 (1987), using as a model the outcome of Spring Motors Distrib. v. Ford Motor Co., 489 A.2d 660 (N.J. 1985) (where plaintiff allowed the U.C.C. statute of limitations to pass before filing suit, plaintiff's negligence and strict liability claims were barred by the economic loss rule). *See also* authorities cited at West's ☞ 313A PRODUCTS LIABILITY, k17.1; West's ☞ 343 SALES, k255. Even in U.C.C. actions, courts may find that the product loses its character as a "good" for U.C.C. warranty purposes once it is installed or applied upon or within a structure. *See, e.g.,* Keck v. Dryvit Systems, Inc., 830 So.2d 1, 4 (Ala. 2002); *but see* Johnstone, J. in dissent ("the integration of building materials J340 [as] intended by the manufacturers, suppliers, and sellers in no way detracts from the character of those materials, members, or components as products.") 830 So.2d at 14. *See also* Stoney v. Franklin, 44 UCC Rep. Serv.2d 1211 (Va. Cir. Ct. 2001) ("goods exist if they 'are movable at the time of identification to the contract of sale'").

167. *See, e.g.,* Sullivan Indus., Inc. v. Double Seal Glass Co., 480 N.W.2d 623, 628–29 (Mich. Ct. App. 1991) *citing* Consumer Power Co. v. Mississippi Valley Structural Steel Co., 636 F. Supp. 1100, 1106–08 (E.D. Mich. 1986). *See also* authorities cited at West's ☞ 313A PRODUCTS LIABILITY, k17.1, 20.

recovery in negligence when the parties are in privity of contract, despite damage to property "other than the product itself."[168]

In *Myrtle Beach Pipeline Corp. v. Emerson Electric Co.*,[169] specially made pipe leaked, causing a large fuel spill and subsequent clean-up costs. Despite damage to land adjacent to the pipeline project, tort recovery for the clean-up cost was denied on privity grounds.[170] Other courts may be less direct in referring to privity as a reason to deny tort relief, but use the fact that the affected parties have a direct contract (even though not with the defendant tort feasor) to restrict the type of "other property" whose uncontemplated damage would avoid the application of the economic loss rule.[171]

Many jurisdictions have addressed the issue of whether a manufacturer of a defective construction component incorporated into a structure may be liable in negligence. These courts struggle with whether the defective product has caused bodily injury,[172] or physically damaged "property other than the product itself."[173]

---

168. *See* authorities cited at West's ☞ 272 NEGLIGENCE, k463.

169. 843 F. Supp. 1027 (D.S.C. 1993).

170. *Id.* at 1048–55. The court discussed the economic loss rule, but was more impressed that these were "sophisticated parties" to a "negotiated" contract and added that, even if "other property" were damaged, such damage was contemplated by the parties' contract. *Id.* at 1057. *But see* Tourist Vill. Motel, Inc. v. Massachusetts Eng'g Co., 801 F. Supp. 903 (D.N.H. 1992) (where a fuel drum leak damaged plaintiff's property, the economic loss rule was not applied).

171. *See* Palmetto Linen Serv., Inc. v. U.N.X., Inc., 205 F.3d 126, 129 (4th Cir. 2000) ("sophisticated parties" in privity should have contemplated the type of injury sustained, thereby "rendering other property damage inseparable from the defect in the product itself"); Wausau Tile, Inc. v. County Concrete Corp., 593 N.W.2d 445 (Wis. 1999) (where defective cement from supplier in privity caused manufacturer to fabricate and sell defective pavers that cracked, split, and expanded, no recovery in tort was allowed for the purely economic damages to the "product").

172. Most courts are able to consistently discern the presence or absence of a causal link between a defective construction product and bodily injury. More difficult for courts are determinations of whether a defective construction product has caused damage to "other property." In nontraumatic situations, significant bodily injuries proximately caused by a benignly defective construction product (such as a leaking window) are rare. The proximate causation element of emotional distress claims can be attenuated, to say the least. *See, e.g.,* Erlich v. Menezes, 981 P.2d 978 (Cal. 1999) (reversing an award of damages for emotional distress in negligent construction case).

173. *See* County of Chenango Indus. Dev. Agency v. Lockwood Greene Eng'rs, 494 N.Y.S.2d 832 (App. Div. 1985) (building owners could not recover in tort against roofing manufacturer in tort for cracks, splits, and leaks in roof, held to constitute only economic damage). The majority of courts do not differentiate, when the question is the viability of an action in negligence against a *manufacturer*, between types of owner or uses of the structure. Courts are, however, quick to spot, and deny,

The "other property" analysis is rather simple to articulate. Its application is less so. In the construction arena in particular, often the defective nature of a product[174] can cause "physical damage." Examples include water intrusion from an improperly applied roofing membrane and cracked marble flooring due to a badly deflecting floor truss. Whether these damages are recoverable in negligence depends upon how a particular jurisdiction defines "product" and "other property" damaged by the defective product, whether the parties are in privity, and how the jurisdiction frames its desired exceptions to the rule.

If the integrated structure is the "product," the economic loss rule bars recovery for any damaged part of it.[175] A significant number of courts, and the Restatement of Torts,[176] follow the broad "integrated product" analysis. If the defendant manufacturer of the allegedly defective construction

---

economic *de minimus. See* Veeder v. N.C. Machinery Co., 720 F. Supp. 847 (W.D. Wash. 1989) (damage to rug from oil spray *de minimus*); Wisconsin Public Svc. Corp. v. Ecodyne Corp., 702 F. Supp. 217 (E.D. Wis. 1998) (*de minimus* damage to other property insufficient to overcome economic loss rule).

174. Defective design and construction services can also cause physical damage. *See* discussion in the next section of this chapter.

175. *See, e.g.,* Dakota Gasification Co. v. Pascoe Bldg. Sys., 91 F.3d 1094, 1099 (8th Cir. 1996) (applying North Dakota law); Detroit Edison Co. v. NABCO, Inc., 35 F.3d 236 (6th Cir. 1994) (applying Michigan law); Chicago Heights Venture v. Dynamit Nobel, 782 F.2d 723 (7th Cir. 1986) (where defective roofing material allowed leaks damaging building, building was held to be a completed product); Blagg v. Fred Hunt Co., 612 S.W.2d 321 (Ark. 1981) (house may be a "product" just like an automobile); Casa Clara Condo. Ass'n, Inc. v. Charley Toppino & Sons, Inc., 620 So.2d 1244 (Fla. 1993) (concrete with high salt content corroded reinforcing steel in balconies causing balconies to crumble, but court held no damage to "other property"); Foxcroft Townhome Owners Ass'n v. Hoffman Rosner Corp., 449 N.E.2d 125 (Ill. 1983) (damages resulting from defective siding were not damage to "other property"); Calloway v. City of Reno, 993 P.2d 1259, 1267–68 (Nev. 2000) (roofing and siding defects causing water damage to interior structural components were held to be damage to the "product" only); American Towers Owners v. CCI Mech., 930 P.2d 1182 (Utah 1996) (damage to plumbing pipes in the entire complex were damages to the "product" for purposes of the economic loss rule, no recovery). *See also* authorities cited at West's ☞ 272 NEGLIGENCE, k1250–1251; West's ☞ 313a PRODUCT LIABILITY, k17.1, 42.

176. The RESTATEMENT (THIRD) OF TORTS: PRODUCTS LIABILITY (1998) describes the characterization process (separate or incorporated) when products are incorporated into a system as "difficult." Nonetheless, the RESTATEMENT authors opine: "When the product or system is deemed to be an integrated whole, courts treat such damage as harm to the product itself." RESTATEMENT (THIRD) OF TORTS: PRODUCTS LIABILITY § 21, cmt. e, at 295–96 (1998). But as observed by at least one commentator and several courts, this analysis fails to recognize the duties "that arise independently of the pyramid structure of privity created by the tiers of contracts and subcontracts." Cheezem, *supra* note 157, at 22. *See also* Gilbane Building Co. v. Nemours Foundation, 606 F. Supp. 995, 1005 (D. Del. 1985) (recognizing the interdependence of construction participants).

product convinces the court that the product is so integrated into the structure (or a construction system within the structure) that it loses its identity,[177] then the integrated whole becomes the "product." If the structure is the "product," it cannot be "other property" for the purposes of physical damage sufficient to avoid the economic loss rule protecting the manufacturer. On the other hand, a number of courts have not followed the "integrated structure as a product" analysis. These judges allow recovery against a remote manufacturer for property damage to "other property" when the defective product damages another identifiable construction component.[178]

Some defective products cases (most outside the construction arena) allow recovery of economic damages when the cause of physical property damage to a product is an outside source, such as fire.[179] Courts also have made distinc-

---

177. *See, e.g.*, Nat'l Union Fire Ins. Co. v. Pratt & Whitney, 815 P.2d 601 (Nev. 1991) (a defective part in the engine of a factory-assembled airplane damaged the engine and the airplane; the airplane was held to be the integrated whole, and therefore the "product").

178. *See, e.g.*, Lamb v. Georgia-Pacific Corp., 392 S.E.2d 307, 308 (Ga. Ct. App. 1990) (where allegedly defective particle board installed underneath tile floor caused tile to crack, costs to repair damaged portion of the tile floor were recoverable as damage to "property other than the product itself," but other economic damages would be denied); *see also* authorities cited at West's 🔑 115 DAMAGES, k36, 39; West's 🔑 313A PRODUCTS LIABILITY, k17.1, 42; *see also* Saratoga Fishing Co. v. J.M. Martinac & Co., 520 U.S. 875, 879 (1997) (ship's defective component damaged equipment added to the ship after the ship's initial purchase, held, added equipment was "other property"); Pulte Home Corp. v. Osmose Wood Preserving, Inc., 60 F.3d 734, 741 (11th Cir. 1995) ("to satisfy the other property exception [to the economic loss rule], Pulte must establish damage to property aside from the FRT plywood treated with Osmose chemicals." Other components may have been replaced but not because they were *damaged* by the FRT, but rather as *a consequence* of replacing the FRT plywood); Jimenez v. Superior Court, 58 P.3d 450 (Cal. 2002) (strict liability case against a manufacturer; defective windows caused water damage to walls, floors, etc., which were held to be "other property"); Stearman v. Centex Homes, 92 Cal. Rptr. 2d 761 (Cal. Ct. App. 2000) (in strict liability case, defective foundation construction and inadequate soil compaction caused slab movement, deformation, and cracked walls, which were held to be physical damage to "other property"); Comptech Int'l Inc. v. Milam Commerce Park, Ltd., 753 So.2d 1219 (Fla. 1999) (in negligence claim by tenant against landlord for selection of contractor who damaged tenant's electrical systems, warehouse space, and computers during renovation, existing electrical systems and computers were held to be "other property"); United Air Lines, Inc. v. CEI Indus. of Illinois, Inc., 499 N.E.2d 558 (Ill. App. Ct. 1986) (water leaks in defective roof caused collapse of ceiling; Northridge Co. v. W.R. Grace & Co., 471 N.W.2d 179 (Wis. 1991) (asbestos causes physical harm to structure, held structure is "other property" and outside the economic loss rule); City of La Crosse v. Schubert, Schroeder & Assocs., 240 N.W.2d 124 (Wis. 1976) (in remote purchaser's negligence action against manufacturer of a roof that leaked and required replacement, damages to other parts of the structure were recoverable).

179. *See, e.g.*, Rocky Mountain Fire & Cas. Co. v. Biddulph Oldsmobile, 640 P.2d 851 (Ariz. 1982) (where a Winnebago was destroyed by fire, court held economic loss rule does not apply to

tions when damaged property is contained within, but not integrated into, the structure.[180] In *Scott & Fetzer Co. v. Montgomery Ward & Co.*,[181] fire warning systems malfunctioned in a large warehouse occupied by several tenants. The fire spread throughout the warehouse, causing damage to the premises leased by various tenants and to their personal property. The court went so far as to deem the loss of the value of the tenants' leasehold and their personal items to be "not economic," because the damage was for "loss of property other than the defective product."[182]

Courts also struggle with the situation where the product is defective, and potentially dangerous, but has not yet injured anyone. In the *Whiting-Turner* case,[183] the Court of Judicial Appeals of Maryland carved out an exception to the otherwise accepted economic loss rule (barring recovery if the defective product has not caused physical injury) for a defect that can lead to a "serious risk of creating a dangerous condition."[184] There, the defect was both in the product and in the construction installation services of the contractors.

The Maryland court, drilling down into the facts, exposed one of the economic loss rule's major weaknesses when applied in the construction context—that a defective product or condition may be potentially dangerous without causing

---

property damage, but would apply to claim for loss profits or other commercial losses); Gherna v. Ford Motor Co., 55 Cal. Rptr. 94 (Cal. Ct. App. 1966) (where fire in the engine compartment destroyed an entire automobile, some economic losses allowed). *But see* Lloyd Wood Coal Co. v. Clark Equip. Co., 543 So.2d 671 (Ala. 1989) (front end loader's hydraulic hose ruptured, causing a fire, but damage was only to the product itself, and economic losses barred).

180. *See* 2-J Corp. v. Tice, 126 F.3d 539, 544 (3d Cir. 1997) (applying Pennsylvania law) (a collapsed metal building caused damage to stored inventory, which was held "other property" from defective metal building, and manufacturer was liable for economic losses).

181. 493 N.E.2d 1022 (Ill. 1986).

182. *Id.* at 1026. The court also noted that the damage was caused by a "sudden and dangerous conflagration."

183. Council of Co-Owners Atlantis Condo., Inc. v. Whiting-Turner Contracting Co., 517 A.2d 336, 345 (Md. 1986) (electrical utility shafts did not contain required insulation, creating a building code violation and potential hazard).

184. *Id.* Although the project was multifamily residential, the Maryland court did not limit the exception strictly to claims for damage to residential properties.

physical (and therefore recoverable) damage.[185] Even when a defect creates an inherently dangerous situation, the economic loss rule, strictly applied, bars any recovery (and therefore without bodily injury would prevent an action) for the repair or replacement of the defective product.[186] The Maryland court determined that focusing upon the "fortuitous circumstance of the nature of the resultant damage" was the wrong approach.[187]

Other cases have reached just the opposite result. In an economic loss products case involving potentially dangerous corroding steel wall panels,[188] the U.S. Court of Appeals for the Seventh Circuit strictly applied the economic loss rule to the owner's negligence count. Writing for the court, Judge Posner acknowledged that allowing recovery for bodily injuries caused by a defective product (including economic damages arising from the injuries), but barring recovery for economic damages in the absence of bodily injury caused by the same defective product, was a matter of fortuity. Still, Judge Posner observed, the court "could not recast this case as if one of the corroded wall panels had fallen and broken [the plaintiff's] foot."[189]

---

185. In *Whiting-Turner, supra* note 182, the court observed: "Why should a buyer have to wait for a personal tragedy to occur in order to recover damages to remedy or repair defects?" 517 A.2d at 345.

186. One court has opined that only a few jurisdictions allow direct negligence actions for purely economic losses, or have recognized tort-based warranties, against *product manufacturers* of defective construction components not in privity of contract with the plaintiff absent a showing of physical harm or the serious risk of harm. *See* Wilson v. Dryvit Sys., Inc., 206 F. Supp. 2d 749 (E.D.N.C. 2002) (where the structure as a whole suffered only economic damages even though water intrusion allowed by defective cladding caused structural damage, the court held that the economic loss rule applied to claim against a remote manufacturer) (citing cases). *Compare* the application of the rule to construction service providers, at note 231.

187. *Id.; see also* Kennedy v. Columbia Lumber & Mfg. Co., 384 S.E.2d 730, 737 (S.C. 1989), where the court opined: "We find that this legal framework [focusing only upon the type of damage incurred] generates difficulties. This is so because the framework's focus is on consequences, not action. ... The framework we adopt focuses on activity, not consequence."

188. Miller v. United States Steel Corp., 902 F.2d 573 (7th Cir. 1990).

189. *Id.* at 574. Interestingly, less than two years later, in a somewhat analogous case involving commercial general liability coverage for "property damage," Judge Posner wrote, "The incorporation of a defective product into another product inflicts *physical injury* in the relevant sense [insurance coverage] on the latter [the nondefective product] at the moment of incorporation—here, the moment when the defective Qest systems were installed in homes" (emphasis added); *see* Elger Mfg., Inc. v. Liberty Mut. Ins. Co., 972 F.2d 805, 814 (7th Cir. 1992) (declaratory judgment action brought

Other courts have created an exception for buildings, especially schools or governmental offices, that contain asbestos.[190] The cost of removing asbestos, clearly only an economic damage, has been awarded even in jurisdictions that otherwise strongly endorse the economic loss rule.[191]

The courts in Illinois, for instance, seem to be firm supporters of the economic loss rule. Illinois has consistently denied recovery when a defective condition exists but no physical harm has been caused by a defective product other than to itself.[192] When schools and asbestos were involved, however, Illinois found that asbestos fibers in the asbestos-containing materials "may, in certain circumstances, be harmful."[193] In the "circumstance" of the thirty-four school districts in the Chicago area that had removed asbestos-containing materials and were seeking to recover their economic removal costs, the court found the requisite harm.[194] The court admonished, however, that the presence of asbestos "should not be construed as an invitation to bring economic loss contract actions within the sphere of tort law through the use of some *fictional* property damage."[195] [emphasis added]

---

to determine if physical injury occurred for the purposes of property damage triggering commercial general liability coverage); *see also* Roger H. Proulx & Co. v. Crest Liners, Inc., 119 Cal. Rptr. 2d 442 (Cal. Ct. App. 2002) (insurance broker was sued in negligence for failure to procure coverage, and defended on basis that the underlying claims were barred by economic loss rule; court held that claimed damages raised triable issue).

190. *See* authorities cited at West's ⬤ 313A PRODUCT LIABILITY, k42.

191. *See, e.g.,* United States Fid. & Guar. Co. v. Wilkin Insulation Co., 550 N.E.2d 1032 (Ill. App. Ct. 1989) (the installation of insulation containing asbestos in schools and other public buildings was property damage for general liability insurance purposes); Bd. of Educ. v. A, C & S, Inc., 546 N.E.2d 580 (Ill. 1989) (citing cases).

192. The leading case in Illinois is Moorman Mfg. Co. v. Nat'l Tank Co., 435 N.E.2d 443 (Ill. 1982) (a grain storage tank cracked, resulting in a sudden and violent ripping, which fortunately did not extend to the full height of the tank, but the court found economic losses only and refused recovery).

193. *A, C & S, Inc., supra* note 189, 546 N.E.2d at 588.

194. *Id.* The thirty-four school districts in the Chicago area constituted a formidable set of plaintiffs.

195. *Id.* At least one jurist has opined that because tort law reduces even bodily injury to monetary damages, the distinction between physical injury and economic loss is in itself a fiction. *See* F. Malcolm Cunningham, Jr. & Amy L. Fischer, *The Economic Loss Rule: Deconstructing the Mixed Metaphor in Construction Cases,* 33 Tort Ins. L.J. 147, 148 (1997), quoting from the dissent in

(continued)

As many courts around the United States have observed, asbestos cases are "unique in the law."[196] A number of the earlier asbestos-in-building decisions conflict with other appellate decisions from the same jurisdictions,[197] as owners were allowed to recover the economic cost of removing asbestos-containing materials without a showing of bodily injury or physical damage other than the "contamination" of the structure itself.[198] Within a decade, however, jurisdictions comfortable with a broader application of the economic loss rule dealt with asbestos-in-building cases by not allowing tort actions until asbestos was airborne within the structure, and dismissing negligence-based claims until the asbestos-containing material was friable.[199] Friable asbestos, which allowed asbestos fibers to be released into the environment of

---

Floor Craft Floor Covering, Inc. v. Parma Cmty. Gen. Hosp. Ass'n, 560 N.E.2d 206, 213–16 (Ohio 1990) (Brown, J. dissenting). *Compare* the opinion in *A, C & S, supra* note 189, at 585–86 *with* that of the same court in Redarowicz v. Ohlendorf, 441 N.E.2d 324, 331 (Ill. 1982) (when defective soil compaction caused the chimney and adjoining wall at plaintiff's residence to pull away from the house, the court held this a mere disappointed expectation: "the only danger to the plaintiff is that he would be forced to incur additional expenses for living conditions that were less than what was bargained for."); *see also* Foxcroft Townhome Owners Ass'n v. Hoffman Rosner Corp., 449 N.E.2d 125 (Ill. 1983) (economic loss rule bars damages resulting from defective siding without personal injury or damage to "other property").

196. *See* San Francisco United Sch. Dist. v. W.R. Grace & Co., 44 Cal. Rptr. 2d 305, 307–08 (Cal. Ct. App. 1995) (citing cases).

197. *Compare* City of Greenville v. W.R. Grace & Co., 827 F.2d 975 (4th Cir. 1987) (applying South Carolina law) (asbestos fireproofing created risk of asbestos-related diseases, and city could maintain negligence action for solely economic losses); *with* 2000 Watermark Ass'n v. Celotex Corp., 784 F.2d 1183,1185 (4th Cir. 1986) (applying South Carolina law) (blistering roof at plaintiff's condominium project constituted mere economic loss, and recovery in negligence was unavailable, *citing* East River S.S. Corp. v. Transamerica Delaval, Inc., 476 U.S. 858 (1986)); and Myrtle Beach Pipeline Corp. v. Emerson Elec. Co., 843 F. Supp. 1027 (D. S.C. 1993).

198. *See, e.g.,* City of Manchester v. Nat'l Gypsum Co., 637 F. Supp. 646, 651 (D.R.I. 1986) (the measure of damages [economic] does not transform the nature of the injury [here, physical injury to "other property"] into solely economic loss; economic loss rule was not applied); Town of Hooksett Sch. Dist. v. W.R. Grace & Co., 617 F.Supp 126 (D.N.H. 1984) (contamination of premises from asbestos constitutes physical injury to other property); *see also* Mt. Lebanon Sch. Dist. v. W.R. Grace & Co., 607 A.2d 756 (Pa. Super. Ct. 1992) (no physical harm, but economic rule not applied as nonprofit involved); Livingston Bd. of Educ. v. U.S. Gypsum, 592 A.2d 653 (N.J. Super. Ct. App. Div. 1991) (although there was no physical harm, economic loss rule did not apply).

199. *See* discussion and survey of cases in *San Francisco United Sch. Dist., supra* note 194, 37 Cal. App. 4th at 1334; *see also* Adams-Arapahoe Sch. Dist. No. 28-J v. GAF Corp., 959 F.2d 868, 871–73 (10th Cir. 1992) (applying Colorado law). *See also* authorities cited at West's ☞ 241 LIMITATION OF ACTIONS, k55 (1)(2).

the structure, "contaminated" the structure; the mere presence of asbestos (e.g., in a relatively inert tile product) did not.[200]

The Economic Loss Rule as Applied to the Work of Contractors

For builders, general contractors, and trade contractors, the economic loss rule can be a boon and a bust. The rule protects contractors from unanticipated tort claims, but also may prevent them from recovering repair and replacement costs caused by defective work or products of others.[201]

Construction involves the delegation and allocation of responsibility by contract. Within the "pyramid" of this process, however, many of the participants are not in privity of contract with others. Their defective work and products[202] can cause economic damage to other providers, and cause other contractors to be targets of claims involving defective work.[203] Strictly applied, the economic loss rule often prohibits direct actions by construction participants against those principally responsible for construction defects.

The economic loss rule regularly bars economic damages asserted in negligence actions brought against construction contractors and subcontractors, whether or not the parties to the action are in privity.[204] Naturally, there are exceptions, and different courts emphasize different legal concepts. The issues taken up by the courts to determine the extent of the rule where construction services are involved differ slightly from those grappled with by courts concerning manufactured

---

200. *Adams-Arapahoe, supra* note 197, 959 F.2d at 872; *see also* Comment, *Asbestos in Schools and the Economic Loss Doctrine*, 54 U. Chi. L. Rev. 277, 298–300 (1987).

201. *See, e.g.,* Pulte Home Corp. v. Parex, Inc., 579 S.E.2d 188 (Va. 2003) (builder repaired cladding defects, but was denied right to pursue indemnity and warranty claim against manufacturer due to lack of privity in contract and the economic loss rule in tort).

202. Construction providers do not manufacture or supply "products," at least for strict liability purposes. *See* Restatement (Third) of Torts: Products Liability, § 19, subd. (b) (1998) ("services, even when provided commercially, are not products" and are governed by the law of negligence.)

203. It is important for contractors of all stripes to be able to quantify exposure for construction defects, especially to the extent insurance carriers will deny coverage. The economic loss rule accomplishes this goal, although in rough and irregular fashion.

204. *See* authorities cited at West's ☞ 272 NEGLIGENCE, k321, 463.

products.[205] In addition to privity of contract, courts look to the scope of work and duties the service provider has undertaken contractually, whether damage to "other property" has occurred, and whether the defective work can be related to an independent duty. While a few courts deem lack of privity an absolute bar,[206] most states perceive privity as a starting point to discuss scope of services and the presence or absence of an independent duty.

If the plaintiff and the construction service provider are parties to a contract, and the economic damage claimed is to the contractual (or subcontractual) subject matter of the work, the economic loss rule generally bars recovery in negligence for economic damages claimed.[207] If the plaintiff is not in privity with the provider of defective work, but the work was the subject matter of the provider's contract, the rule will also generally bar economic damages to the work.[208] On the other hand, whether privity exists or not, a plaintiff may

---

205. The agreements of construction service providers are, for instance, generally not governed by the U.C.C.

206. See Sensenbrenner v. Rust, Orling & Neal Architects, Inc., 374 S.E.2d 55 (Va. 1988) (homeowners' action against pool subcontractor and architect dismissed for lack of privity). This holding is consistent with the law in the Old Dominion. See discussion infra relating to design professionals, at note 229.

207. See Anderson Elec., Inc. v. Ledbetter Erection Corp., 503 N.E.2d 246 (Ill. 1986) (no recovery for economic losses caused by negligent performance of construction services); Spillman v. American Homes, 422 S.E.2d 740, 741–42 (N.C. App. 1992) ("a tort action does not lie against a party to a contract who simply fails to properly perform the terms of the contract ... when the injury resulting from the breach is damage to the subject matter of the contract"); Atherton Condo. Apartment-Owners Ass'n Bd. of Directors v. Blume Dev. Co., 799 P.2d 250, 262 (Wash. 1990) (en banc) (no recovery in negligence for economic damages caused by faulty construction, despite privity), citing Stuart v. Coldwell Banker Commercial Group, Inc., 745 P.2d 1284 (Wash. 1987). See also authorities cited at West's ⊕═ 272 NEGLIGENCE, k321, 463. See also authorities cited West's ⊕═ 272 NEGLIGENCE, k463.

208. Nastri v. Wood Bros. Homes, Inc., 690 P.2d 158, 163–64 (Ariz. Ct. App. 1984) (despite latent structural defects, remote purchasers could not recover from the builder on a negligence theory, but could recover for implied-in-law warranty of habitability); Jardel Enters., Inc. v. Triconsultants, Inc., 770 P.2d 1301 (Colo. Ct. App. 1988) (restaurant owner could not bring negligence claim against subcontractor for lost profits resulting from delayed opening of restaurant due to initial construction of the restaurant at the wrong location); Calloway v. City of Reno, 993 P.2d 1259, 1261–62 (Nev. 2000) (townhome owners' claims against subcontractors for economic losses caused by defective roofing and siding did not state cause of action in negligence); cf. Real Estate Mktg., Inc. v. Franz, 885 S.W.2d 921 (Ky. 1994) (claim by remote purchaser was barred; court noted that "tort recovery is contingent upon damage from a destructive occurrence as contrasted with economic loss related solely to diminution in value").

avoid the economic loss rule by demonstrating that the defendant breached a tort duty, independent of (although generally related to) the service provider's contract.[209]

Economic injuries caused by the defective work but visited upon "other property" may be enough to allow a negligence action to proceed.[210] Damage to "other property" generally means property unrelated to the service provider's work. Thus, the "incorporation" and "integration" analysis concerning manufactured products also pertains to claims against and among service providers.[211]

Recovery in negligence for purely economic damages requires the breach of a separate, independent tort duty. [212]

---

209. *See* Town of Alma v. Azco Constr., Inc., 10 P.3d 1256, 1264 (Colo. 2000) (en banc) (town was in privity with contractor, other plaintiffs were not; the court made no distinction based on privity, but adopted and applied a "workable" economic loss rule based on the extent of contractual duty and lack of independent tort duty and relied on it to deny liability for the repair of construction defects and other consequential economic damages. The court acknowledged that the rule would not apply to damages from separate tort) (citing cases); Consol. Hardwoods, Inc. v. Alexander Concrete Constr., Inc., 811 P.2d 440, 443 (Colo. Ct. App. 1991) (owner's negligence claim against subcontractor allowed because independent duty was breached); Juliano v. Gaston, 455 A.2d 523 (N.J. 1982) (owner may recover against subcontractor in negligence for economic damages). *See also* authorities cited at West's ⊕═ 379 TORTS, k5, 1251.

210. *See, e.g.,* Aas v. Superior Court, 12 P.3rd 1125, 1130 (Cal. 2000) (homeowners' association and individual homeowners could not bring negligence actions against developer, contractor, or subcontractors for construction defects or diminution in value, unless damage to "other property" could be shown. "Any construction defect can diminish the value of a house. But the difference between price paid and value received, and deviations from standards of quality that have not resulted in property damage or personal injury, are primarily the domain of contract and warranty law or the law of fraud, rather than of negligence") (citing cases).

211. *See* discussion earlier in this chapter as to the incorporation of products and services to form an "integrated product"—the structure. *But see* Comptech Int'l, Inc. v. Milam Commerce Park, Ltd., 753 So.2d 1219 (Fla. 1999) (tenant sued landlord for negligent selection of contractor, who, in renovating tenant space in warehouse, damaged electrical and computer equipment; the court held that the contract was for a service, the renovation, and suggested that services do not involve "other property," however to the extent that the warehouse was the object of the contract, the wiring and computers were "other property"); McDonough v. Whalen, 313 N.E.2d 435, 439 (Mass. 1974) (owner could recover against subcontractor for negligent design and installation of septic system and recover economic damages despite lack of privity; sewage "flowing over their land" is damage to 'other property' for purposes of avoiding the economic loss rule. The implied warranty of habitability was not discussed).

212. *See* Town of Alma, *supra* note 147, and cases cited therein; *see also* authorities cited at West's ⊕═ 379 TORTS, k5, 1251. *see also* United Int'l Holdings, Inc., v. Wharf (Holdings) Ltd., 210 F.3d 1207 (10th Cir. 2000) (deliberate or negligent conduct inducing reliance constitutes an independent tort); Olympic Prods. Co. v. Roof Sys., Inc., 363 S.E.2d 367 (N.C. App. 1988) (manufacturer's failure to properly inspect installation or thereafter to report improper installation was negligent, and economic damages were allowed); Raynor Steel Erection v. York Constr. Co., 351 S.E.2d

(continued)

If the plaintiff is in privity of contract with the defendant, breach of the obligations of the contract ordinarily cannot be relied upon to support an action in negligence; the parties have already selected a contractual remedy. Failure to perform one's contract, even carelessly, may not support a negligence action for economic damages.[213]

In construction defect cases, many courts distinguish on public policy grounds between homeowner residences and commercial projects. Most states recognize implied-in-law warranties in the sale of new residences by builder-vendors.[214] A few courts recognize a general exception to the economic loss rule in negligence actions against builders and sub-contractors arising out of new residential construction. In *Kennedy v. Columbia Lumber & Manufacturing Co.*,[215] the Supreme Court of South Carolina held that to apply the economic loss rule to insulate contractors from liability for building code violations would be "repugnant" to South Carolina's public policy.[216] While the principal example within the *Kennedy* opinion was the residential builder whose work did not meet minimum building codes,[217] this court later

---

allowed in negligence due to general contractor's failure to properly install); Oates v. JAG, 333 S.E.2d 222, 224–26 (N.C. 1985) (remote homeowner may recover economic damages against original builder in negligence action); Brown v. Fowler, 279 N.W.2d 907 (S.D. 1979) (remote residence purchaser has a negligence claim against builder for economic damages due to breach of separate duty. This was not an action on an implied warranty of habitability, which under South Dakota law extends only to the initial purchaser).

213. *See, e.g.*, Palmetto Linen Service, Inc. v. U.N.X., Inc., 205 F.3d 126, 129 (4th Cir. 2000) (applying South Carolina law), *quoting from* Kennedy v. Columbia Lumber & Mfg. Co., 384 S.E.2d 730, 737 (S.C. 1989) ("the 'economic loss' rule will still apply where duties are created *solely* by contract") (emphasis in original). *See also* authorities cited at West's ☞ 313A PRODUCTS LIABILITY, k17.1.

214. Many courts have recognized implied-in-law construction-related warranties to homeowners, including implied warranties of habitability and of workmanlike construction. These are frequently measured by minimum building codes. Although related to negligence actions, these warranties permit a cause of action based on an implied duty, thereby avoiding the economic loss rule.

215. 384 S.E.2d 730 (S.C. 1989).

216. *Id.* at 734.

217. *Id.* The precise holding in *Kennedy* did not concern a general contractor. A supplier who acquired title to a new residence by lien foreclosure settlement (against the builder) and who then sold the residence to the Kennedys was held not to be a builder-vendor for purposes of the implied warranty of habitability. Nevertheless, the cause of the lawsuit—the general contractor's defective foundation—became the launching pad for the court to announce its rejection of the economic loss

expanded its holding to include developers and those providing defective professional construction services in the new home market.[218]

For those jurisdictions that recognize negligence actions against builders and trade contractors, regardless of privity, upon a showing of an "independent tort," some plaintiffs have found a valuable ally in the state building codes. A violation of a minimum building code is generally regarded as more than "mere discomfort."[219] Such transgressions have proven durable in supporting claims based in negligence[220] as well as implied-in-law warranties (such as habitability).[221]

The building code standard can prove powerful, because repair costs to meet it are certain and diminution in value to a home is easily understood. Further, it must be remembered that jurists (and jurors) are homeowners and tend to sympathize (if not empathize) with homeowners, who generally do not select structural materials or draft the construction contract.

---

rule in the new home residential construction context where the work of contractors did not meet minimum building codes. Code compliance was determined to be a separate duty actionable in negligence, and economic damages were recoverable for the breach of that separate duty. *Id.*

218. *Id.* at 735; *see also* Beachwalk Villas Condo. Ass'n, Inc. v. Martin, 406 S.E.2d 372 (S.C. 1991) (condominium owners could sue architect for negligent design and contract administration). The court's negligence liability net captures other construction service providers, including subcontractors and suppliers.

219. *Compare* Sullivan v. Smith, 289 S.E.2d 870, 873 (N.C. Ct. App 1982) (general contractor and masonry subcontractor were both liable in negligence action for economic damages, for breach of independent tort duty to build fireplace and chimney to minimum building codes) *with* Redarowicz v. Ohlendorf, 441 N.E.2d 324 (Ill. 1982) (remote homeowner's claim against builder did not sound in negligence but in implied warranty of habitability although court held it was "mere discomfort" to have chimney pull away from house due to defective construction).

220. *See* Cosmopolitan Homes, Inc. v. Weller, 663 P.2d 1041 (Colo. 1983) (en banc) (fourth purchaser may recover economic damages in negligence based on builder's latent defects in residence); Kristek v. Catron, 644 P.2d 480 (Kan. Ct. App. 1982) (builder was liable to remote purchaser in negligence for economic damages caused by defective roof). *See also* authorities cited at West's ☞ 272 NEGLIGENCE, k1025.

221. *See* Keyes v. Guy Bailey Homes, Inc., 439 So.2d 670 (Miss. 1983) (remote purchaser may recover in negligence for economic damages and for breach of implied-in-law warranties against builder despite lack of privity, economic loss rule not discussed); Moxley v. Laramie Builders, Inc., 600 P.2d 733 (Wyo. 1979) (negligence action and implied warranty of habitability claim by remote home purchaser against builder for economic damages caused by latent defects were allowed, even though builder's work was accepted by first owner before damages were made manifest. Wyoming also applies implied warranty to second purchaser). *See also* authorities cited at West's ☞ 95 CONTRACTS, k205.35.

The Economic Loss Rule as Applied to Professional Services

Professional services in the construction context are supplied by architects, engineers, and related consultants.[222] Their negligence creates a conundrum for the economic loss rule.

Negligent professional services, including design and construction administration services, can economically injure any construction participant, from the owner to a second-tier supplier. The harm can be direct or involve principles of indemnification. The foreseeable class of economically damaged plaintiffs with legitimate negligence claims against design professionals is large, greater even perhaps than against a negligent trade contractor. The set of individuals adversely affected economically by a contractor's faulty work normally is limited to the users of such project, whereas a design professional's negligence can cause economic losses to owners, users, and project participants.

As discussed in Chapters 7 and 8, the scope of services undertaken by a design professional directly affects the breadth of the duty required of the professional. Once the obligation is identified, the architect or engineer must meet the standard of care for the services undertaken. To recover in negligence against a design professional, there must be proof of a breach of the standard of care owed. Similarly, most contract-based actions against design professionals also require plaintiffs to demonstrate a breach of the professional standard of care assumed for the activity in question.[223] On these points, jurisdictions generally agree. Beyond this legal framework, courts part company. Who may and who may not maintain a negligence action against a design professional for economic loss is a matter as much of local legal inference as legal analysis.[224]

---

222. Hydrologists, geotechnical engineers, and geologists are examples of related professional consultants. Licensure or registration with a state governing board normally determines a consultant's status.

223. See Chapter 7 of this text.

224. The discussion in this chapter concerns economic losses sustained by owners, end users, and project participants. Instances of bodily injury and physical property damage can also occur, and

It is in the context of construction design professional services that the application of the economic loss rule is most difficult to reconcile. No analytical theme predominates. It is almost as if someone had written the words "privity," "special relationship," "foreseeability," "supervising architect," "no duty," and "covered by another contract" on the six sides of a die, and then passed the die around the appellate judiciaries of various states. The only constant is that economic damages are the subject of the claim.

Some courts find that if an owner has reached a bargain with the design professional as to the scope and standard of professional services, the owner must look to that agreement for resolution of economic disputes.[225] Other jurisdictions, however, allow a party in privity with a design professional, such as an owner, to bring simultaneously an action for breach of contract and one for professional negligence.[226] This can be significant, as statutes of limitation and other procedural rules vary between contract and tort-based causes of action.[227] Also, disclaimers in contractual language may

---

are discussed in Chapter 8. The issue of damage to property "other than the product itself," which pervades the discussion of the economic loss rule in the manufactured product context, is recast in the services context, reappearing as the issue of whether the damage was contemplated by "a contract."

225. *See, e.g.*, City Express, Inc. v. Express Partners, 959 P.2d 836 (Haw. 1998) (economic loss rule barred owner's negligence action against a design professional where the two were in privity of contract); Brushton-Moira Cent. Sch. Dist. v. Alliance Wall Corp., 600 N.Y.S.2d 511 (App. Div. 1993) (where panels selected by architect were inappropriate for school project, the contract action was allowed and the tort action dismissed); Key Int'l Mfg. v. Morse/Diesel, Inc., 536 N.Y.S.2d 792 (App. Div. 1988) (owner cannot sue architect or prime contractor in negligence for economic loss since the damages sought are of the type remediable in contract). *See also* authorities cited at West's ⊕═ 272 NEGLIGENCE, k1251; West's ⊕═ 184 FRAUD, k13(3).

226. *See, e.g.*, Consol. Edison Co. v. Westinghouse Elec. Corp., 567 F.Supp 358 (S.D.N.Y. 1983) (architect was liable to owner in contract and in negligence); Kellogg v. Pizza Oven, Inc., 402 P.2d 633, 635 (Colo. 1965) (claim sounds in negligence separate from contract); Robinson Redevelopment Co. v. Anderson, 547 N.Y.S.2d 458 (App. Div. 1989) (negligence action allowed); Housing Vermont v. Goldsmith & Morris, 685 A.2d 1086 (Vt. 1996) (malpractice action allowed when site grading plan was insufficient for construction purposes). *See also* authorities cited at West's ⊕═ 272 NEGLIGENCE, k321. Design professionals may also be individually liable in negligence even though they practice through a corporation. *See Moransais, supra* note 156 (owner was allowed to bring a negligence action against the individual professional engineers and a contract action against the engineering services company with which the owner had contracted); *see generally* discussion in Chapter 7 of this text.

227. *See* Milwaukee Partners v. Collins Eng'rs, Inc., 485 N.W.2d 274 (Wis. Ct. App. 1992) (owner's contract claim was barred by statute of limitations but its tort action was allowed to proceed).

govern the contract action, but not the action for professional negligence.[228]

For third parties not in privity with the design professional, the reported cases go both ways, and the legal bases for the decisions are mixed. A number of courts hold that no action for economic losses may be maintained by a third party against a construction design professional, regardless of the scope of its services or the foreseeability of harm.[229] In the majority of these jurisdictions, the economic loss rule (generally the "no duty" or "covered by another contract" side of the die rather than the "privity" side) is invoked to reach this result.[230]

These courts do not dismiss third-party actions because they lack privity as such, but instead deduce that plaintiffs not in privity are not owed a duty by the design professional—thereby cutting off all damages.[231] To these judges, it is often at least noteworthy that the contract between the contractor and the owner contains provisions (including limitations) relating to foreseeable economic losses.[232] At least one juris-

---

228. *See* Diocese of Rochester v. R-Monde Contractors, 562 N.Y.S.2d 593 (Sup. Ct. 1989) (exculpatory terms within the owner/architect contract did not bar a claim for professional negligence); Bd. of Educ. v. Sargent, Webster, Crenshaw & Folley, 539 N.Y.S.2d 814 (App. Div. 1989) (disclaimers in architect's agreement with owner did not absolve architect from duty to alert owner of defective construction).

229. *See* authorities cited at West's ⊕═ 272 NEGLIGENCE, k1205(4), 1251.

230. *See, e.g.,* Fireman's Fund Ins. Co. v. SEC Donohue, Inc., 679 N.E.2d 1197 (Ill. 1997) (economic loss rule applies to engineers and architects, barring any recovery in tort for economic losses); 2314 Lincoln Park West Condo. Ass'n v. Mann, Gin, Ebel & Frazier Ltd., 555 N.E. 2d 346 (Ill. 1990) (same); Border Brook Terrace Condo. Assoc. v. Gladstone, 622 A.2d 1248 (N.H. 1993) (economic loss doctrine applied). Floor Craft Floor Covering, Inc. v. Parma Community Gen. Hosp. Ass'n, 560 N.E.2d 206 (Ohio 1990) (in accord with *Widett*); American Towers Owners Ass'n, Inc., v. CCI Mech., Inc. 930 P.2d 1182, 1192 (Utah 1996) (same); Atherton Condo. Apartment-Owners Ass'n Bd. of Directors v. Blume Dev. Co., 799 P.2d 250, 262 (Wash. 1990) (en banc) (same); Widett v. U.S. Fid. & Guar. Co., 815 F.2d 885, 886–87 (2d Cir. 1987) (absent privity, architect was not liable for professional negligence to subcontractors that detrimentally relied on erroneous site plans).

231. *See, e.g.,* Fleischer v. Hellmuth, Obata & Kassabaum, Inc., 870 S.W.2d 832 (Mo. Ct. App. 1993) (architect had no duty to construction manager); Rissler & McMurray Co. v. Sheridan Area Water Supply Joint Powers Bd., 929 P.2d 1228 (Wyo. 1996) (engineer's duty under its contract with the water board did not extend to the contractor either under a design negligence theory or a negligent misrepresentation theory; *but see* Miller v. Big River Concrete, LLC, 14 S.W.3d 129, 134 (Mo. Ct. App. 2000) (engineer's negligence in conducting tests was actionable in negligence and negligent misrepresentation despite lack of privity).

232. *See also* Berschauer/Phillips Constr. Co. v. Seattle Sch. Dist. No.1, 881 P.2d 986 (Wash. 1994) (en banc) (limiting contractor's recovery of economic damages to remedies provided and disclaimed in owner/contractor contract).

diction, however, has not employed the economic loss rule (denominated as such) in professional negligence actions, but instead has relied consistently and strictly upon privity of contract to reject a third-party cause of action for professional negligence.[233]

Other jurisdictions allow third parties to assert professional negligence actions for economic damages.[234] The legal basis cited in these decisions rests in the reasonable foreseeability that harm may result to a particular group from the design professional's negligent conduct.[235] This foreseeability creates a duty to use due professional care. Some courts distinguish between design services that predate the commencement of construction and professional services performed during the project. Several of these opinions refer to a "special relationship" between an architect who has contract administration duties and the project participants.[236] California was one of the first jurisdictions to recognize that a "supervising architect," who holds the power of the purse against the contractor, has power "tantamount to life or

---

233. *See* Bryant Elec. Co. v. City of Fredricksburg, 762 F.2d 1192 (4th Cir. 1985) (there is no cause of action for a contractor to recover against an engineer for economic loss in the absence of privity under Virginia law); Blake Constr. Co. Inc. v. Alley, 353 S.E.2d 724, 727 (Va. 1987). Unlike other jurisdictions, Virginia is uniformly strict in its privity requirement, for all professionals. *See, e.g.,* Ward v. Ernst & Young, 435 S.E.2d 628 (Va. 1993) (action against CPA requires privity); Copenhaver v. Rogers, 384 S.E.2d 593 (Va. 1998) (privity required in claim against attorney). Virginia also requires privity for most indemnification actions. *See* Pulte Home Corp. v. Parex, Inc., 579 S.E.2d 188 (Va. 2003).

234. See generally Matthew S. Steffey, *Negligence, Contract, and Architect's Liability for Economic Loss,* 82 KY. L.J. 659, 662 (1993); Annotation, *Tort Liability of Project Architect for Economic Damages Suffered by Contractor,* 65 A.L.R.3D 249 (1975).

235. *See, e.g.,* Ins. Co. of N. Am. v. Town of Manchester, 17 F. Supp. 2d 81, 84 (D. Conn. 1998) (applying Connecticut law) ("foreseeability is key to the determination of a cause of action in negligence").

236. *See* E.C. Ernst, Inc. v. Manhattan Constr. Co., 551 F.2d 1026 1031–32 (5th Cir. 1977) (applying Alabama law); Donnelly Constr. Co. v. Oberg/Hunt/Gilleland, 677 P.2d 1292, 1295–97 (Ariz. 1984); Hewett-Kier Constr., Inc. v. Lemuel Ramos & Assocs., Inc., 775 So.2d 373 (Fla. App. 2002); A.R. Moyer, Inc. v. Graham, 285 So.2d 397 (Fla. 1973) ("supervising architect"); Craig v. Everett M. Brooks Co., 222 N.E.2d 752, 755 (Mass. 1967) (engineer was not liable for mistakes in his plans, but was for professional negligence in improperly placing stakes needed to locate and direct construction); Pritchard Bros., Inc. v. Grady Co., 428 N.W.2d 391 (Minn. 1988) (contractor may sue architect for professional negligence and for purely economic loss); Tommy L. Griffin Plumbing & Heating Co. v. Jordan, Jones & Goulding, Inc., 463 S.E.2d 85 (S.C. 1995) (engineer owed contractor a duty not to negligently design or negligently supervise project and was liable to contractor even absent privity for economic losses).

death."[237] Other jurisdictions decline to draw so fine a distinction,[238] and enforce provable economic loss actions against construction design professionals for various sorts of professional conduct.[239]

In allowing negligence actions to proceed against design professionals in the absence of privity, courts follow precedent established in other professional liability situations.[240] The construction process, however, is viewed by some jurisdictions as a different area of commerce, needing different legal rules. Illinois, for instance, allows nonprivity negligence actions against other professionals and nonprofessionals outside the construction process, including accountants,[241] attorneys,[242] and stock market indexing services,[243] but not against architects.

---

237. United States *ex rel.* Los Angeles Testing Lab. v. Rogers & Rogers, 161 F. Supp. 132, 136 (S.D. Cal. 1958).

238. *See* Bagwell Coatings, Inc. v. Middle South Energy, Inc., 797 F.2d 1298 (5th Cir. 1986) (contractor's negligence action allowed against architect who was aware contractor would be harmed if architect did not properly perform his contractual duties to owner); Mayor & City Council v. Clark-Dietz & Assocs. Engrs, Inc., 550 F. Supp. 610, 623 (N.D. Miss. 1982) (architect owes duty to those parties proximately suffering economic losses as a result of architect's negligent design); Stone's Throw Condo. Ass'n, Inc. v. Sand Cove Apartments, Inc., 749 So.2d 520, 522 (Fla. Dist. Ct. App. 1999) (architect's failure to design to state minimum building code and for negligent misrepresentation are not barred by economic loss rule despite lack of privity); Moransais v. Heathman, 744 So.2d 973, 983 (Fla. 1999) ("the mere existence of such a contract should not serve per se to bar an action for professional malpractice"); Magnolia Constr. Co. v. Mississippi Gulf S. Eng'rs, Inc., 518 So.2d 1194, 1202 (Miss. 1988) (third parties are entitled in Mississippi to rely on a design professional's contractual obligation to the owner and may recover economic losses for architect's negligence); Conforti & Eisele, Inc. v. John C. Morris Assoc., 418 A.2d 1290 (N.J. Super. 1980) (contractors may sue architects for professional negligence despite lack of privity); Shoffner Indus., Inc. v. W.B. Lloyd Constr. Co., 257 S.E.2d 50, 55–59 (N.C. Ct. App. 1979). *But see* R.H. Macy & Co. v. Williams Tile & Terrazo, Inc. 585 F. Supp. 175, 180 (N.D. Ga. 1984) (applying Georgia law, architect owes no tort duty to subcontractor if their relationship does not "approach" that of privity or reliance).

239. *See, e.g.,* Dufficy & Sons, Inc. v. BRW, Inc., No. 01CA2201, 2002 WL 31601023 (Colo. Ct. App. Nov. 21, 2002) (citing cases).

240. *See, e.g.,* Ins. Co. of N. Am. v. Town of Manchester, 17 F. Supp. 2d 81 (D. Conn. 1998) (design professionals, like other professionals such as accounting firms and attorneys, are liable for economic damages regardless of privity where reliance by the plaintiff was reasonably foreseeable); Seigle v. Jasper, 867 S.W.2d 467 (Ky. Ct. App. 1993) (Restatement applied to sustain a claim against title abstracter by claimant not in privity with defendant).

241. Congregation of the Passion, Holy Cross Province v. Touche Ross & Co., 636 N.E.2d 503 (Ill. 1994); *see also* Ingram Indus., Inc. v. Nowicki, 527 F. Supp. 683 (E.D. Ky. 1981) (adopting Restatement view as applied to accountants).

242. Collins v. Reynard, 607 N.E.2d 1185 (Ill. 1992) (an attorney's duty of competence exists "without regard to the terms of any contract of employment").

243. Rosenstein v. Standard & Poor's Corp., 636 N.E.2d 665 (Ill. App. Ct. 1993).

The Economic Loss Rule as Applied to the Tort
of Negligent Misrepresentation

As discussed in Chapter 8, the separate negligence-based tort of negligent misrepresentation may be asserted against any construction project participant who disseminates project-related information. Owners, construction managers, general and trade contractors, and design professionals may be alleged to have negligently supplied inaccurate information for the guidance of others.[244] The Restatement specifically allows the tort to be maintained whether or not the injured party has a contract with the information-disseminating party.[245] In place of privity, the Restatement emphasized foreseeability, requiring that the party providing the information know the class of those intended to receive and use the information.[246]

Many judges are less than comfortable with the breadth of the Restatement's pronouncements. To them, the Restatement's foreseeability standard is a poor substitute for contractual responsibility. As noted by one court, it is "a standard that sweeps too broadly in a professional or commercial context, portending liability that is socially harmful in its potential scope and uncertainty."[247] In the construction setting in particular, courts have been uneasy assessing responsibility for economic damage based on the transmission of inaccurate information related to a contractual undertaking.

A number of courts maintain that where there is privity of contract and only economic damages, there is no need for an additional tort of negligent misrepresentation.[248] Other courts have chosen not to allow negligent misrepresentation claims when there is a contract—any contract—that relates to the subject matter of the claimed damages.

---

244. *See* Restatement (Third) of Torts: Products Liability § 552 (1998).

245. *Id.*, cmt. g.

246. *Id.*, cmt. h.

247. Local Joint Executive Bd. v. Stern, 651 P.2d 637, 638 (Nev. 1982).

248. *See, e.g.*, Marvin Lumber and Cedar Company v. PPG Industries, Inc., 223 F.3d 873, 884–885 (8th Cir. 2000); Duquesne Light Co. v. Westinghouse Elec. Corp., 66 F.3d 604 (3rd Cir. 1995); City Express, Inc. v. Express Partners, 959 P.2d 836 (Haw. 1998). *See also* authorities cited at West's ☞ 184 FRAUD, k25, 27.

In *Berschauer/Phillips Construction Co. v. Seattle School District No. 1*,[249] a delayed general contractor settled with the owner, reserving claims against the design professionals for professional negligence and negligent misrepresentation that caused or contributed to the project delay.[250] Noting that no physical property damage or bodily injury was alleged, the court dismissed all negligence-based claims against the design professionals, including the claim for negligent misrepresentation.[251] In so doing, the court acknowledged that Section 552 of the Restatement was recognized in the State of Washington, but held that "in the construction industry, contract principles override the tort principles in Section 552 and, thus, purely economic damages are not recoverable."[252] The fact that the general contractor had a contractual remedy against the owner was dispositive for the court.[253]

Other courts limit the expanse of the Restatement's class of potential plaintiffs by making fine distinctions, on behalf of design professionals, concerning what constitutes "information in the course of one's business or profession."[254] Illinois, for instance, specifically recognizes an exception to the economic loss rule outside the construction context for damages caused by another's negligent misrepresentation as described in the Restatement (Third) of Torts Section 552.[255] When presented with the case of a professional engineer whose

---

249. 881 P.2d 986 (Wash. 1994) (en banc).

250. The contractor alleged that the design professionals supplied inaccurate information, which caused the contractor to incur extra costs and delay damages in connection with the performance of the construction contract.

251. *Id.*

252. *Id.* at 993.

253. That there may have been contract provisions in the owner/general contractor agreement that severely limited the general contractor's right to recover foreseeable and substantial delay damages was apparently irrelevant to the court.

254. Restatement (Third) of Torts: Product Liability § 552 (1998).

255. *See* Moorman Mfg. Co. v. Nat'l. Tank Co., 435 N.E.2d 443, 449 (Ill. 1982), and its progeny. This exception is one of three to the economic loss rule recognized in *Moorman*. The other two are fraud and property damage from a sudden or dangerous occurrence. *Id.* at 450; *see also* Rozny v. Marnul, 250 N.E.2d 656, 660 (Ill. 1969) (plaintiffs not in privity were allowed to recover economic damages against a surveyor for inaccurate information on survey).

plans for a tunnel location were inaccurate by seventy-five yards, not only causing the contractor to incur additional costs but also causing damage to other property, the Illinois court nevertheless held that the engineer was not "in the business of supplying information."[256] In a concluding remark, the court noted that the remedy for inaccurate plans could be expressed "in contract terms."[257]

Courts that allow the tort of negligent misrepresentation in the construction setting also tend to inquire rather deeply into the facts of a contested case, in order to satisfy themselves that economic damage to a certain class of recipients was foreseeable. As in the analysis of the "supervising architect" exception in cases of design professional negligence discussed above, many courts look for a relationship between the parties that is "so close as to be the functional equivalent of contractual privity."[258] If it is found, the economic loss rule is often not applied.[259]

The concern of Restatement (Third) of Torts Section 552 is with foreseeability of the class of recipients of information. Foreseeability supplies consistency in the identity of potential plaintiffs similar to the bargained-for protection

---

256. Fireman's Fund Ins. Co. v. SEC Donohue, Inc., 679 N.E.2d 1197, 1201–02 (Ill. 1997) (a design professional's plans and drawings were incidental to the tangible product, the water pipe project); *see also* 2314 Lincoln Park West Condo. Ass'n v. Mann, Gin, Ebel & Frazier, Ltd., 555 N.E.2d 346 (Ill. 1990) (architect's information is incidental to a tangible product, *i.e.*, a structure and details on plans are normally transformed into the structure) (*dicta*). *But see* Tolan & Son, Inc. v. KLLM Architects, Inc. 719 N.E.2d 288, 298 (Ill. App. Ct. 1999) (refining the "incidental" analysis to design professionals; project design architects were not "providers of information," but a consulting engineer could be).

257. SEC Donohue, *supra* note 252, 679 N.E.2d at 1202. Apparently, this parsing of the Restatement requirements is limited to the court's resentment of tort claims in the construction sector, and not in other commercial transactions. *See* Rosenstein v. Standard & Poor's Corp., 636 N.E.2d 665 (Ill. App. Ct. 1993) (negligent misrepresentation claim allowed against stock market indexing service by those not in privity). Illinois also allows negligent misrepresentation claims against attorneys and CPAs. *See* notes 237, 238, *supra*. This distinction has drawn the criticism of a number of commentators, and three of the state's Supreme Court Justices. *See* SEC Donohue, 679 N.E.2d at 1202 (Heiple, J. in dissent).

258. Ossining Union Free Sch. Dist. v. Anderson LaRocca Anderson, 539 N.E.2d 91 (N.Y. 1989).

259. *Id.* at 92. *See also* authorities cited at West's ⊕═ 184 FRAUD, k29.

of a contract. Foreseeability is vital to courts that uphold a plaintiff's right to sue for negligent misrepresentation, regardless of privity, when harmed only economically.[260] Thus, despite the economic loss rule, negligent misrepresentation claims have been maintained against builders and developers,[261] construction managers,[262] design professionals,[263] and construction product manufacturers.[264]

Sovereign Immunity

The doctrine of sovereign immunity originated in the notion at common law that "the king can do no wrong."[265] Sovereign immunity in the federal realm is a judicial doctrine that shields the federal government and its agencies from suit, absent a waiver.[266] To allow what it considers proper claims to be prosecuted, Congress has authorized a wide range of suits under the Federal Tort Claims Act (FTCA),[267] the Tucker Act,[268] and the Contract Disputes Act (CDA),[269]

---

260. *See, e.g., Borough of Lansdowne, supra* note 152, 2000 WL 1886578, at *2 ("Section 552 has supplanted the need for contractual privity as the device by which liability is limited from the world at large to those whom the actor should reasonably foresee might be harmed by his negligent provision of false information").

261. Council of Co-Owners Atlantis Condo., Inc. v. Whiting-Turner Contracting Co., 517 A.2d 336, 348 (Md. 1986).

262. John Martin Co. v. Morse/Diesel, Inc. 819 S.W.2d 428 (Tenn. 1991) (subcontractor was allowed to maintain negligent misrepresentation claim against construction manager for improper information in directing the subcontractor's work).

263. Guardian Constr. v. Tetra Tech, Inc., 583 A.2d 1378 (Del. Super. 1990) (plaintiffs not in privity were allowed to maintain action for negligent misrepresentation against engineer); Nota Constr. Corp. v. Keyes Assocs., Inc., 694 N.E.2d 401 (Mass App. Ct. 1998) (mistakes and misinformation in architect's plans could give rise to negligent misrepresentation action despite lack of privity).

264. *See* Vill. of Cross Keys, Inc. v. U.S. Gypsum Co., 556 A.2d 1126, 1133 (Md. 1989) (negligent misrepresentation claim against designer/manufacturer of curtain wall system not barred by economic loss rule, although recovery was denied due to failure to follow manufacturer's specifications); *see also* State *ex rel.* Bronster v. United States Steel Corp., 919 P.2d 294, 302 (Haw. 1996) (economic loss rule properly disregarded, and recovery allowed, in negligent misrepresentation case against steel manufacturer where there was privity).

265. WILLIAM BLACKSTONE, COMMENTARIES 254 (1813 ed.).

266. *See* Dep't of Army v. Blue Fox, Inc., 525 U.S. 255, 260 (1999); FDIC v. Meyer, 510 U.S. 471, 475 (1994); cases cited at West's 🔑 393 UNITED STATES k125(3).

267. 28 U.S.C.A. §§ 2671 *et seq.*

268. 28 U.S.C.A. § 1491 (2003).

269. 41 U.S.C.A. §§ 601 *et seq.* (2003).

among others not likely to involve construction claims. Not surprisingly, courts strictly construe the scope of a waiver of sovereign immunity, in favor of the government.[270] Further, any exception to the federal government's immunity from suit must be unequivocally expressed in the statutory text;[271] it will not be implied.[272]

The Tucker Act provides a mechanism for government contractors to pursue their claims against the federal government:

> The United States Court of Federal Claims shall have jurisdiction to render judgment upon any claim against the United States founded either upon the Constitution, or any Act of Congress or any regulation of an executive department, or upon any express or implied contract with the United States, or for liquidated or unliquidated damages in cases not sounding in tort.[273]

The Tucker Act and the CDA waive the government's sovereign immunity only for claims seeking monetary damages.[274]

While the Tucker Act and the CDA apply to direct claims by contractors, suits by contractors or subcontractors lacking a contractual relationship with the federal government can be brought only in tort, under the FTCA. The latter provides, subject to certain exceptions, that "[t]he United States shall be liable, respecting the provisions of this title relating to tort claims, in the same manner and to the same extent as a private individual under the circumstances."[275]

---

270. *See Blue Fox, supra* note 262, 525 U.S. at 261; Lane v. Pena, 518 U.S. 187, 192 (1996); United States v. Williams, 514 U.S. 527, 531 (1995) (when confronted with a purported waiver of the Federal Government's sovereign immunity, the Court will "constru[e] ambiguities in favor of immunity"); cases cited at West's ⬥══ 393 UNITED STATES, k125(6).

271. *Blue Fox, supra* note 262, 525 U.S. at 261; *Lane, supra* note 266, 518 U.S. at 192; United States v. Nordic Vill., Inc., 503 U.S. 30, 33–34, 37 (1992); *see* cases cited at West's ⬥══ 393 UNITED STATES, k125(5).

272. *See* Irwin v. Dep't of Veterans Affairs, 498 U.S. 89, 95 (1990).

273. 28 U.S.C.A. § 1491(a)(1) (2003).

274. See C. Stanley Dees, *The Future of the Contract Disputes Act: Is It Time to Roll Back Sovereign Immunity?*, 28 Pub. Cont. L.J. 545, 549 (1999).

275. 28 U.S.C.A. § 2674 (2003).

The FTCA's waiver of sovereign immunity carves out major exceptions, such as decisions falling within a governmental discretionary function[276] and acts by independent contractors.[277] The utility of the FTCA for claims by contractors and subcontractors is severely limited, since it applies only to torts and not to contract disputes.

Sovereign immunity was first extended to an American local government in 1812 in *Mower v. Inhabitants of Leicester*[278] and has been adopted by most jurisdictions in the United States.[279] While state and local sovereign immunity originally was absolute, state courts created exceptions to avoid harsh results.[280] The primary exception to sovereign immunity for states and municipalities was created by a nineteenth-century distinction between "governmental" and "proprietary" functions.[281] When an activity benefits the general public, courts characterize it as "governmental," and the government remains shielded from liability. When an activity primarily benefits a municipality, courts deem it "proprietary," and the sovereign may be sued.[282] This distinction has been called "one of the most unsatisfactory known to law."[283]

More recently, courts have gone beyond merely carving out exceptions and abolished the doctrine of sovereign immunity

---

276. *See id.* § 2680(a); cases cited at West's ☞ 393 UNITED STATES, k78(12). *But see* Bell v. United States, 127 F.3d 1226, 1230 (10th Cir. 1997) (where government employee lacks discretion due to terms in the contract specification, the exception for discretionary function was inapplicable to a tort claim).

277. *See* Roditis v. United States, 122 F.3d 108, 111 (2d Cir. 1997) (FTCA precluded United States Postal Service's liability for injuries plaintiff suffered on premises controlled by independent contractor on post office construction project); cases cited at West's ☞ 393 UNITED STATES, k78.

278. 9 Mass. 247 (1812); see also Scott J. Borth, *Municipal Tort Liability for Erroneous Issuance of Building Permits: A National Survey*, 58 WASH. L. REV. 537, 539 (1983).

279. *See* Fleming James, Jr., *Tort Liability of Governmental Units and Their Officers*, 22 U. CHI. L. REV. 610, 621–23 (1955).

280. *See* People v. Superior Court, 178 P.2d 1, 2, 4–5 (Cal. 1947) (recognizing potential liability for proprietary conduct); cases cited at West's ☞ 360 STATES, k112.

281. This distinction between government and proprietary functions originated in 1842 in Bailey v. City of New York, 3 Hill 531 (N.Y. 1842). *See* Borth, *supra* note 274, at 539, n.14.

282. *See* Borth, *supra* note 274, at 539–40.

283. 3 KENNETH CULP DAVIS, ADMINISTRATIVE LAW TREATISE § 25.07, at 460 (1958).

for state and local governments altogether. Thus, governmental units could be held answerable in tort on the same basis as private parties, unless a tort immunity statute imposed conditions upon that liability.[284] Today most states have established a comprehensive statutory system of partial tort immunity and designated areas of potential liability. Like federal sovereign immunity, state tort claims acts typically allow states and municipalities to enjoy freedom from suit unless a basis for liability has been explicitly listed in the Act. In these states, the governmental/proprietary distinction has been rejected as unmanageable.[285] In its place, many states employ a widely adopted distinction between discretionary and ministerial decisions or actions.[286] Whether the newer distinction is easier to apply consistently is a matter of debate. Attorneys for public contractors therefore need to consult their state's statutes and decisional law to fully understand the framework for this important limitation on damages.

Mitigation of Damages

The mitigation doctrine, also called the doctrine of avoidable consequences, precludes a plaintiff from recovering damages "for loss that the injured party could have avoided without undue risk, burden or humiliation."[287] A plaintiff need only make "reasonable" efforts to avoid loss, even if those steps turn out to be unsuccessful.[288] The principle of

---

284. *See* cases cited at West's ⊕ 268 MUNICIPAL CORPORATIONS, k723.

285. *See* cases cited at West's ⊕ 268 MUNICIPAL CORPORATIONS, k724–25.

286. *See* cases cited at West's ⊕ 268 MUNICIPAL CORPORATIONS, k728.

287. RESTATEMENT (SECOND) OF CONTRACTS § 350(1) (1981); cases cited at West's ⊕ 115 DAMAGES, k62(4).

288. *See* RESTATEMENT (SECOND) OF CONTRACTS § 350(1) (1981). An example of efforts to mitigate damages that go beyond reasonable can be found in T.C. Bateson Constr. Co. v. United States, 319 F.2d 135, 160 (Ct. Cl. 1963). There, a contractor failed to completely install heating boilers at a project on an air force base, and the government brought in government civil service employees to operate the boilers. This action by the owner caused union construction employees to strike, resulting in a thirty-eight-day delay. The court found that the contractor was not required to take steps to have the picketing enjoined because it was doubtful that the strike was against the prime contractor, and the time necessary to obtain an injunction would have been at least as long as the delay.

minimizing losses "is designed to discourage persons against whom wrongs have been committed from passively suffering economic loss that could be averted by reasonable efforts, or from actively increasing such loss where prudence requires that such activity cease."[289] Failure to mitigate constitutes an affirmative defense that must be pled by the defendant separately from comparative negligence.[290] Although such amelioration frequently is referred to as a plaintiff's "duty," the burden rests on the defendant to demonstrate the plaintiff's failure to curtail its damages.

The mitigation doctrine applies to construction contracts.[291] For instance, when an owner terminates a project, the contractor might curtail its losses by laying off employees, returning rented equipment, canceling material deliveries, and reselling unused materials. Likewise, owner-caused delays may trigger the contractor's duty to mitigate damages.[292] Even when a project temporarily halts for a reason unanticipated by either party, the contractor would have the same duties to use resources elsewhere, if reasonable.

When a contractor fails to make these mitigation efforts, its entitlement to damages may be reduced or eliminated. For example, a general contractor who accepted the second low bid (after failing to require performance by the low bidder) was denied recovery of the increased cost of the second low bid.[293] Another contractor was barred from recovering damages arising out of a Small Business Association loan

---

289. Powers v. Miller, 984 P.2d 177 (N.M. Ct. App. 1999) (*quoting* Hickey v. Griggs, 738 P.2d 899, 902 (N.M. 1987)).

290. *See, e.g.*, Atlantic Contracting, Inc. v. Int'l Fid. Ins. Co., 86 F. Supp. 2d 479, 480 (E.D. Pa. 2000) (applying Pennsylvania law).

291. *See, e.g.*, Gaylord Builders, Inc. v. Richmond Metal Mfg. Co., 140 A.2d 358 (Pa. Super. Ct. 1958).

292. For instance, where the contractor's home office was so tied up by the owner's delays that it is unable to estimate and bid on other jobs, one court required the contractor to have hired an additional employee to handle the bidding procedure. If the contractor had thus mitigated its damages, the contractor would have been entitled only to damages for the cost of one employee, rather than the entire costs for its inability to estimate and bid other projects. Manshul Constr. Corp. v. Dormitory Auth. of New York, 444 N.Y.S.2d 792, 804 (N.Y. Sup. Ct. 1981).

293. *See Gaylord Builders, supra* note 287. *But see* Associated Lathing & Plastering Co. v. Louis C. Dunn, Inc., 286 P.2d 825 (Cal. Ct. App. 1955) (contractor could not be charged with failing to

because the contract was terminated two months before the loan was accepted; the contractor could have avoided liability but failed to do so.[294] Still another contractor was barred from back-charging his flooring subcontractor for post-installation repairs when the contractor did not notify the subcontractor of the defects and provide the sub an opportunity to correct them.[295] Contractors also may improperly neglect to prevent losses where they continue construction after learning that certain necessary tests have not been done on the site.[296] So long as the contractor's efforts have been reasonable, however, it likely will not have violated its duty to minimize damages.[297]

For an owner, the duty to curtail losses can arise when a contractor abandons a project: The owner generally must make reasonable efforts to keep the project moving forward. In contrast to a need to act affirmatively, mitigation of damages also may require an owner not to interfere with the contractor's right and duty to cure bad workmanship. Thus, an owner violates that obligation, and may forfeit a claim for loss of use, if it prevents the contractor from correcting defects in the construction or completing the building.[298] The owner's duty, however, cannot be equated with a duty to preserve the contractor's part performance.[299] Essentially, an

---

minimize damages by accepting next highest bid instead of soliciting new bids following breach by subcontractor when solicitation of new bids would have unreasonably delayed the entire project). Thus, a key element in mitigating damages is whether the contractor acted "reasonably."

294. *See* MLK, Inc. v. Univ. of Kansas, 940 P.2d 1158 (Kan. Ct. App. 1997).

295. *See* Raleigh Paint & Wallpaper Co. v. James T. Rogers Builders, Inc., 327 S.E.2d 36 (N.C. Ct. App. 1985).

296. *See* Richardson v. Collier Bldg. Corp., 793 S.W.2d 366 (Mo. Ct. App. 1990) (contractor could not recover damages from subcontractors hired to compact and to test such compaction).

297. *See* Turner Constr. Co. v. First Indem. of Am. Ins. Co., 829 F. Supp. 752, 761–62 (E.D. Pa. 1993) (contractor did not violate duty to mitigate damages to be reimbursed by performance bond surety by refusing to declare subcontractor [the surety's principal] in default, where the contractor followed its policy of not declaring default until subcontractor had stopped work).

298. *See* Tomlinson Lumber Yard v. Engel, 216 N.W.2d 87, 90 (N.D. 1974).

299. Such a duty is not required by law. *See* Herbert W. Jaeger & Assocs. v. Slovak American Charitable Ass'n, 507 N.E.2d 863, 867 (Ill. App. Ct. 1987) (after the contractor abandoned project, owner was not required to sell property or acquire new financing to complete construction; property owner eventually sold property at a much greater profit).

owner may discharge his obligation to mitigate damages by giving the contractor reasonable notice of any defect in construction and an opportunity to repair.[300]

Betterment

A form of unjust enrichment is the involved in concept of "betterment."[301] Contractual damages require the party in breach to compensate the injured party in an amount that will place the nonbreaching party in as good a position as it would have been had the contract not been breached. Remediation "'enhancements' that give the nonbreaching party (1) more than what was originally bargained for, or (2) what was intended and otherwise would have paid for if not inadvertently omitted from the original scope of work" are known as "betterment" and must be credited to the damages claimed.[302] Betterment also provides a defense to architects for faulty designs.[303]

An example of betterment can be found in *St. Joseph's Hospital v. Corbetta Construction Co.*,[304] where the owner brought a suit for damages against the architect, contractor, and supplier of wall paneling because the paneling did not meet city code requirements. Because the owner specified a system that violated code, it could not recover the extra cost for the more expensive paneling or the extra labor required by its more difficult installation.[305] Betterment, then, can provide a substantial limitation on quasi-contractual recovery.

---

300. *See, e.g.,* Heap v. Weber Constr. Co., 407 So.2d 799, 802 (La. Ct. App. 1981) (owner need not make repairs himself if he makes regular contact with contractor to inform him of problem and provides an opportunity to repair).

301. *See* cases cited at West's ⊕ 115 DAMAGES, k45.

302. Philip L. Bruner & Patrick J. O'Connor, Jr., 6 Bruner and O'Connor on Construction Law § 19:26 (2002).

303. *See* Justin Sweet, Sweet on Construction Law § 11.13(e) (1997).

304. 316 N.E.2d 51 (Ill. App. Ct. 1974).

305. *See id.* at 62.

Economic Waste

As discussed in Chapter 5, damages for breach of contract by a contractor have been measured in two ways: (1) the reasonable cost of completing performance and (2) the diminution in the market price of the property caused by the breach.[306] The less generous measure of recovery, based on diminution in market price, is awarded when the more generous measure, cost of completion, would result in "economic waste."[307] In many cases, it may make little difference whether damages are measured by the cost of completion or diminution in value. The doctrine of economic waste comes into play where extremely divergent outcomes are produced in applying the two measures.

Reduction by Collateral Source Recovery

The collateral source rule itself is not a limitation on damage recovery, but in fact the opposite. Generally, payments or benefits received by a plaintiff from a source other than the party who breaches a contract are not credited against the breaching party's liability.[308] This collateral source rule applies even where the plaintiff has received compensation as a result of the defendant's action measured by the plaintiff's losses.[309] Collateral sources include insurance, pensions, continued wages, disability payments for which the plaintiff actually or constructively had paid, and payments from another source that will be repaid from the tort recovery through subrogation, refund of benefits, or some other arrangement.[310] A plaintiff can prevent a defendant from introducing evidence

---

306. *See* RESTATEMENT (SECOND) OF CONTRACTS § 348(2) (1981).

307. E. ALLAN FARNSWORTH, CONTRACTS § 12.13, at 910 (2d edition 1990); *see* cases cited at West's 95 CONTRACTS, k320; 15 DAMAGES, k123.

308. *See* RESTATEMENT (SECOND) OF TORTS § 920A(2) (1979); cases cited at West's 15 DAMAGES, k159.

309. *See* DAN B. DOBBS, HANDBOOK ON THE LAW OF REMEDIES § 3.6, at 185 (1973).

310. *See, e.g.,* Helfend v. S. Cal. Rapid Transit Dist., 465 P.2d 61 (Cal. 1970).

of such payments made either to the plaintiff or on his behalf.[311]

Collateral source compensation may, however, create limitations on damage recoveries in some instances arising from construction disputes. Many courts hold that the collateral source rule does not apply to breach of contract claims, unless the breach was willful.[312] "In 1955, the Seventh Circuit Court of Appeals observed that it was unable to find 'a single case in which [the collateral source rule had] been carried over to contract damages.'"[313] The rationale for not extending this protection to plaintiffs in contract actions has been stated as follows:

> The collateral source rule is punitive; contractual damages are compensatory. The collateral source rule, if applied to an action based on breach of contract, would violate the contractual damage rule that no one shall profit more from the breach of an obligation than from its full performance.[314]

Since that time, other decisions have applied the rule to contract claims and thereby prevented a breaching party from reducing its liability by amounts received by the plaintiff from alternate sources.[315] In *Hall*, the Vermont Supreme Court gave the following rationale for applying the collateral

---

311. *See id.;* Arambula v. Wells, 85 Cal. Rptr. 2d 584 (Cal. Ct. App. 1999).

312. *See* In re Future Mfg. Co-Op, Inc., 165 F. Supp. 111 (N.D. Cal. 1958) (plaintiff suing on contract could recover amount of damages less insurance proceeds); Grover v. Ratliff, 586 P.2d 213, 215 (Ariz. Ct. App. 1978); Helfend (In re Exterstein's Estate), 2 Cal. 2d 13 (1934); Corl v. Huron Castings, Inc., 544 N.W.2d 278 (Mich. 1996) (extending collateral source rule to contract law would be in direct conflict with the fundamental precept that the remedy for breach of contract focuses on making the nonbreaching party whole).

313. Hall v. Miller, 465 A.2d 222, 226 (Vt. 1983) (quoting United Protective Workers v. Ford Motor Co., 223 F.2d 49, 54 (7th Cir.1955)).

314. Patent Scaffolding Co. v. William Simpson Constr. Co., 64 Cal. Rptr. 187, 191 (Cal. Ct. App. 1967).

315. Klein v. United States, 339 F.2d 512, 517–18 (2d Cir.1964) (applying New York law); Seibel v. Liberty Homes, Inc., 752 P.2d 291, 293 (Or. 1998) (holding that, for breach of an employment contract, the judgment should not be reduced by sums that plaintiff later received in social security disability benefits); Hall v. Miller, 465 A.2d 222 (Vt. 1983). *See also* NLRB v. Gullett Gin Co., 340 U.S. 361, 364 (1951) (despite potential double recovery, collateral state unemployment compensation benefits need not be deducted from back pay award).

source rule to contract actions: "as between the two parties, it is better that the injured plaintiff recovers twice than that the breaching defendant escape liability altogether."[316] In many of the situations cited in these cases, where the plaintiff must reimburse the collateral source from the award recovered from the defendant, the collateral source rule logically should apply because the plaintiff has not gained a windfall.[317]

Where rights of subrogation pertain, the collateral source rule may protect those principles. In effect, plaintiff does not receive any untoward benefit of the collateral source rule when its rights against the wrongdoer have been subrogated to an indemnitor.[318] Application of the collateral source rule to construction claims thus will likely depend on the presence of subrogation clauses.

Contributory Negligence and Comparative Fault

Contributory negligence and comparative fault arise when conduct on the part of the plaintiff falls below the standard to which he should conform for his own protection and when that conduct is a legally contributing cause of the plaintiff's loss for which damages are sought from the defendant.[319] Contributory and comparative fault defenses apply only to negligence actions, such as suits for design professional liability, and not to claims for the breach of a (nonprofessional services) contract.

---

316. 465 A.2d at 226.

317. *See* John G. Fleming, *The Collateral Source Rule and Contract Damages,* 71 CAL. L. REV. 56, 57 (1983). Fleming cites "indemnity insurance, workers' compensation entitling the insurer to subrogation for benefits paid, contractual stipulations for repayment under certain prepaid medical plans, loans made to the victim on condition of repayment in case of a successful tort recovery, and other instances permitting the collateral source a direct claim for reimbursement from the tortfeasor." *Id.*

318. *See* Carter v. Berger, 777 F.2d 1173, 1175 (7th Cir.1985) ("The 'collateral benefit' rule of tort law rests on the belief that the wrongdoer should be made to pay [the victim—the better to deter like conduct—whether or not the victim has providently supplied another source of compensation, unless the supplier of the compensation has a subrogation clause."); Austin Co. v. Int'l Bhd of Elec. Workers, Local Union No. 701, 665 F. Supp. 614, 621 (N.D. Ill, 1987).

319. *See* RESTATEMENT (SECOND) OF TORTS § 463 (1979); cases cited at West's 🔑 272 NEGLIGENCE, k501.

One possible area of ambiguity as to whether comparative fault principles will apply is to claims for breach of warranty.

> An action for breach of warranty is held to sound sometimes in tort and sometimes in contract. There is no intent to include in the coverage of the [Comparative Fault] Act actions that are fully contractual in their gravamen and in which the plaintiff is suing solely because he did not recover what he contracted to receive. The restriction of coverage to physical harms to person or property excludes these claims.[320]

---

320. Flom v. Stahly, 569 N.W.2d 135, 141 (Iowa 1997) (*quoting* Uniform Comparative Fault Act § 1(b) cmt., 12 U.L.A. 128 (1996)); *see also* Roger W. Stone, *Architects' and Engineers' Liability Under Iowa Construction Law*, 50 DRAKE L. REV. 33, 42 (2001); cases cited at West's ⊕═ 95 CONTRACTS, 328(1).

Proof of Damages

DOUGLAS S. OLES

10

EQUITABLE COMPENSATION

As outlined in the preceding chapters of this book, U.S. law recognizes a variety of theories and causes of action by which a construction industry claimant may recover damages for breach of contract or pursuant to a contractually specified remedy. A common thread of these alternative approaches is the goal of restoring the injured party to the position it would have occupied but for the breach and/or other compensable event.

The standard federal Changes Clause for fixed price contracts provides that when the cost or time of contract performance is changed, "the Contracting Officer shall make an equitable adjustment in the contract price, the delivery schedule, or both, and shall modify the contract."[1]

---

1. *See* Federal Acquisition Regulation [hereinafter FAR] 52.243-4(d). The FAR is generally located at Title 48 of the CODE OF FEDERAL REGULATIONS. Citations in this text are to the September 2001 edition.

A similar promise of "equitable adjustment" appears in the federal Differing Site Condition Clause.[2] This principle is consistent with traditional common law remedies for breach of contract that were designed to make an injured party whole for foreseeable economic losses reasonably incurred.[3] By contrast, federal regulations use the simpler term "adjustment" in circumstances where a contractor is entitled to recover costs but no markup for profit.[4]

Earlier in this book, we have seen that contract damage remedies in some cases do not make the injured party whole. They generally exclude certain remote or unforeseeable consequential damages, and they almost always fail to compensate for the kinds of general damages (e.g., pain and suffering) that are typically available in tort-based actions. Sometimes, they fall short of making the injured party whole because of specific limits on recovery that were negotiated in the parties' contract (e.g., liquidated delay damages or specified limits on recoverable markups). They may also fail to reimburse an injured contract party for the full extent of legal fees and costs that were reasonably expended to vindicate its rights. Nonetheless, the American judicial process generally favors a result that makes an injured party whole, and contract clauses or legal rules in derogation of that principle tend to be narrowly construed.

PROVING THE FACT AND AMOUNT OF DAMAGES

A party claiming damages bears the burden of proving by competent evidence to the requisite standard of proof both the fact of damage and the amount of damage.[5] Where the

---

2. *See* FAR 52.236-2(b).

3. *See* Philip L. Bruner & Patrick J. O'Connor, Jr., Bruner & O'Connor on Construction Law § 19:50 (2002).

4. *See, e.g.,* FAR 52.242-14 (Suspension of Work); FAR 52.242-17 (Government Delay of Work).

5. *See, e.g.,* James F. Nagle, Federal Construction Contracting § 24.2, at 346 (1992); Ralph C. Nash Jr. & John Cibinic Jr., Federal Procurement Law at 1384, n.1 (3d edition 1980).

fact of damage is established, the claimant's inability to prove the amount of its damages with accuracy is generally not a bar to recovery. Professor Corbin summarized this proposition as follows:

> There are many cases in which, by reason of the ordinary experience and belief of mankind, the trial court is convinced that substantial pecuniary harm has been inflicted, even though its amount in dollars is incapable of proof. If the defendant had reason to foresee this kind of harm and the difficulty of proving its amount, the injured party will not be denied a remedy in damages because of the lack of certainty.[6]

One familiar standard for the required proof is one of "reasonable certainty."[7] It is applied both in proving that a breach of contract in fact caused monetary damage and also as a standard in proving the amount of damage.[8] In the latter application, the United States Court of Claims articulated the standard in terms that have been widely followed: "This court has enunciated its acceptance of the 'settled principle that where the fact of damage has been established, absolute certainty or precise mathematical accuracy as to the amount of damages is not necessary.' "[9]

In the specific context of claims for labor inefficiency, the same court held: "That loss of productivity of labor resulting from improper delays caused by defendant is an item of damage for which plaintiff is entitled to recover admits of no

6. ARTHUR LINTON CORBIN, CORBIN ON CONTRACTS § 1020, at 108 (interim ed. 2002).

7. See, e.g., Restatement (Second) of Contracts § 352 (1981).

8. See BRUNER & O'CONNOR, supra note 3, § 19:15, at 79 ("the breach must be proven to have been a 'substantial factor' in causing the damages," but "'reasonable certainty' in proof of the amount of damage is a lower burden than 'reasonable certainty' required for proof of causation in fact").

9. Petrovich v. United States, 421 F.2d 1364, 1367 (Ct. Cl. 1970), quoting from Dale Constr. Co. v. United States, 168 Ct. Cl. 692, 729 (1964); see also Elec. & Missile Facilities, Inc. v. United States, 416 F.2d 1345 (Ct. Cl. 1969) ("where responsibility for damage is clear, it is not essential that the amount thereof be ascertainable with absolute exactness or mathematical precision: 'It is enough if the evidence adduced is sufficient to enable a court or jury to make a fair and reasonable approximation.' "); Wunderlich Contracting Co. v. United States, 351 F.2d 956, 968 (Ct. Cl. 1965) (it is sufficient if the claimant furnishes the court "with a reasonable basis for computation, even though the result is only approximate").

doubt, nor does the impossibility of proving the amount with exactitude bar recovery for the item."[10]

Where a nonbreaching party is able to convince a court that a profit would have been earned, it is likely to be indulged even though the amount of anticipated profit cannot be proved.[11]

Claimants who can establish that they in fact suffered damages for which another contract party is liable (regardless of whether such damages arise under the contract or result from breaches thereof) will generally find support in the many cases that excuse them from having to prove the amounts of their damages with mathematical certainty. By contrast, the defendant in a construction dispute should make an effort to isolate the specific events giving rise to the claim and attempt (by segregating them) to limit the resulting damages that can be proved with reasonable certainty.

In many cases, the resulting issues of valuation are proved with aid of expert witnesses.[12] What Corbin notes about valuation should be generally applicable to proof of construction damages:

> The process of valuation or appraisal [in proof of damages] always involves an expression of "opinion" and "judgment." The fact that these are variable, among "experts" as well as among men in general, is not sufficient ground for rejecting their testimony or for nonacceptance of their results. If the end to be attained is properly kept in view (e.g., compensation instead of punishment), the courts permit a considerable degree of variation in the method of attaining it.[13]

---

10. Luria Bros. & Co. v. United States, 369 F.2d 701, 712 (Ct. Cl. 1966) (citations omitted).

11. *See, e.g.,* V.C. Edwards Contracting Co. v. Port of Tacoma, 514 P.2d 1381 (Wash. 1973) ("If a court believes profits would have been made if there had been no breach by the defendants, recovery has been allowed where 'the amount of profits prevented is scarcely subject to proof at all'"); *see generally* authorities cited at West's ⊕ 115 DAMAGES, k6.

12. *See, e.g.,* NASH & CIBINIC, *supra* note 5, at 1386 n.3 ("One use of expert testimony is to link estimated cost data to the circumstances giving rise to the Government liability thus establishing causation. Ordinarily, expert testimony is discounted if the expert is not familiar with the facts of performance.").

13. CORBIN, *supra* note 6, § 1020, at 107.

ACTUAL SEGREGATED COSTS VERSUS TOTAL COST CLAIMS

Although a claimant generally is not required to prove its damages with mathematical certainty, it must make reasonable efforts to prove how the dollar amounts claimed result from the acts or omissions on which liability is based. To the greatest extent reasonably possible, the claimant must therefore attempt to segregate the portion of its damages allocable to each compensable event.

This type of cost segregation is generally easiest when the dispute involves only a limited portion of the work. For example, costs arising from owner changes in materials or finishes may affect only certain specific procurement costs plus any associated direct labor and equipment required to perform the changes. When changes or delays affect the overall scope or sequence of performance, however, they can significantly reduce labor productivity while pushing subsequent activities into seasons and conditions that were not anticipated when the project was bid. As changes and delays become overlapping or more pervasive, proof of resulting monetary damages becomes more difficult, because the claimant becomes correspondingly less able to segregate and calculate damages from individual causes.

As indicated above, the preferred method of proving damages is to offer evidence of actual costs arising from each event for which compensation is sought. Within the budgetary constraints imposed by the amount of money at issue, a claimant should segregate its damages to the extent reasonably permitted by the project records. When a claimant can establish entitlement to compensation but is unable to segregate its actual damages, however, it may in some circumstances obtain an award based on a broader analysis of its project cost overruns. One such approach is the so-called "total cost method." This method calculates damages based on the difference between a claimant's total costs of performance and its original estimate for the work at issue. This method is widely disfavored by courts, boards, and arbitrators, because it assumes that the defendant should bear responsibility for every cost that overran a pre-bid estimate.[14]

In *WRB Corp. v. United States*,[15] the Court of Claims outlined four safeguards for using the "total cost method" that have been widely followed:

> The acceptability of the method hinges on proof that (1) the nature of the particular losses make it impossible or highly impracticable to determine them with a reasonable degree of accuracy; (2) the plaintiff's bid or estimate was realistic; (3) its actual costs were reasonable; and (4) it was not responsible for the added expenses. *See* J.D. Hedin Construction Co. v. United States, *supra*, 171 Ct. Cl. at pages 86–87, 347 F.2d at pages 246–47; Oliver-Finnie Co. v. United States, *supra*, 150 Ct. Cl. at pages 197, 200, 279 F.2d at pages 505–06; F.H. McGraw & Co. v. United States, *supra*, 131 Ct. Cl. at page 511, 130 F. Supp. at page 400.[16]

With respect to each of these fact-based elements, the claimant bears the burden of proof.

The claimant's ability to prove segregated damages with accuracy will generally depend on the availability of detailed cost records and the extent to which the compensable events affected the overall scope, duration, and sequence of work. The reasonableness of a claimant's estimate is often established by reference to competing bids and the claimant's ability to withstand cross-examination as to any elements of required work that were allegedly omitted in the bid. Actual costs incurred are often presumed to be reasonable, but this presumption may be rebutted if the defendant can offer evidence that the claimant incurred needless expenses.

---

14. *See, e.g.*, Servidone Constr. Corp. v. United States, 931 F.2d 860, 861–62 (Fed. Cir. 1991) ("total cost" method used "with caution and as a last resort" and in "extraordinary circumstances"); Integrated Logistic Support Sys. Int'l, Inc. v. United States, 47 Fed. Cl. 248, 260 (2000) (total cost method is "universally disfavored" and should be "circumscribed carefully"); Neal & Co. v. United States, 36 Fed. Cl. 600, 638 (1996); Youngdale & Sons Constr. v. United States, 27 Fed. Cl. 516, 540–42 (1993); Huber, Hunt & Nichols, Inc. v. Moore, 67 Cal. App. 3d 278, 304 (Cal. Ct. App. 1977).

15. 183 Ct. Cl. 409, 426 (1968).

16. *See also* NASH & CIBINIC, *supra* note 5, at 1387–90.

The claimant's ability to prove that it did not cause its own cost overruns is generally an issue for fact witnesses and experts, depending in part on whether the job records indicate cost overruns for which neither contract nor applicable law provides compensation. Because these factors are necessarily dependent on factual evidence, the viability of a "total cost" claim normally is not determined via pre-trial summary judgment.

Total cost claims have been considered in a variety of federal[17] and state[18] decisions. In both venues, the pure "total cost method" is likely to be rejected when the claimant fails to carry its burden of proof on each element outlined in the *WRB Corporation* decision. Total cost claims are also likely to be rejected when credible expert testimony provides a reasonable basis for segregating the cost overruns allocable to the events for which compensation is owed.

When a claimant is unable to segregate damages resulting from each compensable event, somewhat greater acceptance is accorded to the so-called "modified total cost method." Under this approach, the claimant's initial bid price is used as a baseline to measure damages, but it is adjusted to compensate for inaccuracies in the original bid estimate and for cost overruns that are not the responsibility of the defendant.[19] Such adjustments should include reasonable credits for costs of unbudgeted rework, inefficiencies, and delays not caused by the defendant.

In federal contracting, another alternative to the "total cost" method is referred to as a "jury verdict" approach. Although juries are generally not available in federal contract litigation, federal courts and boards have applied this label

---

17. Cases allowing "total cost" awards include Neal & Co. v. United States, 945 F.2d 385, 389 (Fed. Cir.1991) and J.D. Hedin Constr. Co. v. United States, 347 F.2d 235, 247 (Ct. Cl. 1965). For other cases, *see* authorities cited at West's ◈══ 393 UNITED STATES, k74, k95.

18. *See* S.L. Rowland Constr. Co. v. Beall Pipe & Tank Corp., 540 P.2d 912 (Wash. Ct. App. 1975), and other authorities cited at West's ◈══ 115 DAMAGES, k117.

19. *See* Great Lakes Dredge & Dock Co. v. United States, 96 F. Supp. 923 (Ct. Cl. 1951) and discussion in NAGLE, *supra* note 5, § 350–51; *see also* authorities cited in BRUNER & O'CONNOR, *supra* note 3, § 19:95, at 299 n.4.

when they award a rough allocation of damages in cases where a claimant can clearly prove entitlement to compensation but cannot prove the amount due. This alternative was discussed by the United States Court of Claims in *Boyajian v. United States*, a case often cited as authority for the safeguards applied to "total cost" claims:

> In situations where the court has rejected the "total cost" method of proving damages, but where the record nevertheless contains reasonably satisfactory evidence of what the damages are, computed on an acceptable basis, the court has adopted such other evidence, ... or where such other evidence, although not satisfactory in and of itself upon which to base a judgment, has nevertheless been considered at least sufficient upon which to predicate a "jury verdict" award, it has rendered a judgment based on such a verdict.[20]

In federal cases, this "jury verdict" approach has been used to support a rough quantification of damages (often a percentage of the amounts claimed) where the "total cost" method has been expressly rejected[21] and in other cases.[22] As in the case of "total cost" calculations, however, the "jury verdict" approach may be used only when "the claimant can demonstrate a justifiable inability to substantiate the amount of his resultant injury by direct and specific proof."[23]

A few state courts allow the equivalent of a federal "jury verdict" under the label of *quantum meruit* recovery. Under this theory, the original pricing of a construction or supply contract can effectively be replaced by a cost-based damage

---

20. 423 F.2d 1231, 1244 (Ct. Cl. 1970).

21. *See, e.g.*, S.W. Elec. & Mfg. Corp. v. United States, 655 F.2d 1078, 1088 (Ct. Cl. 1981); Meva Corp. v. United States, 511 F.2d 548, 558 (Ct. Cl. 1975).

22. *See, e.g.*, Salem Eng. & Constr. Corp. v. United States, 2 Cl. Ct. 803, 808 (1983); Tektronix, Inc. v. United States, 575 F.2d 832, 836 (Ct. Cl. 1978); Inland Container, Inc. v. United States, 512 F.2d 1073, 1082 (Ct. Cl. 1975) ("In estimating damages, this court 'occupies the position of a jury under like circumstances'"); Appeal of B & M Roofing & Painting Co., 93-1 BCA ¶ 25,504 (ASBCA 1992) (jury verdict method resorted to only where clear proof of injury, no more reliable method of damage computation, and sufficient evidence to allow fair and reasonable approximation of damage); *see also* discussion of "total cost" and "jury verdict" claims in Chapter 6 of this text.

23. Joseph Pickard's Sons Co. v. United States, 532 F.2d 739, 742 (Ct. Cl. 1976).

award when the planned scope and/or schedule of work are substantially altered by causes for which a defendant project owner is liable. For example, the Supreme Court of Washington held in *Bignold v. King County*[24] that the *quantum meruit* approach "provides an appropriate basis for recovery when substantial changes occur which are not covered by the contract and were not within the contemplation of the parties, if the effect is to require extra work and materials or to cause substantial loss to the contractor."

The Supreme Court of Oregon approved a similar approach in *City of Portland v. Hoffman Construction Co.*[25] In California, this kind of *quantum meruit* recovery seems to be limited to private contracts.[26] Where *quantum meruit* recovery is allowed even though the parties had a written contract in place, it may be explained in terms of "cardinal change"[27] or the parties' abandonment[28] or implied modification of the original terms.[29] While state courts may apply a variety of

---

24. 399 P.2d 611, 617 (Wash. 1965); *see also* V.C. Edwards Contracting Co. v. Port of Tacoma, 514 P.2d 1381, 1385–86 (Wash. 1973); Kieburtz v. City of Seattle, 146 P. 400 (Wash. 1915) (radical or material changes in plans or changes not within contemplation of the original contract entitled the contractor to recover its increased costs of work).

25. 596 P.2d 1305, 1310 (Or. 1979); *see also* Hayden v. City of Astoria, 145 P. 1072, 1074 (Or. 1915) (owner's changes beyond contemplation of the parties allowed contractor to recover under *quantum meruit*).

26. *See* C. Norman Peterson Co. v. Container Corp. of America, 218 Cal. Rptr. 592, 598, 602 (Cal. Ct. App. 1985) (changes beyond the scope of originally contemplated work entitled contractor to utilize the total cost method in recovering the reasonable value of its work on a *quantum meruit* basis). *But see* Amelco Elec. v. City of Thousand Oaks, 38 P.3d 1120, 1128 (Cal. 2002) (on public contracts, contractors may not recover under *quantum meruit*, because it would contradict requirements of competitive bidding statutes).

27. "Cardinal change" is originally a federal doctrine authorizing equitable compensation when the changes or delays on a project exceed the scope that a bidding contractor could reasonably anticipate. *See, e.g.,* Edward R. Marden Corp. v. United States, 442 F.2d 364, 369–70 (Ct. Cl. 1971); Air-A-Plane Corp. v. United States, 408 F.2d 1030 (Ct. Cl. 1969). The "cardinal change" theory has been applied in some courts applying state law. *See, e.g.,* Westinghouse Elec. Corp. v. Garrett Corp., 437 F. Supp. 1301, 1332 (D. Md. 1977) (delay constituted cardinal change and breach of contract); Housing Auth. of Texarkana v. E.W. Johnson Constr. Co., 573 S.W.2d 316 (Ark. 1978).

28. *See, e.g.,* HTC Corp. v. Olds, 486 P.2d 463, 467 (Colo. Ct. App. 1971); Schwartz v. Shelby Constr. Co., 338 S.W.2d 781, 788–91 (Mo. 1960); Corinno Civetta Constr. Corp. v. City of New York, 493 N.E.2d 905, 912 (N.Y. 1986).

29. *See generally* authorities cited at West's ⊕⇒ 205H IMPLIED AND CONSTRUCTIVE CONTRACTS, k1–124.

legal labels to this kind of equitable remedy,[30] most of them are likely to follow the general principle that contractors who suffer substantial financial losses from pervasive changes, differing site conditions, delays, accelerations, or other disruptions will not be precluded from recovering damages by their reasonable inability to segregate their costs arising from each of the causes for which the defendant is liable.

From the standpoint of an owner or other defendant, of course, it is important to rebut any aggregated cost claim by attempting to argue one or more of the following:

- If the events giving rise to the claim did not affect all work, the claimant should be barred from recovering cost overruns on activities that were not logically affected.

- Customary and reasonable cost accounting during the project would have allowed segregation of the resulting costs, and claimant's recovery should be discounted to the extent that failure to maintain such accounting caused its lack of proof.

- Remedies specified under the contract (e.g., unit prices) provide an adequate and fair remedy for the events on which the claimant's claim is based.[31]

- The conditions imposed on "total cost" or "jury verdict" recovery under federal law should be imposed as conditions to similar claims under state law.

---

30. *See, e.g.,* State *ex rel.* DOT v. Guy F. Atkinson Co., 231 Cal. Rptr. 382, 385–86 (Cal. Ct. App. 1986) (using a jury verdict method "to determine a rough approximation of damages"); Fairbanks North Star Borough v. Kandik Constr., Inc., 795 P.2d 793, 799–800 (Alaska 1990) (when the parties have an express written contract, *quantum meruit* recovery is unavailable, but a contractor compelled to perform work beyond that contemplated in original contract may nonetheless be able to recover the reasonable value of such work).

31. *See, e.g.,* R.M. Taylor, Inc. v. Gen. Motors Corp., 187 F.3d 809, 813–14 (8th Cir. 1999) (federal appeals court declined to hold that numerous change orders constituted implied abandonment under Michigan state law); L. K. Comstock & Co. v. Becon Constr. Co., 932 F. Supp. 906, 935–36 (E.D. Ky. 1993) (changes within parties' contemplation did not qualify as cardinal change); Litton Sys., Inc. v. Frigitemp Corp., 613 F. Supp. 1377 (S.D. Miss. 1985) (remedy provided by contract changes clause was held to preclude claim of cardinal change); Hensel Phelps Constr. v. King County, 787 P.2d 58 (Wash. Ct. App. 1990) (when painter's work was compressed from 45 days to 19 days per floor, remedy clauses under contract precluded *quantum meruit* recovery).

ALLOCATING DELAY DAMAGES
IN CASES OF MIXED CAUSATION

Delay claims pose some special problems in pricing damages, especially where the evidence indicates that both claimant and defendant contributed to causing the delays or schedule disruptions at issue.[32] The claimant in a delay case generally has the burden of proving (a) the extent of the delay, (b) that the delay was proximately caused by the defendant, and (c) that the delay harmed the claimant.[33] This burden of proof generally falls both on contractors who seek delay damages and on owners who seek to assess liquidated or actual delay damages.

If the evidence indicates that both claimant and defendant contributed to critical path delays[34] during the time period at issue, the modern tendency is for courts to make an allocation between the parties.[35] As the United States Court of Federal Claims ruled in *Tyger Construction Co. v. United States:*[36]

> In cases of concurrent delay, where both parties contributed significantly to the delay period by separate and distinct actions, justice requires that the cost of the delay be allocated between the two parties proportionally. ... Apportioning liability when delay is caused by separate and independent actions of the Government and the contractor is supported by abundant precedent. If the delays can be segregated, responsibility can be allocated between the parties. *Fischbach & Moore Int'l Corp.*, ASBCA No. 18146, 77-1 BCA ¶ 12,300, at 59,224 (1976), *aff'd*, 223 Ct. Cl. 119, 617 F.2d 223 (1980).

If the evidence clearly indicates concurrent critical path delays by both litigants, a court will generally look for some

---

32. *See, e.g.,* Peter M. Kutil & Andrew D. Ness, *Concurrent Delay: The Challenge to Unravel Competing Causes of Delay,* 17:4 CONSTR. LAW. 18 (Oct. 1997); authorities cited at West's ⊕═ 393 UNITED STATES, k53, k75, k95.

33. *See, e.g.,* Wilner v. United States, 24 F.3d 1397, 1401 (Fed. Cir. 1994).

34. "Critical path delays" are those which, because of the necessary logic of the sequence of performance, will produce delay in overall completion.

35. *See, e.g.,* NAGLE, *supra* note 5, § 21.4, at 286 ("Most cases ...follow principles of comparative negligence and apportion delays and resulting damages when proof permits apportionment.").

36. 31 Fed. Cl. 177, 259 (1994).

factual basis to apportion liability. In complex cases, such evidence may be presented through expert witnesses and critical path schedule analyses. In smaller cases, courts will at least look for some reasonable opinion testimony to help quantify the parties' respective contributions to delay. In the absence of any reasonable basis to allocate between concurrent critical path delays, a court may deny delay damages to both the contractor and the owner.[37] In *Commerce International Co. v. United States*,[38] which involved claims alleging government delays in supplying parts and drawings for rebuilding M36 tanks, the United States Court of Claims outlined the types of proof that it expected to see:

> We are reminded in general terms that for want of a nail a kingdom could be lost, but there is no evidence or attempt to show, even by illustration, that the delay on this-or-that part held up work on so many tanks for such-and-such an approximate period. We are not told what inventories plaintiff had at various times, what parts it needed from time to time, or when it needed them. There is no effort to differentiate, even by general classes, between the reasonable and the unreasonable Government delays, and to show the special effect of the unreasonable delays. Other important causes of delay (such as dilatory subcontractors) are ignored. The whole subject is left to the general inference that long delays with respect to some parts *must* have caused damage. ... There is an affirmative showing that other causes, for which the defendant was not responsible, contributed most materially to the delay in production. Plaintiff has not separated these delays from that charged to the defendant, and, on this record, the Commissioner has been unable to do so.

---

37. *See, e.g.,* William F. Klingensmith, Inc. v. United States, 731 F.2d 809–10 (Fed. Cir. 1984) ("The general rule is that '[w]here both parties contribute to the delay neither can recover damage[s], unless there is in the proof a clear apportionment of the delay and expense attributable to each party.'") (citing Blinderman Constr. Co. v. United States, 695 F.2d 552, 559 (Fed. Cir. 1982)). *But see* Raymond Constructors of Africa, Ltd. v. United States, 411 F.2d 1227, 1236 (Ct. Cl. 1969) (if the record provides no basis for a precise allocation of responsibility, an estimated "jury verdict" allocation may be made).

38. 338 F.2d 81, 89–92 (Ct. Cl. 1964).

Although a delay claim may effectively be undermined (or at least partially reduced) by a showing that the claimant contributed to critical path delays, it is not enough merely for a defendant to contend that parts of claimant's work were performed later than scheduled. In many cases, a party suffering delay will mitigate that delay by revising its own schedule sequences or by postponing delivery of certain materials until they are needed. For this reason, a defendant alleging concurrent delay should generally bear the burden of proving that such delay (a) affected the critical path schedule and (b) did not occur merely as a result of defendant's own delay.[39] This issue was explained by the Engineering Board of Contract Appeals in *Appeal of John Driggs Co.*:[40]

> WMATA maintains that Appellant was in no position to commence installation of its support of excavation drawings on August 20, 1981. ... The Authority further alleges that Appellant was concurrently-delayed as a result of ongoing negotiations with proposed support of excavation subcontractors and obtaining insurance certificates and subcontractor approval for Appellant's asphalt subcontractor.
>
> A common thread running through all of these alleged "delays" is that Driggs did not complete these particular tasks on the originally-planned and scheduled date. From this, WMATA concludes that they represent concurrent, contractor-caused delays insulating WMATA from liability for the RW 11 design conflict. We disagree. More proof is required to establish WMATA's defense of concurrent delay. When a significant owner-caused, construction delay such as the RW 11 design conflict occurs, the contractor is not necessarily required to conduct all of his other construction activities

---

39. *See, e.g.,* Appeal of Utley-James, Inc., 85-1 BCA ¶ 17,816, at 89,109 (GSBCA 1984) ("we will not require a contractor claiming a compensable delay to prove that in the absence of the government's delaying actions, it would have completed the job on schedule"). *But see* Appeal of Arntz Contracting Co., Beacon Constr. Co., K.A. Constr. Co., & Teaco, Inc. JV, 84-3 BCA ¶ 17,604, at 87,704 (ENG BCA 1984) (contractor must demonstrate that government-caused delays were not concurrent).

40. 87-2 BCA ¶ 19,833, at 100,388 (ENG BCA 1987).

exactly according to his pre-delay schedule, and without regard to the changed circumstances resulting from the delay. For example, in this case, WMATA's theory would require Driggs to have purchased the soldier piles in accordance with its As-Planned Schedule and have them delivered to the site, even though it was obvious that because of the RW 11 design conflict they could not be installed for weeks.

The occurrence of a significant delay generally will affect related work, as the contractor's attention turns to overcoming the delay rather than slavishly following its now meaningless schedule. WMATA is required to demonstrate that, but for the delay caused by WMATA, the contractor could not have performed the project in less time, and would necessarily have been delayed to the same extent in any case. Respondent has failed to meet this burden. Merely speculative or theoretical contractor-caused delays are not adequate to establish a concurrent delay defense.

INTRODUCING DAMAGE EVIDENCE AT TRIAL

Because construction cases often involve multiple parties with complex damage claims, it is essential that parties be permitted to present their damage calculations in summarized or synthesized formats to make them comprehensible to the trier of fact. Cost records may comprise towering stacks of time sheets or computer printouts, or they may reside in electronic formats that are not easily accessed by a judge, jury, or arbitrator. The need to condense such information for presentation at trial creates certain problems under traditional evidentiary rules.

Strictly speaking, summaries prepared for use as exhibits— i.e., not qualifying as business records under Federal Rule of Evidence 803(6)—are inadmissible hearsay. Under Federal Rule of Evidence 1006, however,

> [t]he contents of voluminous writings, recordings, or photographs which cannot conveniently be examined in court may be presented in the form of a chart, summary, or calculation. The originals, or duplicates, shall be made available for examination or copying, or both, by other parties at reasonable

time and place. The court may order that they be produced in court.

Under this rule, a party should have no difficulty using as an exhibit a document that merely summarizes costs or other fact data. For example, a party who wishes to present a summary of a bid estimate or certain categories of actual costs incurred should be permitted to do so, subject to verification (via voir dire or cross-examination) as to its accuracy. Problems arise, however, when parties wish to mix their factual summaries with claim arguments or opinion evidence from experts.

Defendants often object to admission of damage summaries unless they qualify as contemporaneous business records. Thus, a contractor's change order proposal or claim for compensation during a project is generally admissible, but a condensed summary of such proposals prepared for trial is often admitted only for illustrative purposes.[41] Particularly in cases where damages are evaluated by a jury, however, this type of exclusion does not make much sense. Provided that a claim summary is clearly labeled as such, and further provided that it does not include text arguing ultimate issues in the case, justice is usually well served by allowing each side to present the trier of fact with a summary of its position on the costs at issue. The alternative is that trial judges or jurors must prepare laborious (and perhaps erroneous) handwritten notes to be sure that they understand each side's position on each item of disputed costs.

It is of course reasonable to exclude from evidence illustrative exhibits that merely argue one side's interpretations of project cost records or other matters at issue in the case. The authors of this text suggest, however, that courts should exercise their discretion to allow into evidence (under Federal Rule of Evidence 1006) at least one summary of

---

41. *See, e.g.,* Frederic R. Miller, Andrew D. Ness & Todd J. Wagnon, *Daubert and Kumho Tire: The Future of the Expert Witness,* in John D. Carter, Robert F. Cushman, Douglas F. Coppi & Paul J. Gorman, Proving and Pricing Construction Claims Chapter 17 (3d edition 2001); Melvin C. Cohen & Anna H. Oshiro, *Obstacles to Admitting Evidence in Construction Cases,* 20:1 Constr. Law. 39 (Jan. 2000).

each party's position as to the amount of damages (if any) that should be awarded. If a party wishes to amend its position in light of evidence presented during the course of a trial, an amended exhibit should be allowed, provided that it meets all of the following tests:

- Damage figures are reasonably supported by documentary evidence or testimony at trial (which may include admitted deposition transcripts).

- The exhibit includes clear references to underlying source documents for figures used, including trial exhibit numbers if available.

- Figures in the exhibit are either undisputed or are based on source documents that were provided to the opposing party sufficiently in advance of trial to meet the court's pretrial deadlines and to permit fair analysis and cross-examination.

- The methodology of any calculations or analysis is explained or otherwise indicated on the face of the exhibit.

- The exhibit does not contain text that characterizes the other party's evidence or argues contract interpretation or other ultimate issues in the litigation.

EXPERT AND LAY OPINION TESTIMONY

In areas of "scientific, technical, or other specialized knowledge," parties have long been permitted to offer expert testimony to assist the trier of fact. Alternatively, lay witnesses have been permitted to offer opinion testimony rationally based on their own knowledge and perceptions. The admission or rejection of opinion testimony is generally held to be a matter within the broad discretion of the trial court.[42]

---

42. *See, e.g.*, Richmond Steel, Inc. v. Puerto Rican Am. Ins. Co., 954 F.2d 19, 21 (1st Cir. 1992) (trial court decisions reviewed for clear error); *In re* Merritt Logan, Inc., 901 F.2d 349, 359 (3rd Cir

Courts have often admitted opinion testimony to establish the value of property. Traditionally, the owner of a business has been deemed sufficiently familiar with that business to offer competent testimony on its value,[43] provided that such testimony is subject to cross-examination. Alternatively, such testimony may be offered by a company's financial officer[44] or some other person with independent academic training.[45] In *Soo Line Railroad Co. v. Fruehauf Corp.*,[46] for example, the executive vice president of a railway was permitted to testify as an expert concerning the diminution of value in certain railroad cars after a failure of their structural steel.

Opinion evidence may also be allowed in connection with proving lost profits. In *In re Merritt Logan, Inc.*,[47] for example, the Third Circuit allowed three different witnesses to offer opinions in support of claims for damages against the seller, installer, and manufacturer of a defective refrigeration system. The plaintiff's principal shareholder offered his opinion on lost profits, reinforced by a witness who surveyed sales at the affected grocery store—neither of them having to qualify as an expert witness. The court also allowed expert testimony by a certified public accountant who confirmed that the lost profit calculations were consistent with accounting industry standards. The same court previously allowed a claimant's licensed accountant to testify to lost profits even though the accountant was not disclosed, or qualified at trial,

---

1990) (decisions reviewed for abuse of discretion); LaCombe v. A-T-O, Inc. 679 F.2d 431, 434 (5th Cir. 1982) (decisions reviewed for abuse of discretion); Soo Line R. Co. v. Fruehauf Corp., 547 F.2d 1365, 1374 (8th Cir. 1977) (decisions not reversed unless manifestly erroneous); authorities cited at West's ⟐ 157 EVIDENCE, k470.

43. *See, e.g.*, Shane v. Shane, 891 F.2d 976, 982 (1st Cir. 1989) (admitting valuation from company's chief manager); LaCombe v. A-T-O, Inc., 679 F.2d 431, 433–35 (5th Cir. 1982) (remanding case where trial court excluded owner's testimony regarding depreciated value of items in fire insurance claim, even though witness was partly relying on hearsay); Kestenbaum v. Falstaff Brewing Corp., 514 F.2d 690, 698–99 (5th Cir. 1975) (owner was competent to offer opinion on value of his property).

44. *See, e.g.*, S. Cent. Livestock Dealers, Inc. v. Sec. State Bank, 614 F.2d 1056, 1061–62 (5th Cir. 1980) (chief financial officer of feedlot qualified to testify as to its value).

45. *See, e.g.*, Am. Tech. Res. v. United States, 893 F.2d 651, 656 (3rd Cir. 1990).

46. 547 F.2d 1365, 1376–77 (8th Cir. 1977).

47. 901 F.2d 349, 359–60 (3rd Cir. 1990).

as an expert.[48] The Third Circuit noted, however, that testimony from a lay opinion witness would be more restricted than from an expert, because only experts may offer testimony in answer to hypothetical questions.[49]

In *Walla Walla Port District v. Palmberg*,[50] the Ninth Circuit allowed a dredging contractor to offer opinion testimony as to the amount of extra costs sustained when dredging through cobbles and boulders rather than the sand, silt, and fine gravel that were indicated in the specifications. Rejecting a contention that such testimony was too speculative, the court noted that the contractor based his testimony on "experience and observation, his analysis of the leverman's log, and his observation of the type of materials encountered." Expert testimony has also been allowed in order to prove the reasonable estimated cost of repair work that has not yet been performed.[51]

One of the most common uses of independent construction experts is to support a complex calculation of damages. For example, contractors may seek additional compensation for impacts of delays, accelerations, differing site conditions, design errors, or an accumulation of the foregoing events.[52] If compensable problems affect only lmited portions of a project, it is usually preferable to calculate impact by comparing productivity on those portions with productivity on unimpacted work (the so-called "measured mile" approach). If impacts are pervasive through the project or if available records do not permit a greater segregation of cost overruns, however, the claimant may be compelled to fall back on an

---

48. Teen-Ed, Inc. v. Kimball Int'l, Inc., 620 F.2d 399, 402–03 (3rd Cir. 1980).

49. *Id.* at 404.

50. 280 F.2d 237, 249 (9th Cir. 1960).

51. *See, e.g.*, Richard Constr. Co. v. Monongahela & Ohio Dredging Co., 407 F.2d 1170, 1172 (3rd Cir. 1969).

52. *See, e.g.*, Reginald M. Jones, *Update on Proving and Pricing Inefficiency Claims*, 23:3 Constr. Law. 19 (Summer 2003); Lynn Hawkins Patton & Cheri Turnage Gatlin, *Claims for Lost Labor Productivity*, 20:2 Constr. Law. 21 (Apr. 2000); and Geoffrey T. Keating & Thomas F. Burke, *Cumulative Impact Claims: Can They Still Succeed?*, 20:2 Constr. Law. 30 (Apr. 2000); Bruner & O'Connor, *supra* § 19.78, at 258 ff.

unsegregated claim for cost overruns under one or more of the theories discussed earlier in this chapter. Claims for impact may rely in part on industry studies of lost efficiency in similar circumstances,[53] and expert testimony is often helpful in explaining how productivity was impacted and why published studies should be considered.

On the other hand, expert testimony on damage issues is not always admitted.[54] Many construction claimants choose to offer their evidence on damage issues through an expert witness. In recent years, the judicial scrutiny given to expert and opinion testimony is generally perceived to have tightened and the law on expert testimony has undergone significant changes.[55] In *Daubert v. Merrell Dow Pharmaceuticals, Inc.*,[56] the United States Supreme Court held that trial courts should regulate any "scientific" testimony or evidence admitted through experts to ensure that it was both relevant and reliable. The court prescribed four factors to apply to the expert's theory or method:

1. Whether it can be and has been tested

2. Whether it has been subjected to peer review and publication

3. Whether its reliability is limited by a "known or potential rate of error" or by certain operating standards

4. Whether it is generally accepted by the expert's peers[57]

---

53. *See, e.g.*, Hensel Phelps Constr. Co. v. GSA, 01-1 BCA ¶ 31,249 at p. 154,321 (GSBCA 2001) (approving claim that relied on expert who applied published MCAA inefficiency factors).

54. *See, e.g.*, Richmond Steel, Inc. v. Puerto Rican Am. Ins. Co., 954 F.2d 19, 21–22 (1st Cir. 1992) (testimony of certified public accountant properly rejected where it lacked reliability and where witness lacked recent experience auditing construction companies).

55. *See* Paul M. Lurie & Mark R. Becker, *Kumho Tire and Judicial Scrutiny of Expert Testimony by Engineers*, 20:3 Constr. Law. 37 (Jul. 2000).

56. 509 U.S. 579 (1993).

57. *Id.* at 592–93.

In *Kumho Tire Co. v. Carmichael*,[58] the Supreme Court expanded these tests to cover all expert testimony, regardless of whether it is presented on "scientific" issues. Congress subsequently amended Federal Rule of Evidence 702 (Testimony by Experts) to read as follows:

> If scientific, technical, or other specialized knowledge will assist the trier of fact to understand the evidence or to determine a fact in issue, a witness qualified as an expert by knowledge, skill, experience, training, or education, may testify thereto in the form of an opinion or otherwise, if (1) the testimony is based upon sufficient facts or data, (2) the testimony is the product of reliable principles and methods, and (3) the witness has applied the principles and methods reliably to the facts of the case.

The Advisory Committee notes to the 2000 amendment (Federal Rule of Evidence 702) attempt to assure practitioners that the rejection of expert testimony should continue to be "the exception rather than the rule" and that "[v]igorous cross-examination, presentation of contrary evidence, and careful instruction on the burden of proof are the traditional and appropriate means of attacking shaky but admissible evidence." On the other hand, the same notes confirm that "[t]he trial judge in all cases of proffered expert testimony must find that it is properly grounded, well-reasoned, and not speculative before it is admitted."

The 2000 amendments to the Federal Rules of Evidence also added a new qualification to Rule 703 (Bases of Opinion Testimony by Experts):

> Facts or data that are otherwise inadmissible shall not be disclosed to the jury by the proponent of the opinion or inference unless the court determines that their probative value in assisting the jury to evaluate the expert's opinion substantially outweighs their prejudicial effect.

58. 526 U.S. 137 (1999).

It appears that this amendment was largely intended to restrict the flow of hearsay evidence that some litigants insinuate into evidence through the medium of expert testimony.

As the *Daubert* and *Kumho Tire* standards are being applied by lower courts across the United States, some observers perceive a trend toward rejecting testimony from cost or financial experts.[59] Reported cases tend to focus on the most egregious "experts," however, and industry experience suggests that cost experts continue to be widely used in proving and defending damage claims in construction cases.

Where expert witnesses purport to summarize "relevant" documents or other evidence in an exhibit, such summary documents are often challenged. Although they almost always constitute hearsay, they are usually admitted in private arbitrations or other proceedings not governed by the normal rules of evidence. In a trial, the admission of expert reports and charts is a matter of the court's discretion,[60] and they are often admitted only for illustrative purposes during the trial and for argument at the end of the case.[61] As in the case of other damage summary exhibits, it would be helpful to the

---

59. *See, e.g.,* ROBERT F. CUSHMAN, JOHN D. CARTER, PAUL J. GORMAN & DOUGLAS F. COPPI, PROVING AND PRICING CONSTRUCTION CLAIMS § 17.03[B][1] (3rd ed. 2001), *citing In re* Tasch, Inc. v. Sabine Offshore Servs., No. 97–15901 JAB, 1999 U.S. Dist. LEXIS 12368 (E.D. La. Aug. 4, 1999) (consulting expert allowed to testify on damage calculation but barred from testifying on contract interpretation or parties' intent, because jury did not need help on the latter issues, and expert was merely offering testimony to "mirror" fact witnesses); DeJagar Constr., Inc. v. Schleininger, 938 F. Supp. 446 (W.D. Mich. 1996) (financial expert testimony excluded due to mathematical mistakes, unsupported assumptions, and "picking and choosing among purported facts to maximize plaintiff's damages"); Tyger Constr. Co. v. Pensacola Constr., 29 F.3d 137, 145 (4th Cir. 1999) (expert testimony too speculative and consisted of "an array of figures conveying a delusive impression of exactness").

60. *See* Contour Constr. & Land Corp. v. Bexar County, No. 04–95–00011-CV, 996 Tex. App. LEXIS 3585 (Tex. Ct. App. Aug. 14, 1996) (upholding trial court exclusion of photographs and videotape that would not aid the jury); authorities cited at West's 🔑 157 EVIDENCE, k546.

61. *See, e.g.,* Tyger Constr. Co. v. Pensacola Constr., 29 F.3d 137, 142 (4th Cir. 1999) (damage expert testimony should be excluded when too speculative and unsupported in trial record); Engelbretsen v. Fairchild Aircraft Corp., 21 F.3d 721, 728–29 (6th Cir. 1994) (expert reports were improperly admitted on direct testimony, although parts of the reports became admissible through cross-examination on their content); DeJager Constr. Inc. v. Schleininger, 938 F. Supp. 446 (W.D. Mich. 1996) (expert testimony excluded due to the witness's perceived lack of objectivity, mathematical mistakes, and unsupported assumptions); Newberry Square Dev. Corp. v. S. Landmark, Inc., 578 So.2d 750 (Fla. Dist. Ct. App. 1991).

trier of fact if each expert illustrative exhibit would include notations identifying its specific sources in the trial record. Documents containing significant errors or argumentative text should be excluded.

One important lesson from the case law is that testimony on damages may come in the form of lay opinions as often as from a qualified expert witness. To avoid facing a surprise damage witness at trial, counsel should consider at least an interrogatory (and perhaps a request for mandatory pre-trial disclosure) of all witnesses through whom the opposing party intends to offer either expert or lay opinion testimony with regard to calculating damages. If a court or arbitrator has not specified a deadline for disclosure of expert reports and damage calculations, it may be prudent to request one.

When a party designates a witness to offer expert or lay opinion testimony on damage issues, counsel for the opposing party should consider taking a deposition where the witness' qualifications can be tested under the current standards of Federal Rules of Evidence 701–03. The federal Advisory Committee notes to Rule 702 offer some useful tests for the qualifications of experts under recent case law.

In the end, it appears that the revised evidentiary rules have not changed the fundamental principle of giving discretion to trial judges in admitting or rejecting expert and lay opinion testimony. The complexity of the damage issues and the apparent integrity of the witness are both likely to be considered when a court exercises this discretion.

Index